Pretty Guardian ★

Sailor Moon

Short Stories 2

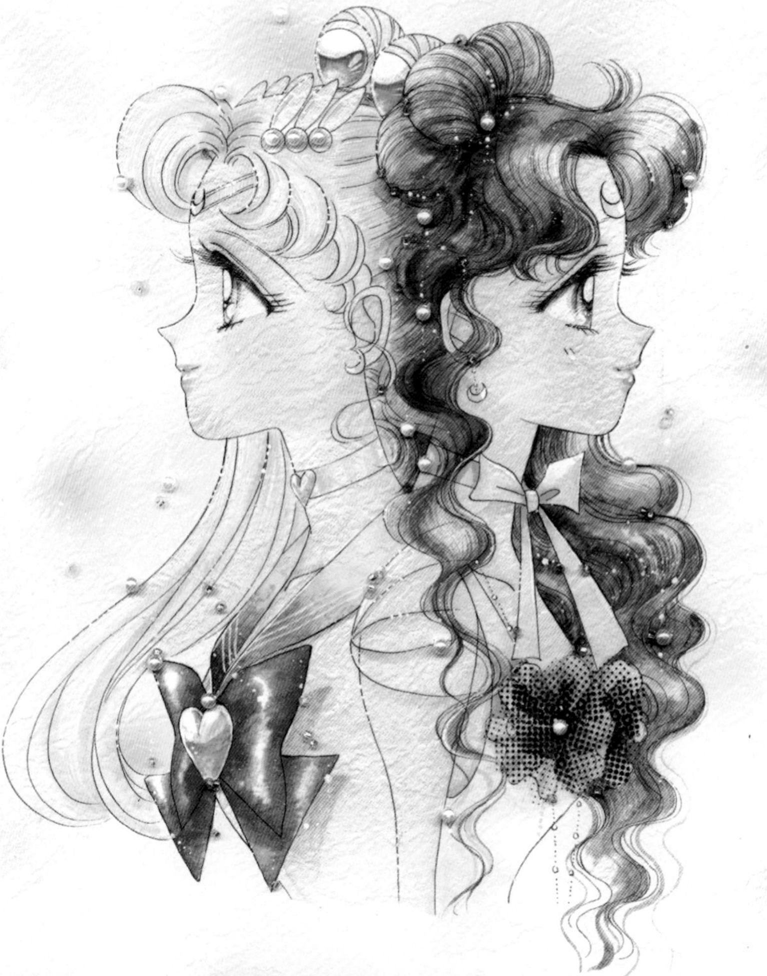

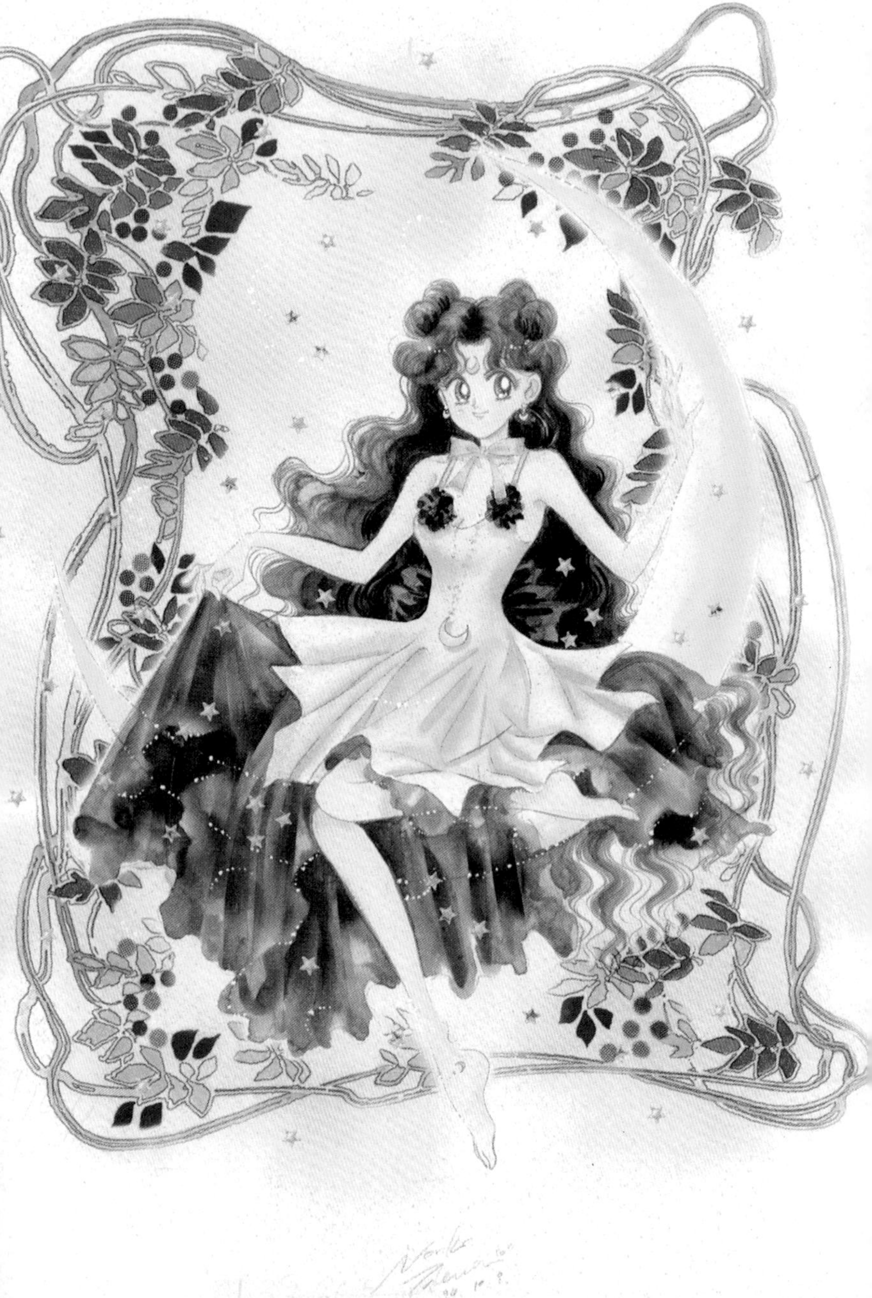

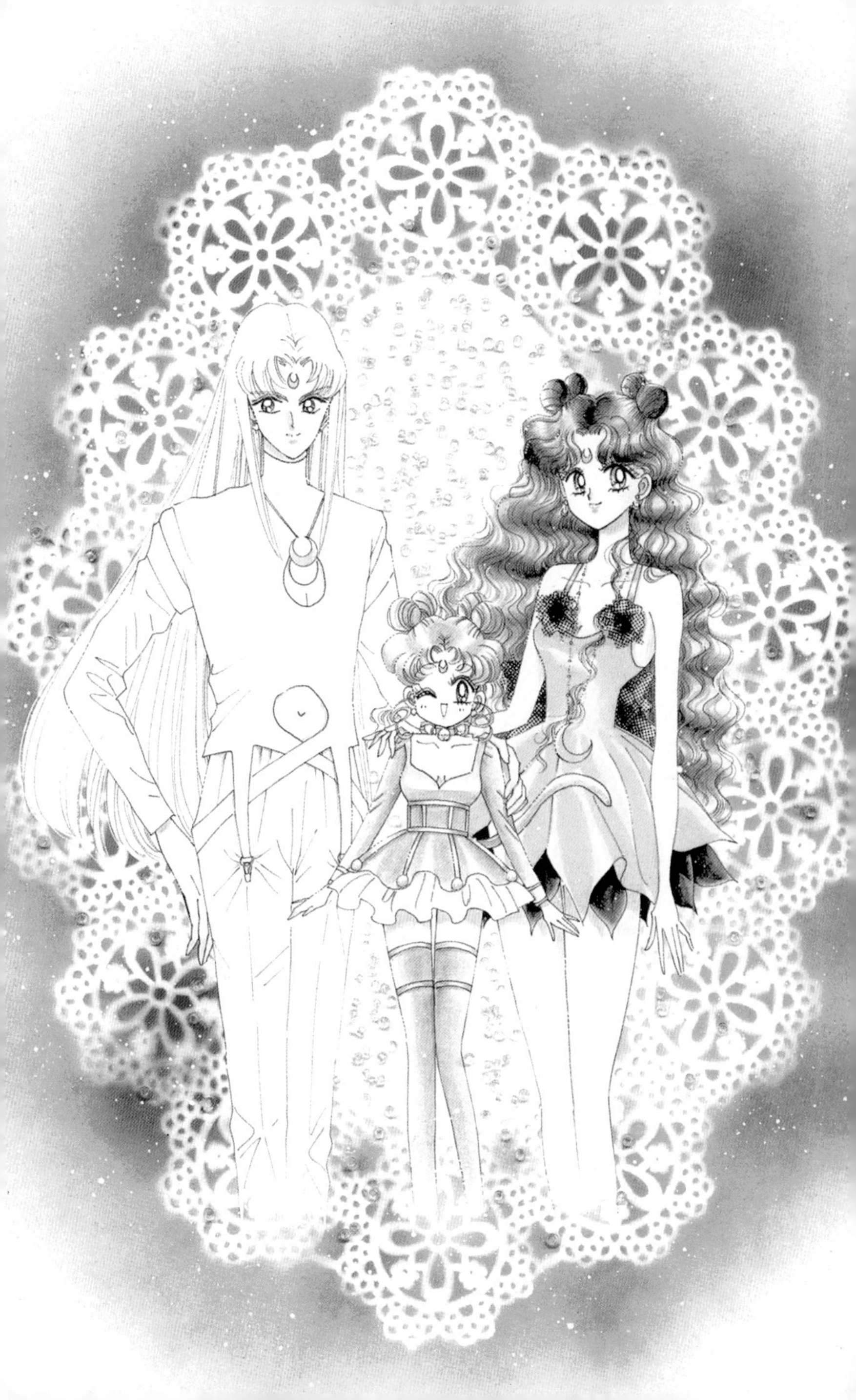

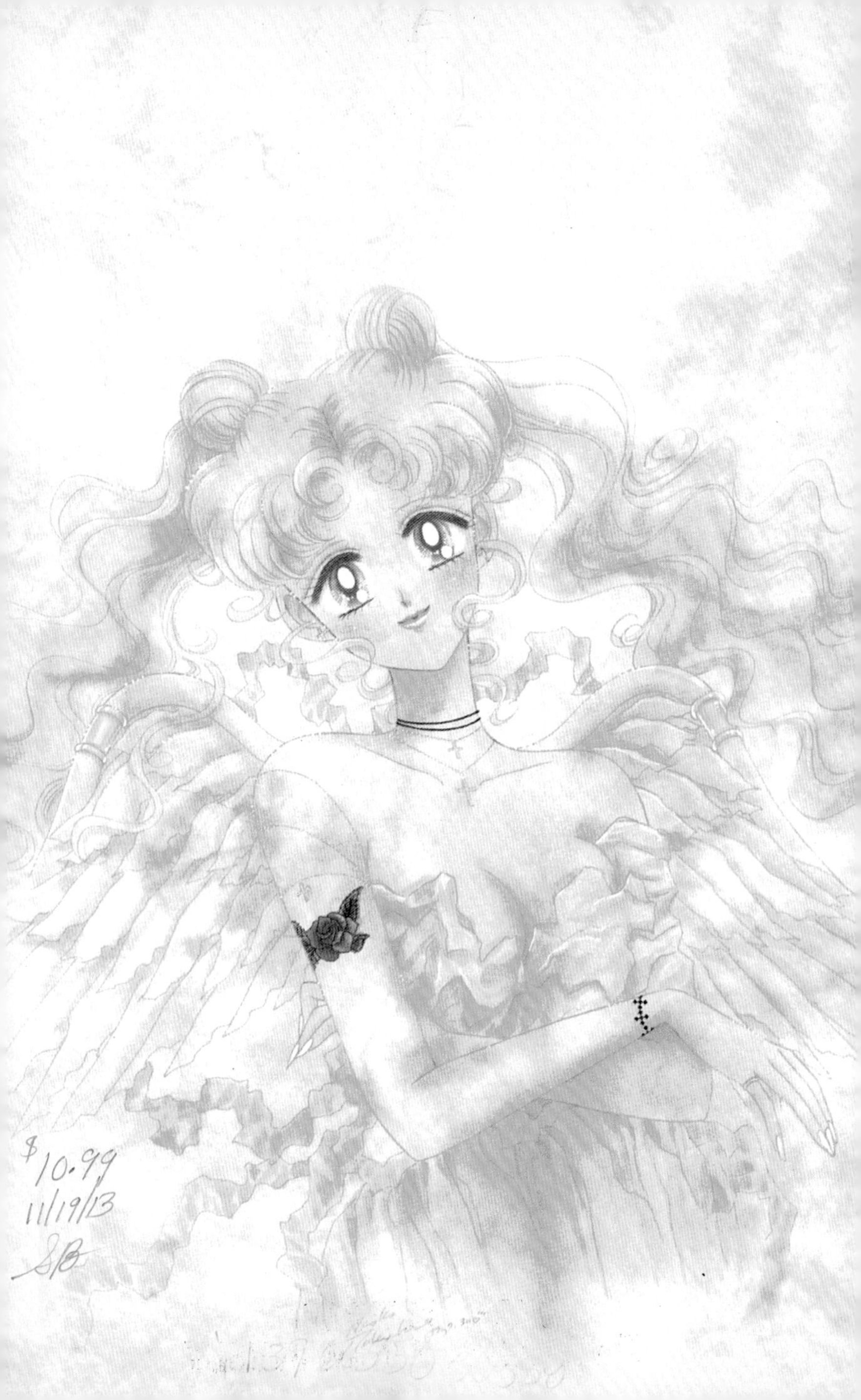

$10.99
11/19/13
SB

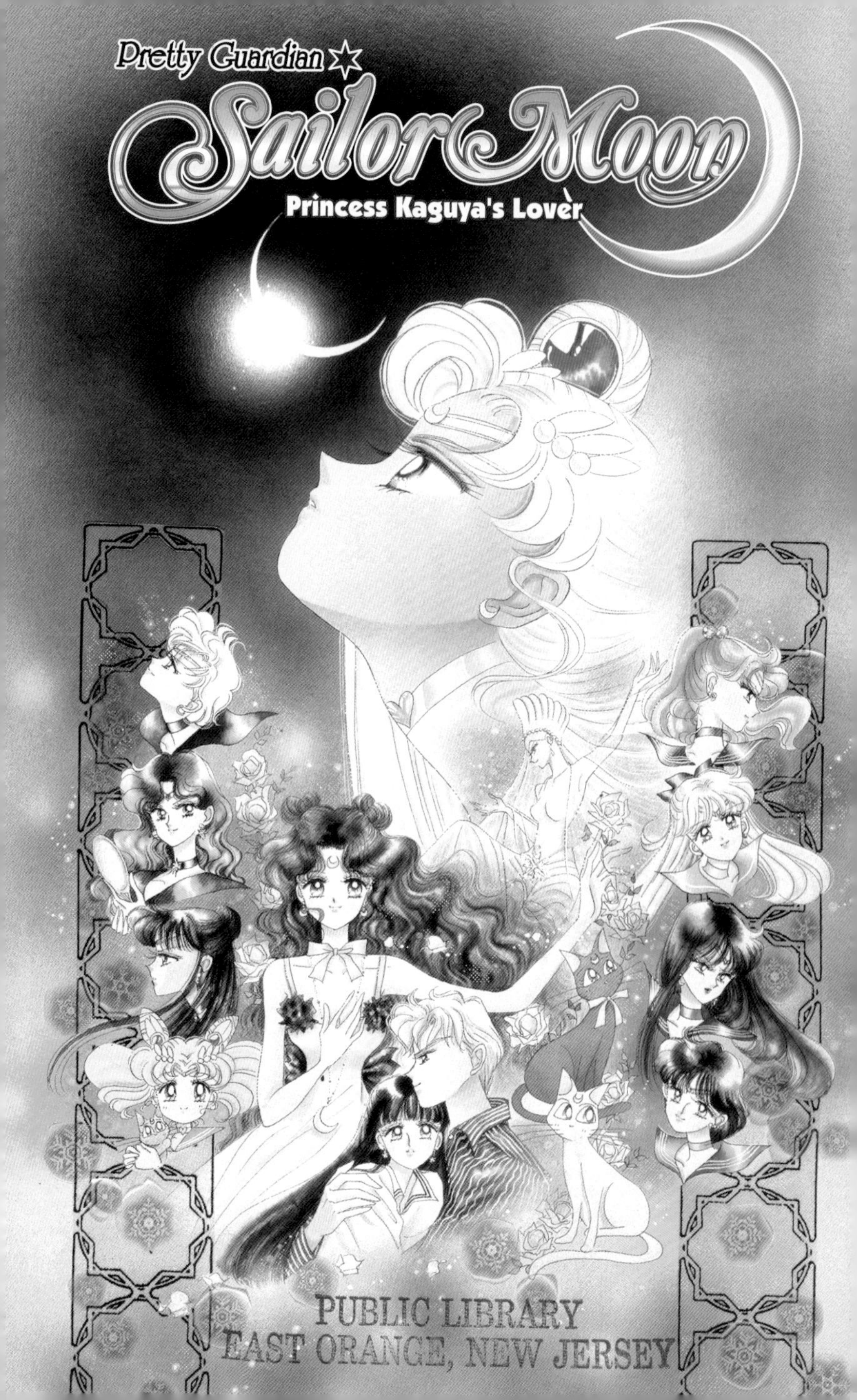
Pretty Guardian
Sailor Moon
Princess Kaguya's Lover

Pretty Guardian
SAILORMOON

Y
SAI
v.2

CONTENTS

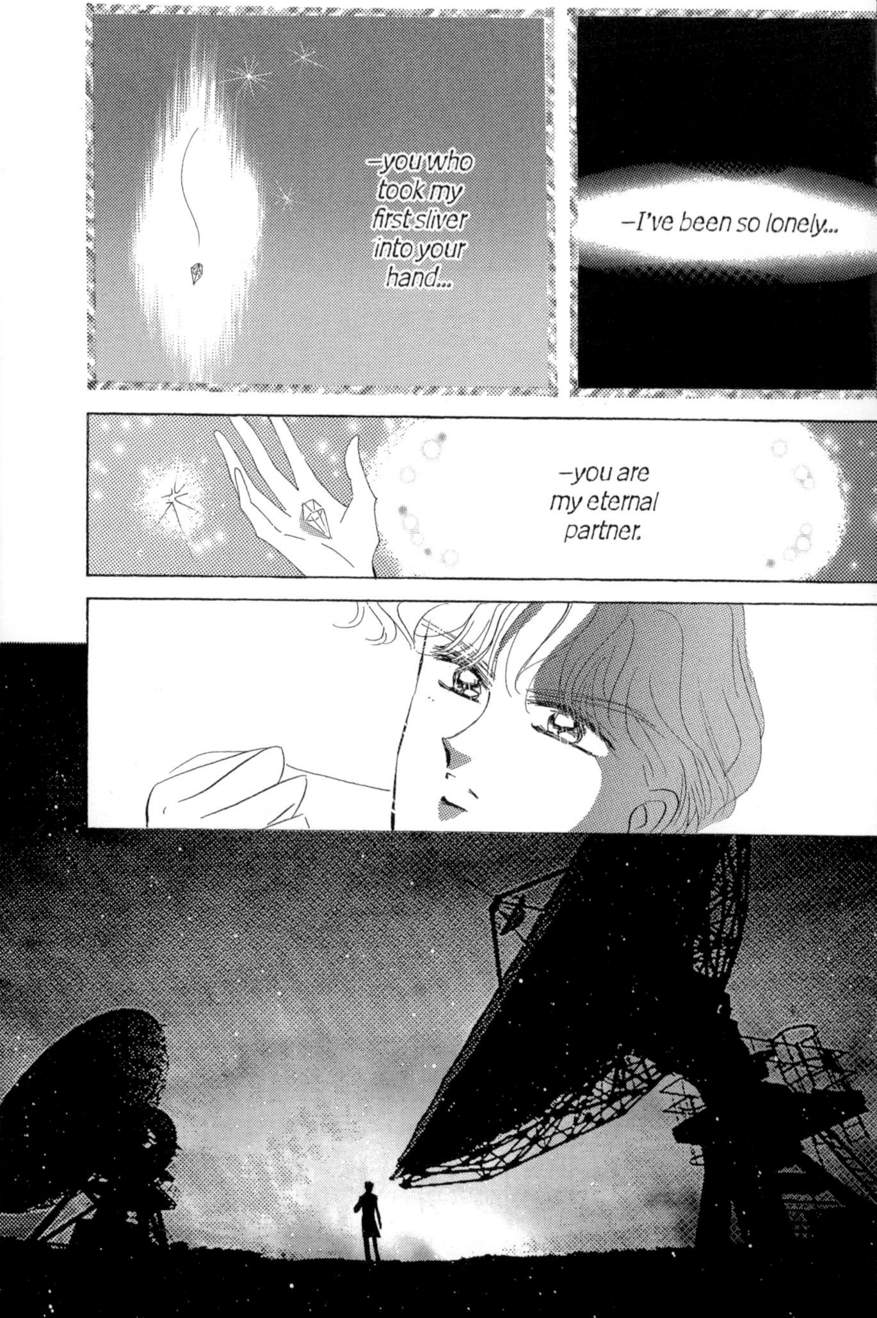
–I've been so lonely...
–you who took my first sliver into your hand...
–you are my eternal partner.

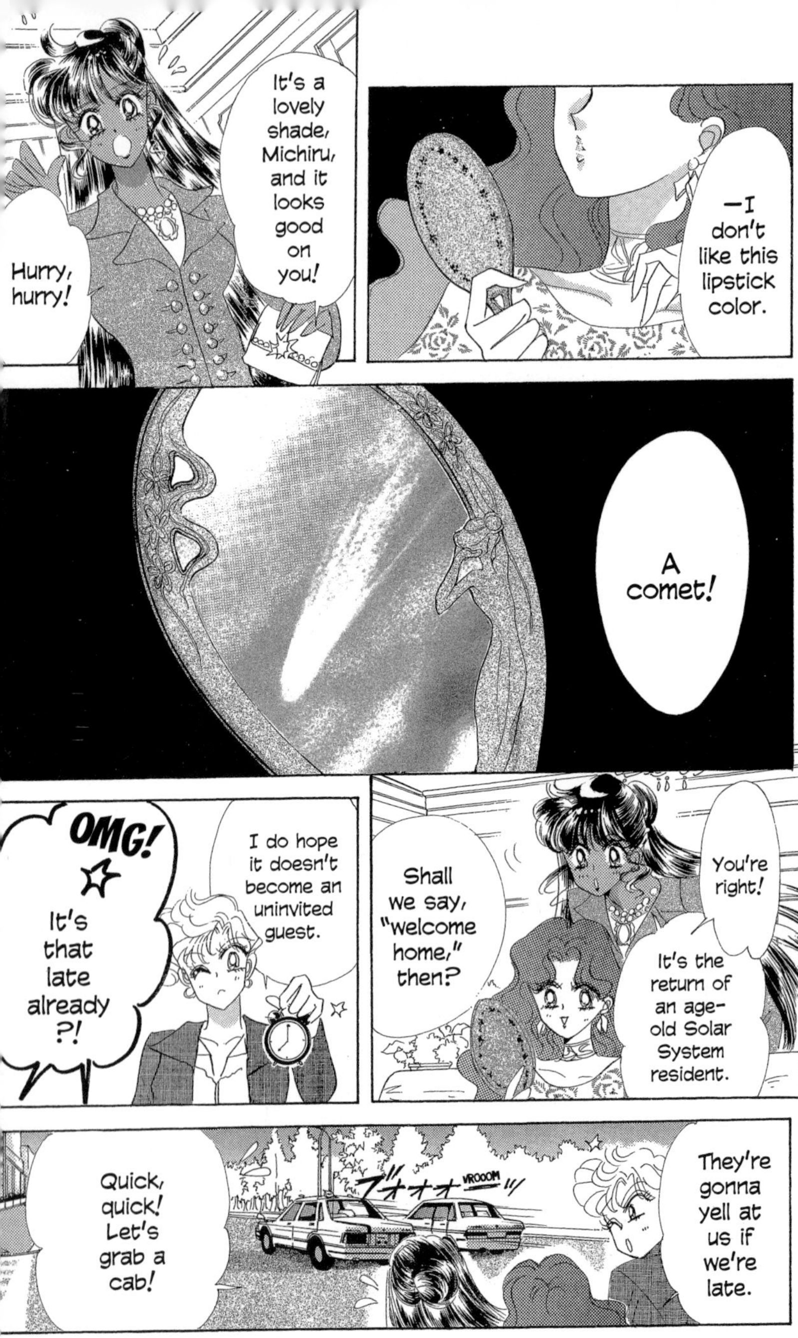
—I don't like this lipstick color.
It's a lovely shade, Michiru, and it looks good on you!
Hurry, hurry!
A comet!
You're right!
It's the return of an age-old Solar System resident.
Shall we say, "welcome home," then?
I do hope it doesn't become an uninvited guest.
OMG!
It's that late already?!
They're gonna yell at us if we're late.
VROOOM
Quick, quick! Let's grab a cab!

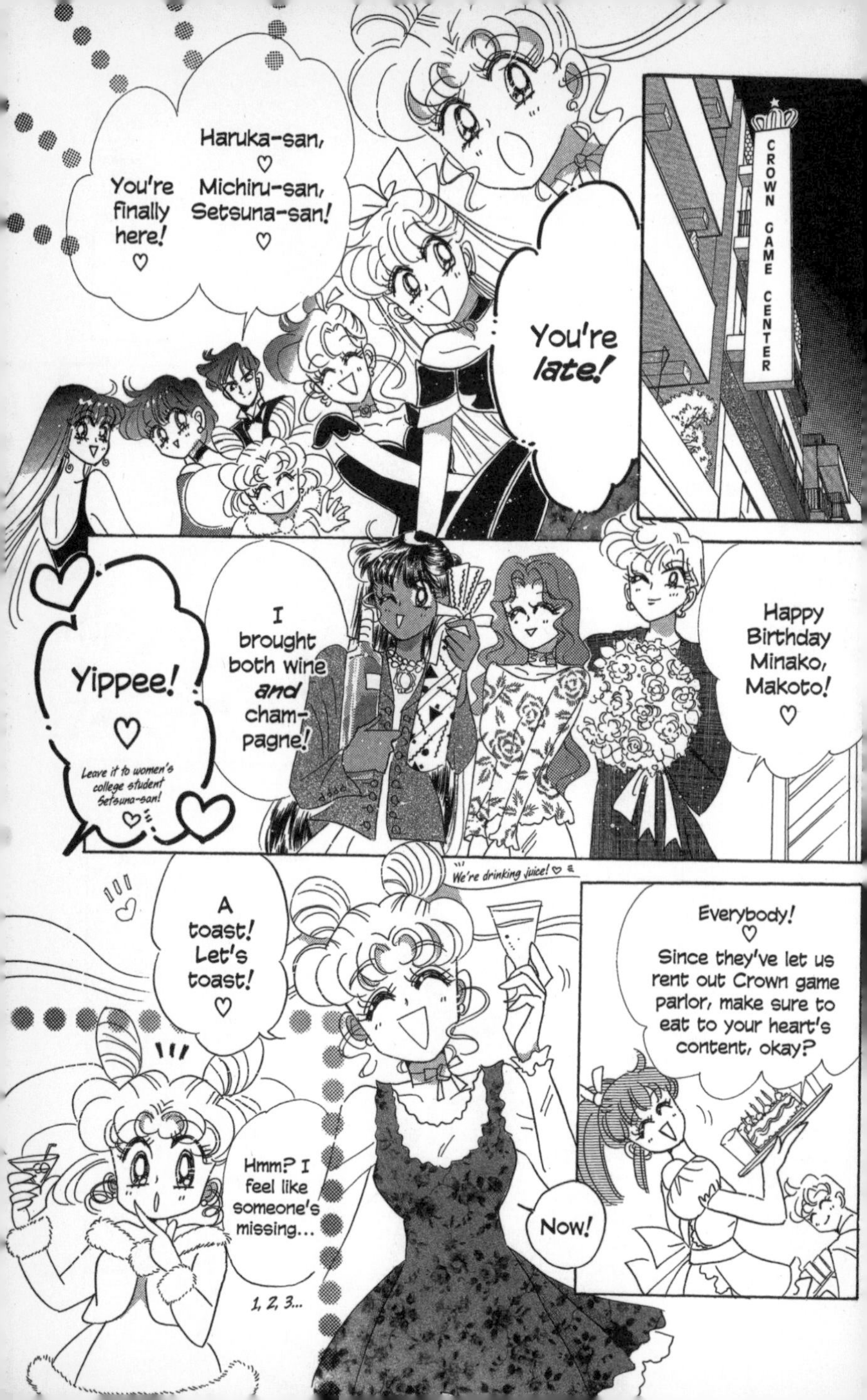

CROWN GAME CENTER
You're *late!*
Haruka-san, ♡ Michiru-san, Setsuna-san! ♡
You're finally here! ♡
Happy Birthday Minako, Makoto! ♡
I brought both wine *and* champagne!
Yippee! ♡
Leave it to women's college student Setsuna-san! ♡
Everybody! ♡ Since they've let us rent out Crown game parlor, make sure to eat to your heart's content, okay?
We're drinking juice! ♡
A toast! Let's toast! ♡
Now!
Hmm? I feel like someone's missing...
1, 2, 3...

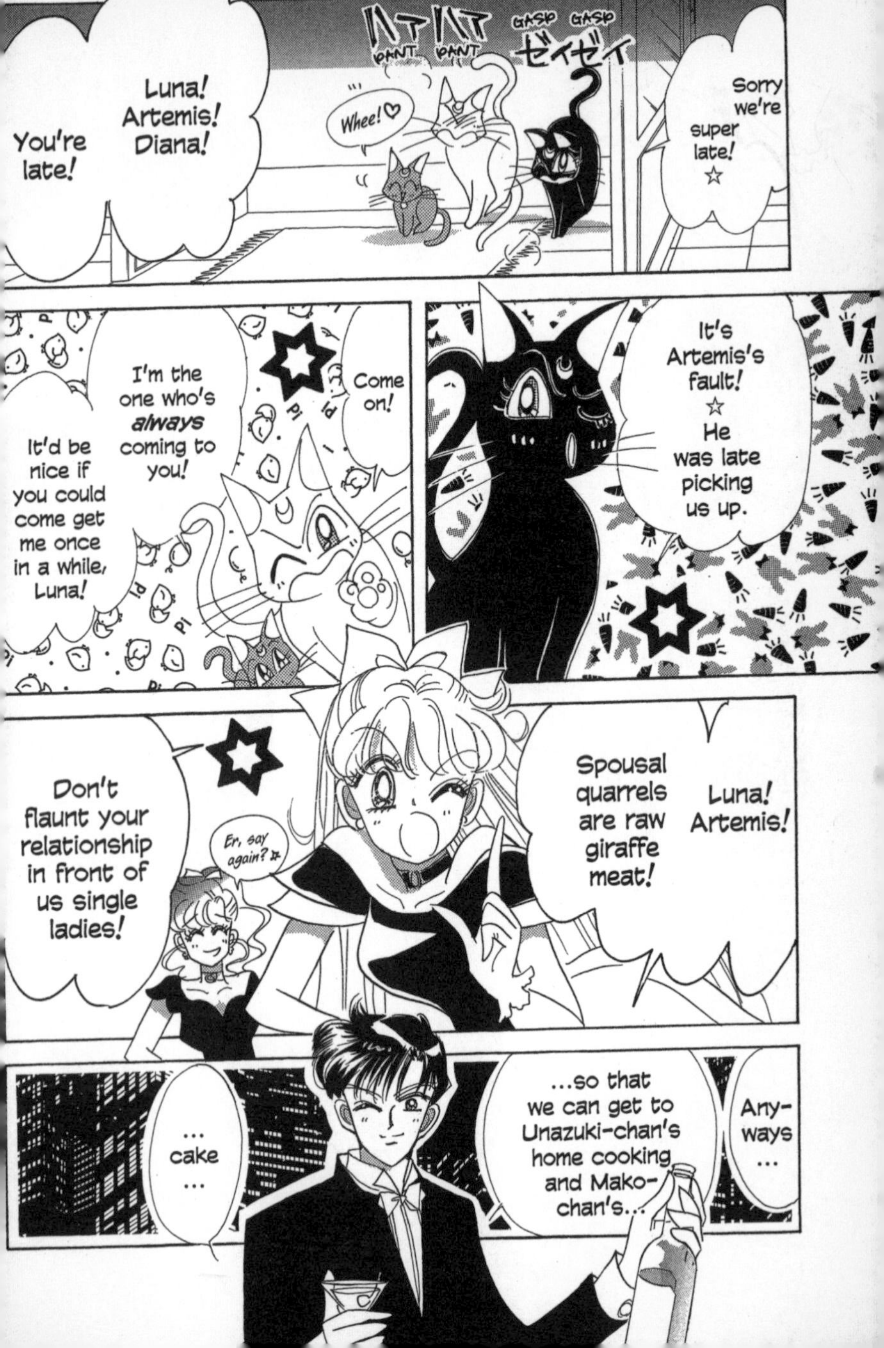
Sorry we're super late! ☆
GASP GASP ゼイゼイ
ハァハァ PANT PANT
Whee! ♡
Luna! Artemis! Diana!
You're late!
It's Artemis's fault! ☆ He was late picking us up.
Come on!
I'm the one who's *always* coming to you!
It'd be nice if you could come get me once in a while, Luna!
Luna! Artemis!
Spousal quarrels are raw giraffe meat!
Er, say again? ☆
Don't flaunt your relationship in front of us single ladies!
Any-ways ...
...so that we can get to Unazuki-chan's home cooking and Mako-chan's...
... cake ...

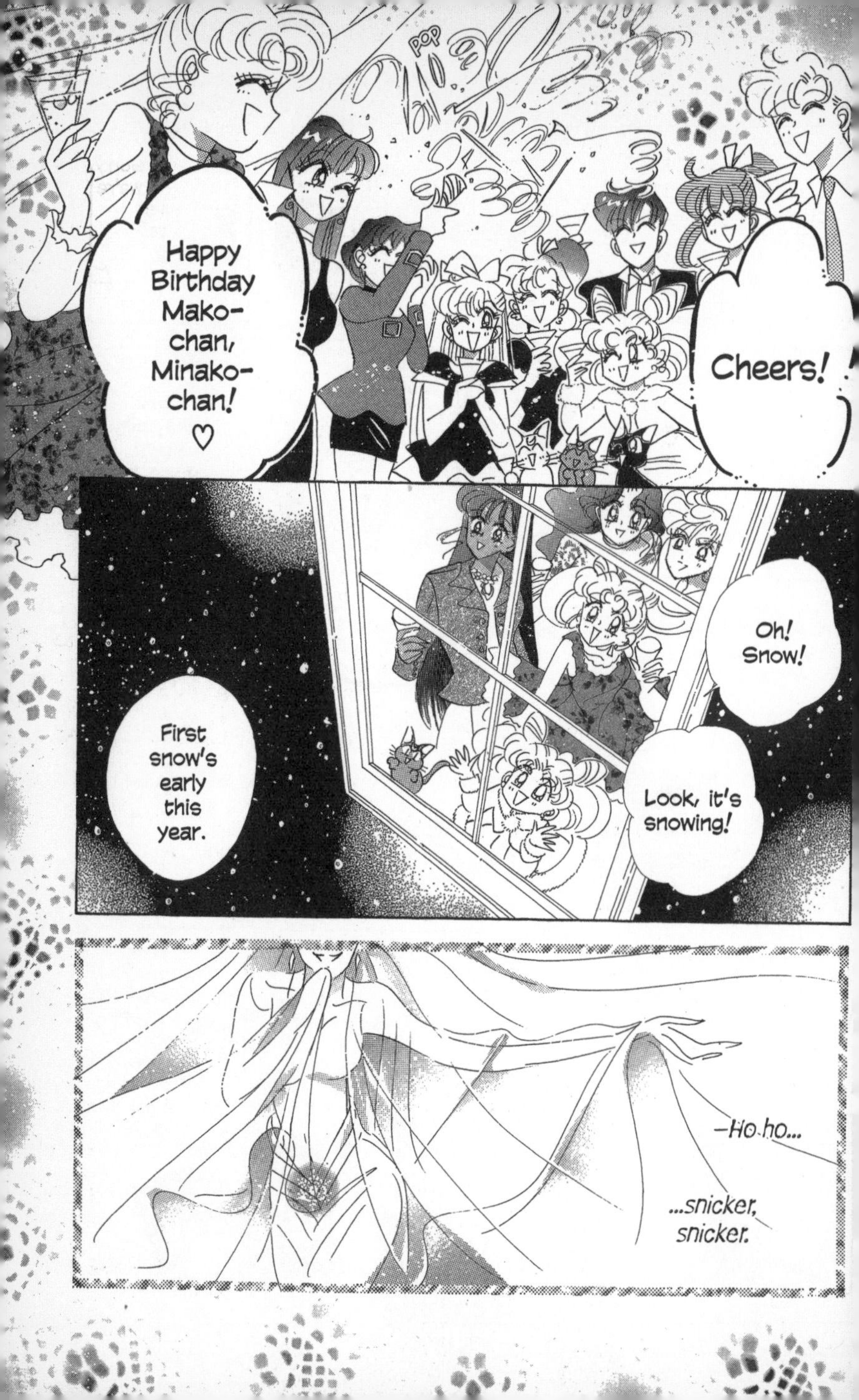
POP
Cheers!
Happy Birthday Mako-chan, Minako-chan! ♡
Oh! Snow!
Look, it's snowing!
First snow's early this year.
—Ho ho...
...snicker, snicker.

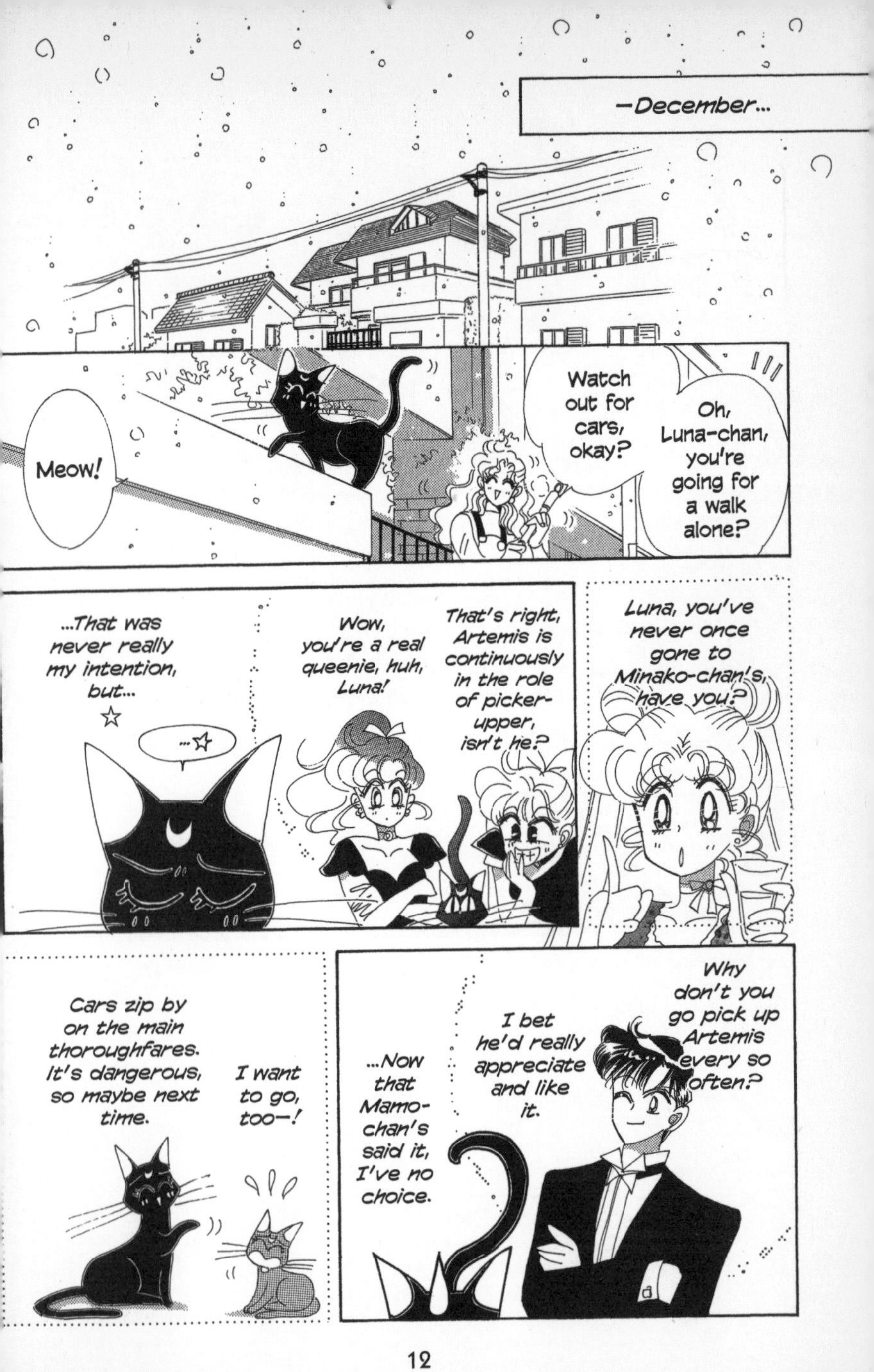
—December...
Oh, Luna-chan, you're going for a walk alone?
Watch out for cars, okay?
Meow!
Luna, you've never once gone to Minako-chan's, have you?
That's right, Artemis is continuously in the role of picker-upper, isn't he?
Wow, you're a real queenie, huh, Luna!
...That was never really my intention, but... ☆
...☆
Why don't you go pick up Artemis every so often?
I bet he'd really appreciate and like it.
...Now that Mamo-chan's said it, I've no choice.
I want to go, too—!
Cars zip by on the main thoroughfares. It's dangerous, so maybe next time.

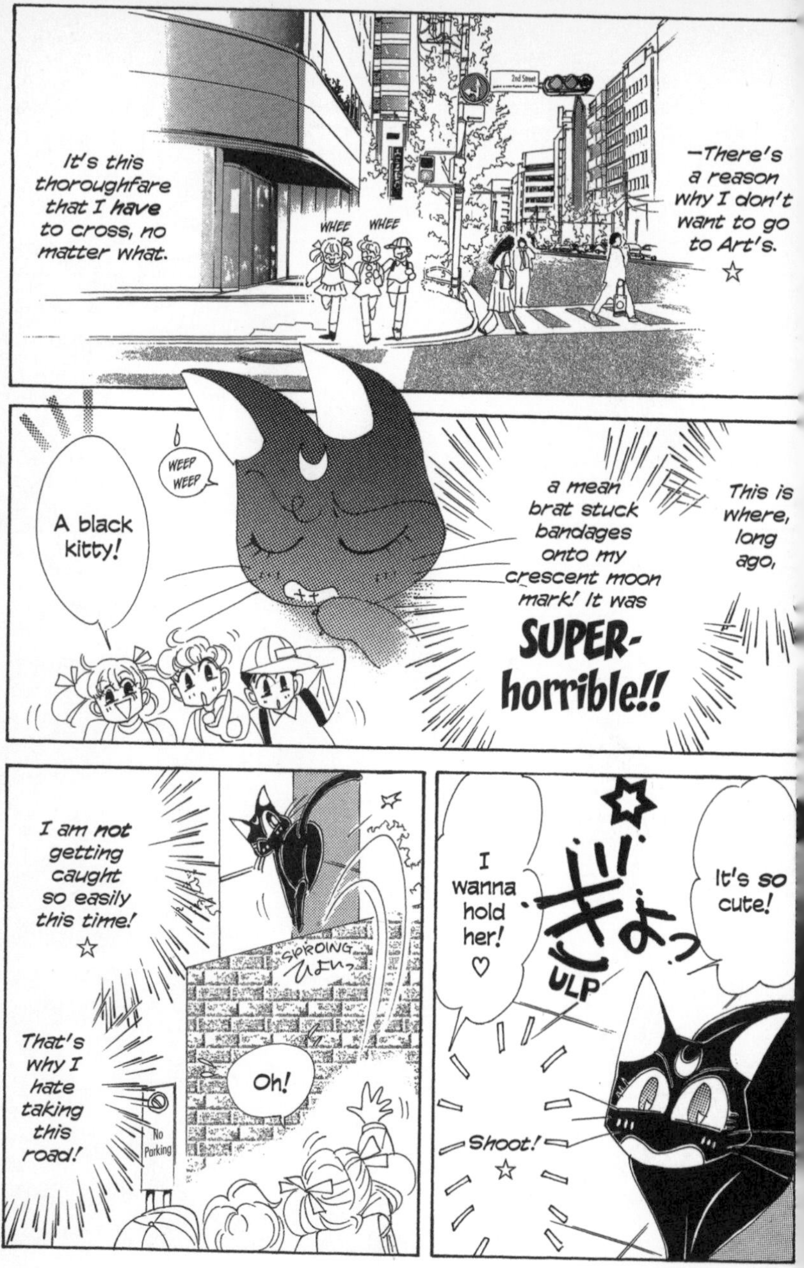
—There's a reason why I don't want to go to Art's. ☆
2nd Street
WHEE WHEE
It's this thoroughfare that I **have** to cross, no matter what.
This is where, long ago,
a mean brat stuck bandages onto my crescent moon mark! It was
SUPER-horrible!!
WEEP WEEP
A black kitty!
It's so cute!
ぎょっ
ULP
I wanna hold her! ♡
Shoot! ☆
I am **not** getting caught so easily this time! ☆
SPROING ひょいっ
Oh!
That's why I hate taking this road!
No Parking

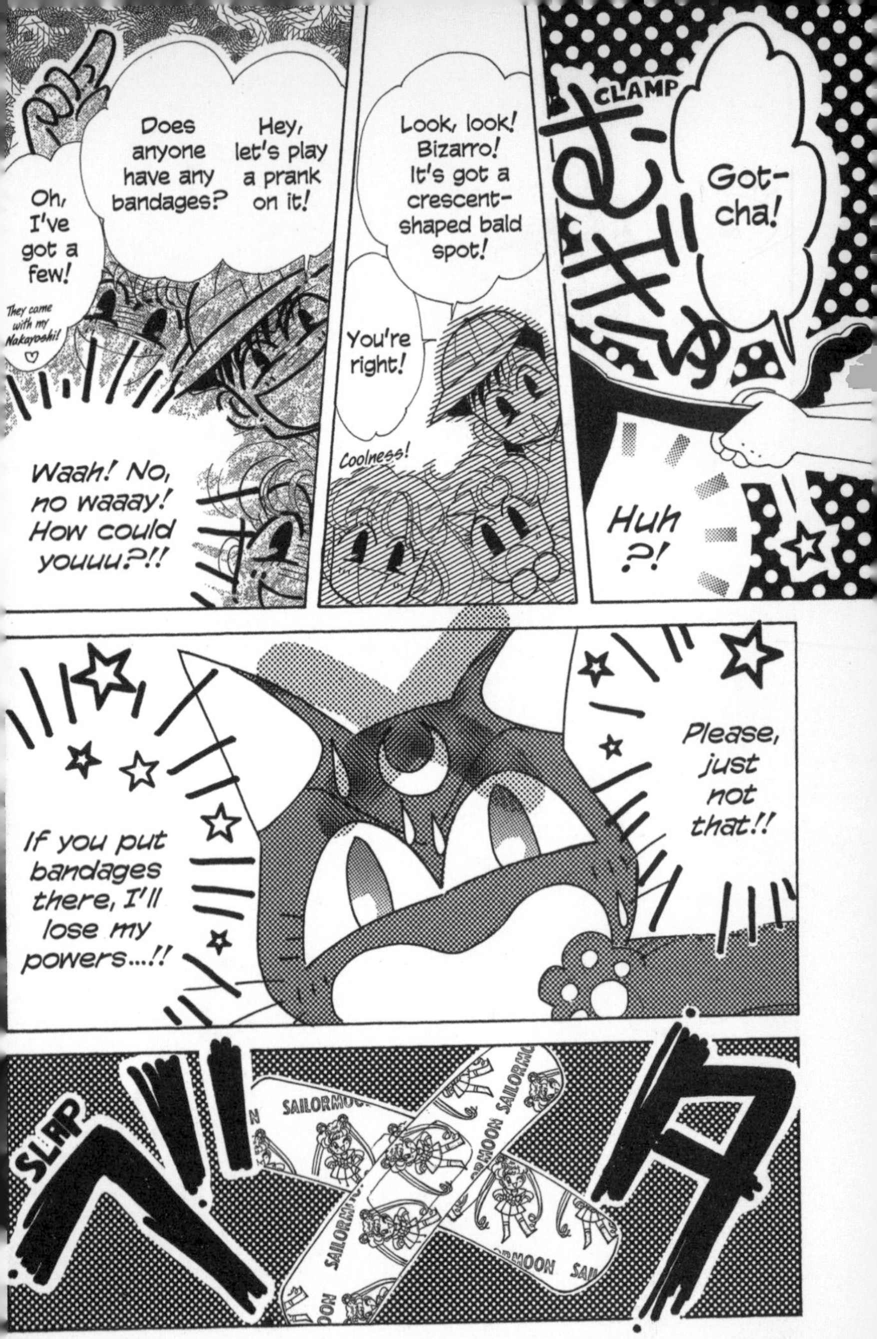

CLAMP
Got-cha!
Huh?!
Look, look! Bizarro! It's got a crescent-shaped bald spot!
You're right!
Coolness!
Hey, let's play a prank on it!
Does anyone have any bandages?
Oh, I've got a few!
They came with my Nakayoshi! ♡
Waah! No, no waaay! How could youuu?!!
Please, just not that!!
If you put bandages there, I'll lose my powers...!!
SLAP
SAILORMOON

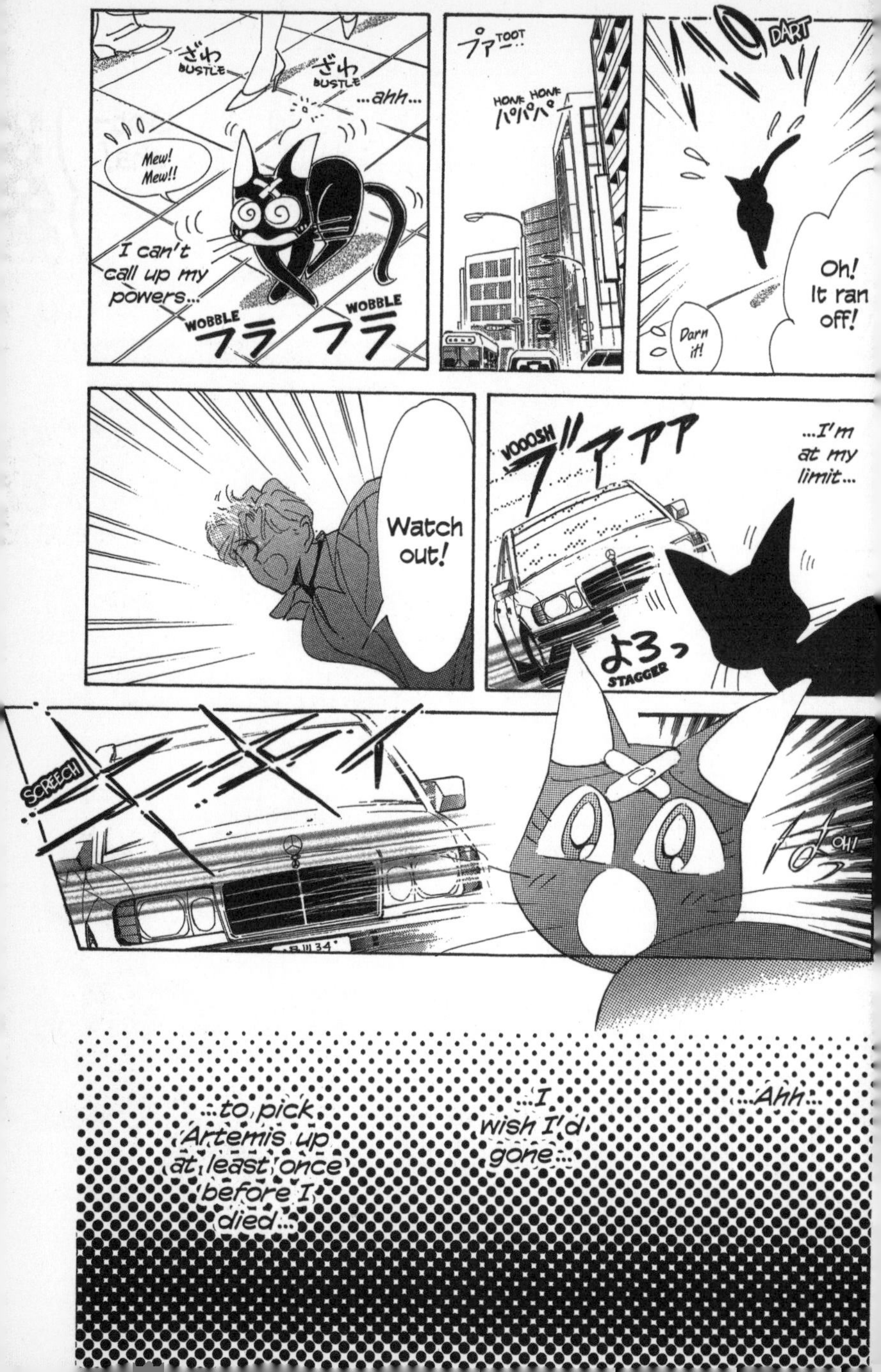
DART
Oh! It ran off!
Darn it!
プァー TOOT
HONK HONK パパパー
ざわ BUSTLE
ざわ BUSTLE
...ahh...
Mew! Mew!!
I can't call up my powers...
WOBBLE フラ
WOBBLE フラ
VOOOSH ヴァアア
...I'm at my limit...
よろっ STAGGER
Watch out!
OH!
SCREECH
...Ahh...
...I wish I'd gone...
...to pick Artemis up at least once before I died...

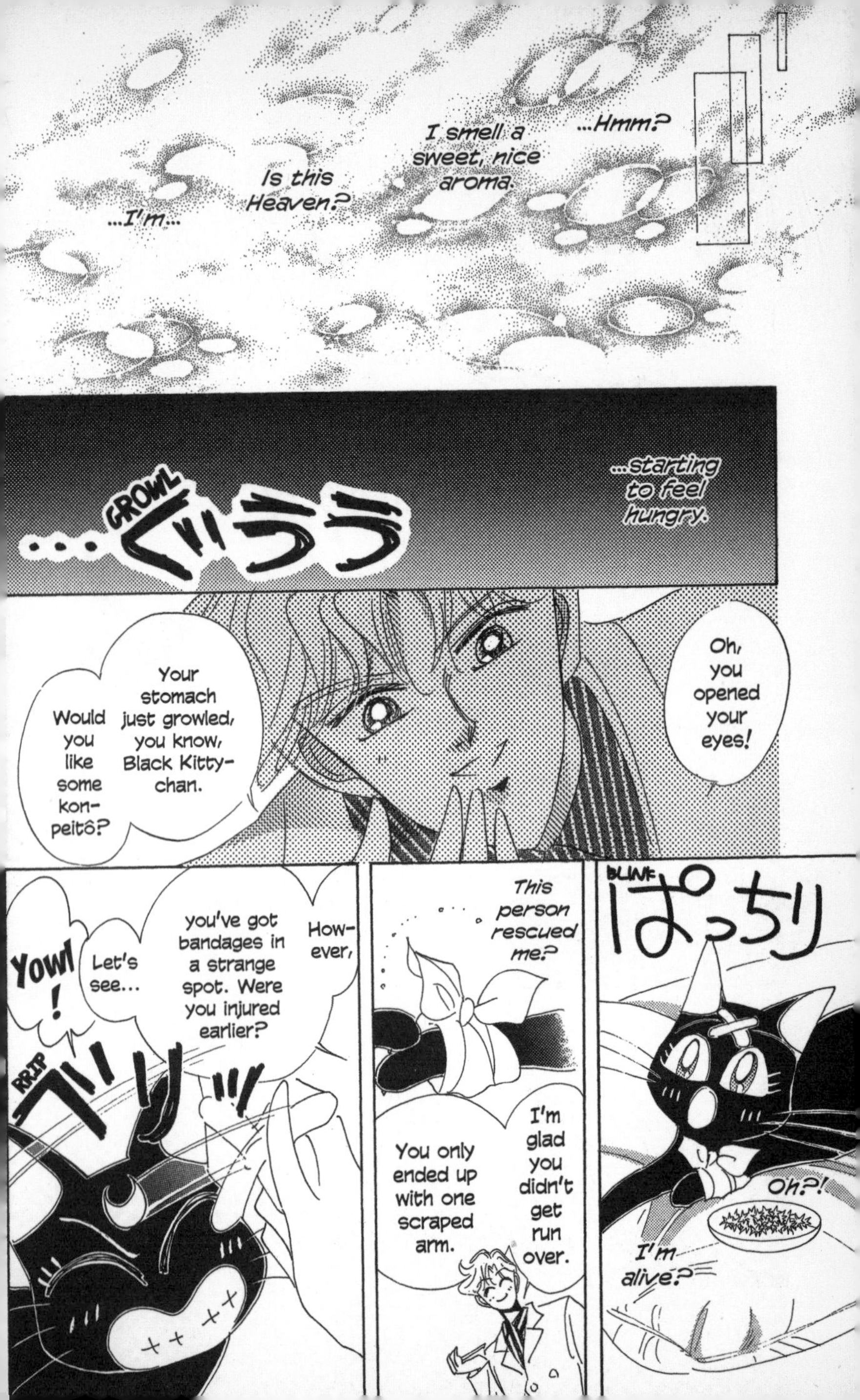

...Hmm?
I smell a sweet, nice aroma.
Is this Heaven?
...I'm...
...starting to feel hungry.
...GROWL ぐうう
Oh, you opened your eyes!
Your stomach just growled, you know, Black Kitty-chan.
Would you like some kon-peitô?
BLINK ぱっちり
Oh?!
I'm alive?
This person rescued me?
I'm glad you didn't get run over.
You only ended up with one scraped arm.
How-ever,
you've got bandages in a strange spot. Were you injured earlier?
Let's see...
YOW!
RRIP

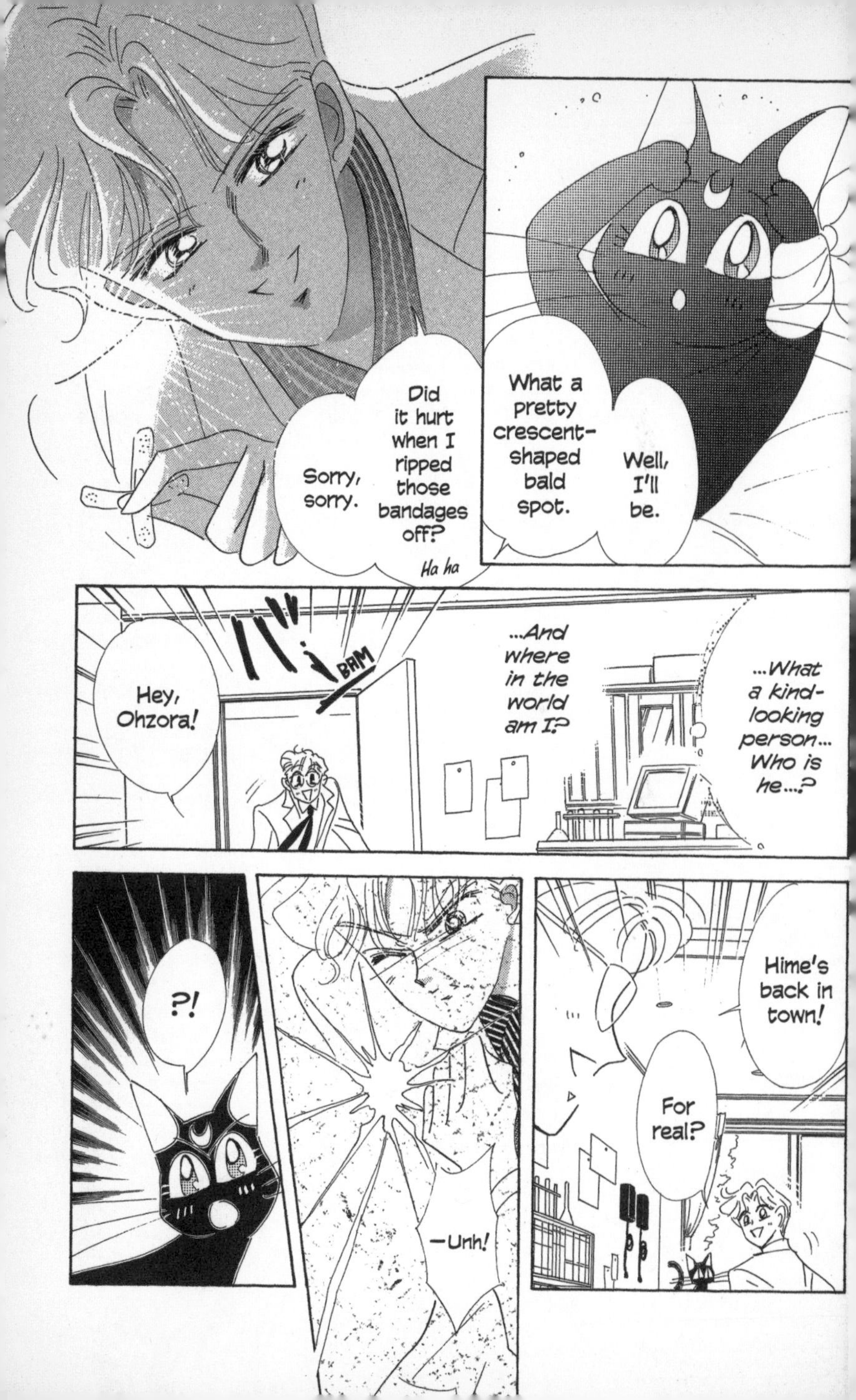
Well, I'll be.
What a pretty crescent-shaped bald spot.
Did it hurt when I ripped those bandages off?
Sorry, sorry.
Ha ha
...What a kind-looking person... Who is he...?
...And where in the world am I?
BAM
Hey, Ohzora!
Hime's back in town!
For real?
—Unh!
?!

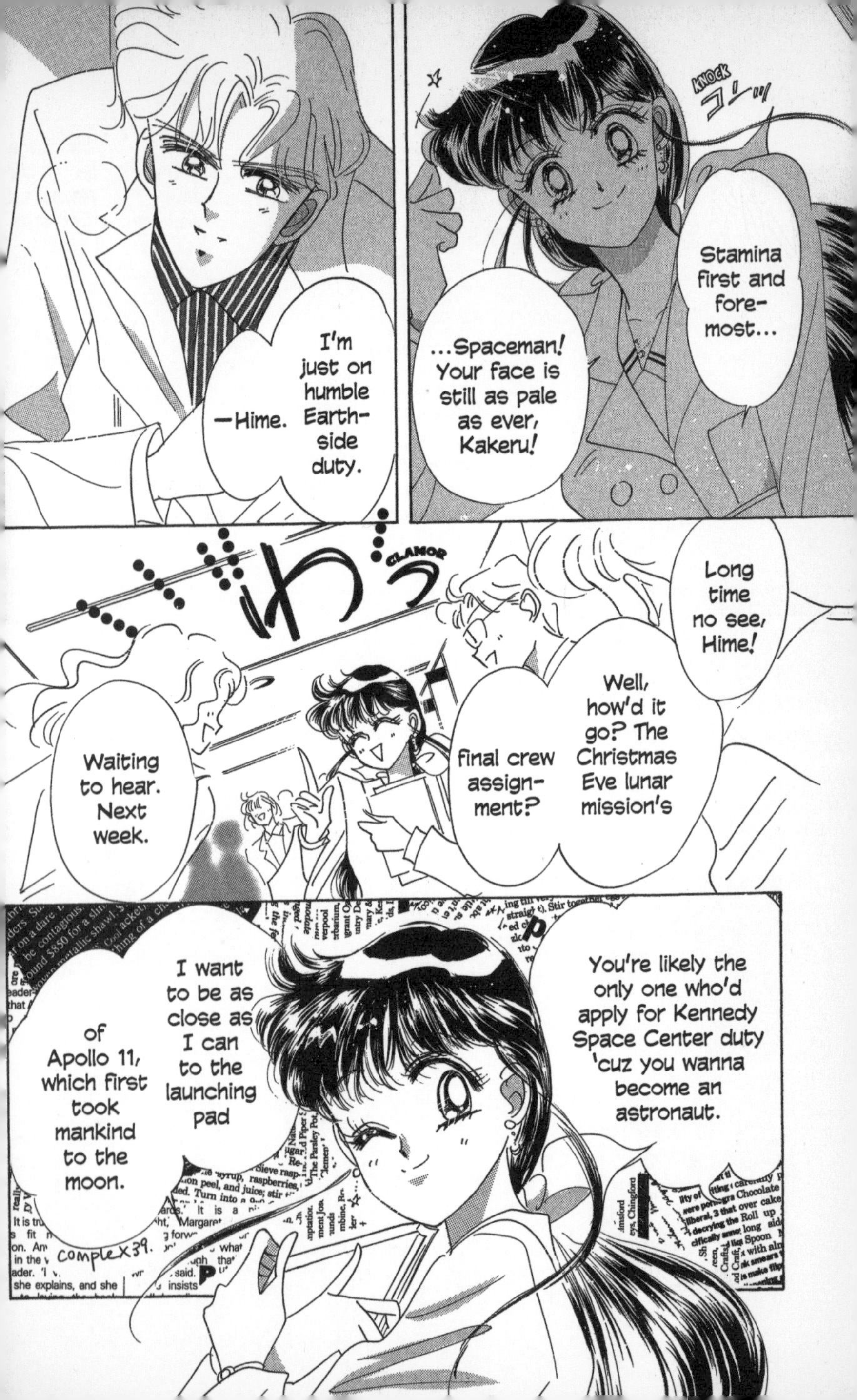
KNOCK
Stamina first and fore-most...
...Spaceman! Your face is still as pale as ever, Kakeru!
I'm just on humble Earth-side duty.
—Hime.
CLAMOR
Long time no see, Hime!
Well, how'd it go? The Christmas Eve lunar mission's final crew assignment?
Waiting to hear. Next week.
You're likely the only one who'd apply for Kennedy Space Center duty 'cuz you wanna become an astronaut.
I want to be as close as I can to the launching pad of Apollo 11, which first took mankind to the moon.
complex39.

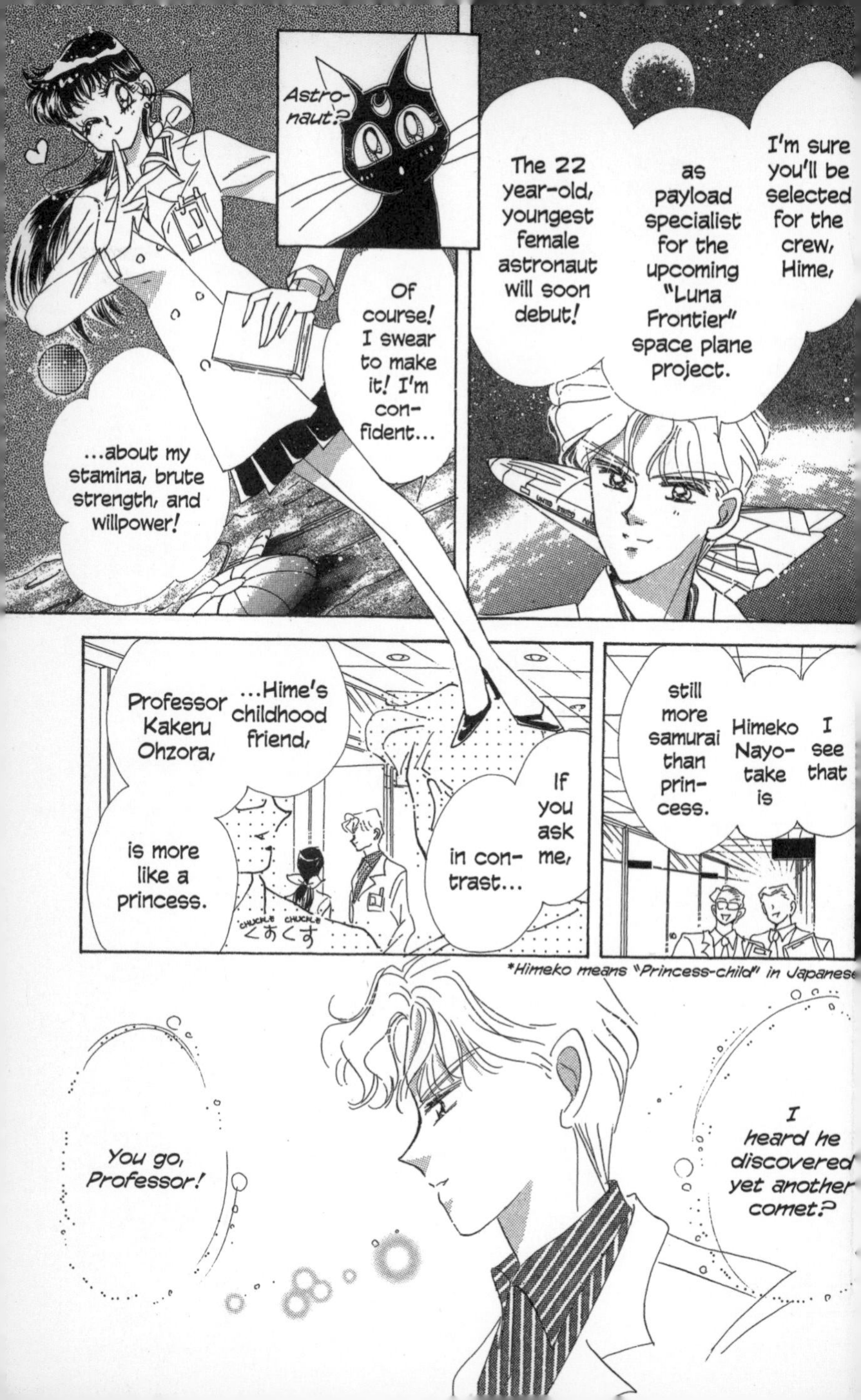
I'm sure you'll be selected for the crew, Hime,
as payload specialist for the upcoming "Luna Frontier" space plane project.
The 22 year-old, youngest female astronaut will soon debut!
Astro-naut?
Of course! I swear to make it! I'm con-fident...
...about my stamina, brute strength, and willpower!
I see that Himeko Nayo-take is
still more samurai than prin-cess.
If you ask me,
in con-trast...
Professor Kakeru Ohzora,
...Hime's childhood friend,
is more like a princess.
CHUCKLE CHUCKLE
くすくす
I heard he discovered yet another comet?
You go, Professor!

*Himeko means "Princess-child" in Japanes

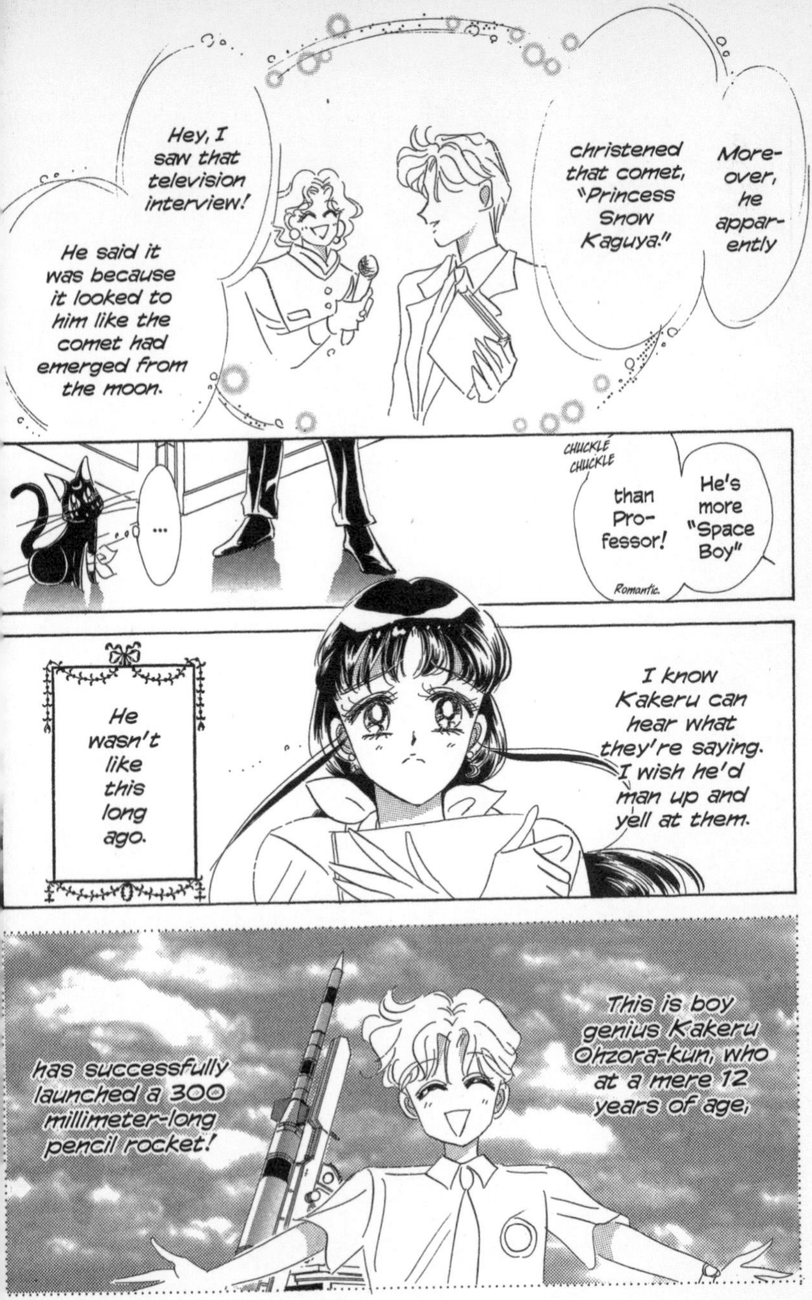
More-over, he apparently
christened that comet, "Princess Snow Kaguya."
Hey, I saw that television interview!
He said it was because it looked to him like the comet had emerged from the moon.
He's more "Space Boy"
than Pro-fessor!
Romantic.
CHUCKLE CHUCKLE
...
I know Kakeru can hear what they're saying. I wish he'd man up and yell at them.
He wasn't like this long ago.
This is boy genius Kakeru Ohzora-kun, who at a mere 12 years of age,
has successfully launched a 300 millimeter-long pencil rocket!

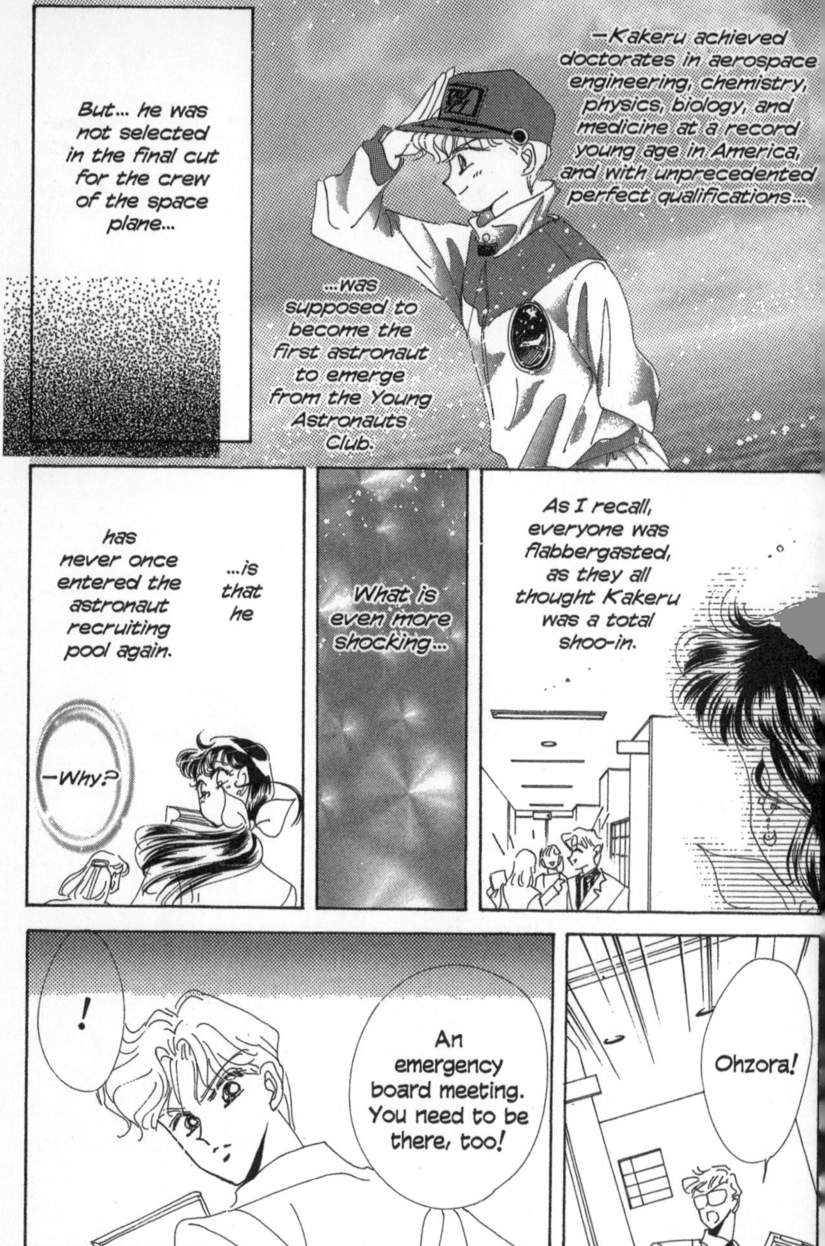
—Kakeru achieved doctorates in aerospace engineering, chemistry, physics, biology, and medicine at a record young age in America, and with unprecedented perfect qualifications...
...was supposed to become the first astronaut to emerge from the Young Astronauts Club.
But... he was not selected in the final cut for the crew of the space plane...
As I recall, everyone was flabbergasted, as they all thought Kakeru was a total shoo-in.
What is even more shocking...
...is that he
has never once entered the astronaut recruiting pool again.
—Why?
Ohzora!
An emergency board meeting. You need to be there, too!
!

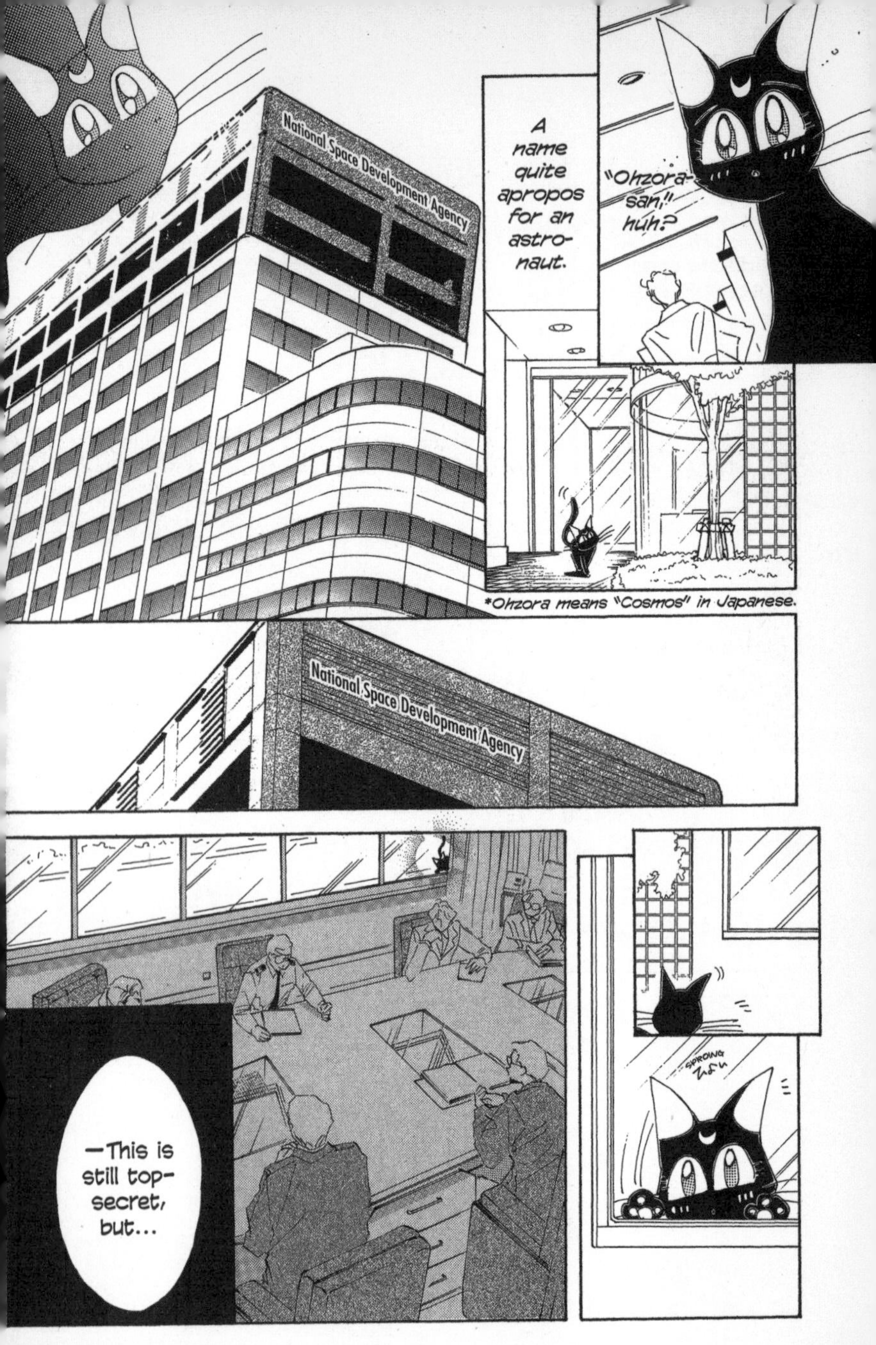
"Ohzora-san,*" huh?
A name quite apropos for an astronaut.
National Space Development Agency
*Ohzora means "Cosmos" in Japanese.
National Space Development Agency
SPROING
—This is still top-secret, but...

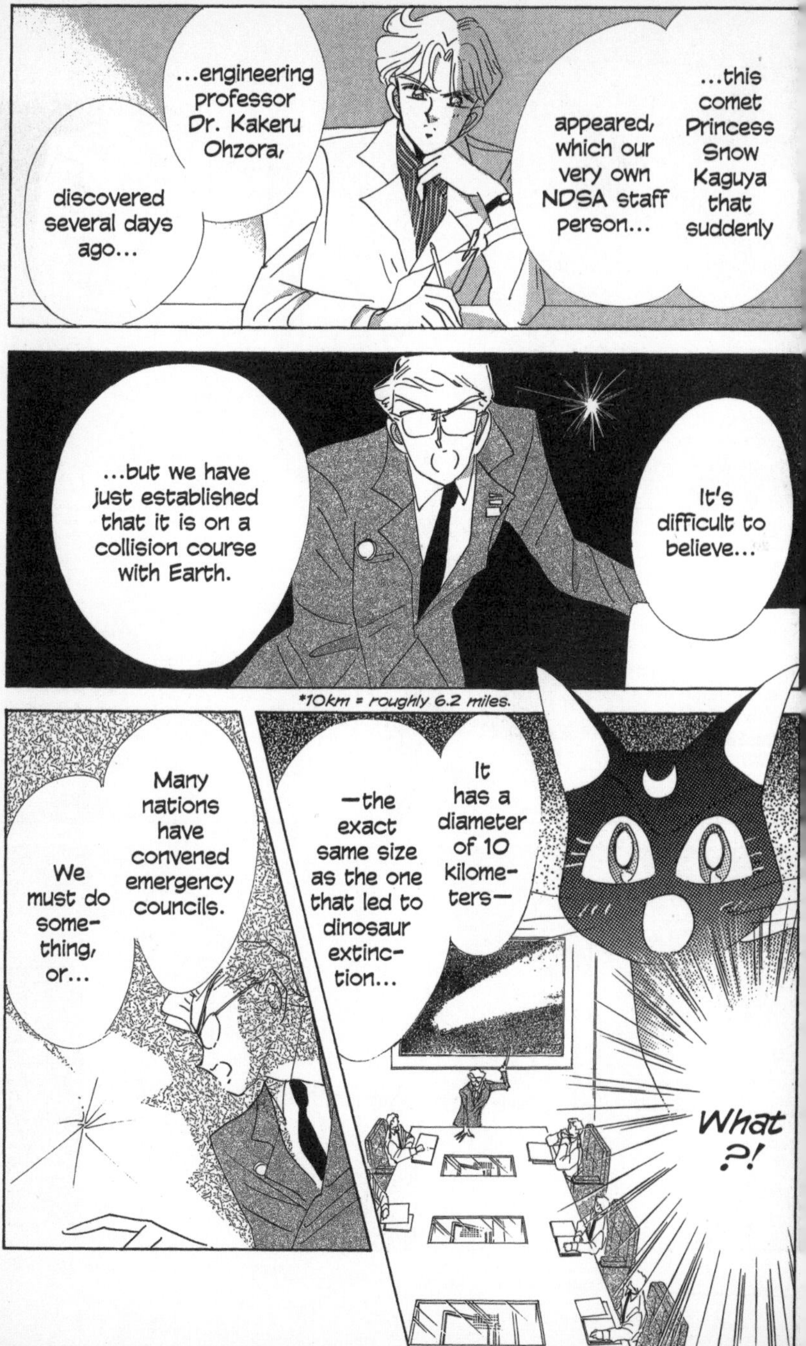
...this comet Princess Snow Kaguya that suddenly
appeared, which our very own NDSA staff person...
...engineering professor Dr. Kakeru Ohzora,
discovered several days ago...
It's difficult to believe...
...but we have just established that it is on a collision course with Earth.
It has a diameter of 10 kilometers—
—the exact same size as the one that led to dinosaur extinction...
What?!
Many nations have convened emergency councils.
We must do something, or...

*10km = roughly 6.2 miles.

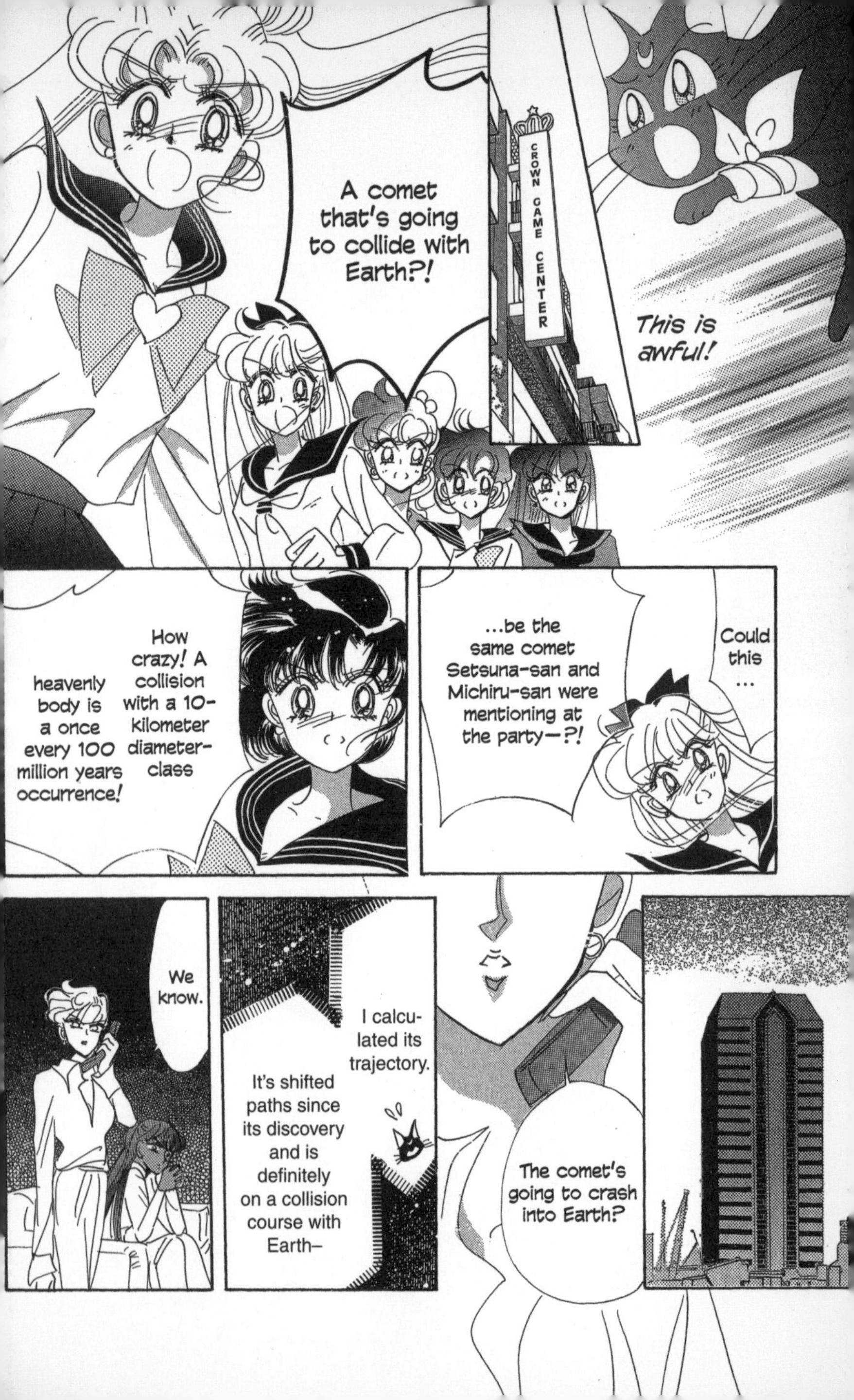
This is awful!
A comet that's going to collide with Earth?!
CROWN GAME CENTER
Could this...
...be the same comet Setsuna-san and Michiru-san were mentioning at the party—?!
How crazy! A collision with a 10-kilometer diameter-class
heavenly body is a once every 100 million years occurrence!
The comet's going to crash into Earth?
I calculated its trajectory.
It's shifted paths since its discovery and is definitely on a collision course with Earth–
We know.

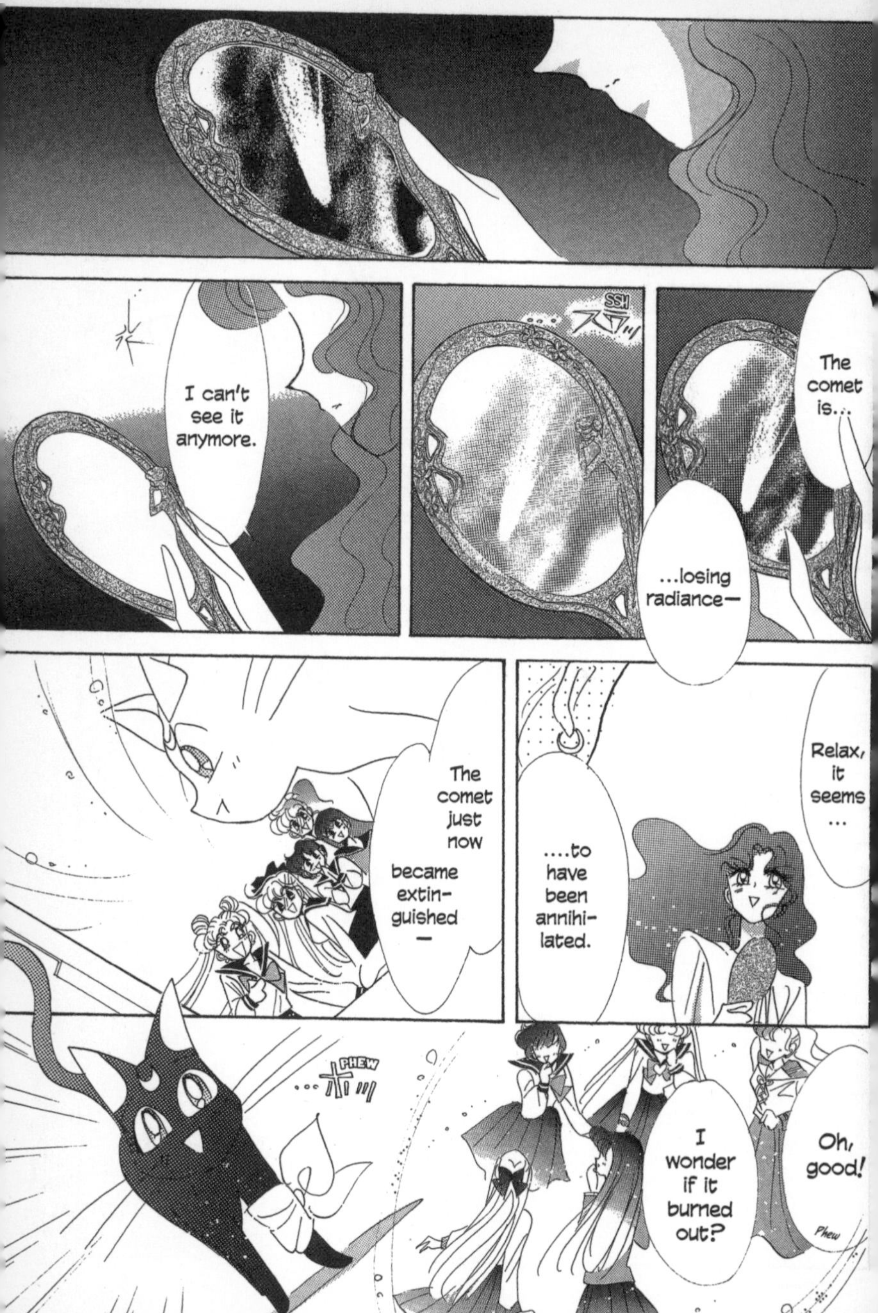
The comet is...
...losing radiance—
SSH
I can't see it anymore.
Relax, it seems ...
....to have been annihilated.
The comet just now became extinguished —
Oh, good!
Phew
I wonder if it burned out?
PHEW

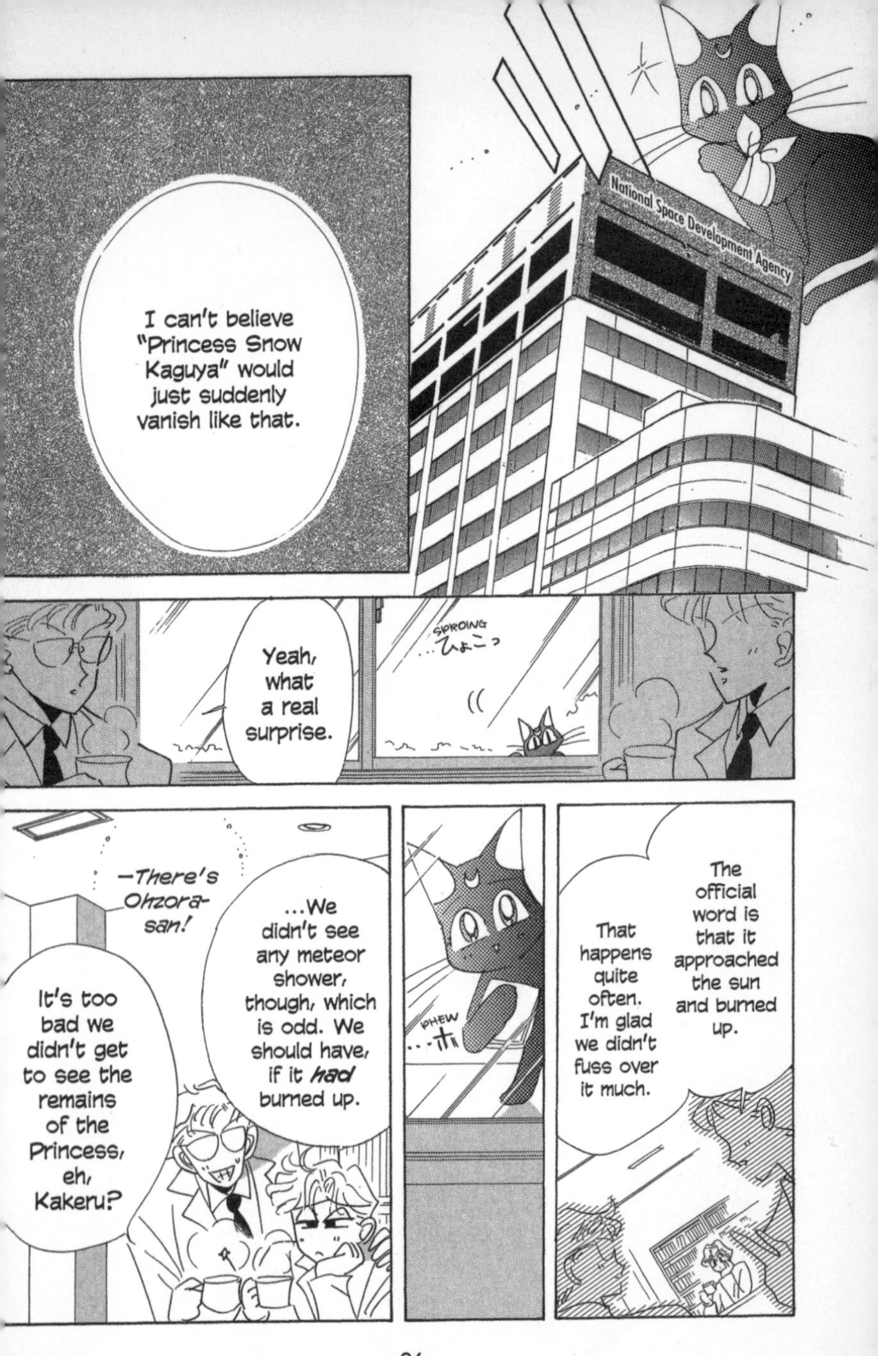
National Space Development Agency
I can't believe "Princess Snow Kaguya" would just suddenly vanish like that.
SPROING ひょこっ
Yeah, what a real surprise.
The official word is that it approached the sun and burned up.
That happens quite often. I'm glad we didn't fuss over it much.
PHEW
—There's Ohzora-san!
...We didn't see any meteor shower, though, which is odd. We should have, if it *had* burned up.
It's too bad we didn't get to see the remains of the Princess, eh, Kakeru?

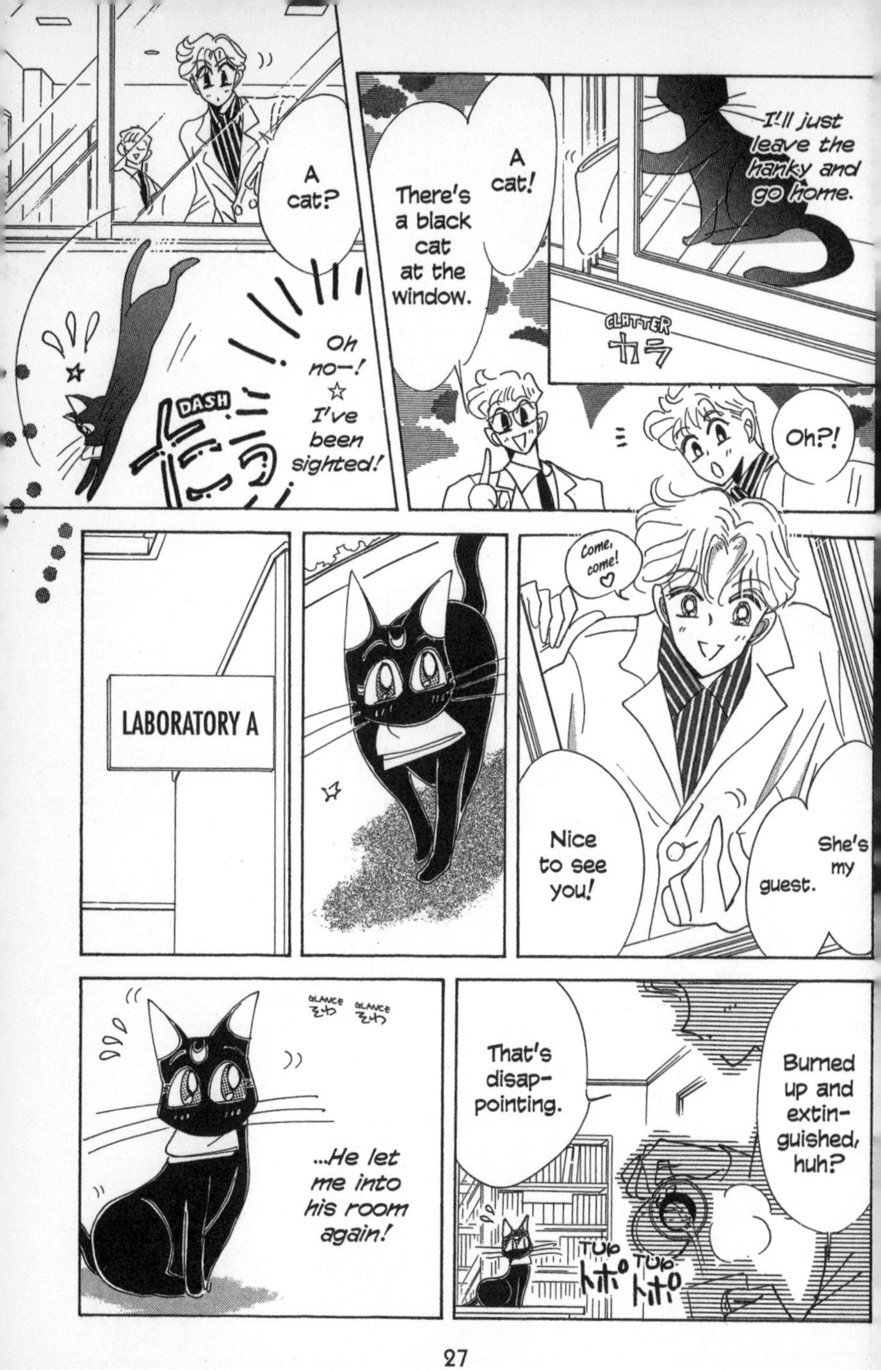
I'll just leave the hanky and go home.
CLATTER
カラ
Oh?!
A cat!
There's a black cat at the window.
A cat?
Oh no—! ☆ I've been sighted!
DASH
Come, come! ♡
She's my guest.
Nice to see you!
LABORATORY A
Burned up and extinguished, huh?
That's disappointing.
TUP
TUP
GLANCE
GLANCE
...He let me into his room again!

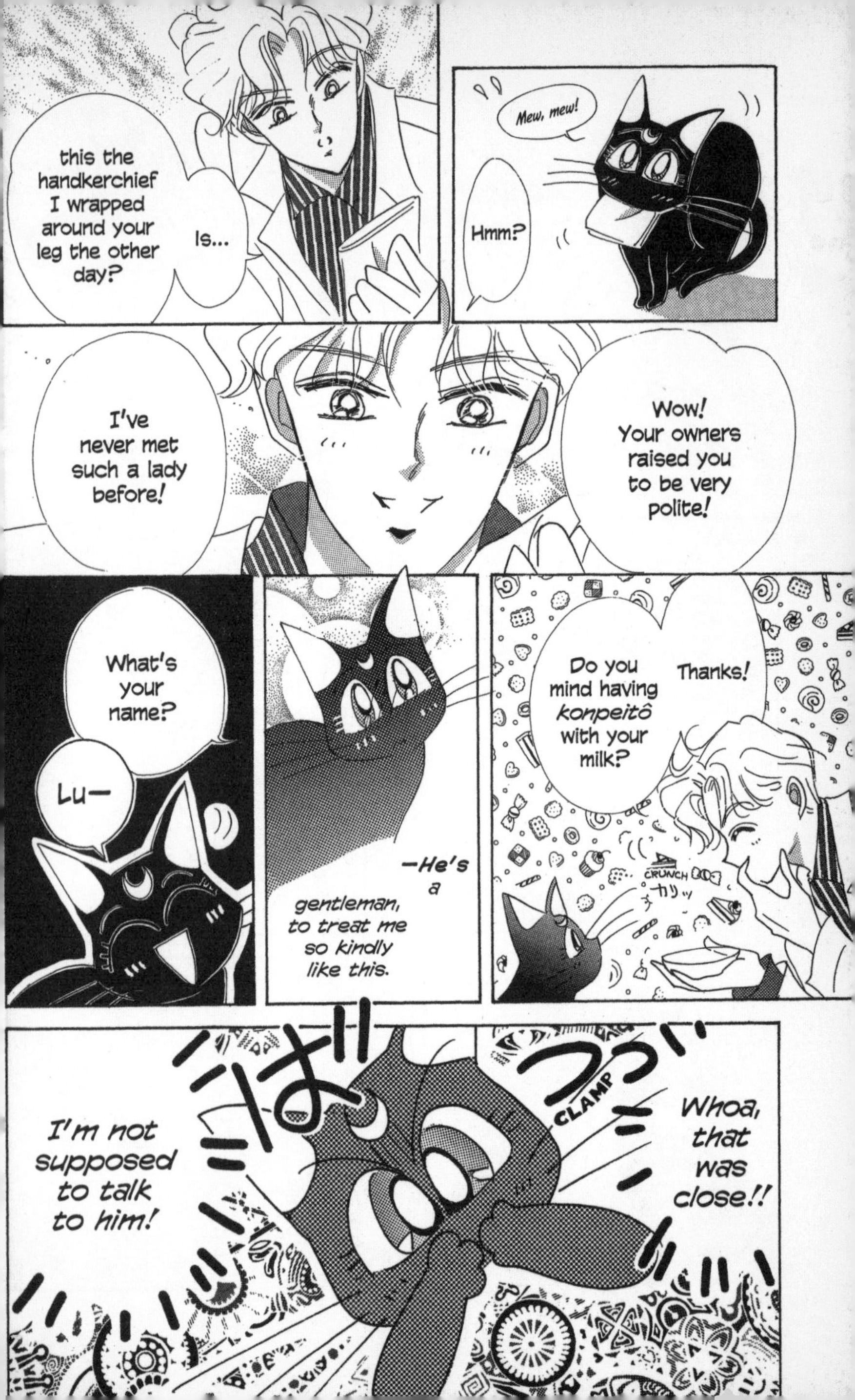
Mew, mew!
Hmm?
Is...
this the handkerchief I wrapped around your leg the other day?
Wow! Your owners raised you to be very polite!
I've never met such a lady before!
Thanks!
Do you mind having *konpeitô* with your milk?
CRUNCH
カリッ
—He's a gentleman, to treat me so kindly like this.
What's your name?
Lu—
Whoa, that was close!!
CLAMP
I'm not supposed to talk to him!

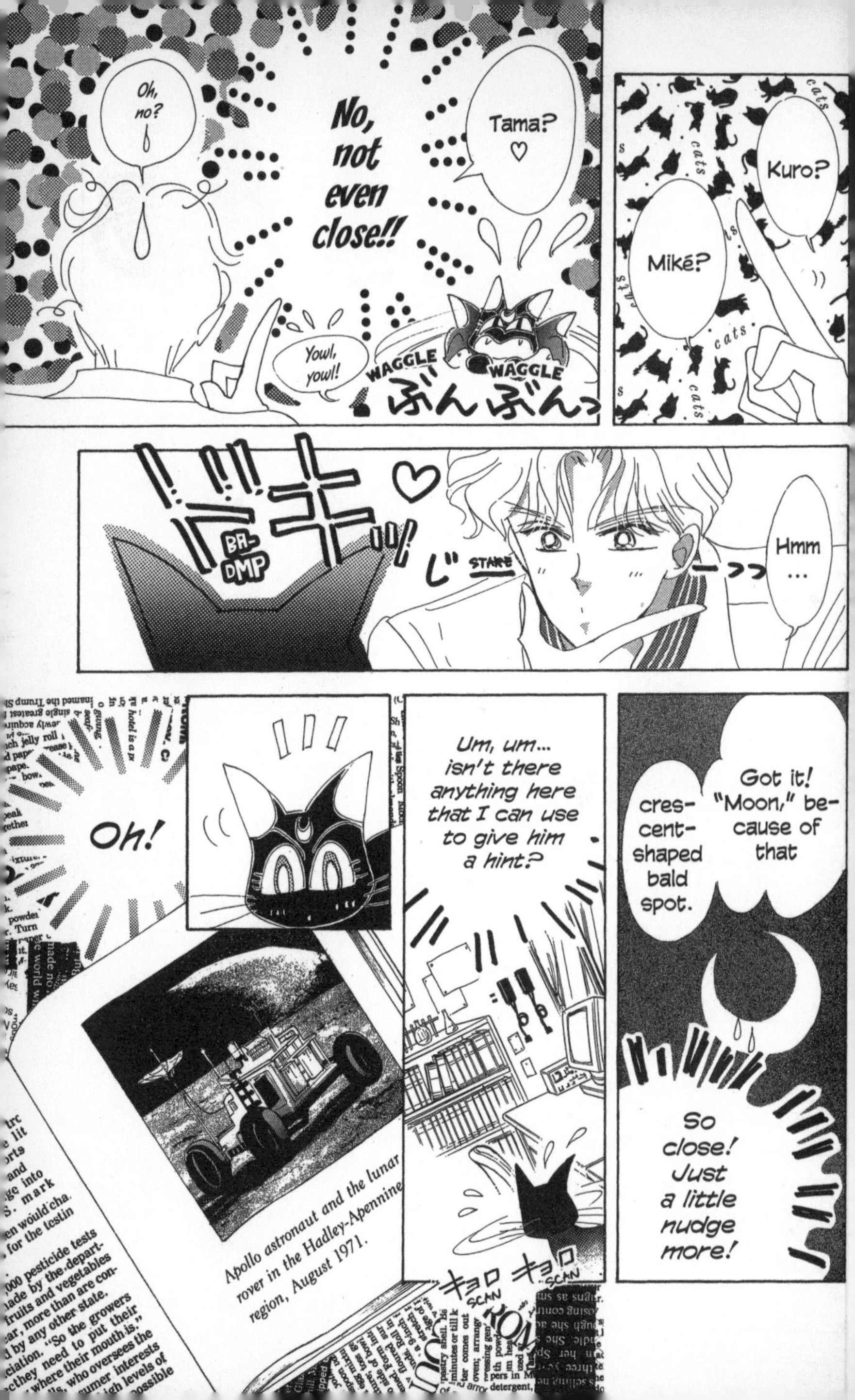
Kuro?
Miké?
Tama? ♥
No, not even close!!
Oh, no?
Yowl, yowl!
WAGGLE WAGGLE
ぶんぶんっ
Hmm...
じーっっ
STARE
ドキッ
BA-DMP
♥
Got it! "Moon," because of that
crescent-shaped bald spot.
So close! Just a little nudge more!
Um, um... isn't there anything here that I can use to give him a hint?
キョロ キョロ
SCAN SCAN
Oh!
Apollo astronaut and the lunar rover in the Hadley-Apennine region, August 1971.

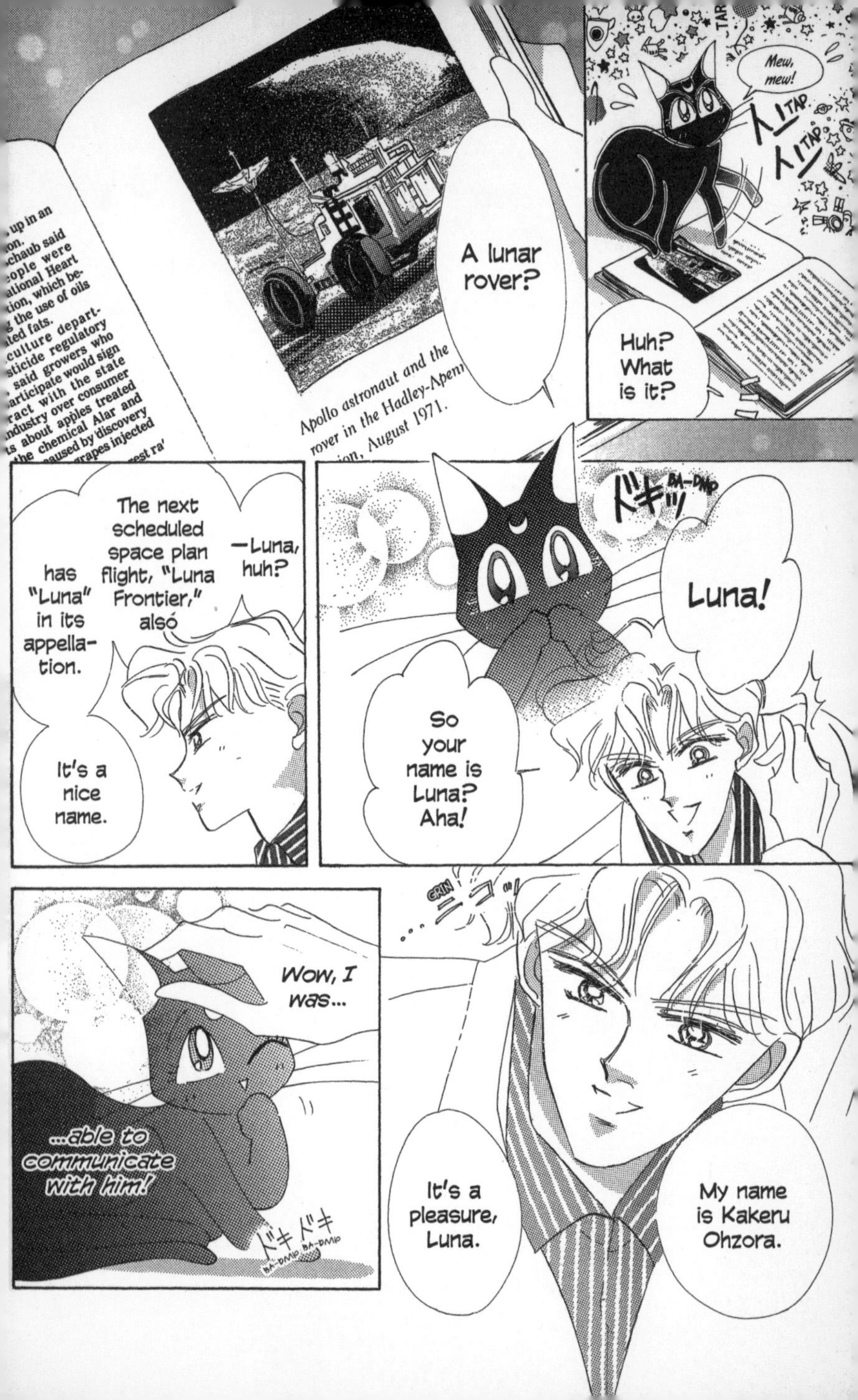

Mew, mew!
TAP
TAP
Huh? What is it?
A lunar rover?
BA-DMP
Luna!
So your name is Luna? Aha!
—Luna, huh?
The next scheduled space plan flight, "Luna Frontier," also has "Luna" in its appellation.
It's a nice name.
GRIN
My name is Kakeru Ohzora.
It's a pleasure, Luna.
Wow, I was...
...able to communicate with him!
BA-DMP BA-DMP

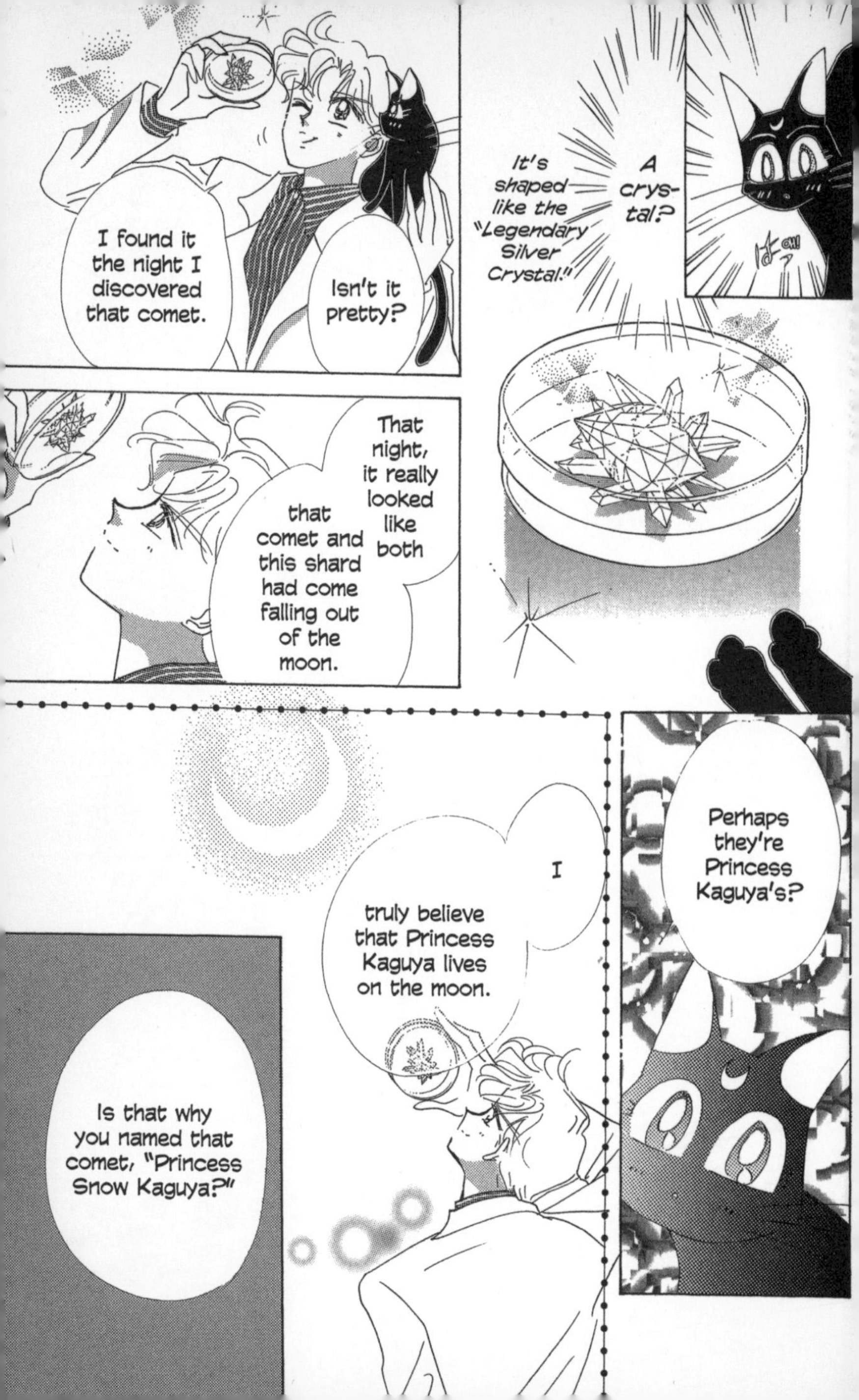
はっ OH!
A crystal?
It's shaped like the "Legendary Silver Crystal!"
Isn't it pretty?
I found it the night I discovered that comet.
That night, it really looked like both that comet and this shard had come falling out of the moon.
Perhaps they're Princess Kaguya's?
I truly believe that Princess Kaguya lives on the moon.
Is that why you named that comet, "Princess Snow Kaguya?"

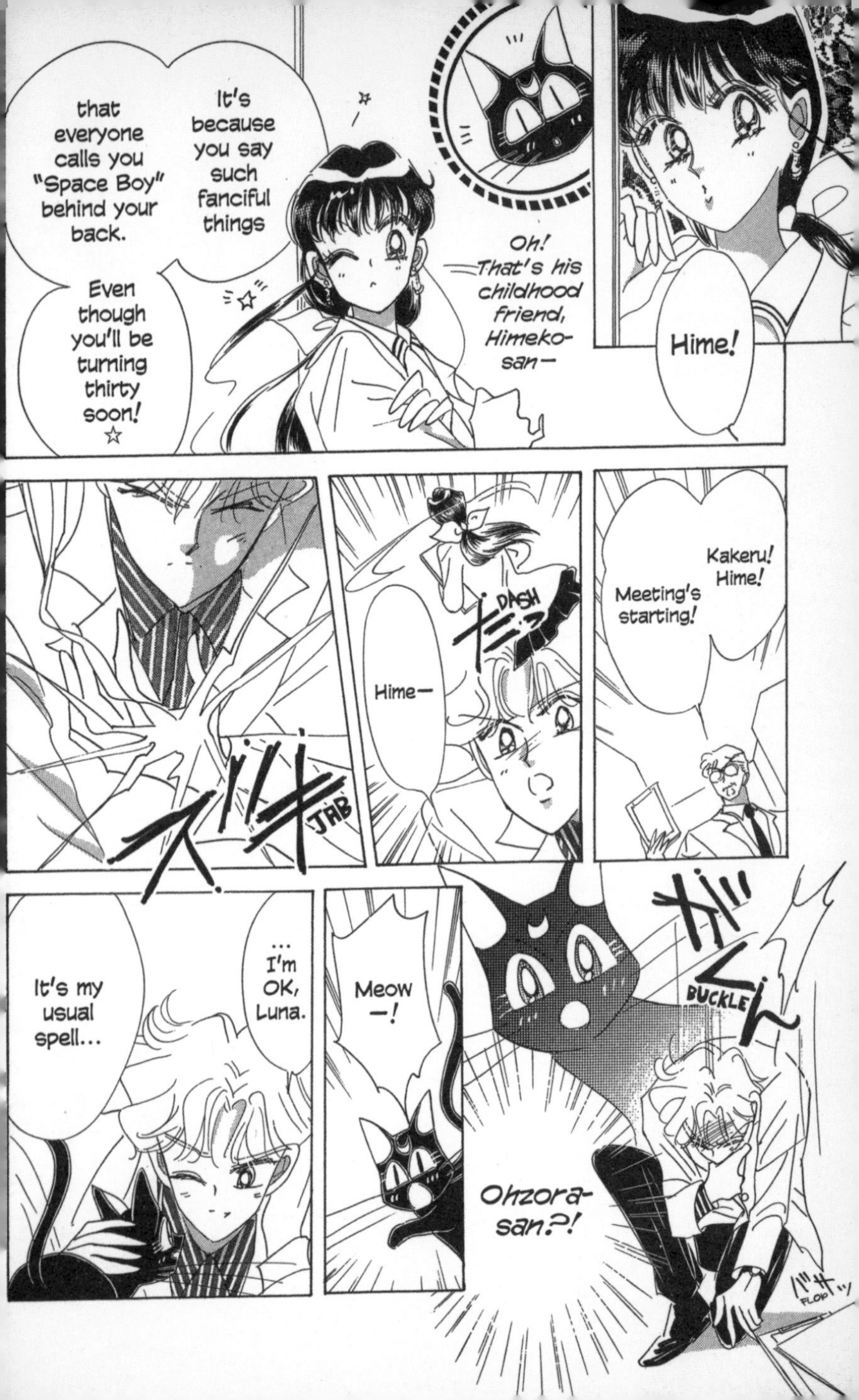
Hime!
Oh! That's his childhood friend, Himeko-san—
It's because you say such fanciful things
that everyone calls you "Space Boy" behind your back.
Even though you'll be turning thirty soon! ☆
Kakeru! Hime!
Meeting's starting!
DASH
Hime—
JAB
BUCKLE
Ohzora-san?!
FLOP
Meow—!
... I'm OK, Luna.
It's my usual spell...

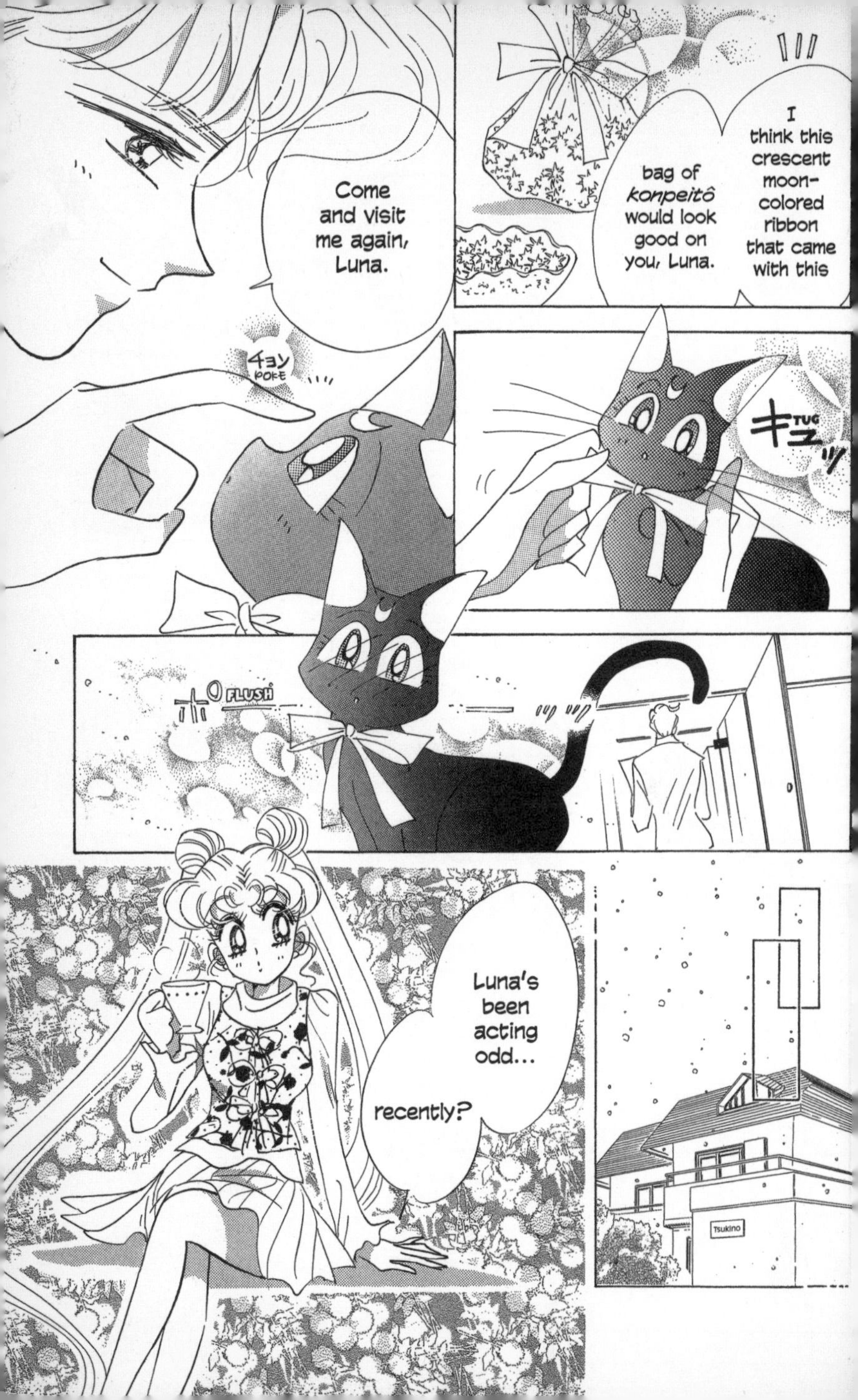

I think this crescent moon-colored ribbon that came with this
bag of *konpeitô* would look good on you, Luna.
TUG
Come and visit me again, Luna.
POKE
FLUSH
Tsukino
Luna's been acting odd...
recently?

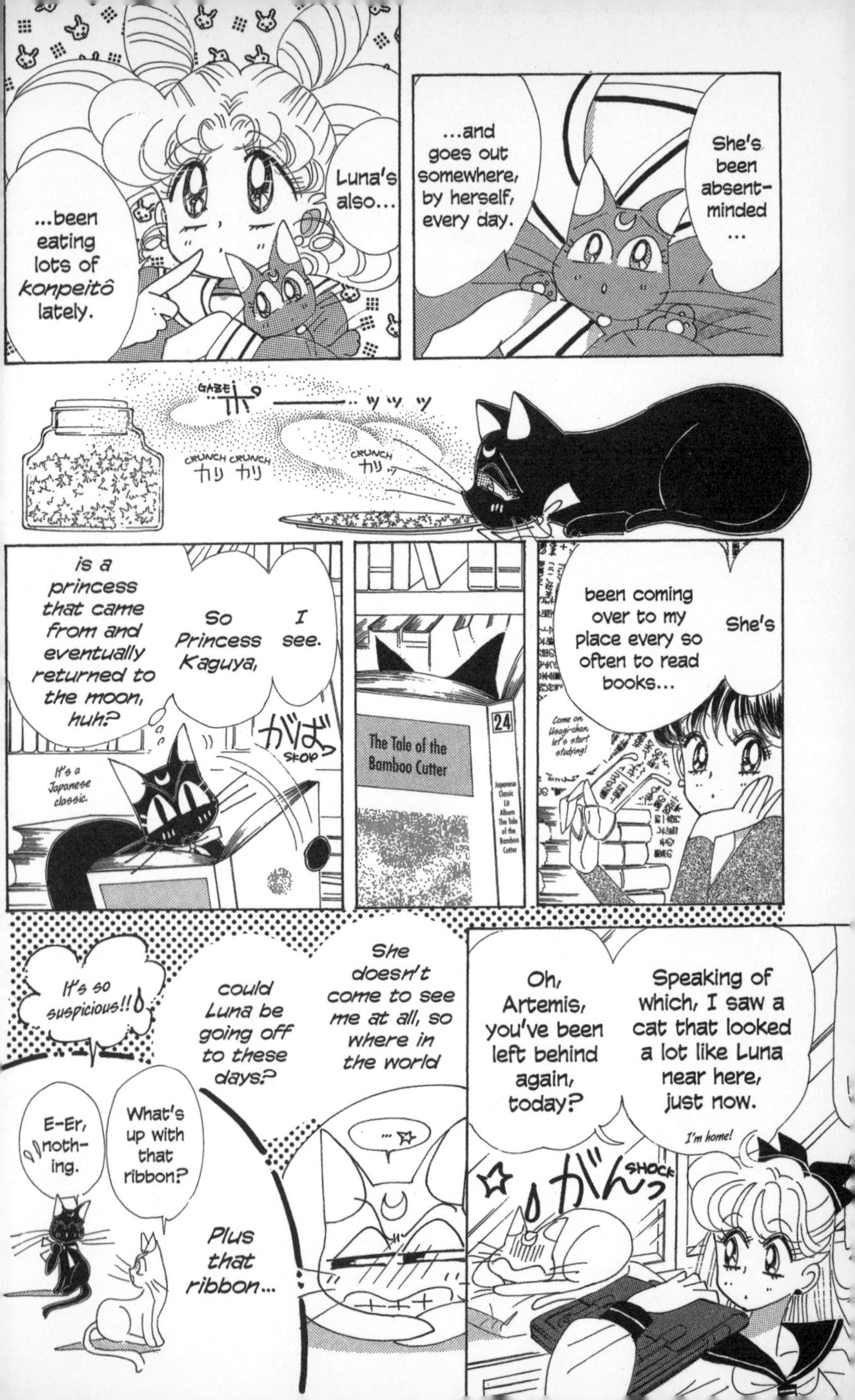
She's been absent-minded ...
...and goes out somewhere, by herself, every day.
Luna's also...
...been eating lots of *konpeitô* lately.
GAZE ポー……ッツッ
CRUNCH カリッ
CRUNCH CRUNCH カリ カリ
She's
been coming over to my place every so often to read books...
Come on, Usagi-chan, let's start studying!
24
The Tale of the Bamboo Cutter
Japanese Classic Lit Album The Tale of the Bamboo Cutter
I see.
So Princess Kaguya,
is a princess that came from and eventually returned to the moon, huh?
がばっ STOP
It's a Japanese classic.
Speaking of which, I saw a cat that looked a lot like Luna near here, just now.
Oh, Artemis, you've been left behind again, today?
I'm home!
がんっ SHOCK
She doesn't come to see me at all, so where in the world
could Luna be going off to these days?
It's so suspicious!!
...
Plus that ribbon...
What's up with that ribbon?
E-Er, noth-ing.

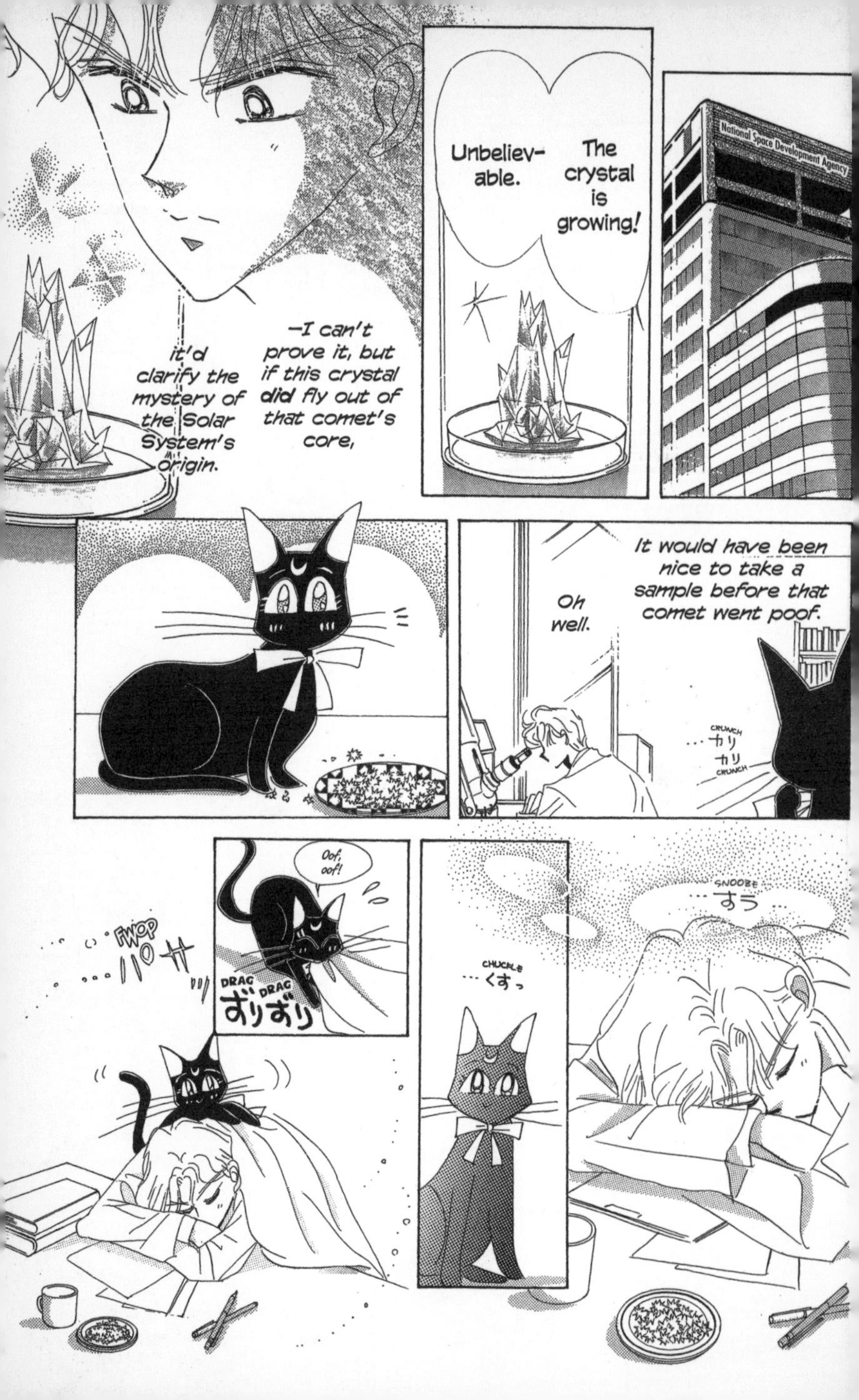
National Space Development Agency
Unbeliev-able.
The crystal is growing!
—I can't prove it, but if this crystal did fly out of that comet's core,
it'd clarify the mystery of the Solar System's origin.
It would have been nice to take a sample before that comet went poof.
Oh well.
CRUNCH
…カリ
カリ
CRUNCH
SNOOZE
…すう…
CHUCKLE
…くすっ
Oof, oof!
DRAG DRAG
ずりずり
FWOP
パサ

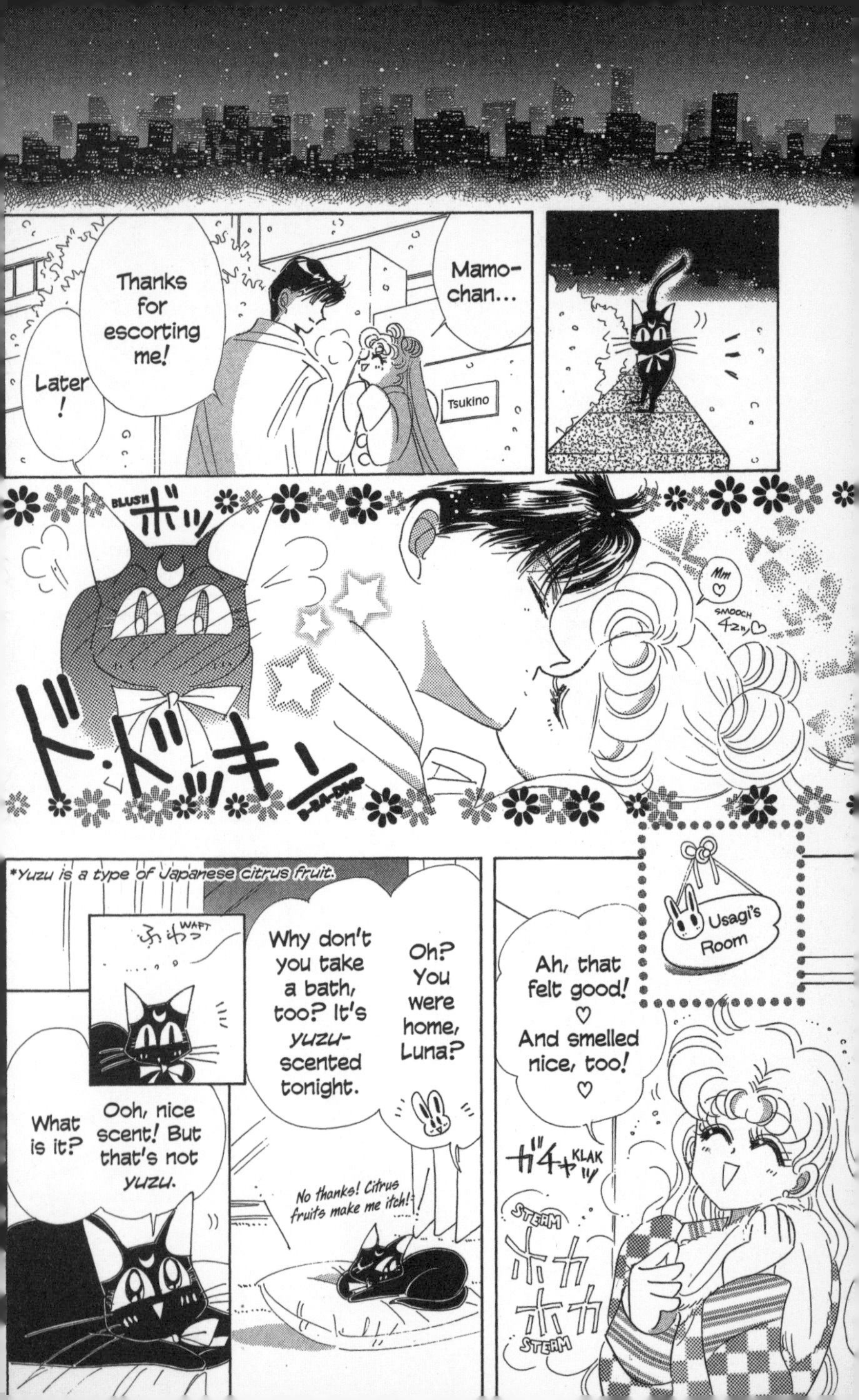
Mamo-chan...
Tsukino
Thanks for escorting me!
Later!
Mm ♡
SMOOCH
BLUSH
D-DA-DMP
Usagi's Room
Ah, that felt good! ♡ And smelled nice, too! ♡
KLAK
STEAM
STEAM
Oh? You were home, Luna?
Why don't you take a bath, too? It's *yuzu*-scented tonight.
No thanks! Citrus fruits make me itch!
*Yuzu is a type of Japanese citrus fruit.
WAFT
......
Ooh, nice scent! But that's not *yuzu*.
What is it?

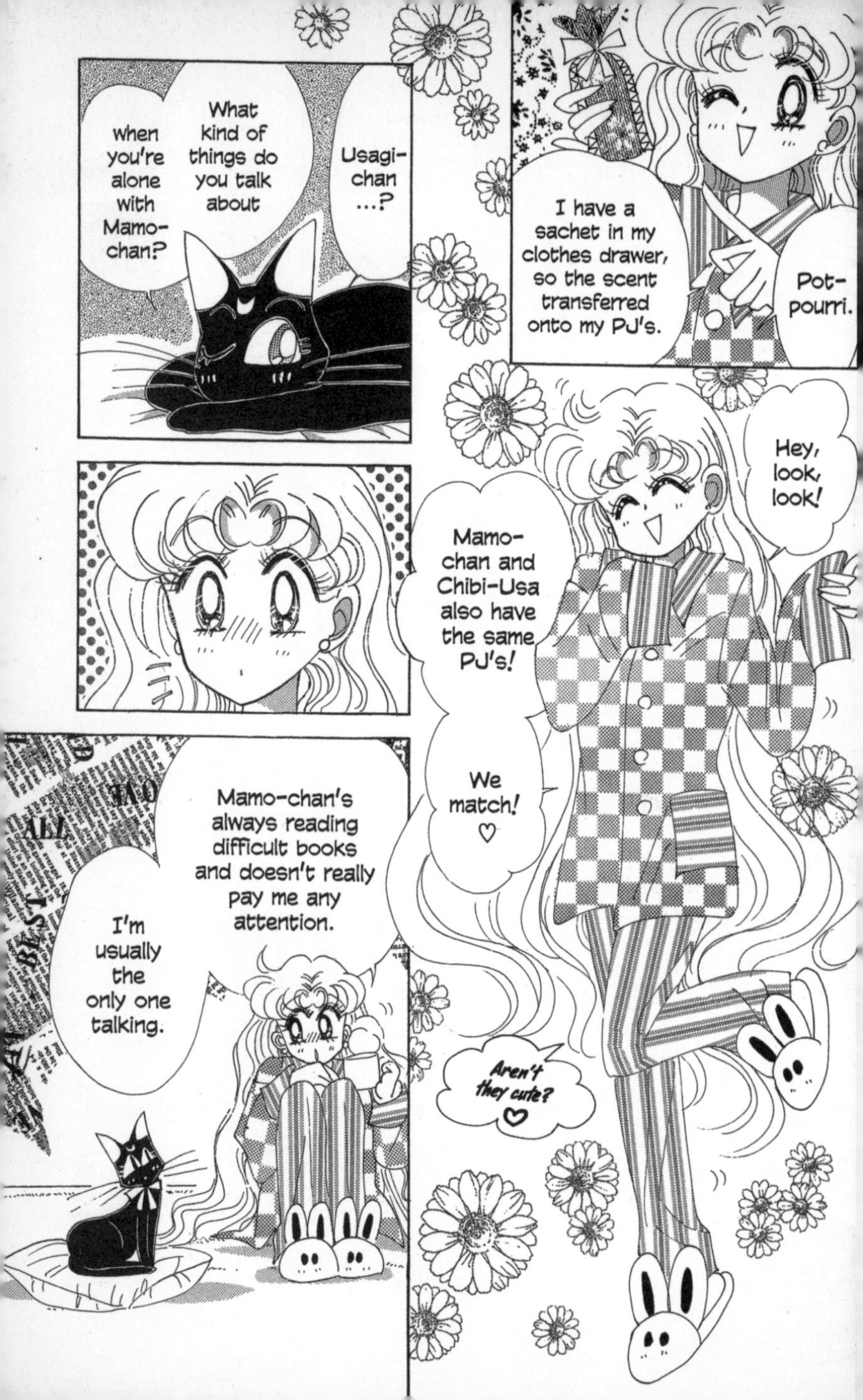
Pot-pourri.
I have a sachet in my clothes drawer, so the scent transferred onto my PJ's.
Hey, look, look!
Mamo-chan and Chibi-Usa also have the same PJ's!
We match! ♡
Aren't they cute? ♡
Usagi-chan ...?
What kind of things do you talk about
when you're alone with Mamo-chan?
Mamo-chan's always reading difficult books and doesn't really pay me any attention.
I'm usually the only one talking.

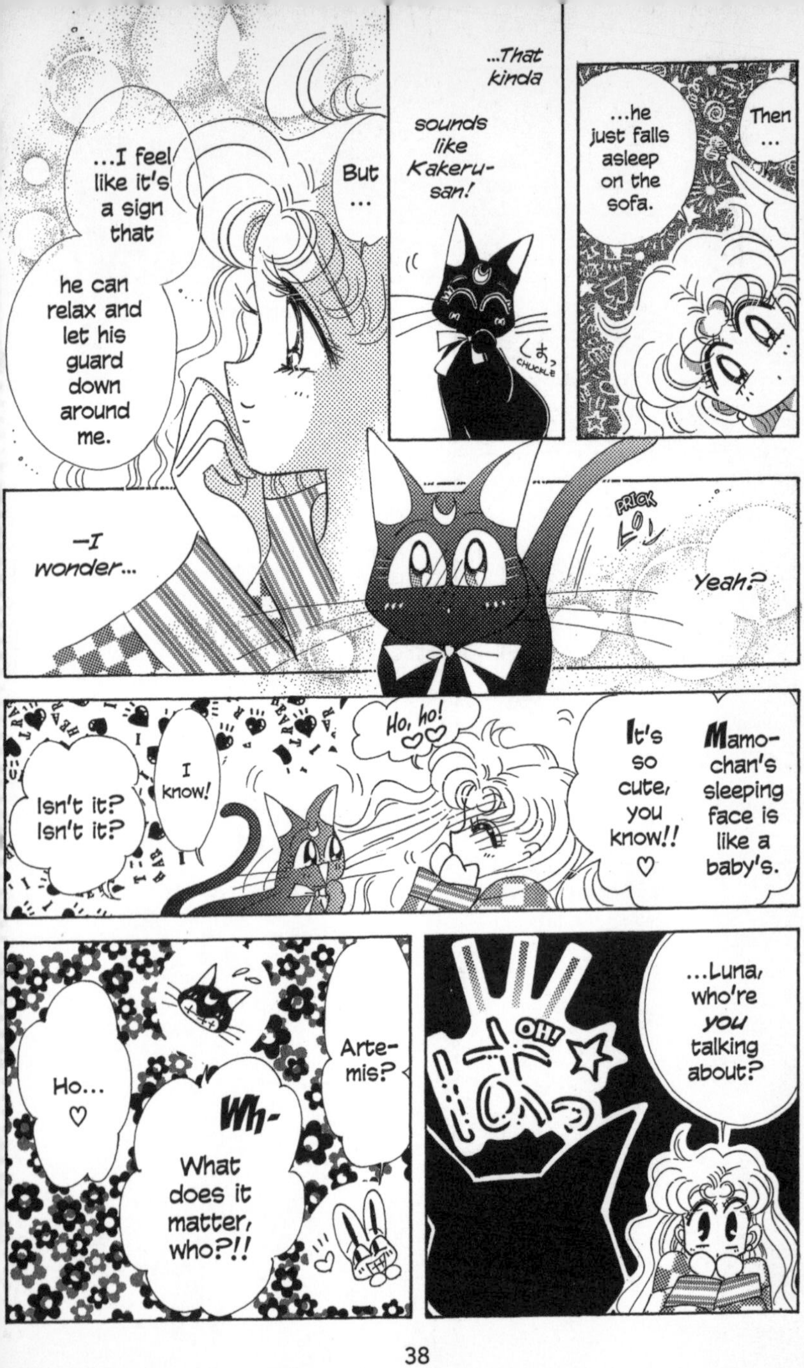
Then...
...he just falls asleep on the sofa.
...That kinda
sounds like Kakeru-san!
CHUCKLE
But...
...I feel like it's a sign that
he can relax and let his guard down around me.
PRICK
Yeah?
—I wonder...
Mamo-chan's sleeping face is like a baby's.
It's so cute, you know!! ♡
Ho, ho! ♡♡
I know!
Isn't it? Isn't it?
...Luna, who're you talking about?
OH!
Arte-mis?
Wh-
What does it matter, who?!!
Ho... ♡

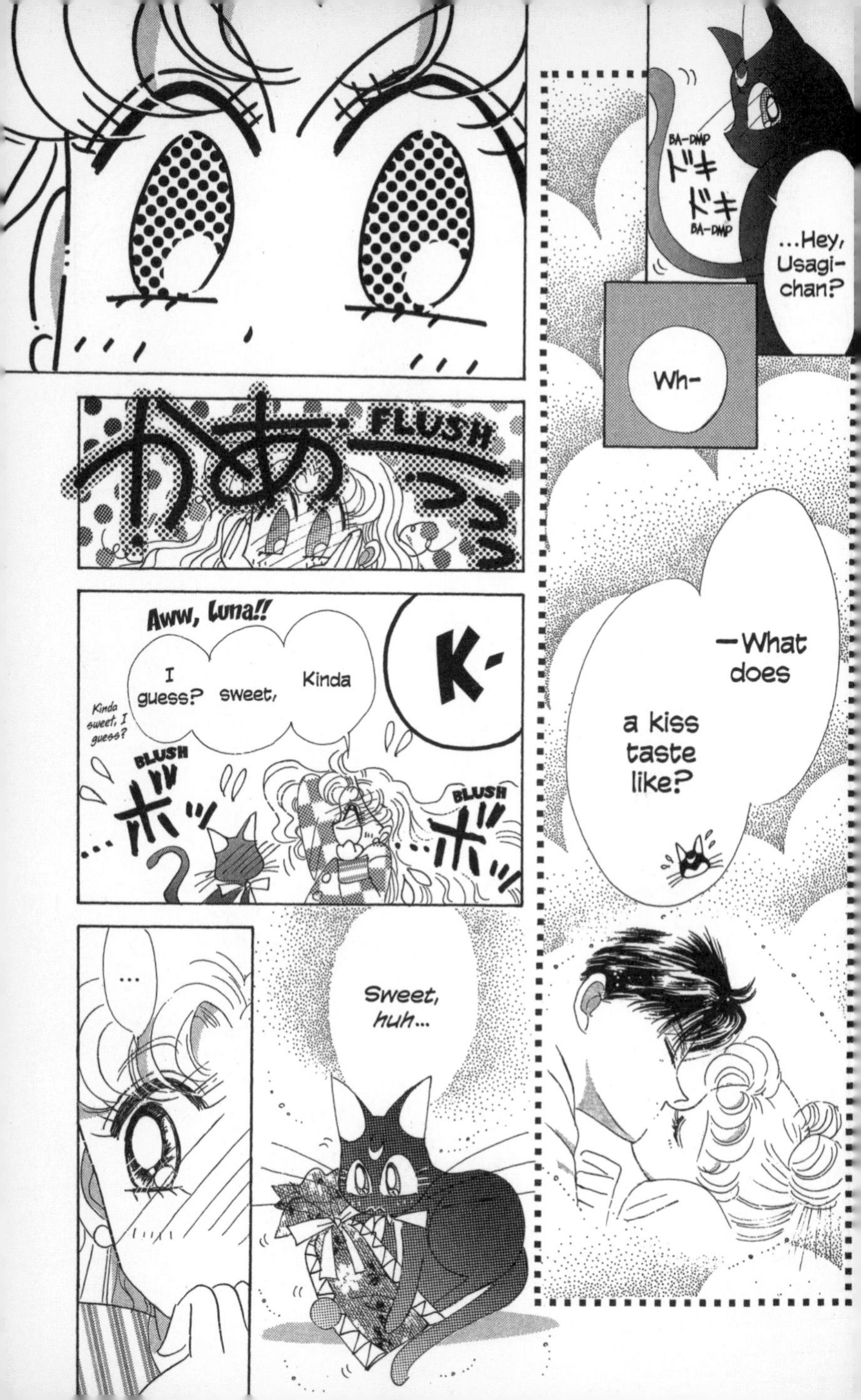

ドキ BA-DMP
ドキ BA-DMP
...Hey, Usagi-chan?
Wh-
—What does a kiss taste like?
かあーっっっ FLUSH
K-
Kinda sweet, I guess?
Kinda sweet, I guess?
Aww, Luna!!
ボッ BLUSH
...ボッ BLUSH
...
Sweet, huh...
...

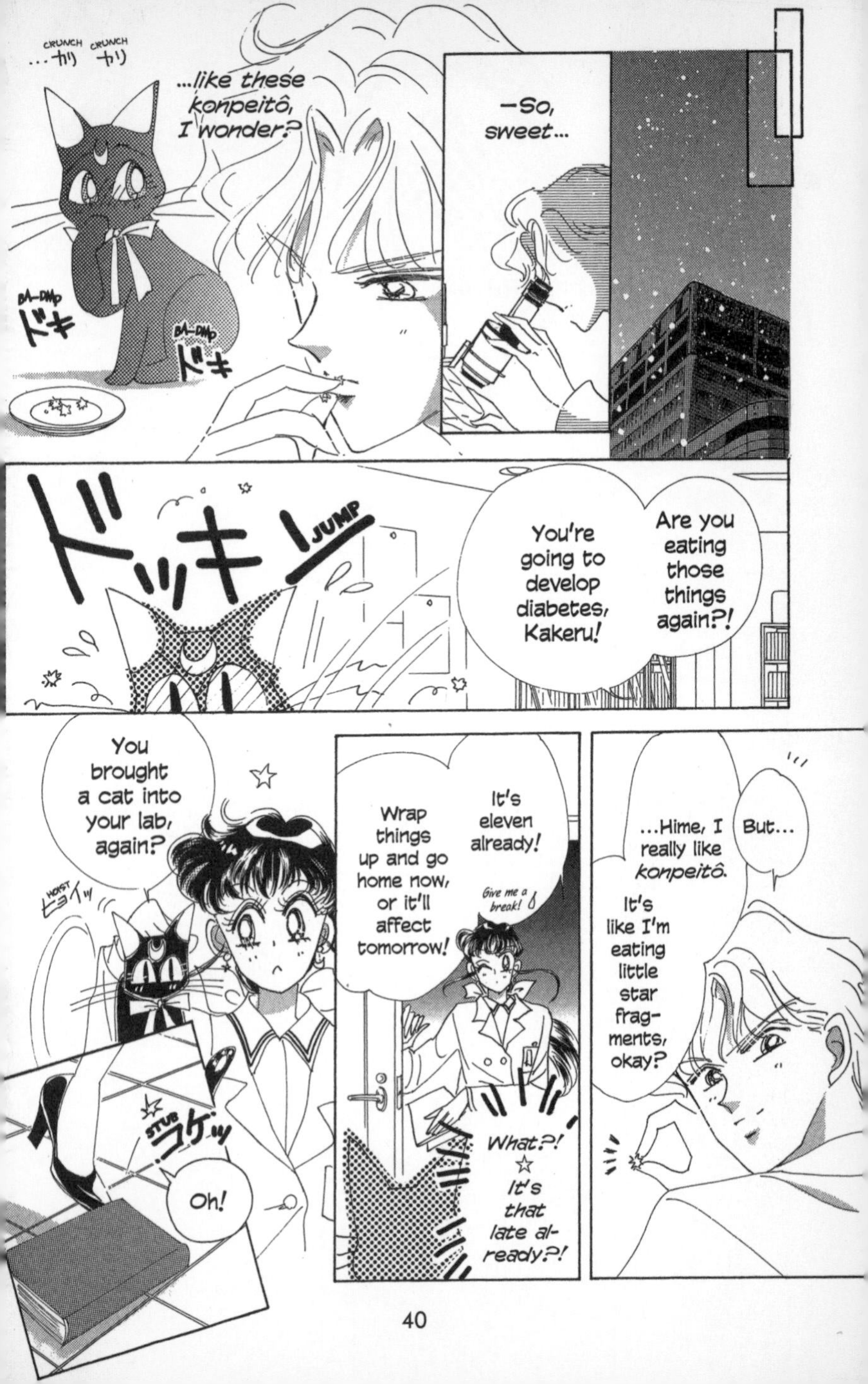
—So, sweet...
...like these konpeitô, I wonder?
CRUNCH CRUNCH ...カリ カリ
BA-DMP ドキ
BA-DMP ドキ
Are you eating those things again?!
You're going to develop diabetes, Kakeru!
JUMP ドッキン
But...
...Hime, I really like konpeitô.
It's like I'm eating little star frag- ments, okay?
It's eleven already!
Wrap things up and go home now, or it'll affect tomorrow!
Give me a break!
What?! ☆ It's that late al- ready?!
You brought a cat into your lab, again?
HOIST ヒョイッ
STUB コケッ
Oh!

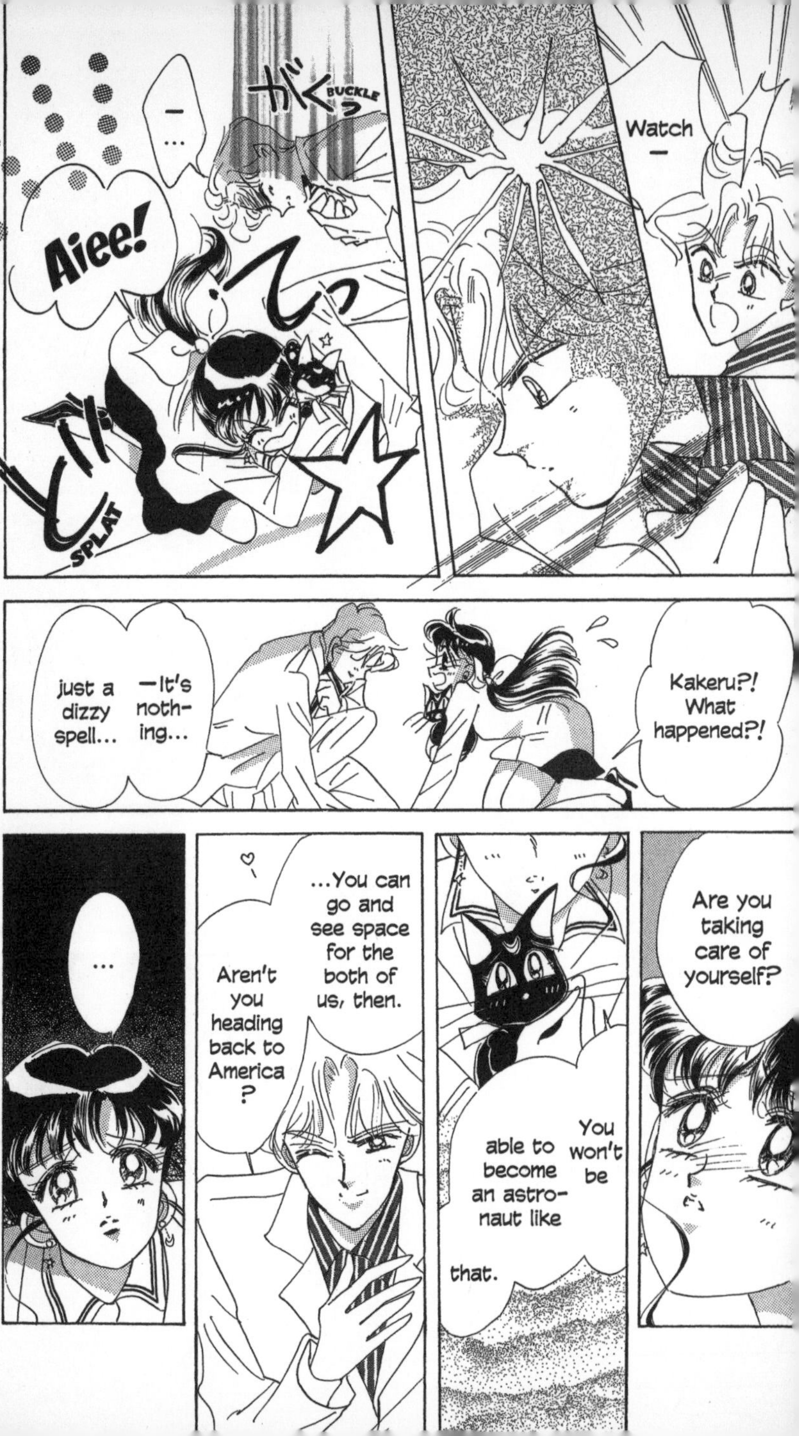

Watch —
— ...
がく BUCKLE
Aiee!
ひっ
SPLAT
Kakeru?! What happened?!
—It's nothing... just a dizzy spell...
Are you taking care of yourself?
You won't be able to become an astronaut like that.
...You can go and see space for the both of us, then.
Aren't you heading back to America?
...

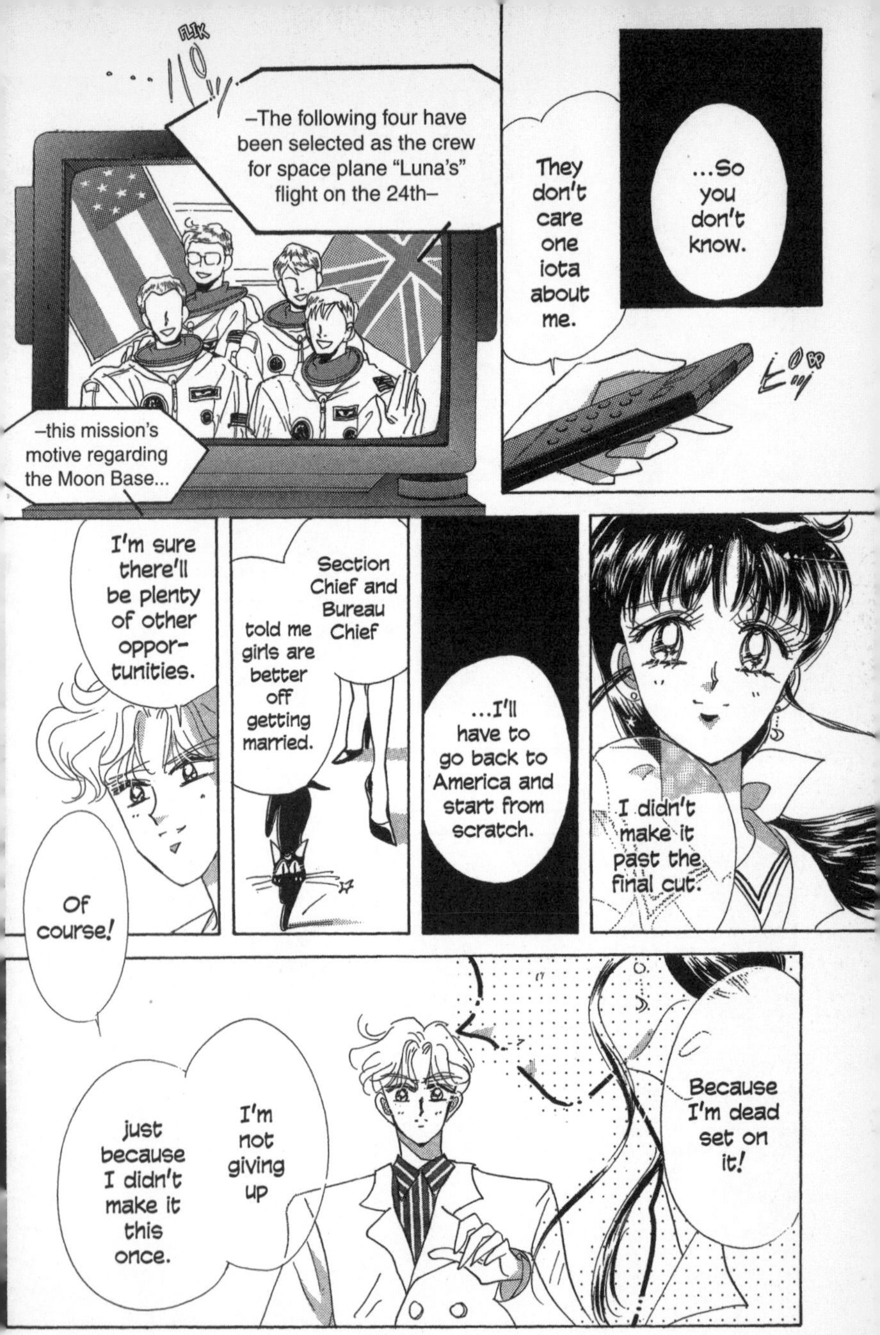
...So you don't know.
They don't care one iota about me.
BP
FLIK
–The following four have been selected as the crew for space plane "Luna's" flight on the 24th–
–this mission's motive regarding the Moon Base...
I didn't make it past the final cut.
...I'll have to go back to America and start from scratch.
Section Chief and Bureau Chief told me girls are better off getting married.
I'm sure there'll be plenty of other opportunities.
Of course!
Because I'm dead set on it!
I'm not giving up just because I didn't make it this once.

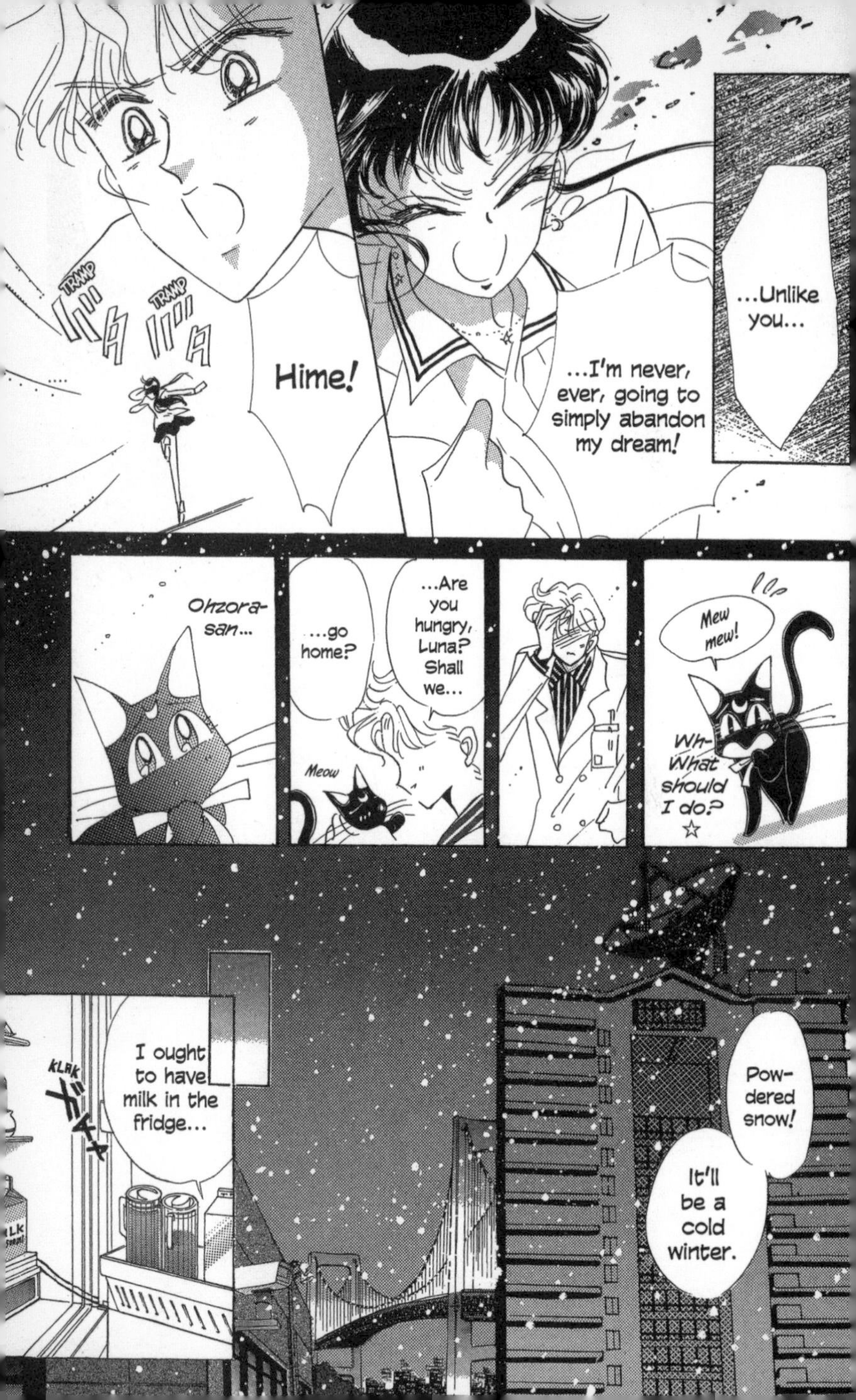
...Unlike you...
...I'm never, ever, going to simply abandon my dream!
Hime!
TRAMP
TRAMP
....
Mew mew!
Wh-What should I do? ☆
...Are you hungry, Luna? Shall we...
...go home?
Meow
Ohzora-san...
Pow-dered snow!
It'll be a cold winter.
I ought to have milk in the fridge...
KLAK

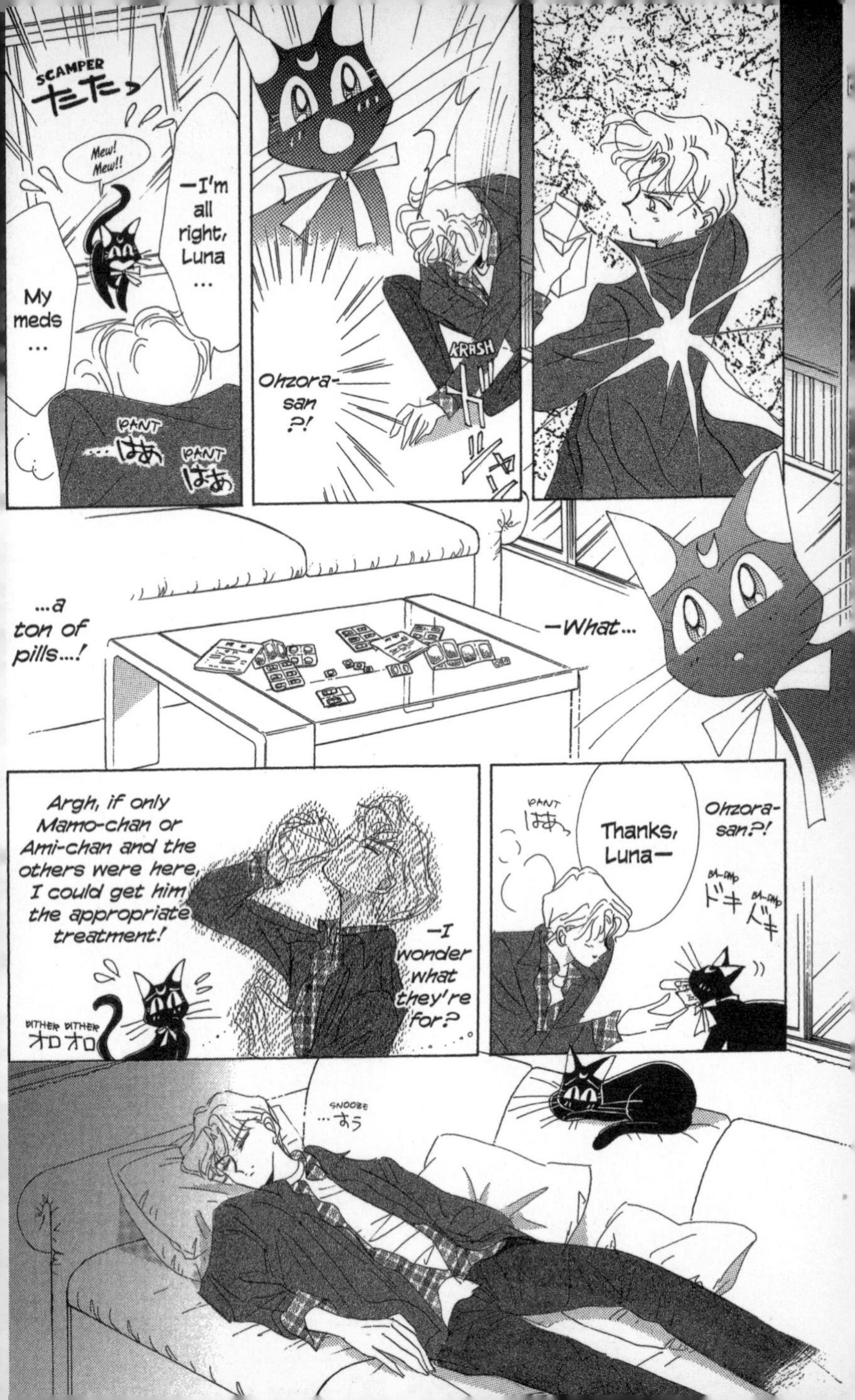
KRASH
Ohzora-san ?!
SCAMPER たたっ
Mew! Mew!!
—I'm all right, Luna ...
My meds ...
PANT はあ
PANT はあ
—What...
...a ton of pills...!
Ohzora-san?!
Thanks, Luna—
PANT はあっ
BA-DMP ドキ
BA-DMP ドキ
—I wonder what they're for?
Argh, if only Mamo-chan or Ami-chan and the others were here, I could get him the appropriate treatment!
DITHER DITHER オロオロ
SNOOZE ...おう

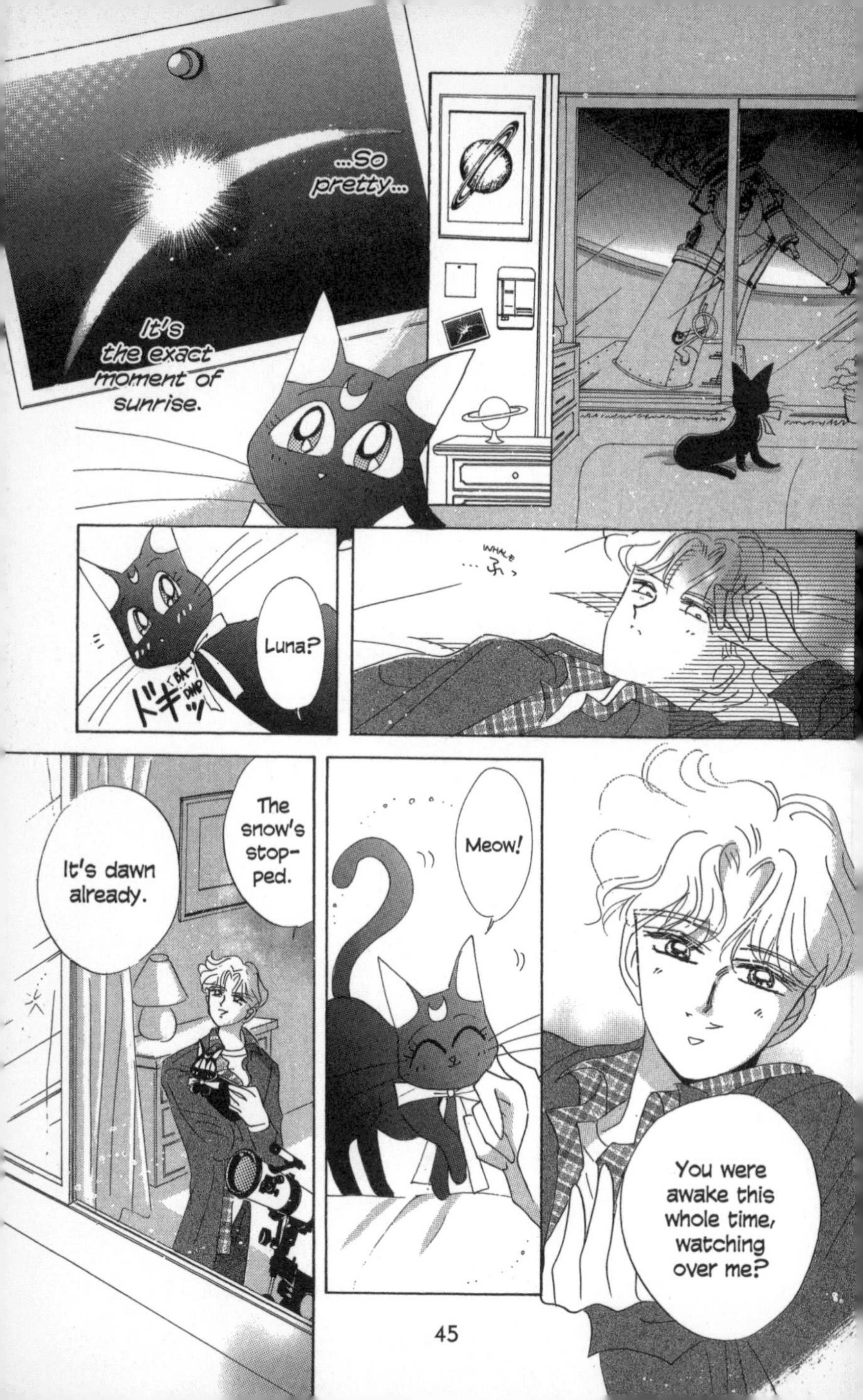
...So pretty...
It's the exact moment of sunrise.
WHALE
...ふっ
Luna?
ドキッ BA-DMP
You were awake this whole time, watching over me?
Meow!
The snow's stop-ped.
It's dawn already.

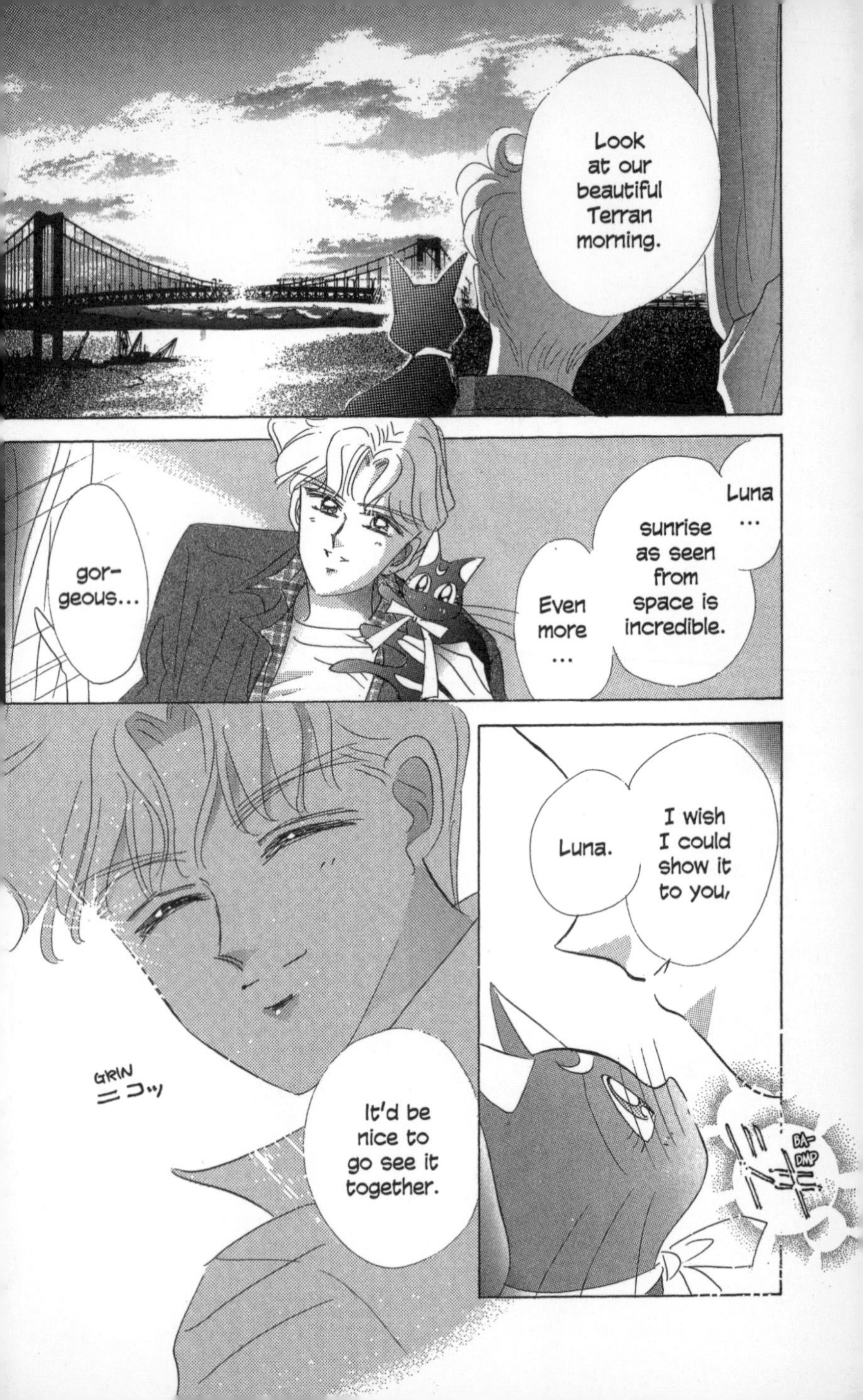

Look at our beautiful Terran morning.
Luna ...
sunrise as seen from space is incredible.
Even more ...
gor-geous...
I wish I could show it to you,
Luna.
BA-DMP
GRIN
It'd be nice to go see it together.

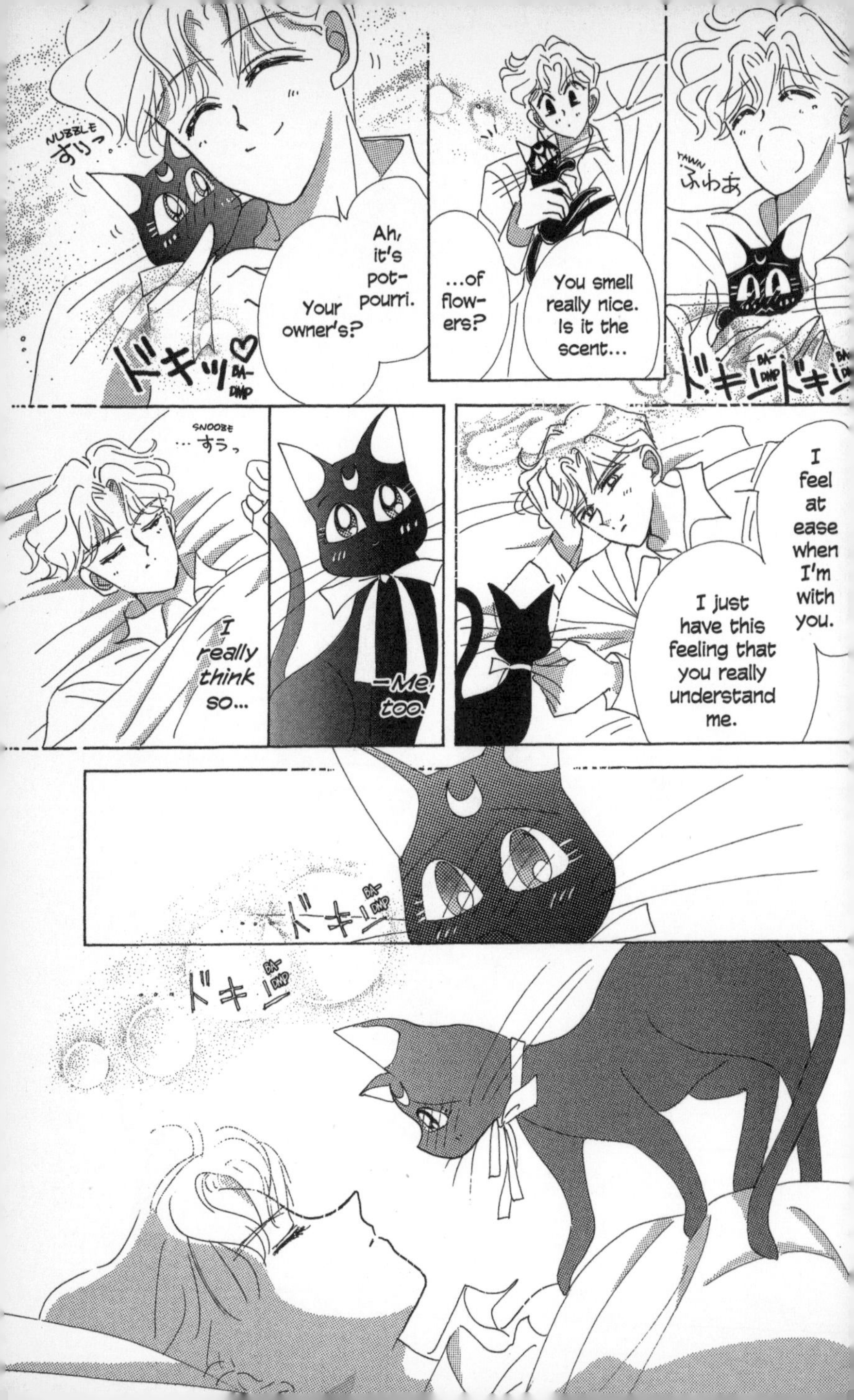
YAWN
ふわあ
BA-DMP
BA-DMP
You smell really nice. Is it the scent...
...of flowers?
Ah, it's pot-pourri.
Your owner's?
NUZZLE
すりっ
BA-DMP
I feel at ease when I'm with you.
I just have this feeling that you really understand me.
—Me, too.
SNOOZE
すうっ
I really think so...
BA-DMP
BA-DMP

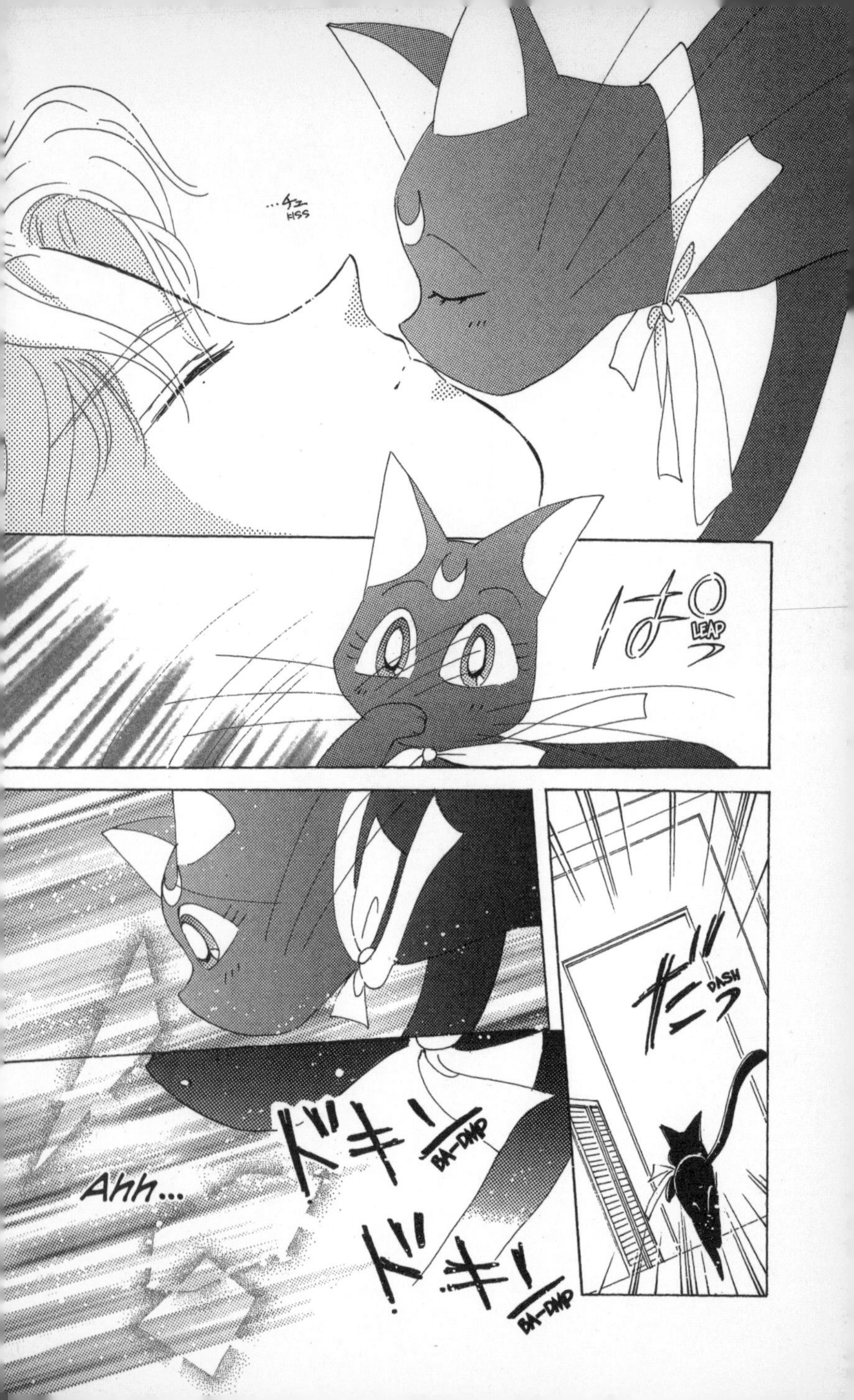
…チュ
KISS
はっ
LEAP
だっ
DASH
ドキン
BA-DMP
ドキン
BA-DMP
Ahh...

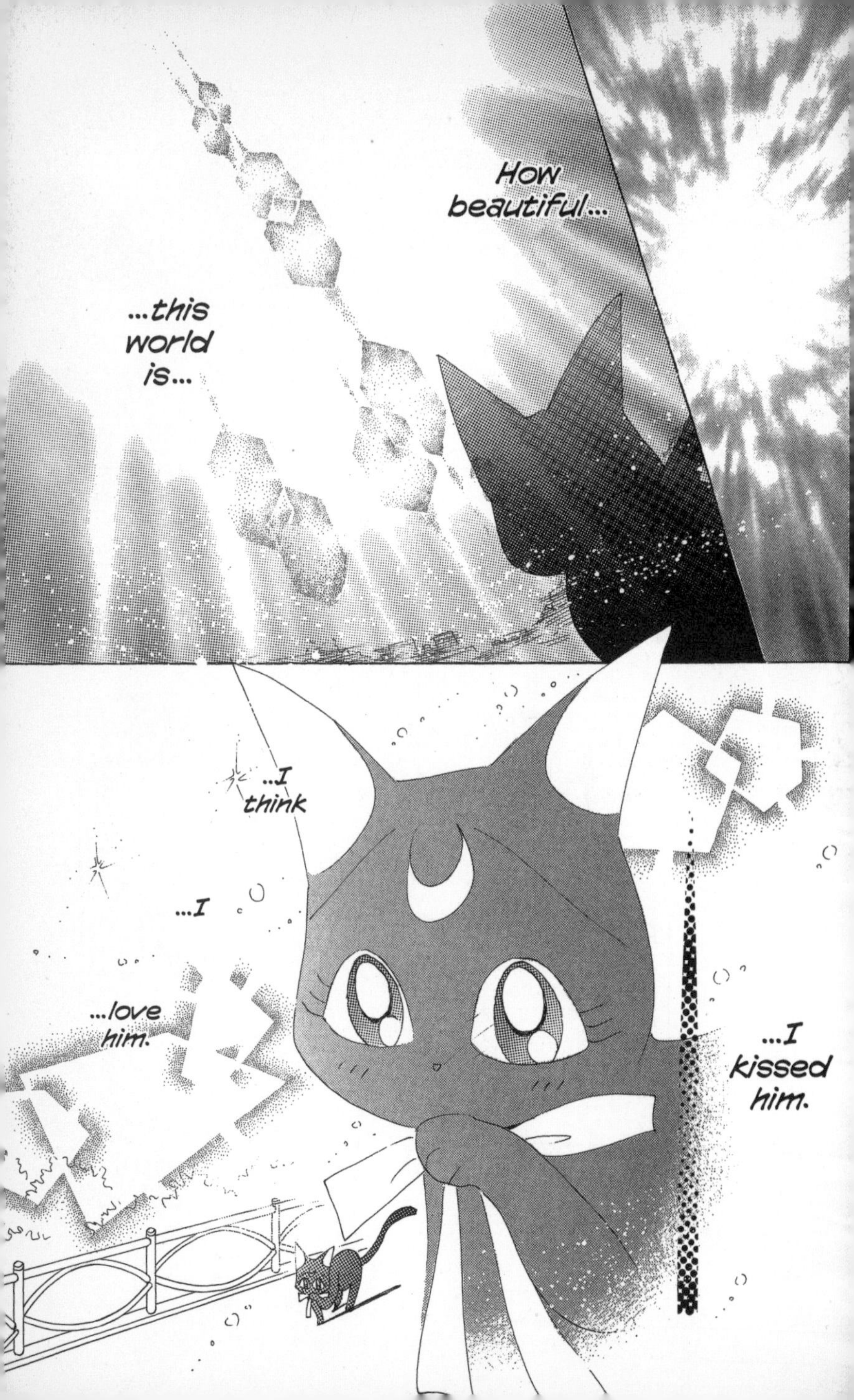
How beautiful...
...this world is...
...I kissed him.
...I think
...I
...love him.

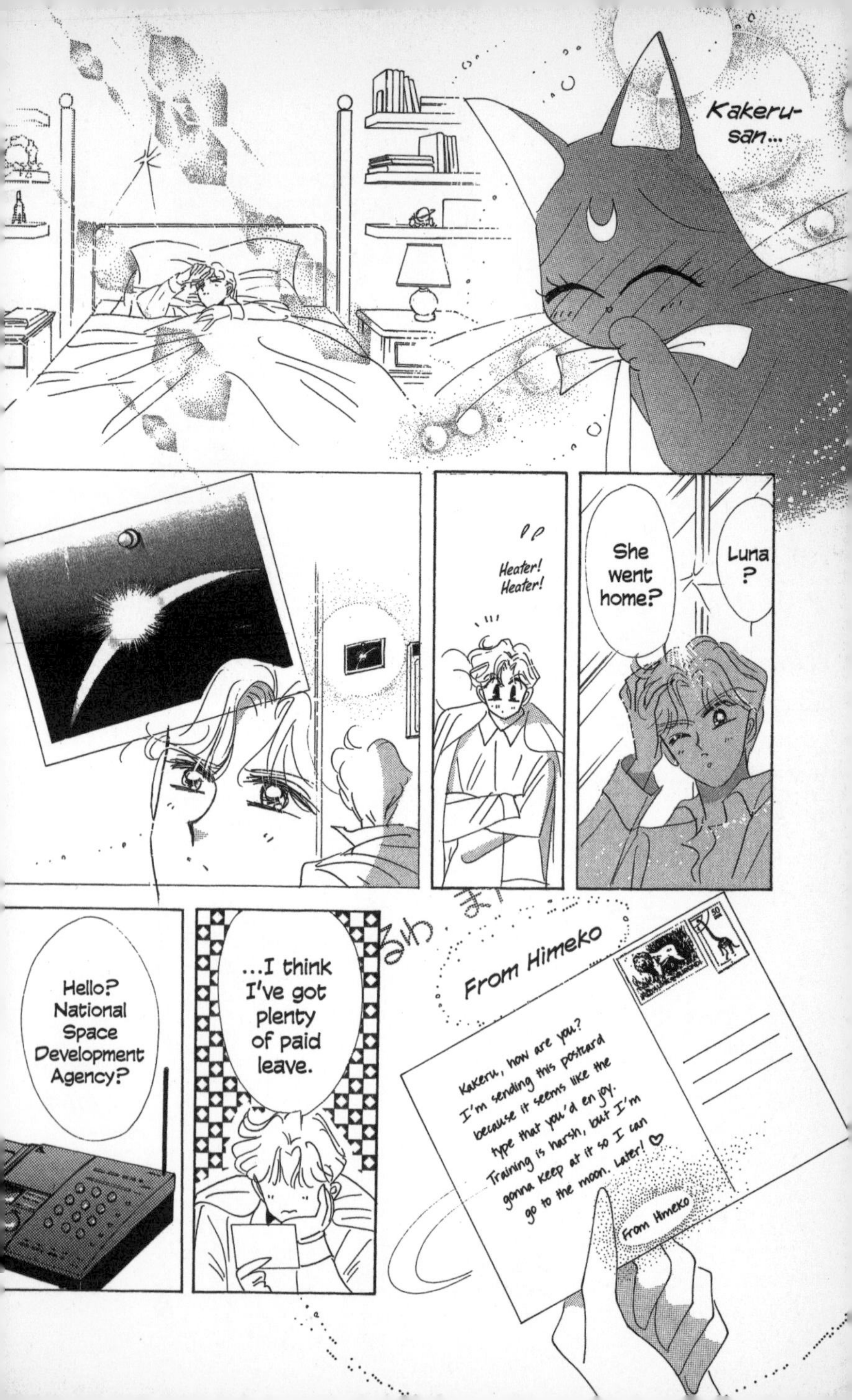
Kakeru-san...
Luna?
She went home?
Heater! Heater!
From Himeko
Kakeru, how are you? I'm sending this postcard because it seems like the type that you'd enjoy. Training is harsh, but I'm gonna keep at it so I can go to the moon. Later! ♡
From Himeko
...I think I've got plenty of paid leave.
Hello? National Space Development Agency?

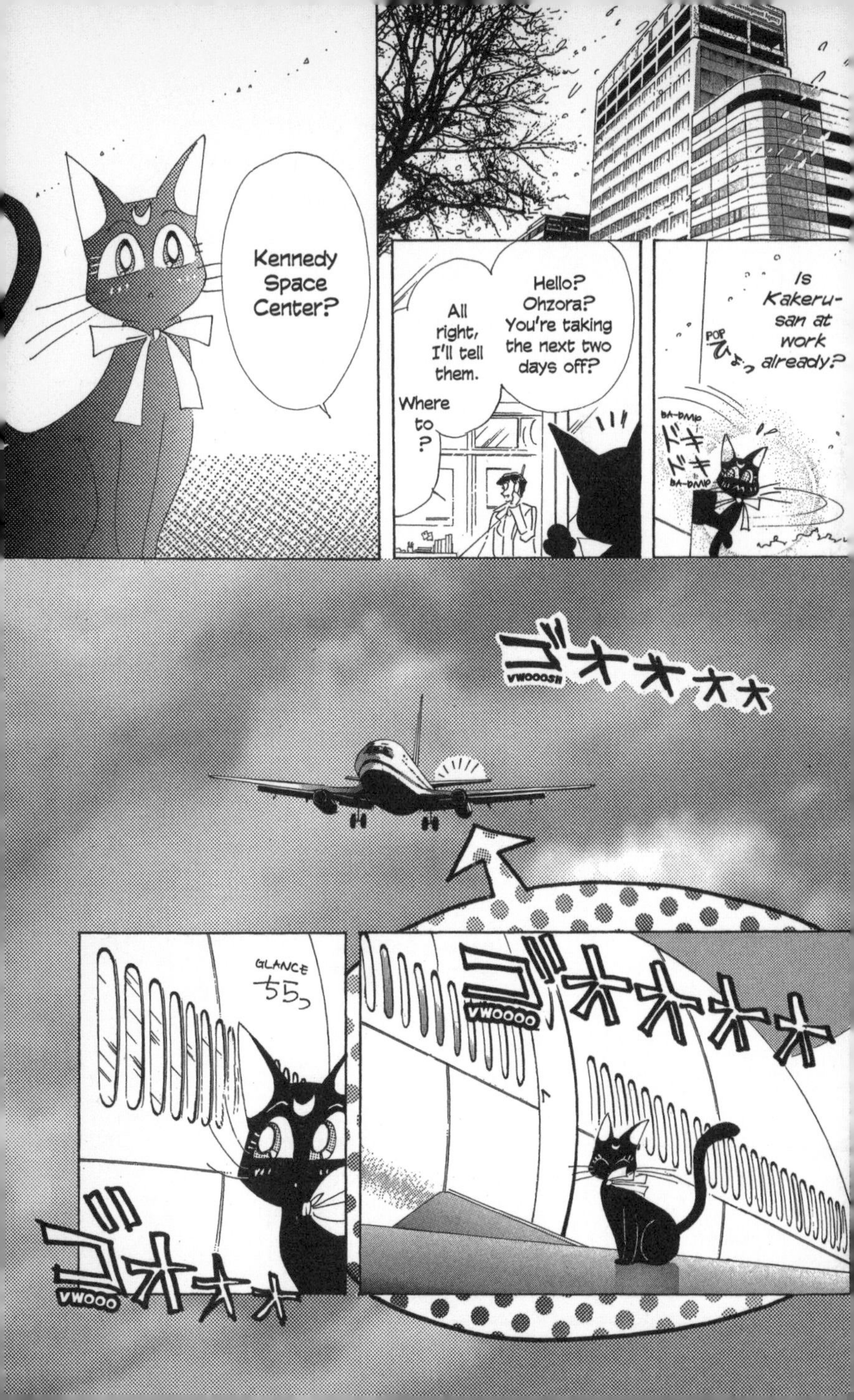
Is Kakeru-san at work already?
POP
ひょっ
BA-DMP
ドキ
ドキ
BA-DMP
Hello? Ohzora? You're taking the next two days off?
All right, I'll tell them.
Where to?
Kennedy Space Center?
VWOOOSH
ゴオオオオ
VWOOOO
ゴオオオオ
GLANCE
ちらっ
VWOOO
ゴオオオ

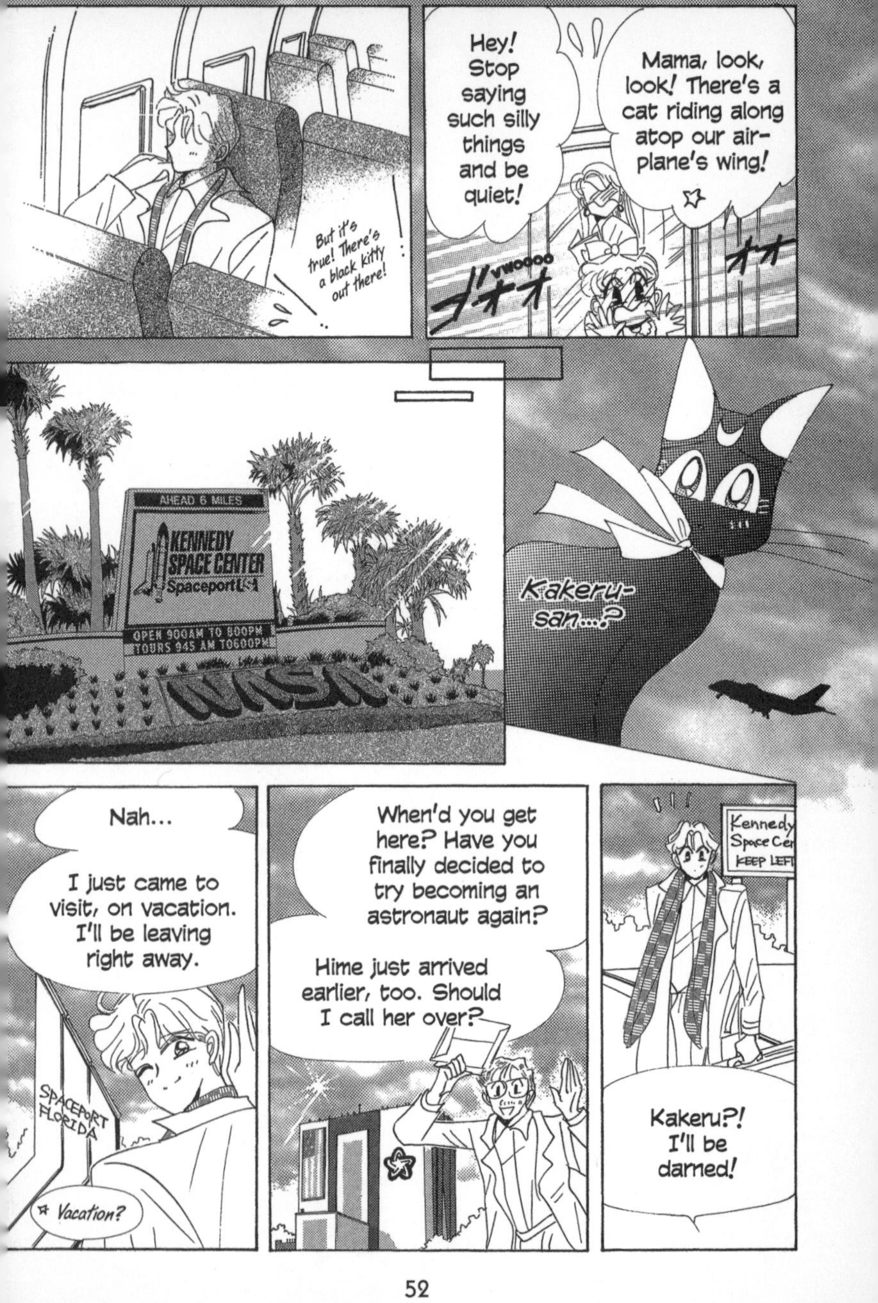
Mama, look, look! There's a cat riding along atop our air-plane's wing!
Hey! Stop saying such silly things and be quiet!
VWOOOO
But it's true! There's a black kitty out there!
Kakeru-san...?
AHEAD 6 MILES
KENNEDY SPACE CENTER Spaceport USA
OPEN 900AM TO 800PM
TOURS 945 AM TO600PM
NASA
Kennedy Space Cen
KEEP LEFT
Kakeru?! I'll be darned!
When'd you get here? Have you finally decided to try becoming an astronaut again?
Hime just arrived earlier, too. Should I call her over?
Nah...
I just came to visit, on vacation. I'll be leaving right away.
SPACEPORT FLORIDA
Vacation?

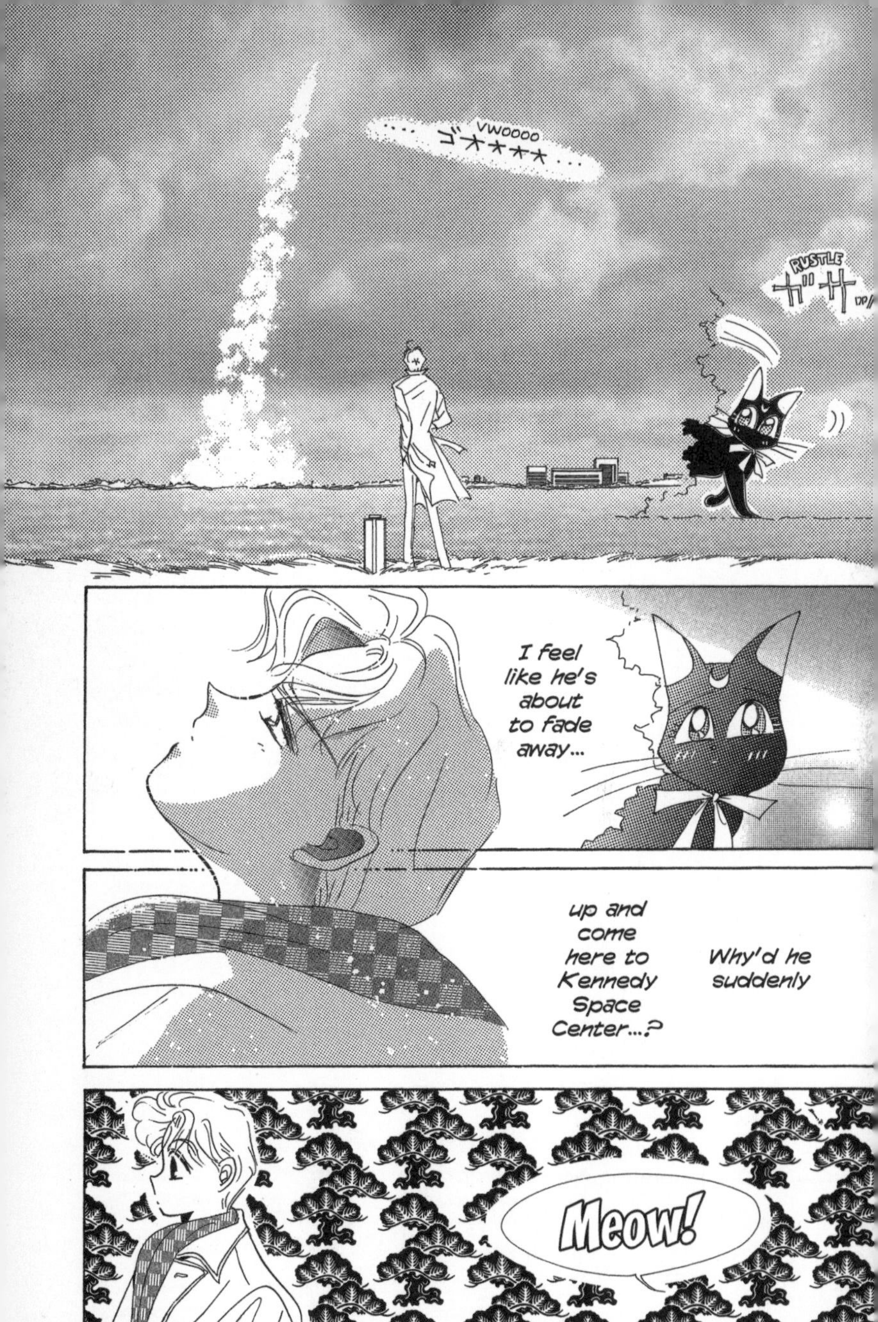
VWOOOO
RUSTLE
I feel like he's about to fade away...
Why'd he suddenly
up and come here to Kennedy Space Center...?
Meow!

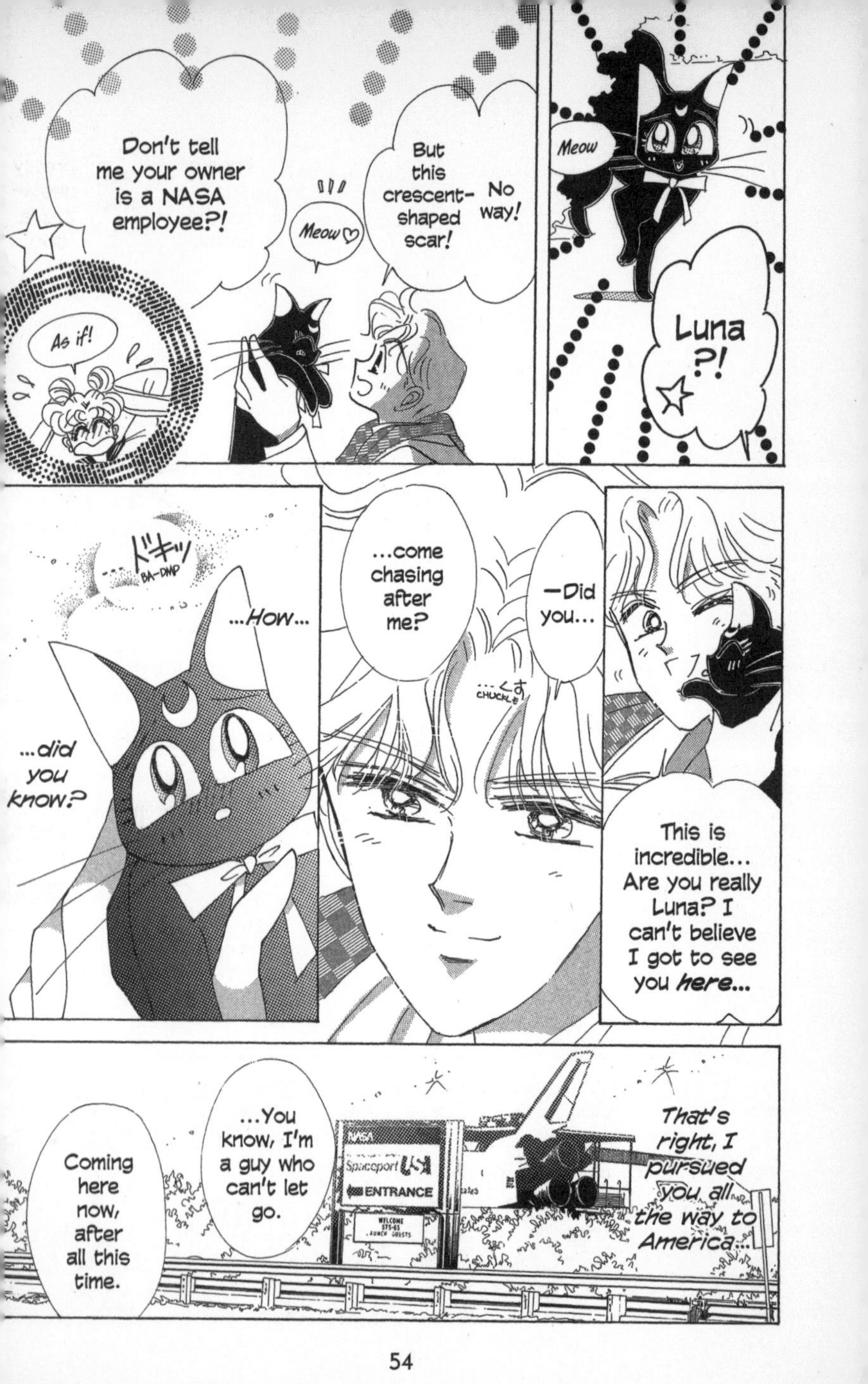
Meow
Luna ?!
No way!
But this crescent-shaped scar!
Meow♡
Don't tell me your owner is a NASA employee?!
As if!
This is incredible... Are you really Luna? I can't believe I got to see you *here*...
—Did you...
...come chasing after me?
...くす CHUCKLE
...ドキッ BA-DMP
...How...
...did you know?
That's right, I pursued you all the way to America...
...You know, I'm a guy who can't let go.
Coming here now, after all this time.
NASA
Spaceport USA
ENTRANCE
WELCOME STS-65 LAUNCH GUESTS

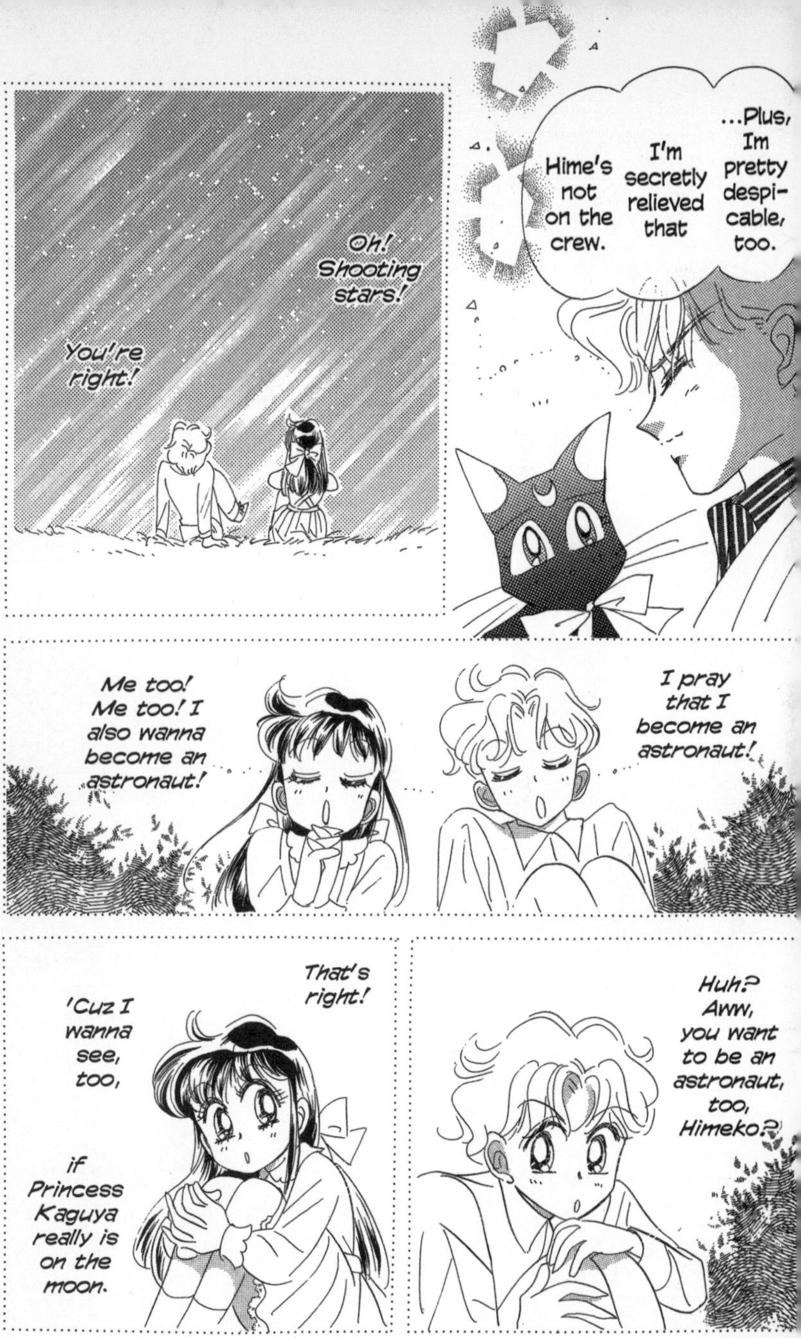
...Plus, Im pretty despi-cable, too.
I'm secretly relieved that
Hime's not on the crew.
Oh! Shooting stars!
You're right!
I pray that I become an astronaut!
Me too! Me too! I also wanna become an astronaut!
Huh? Aww, you want to be an astronaut, too, Himeko?
That's right!
'Cuz I wanna see, too,
if Princess Kaguya really is on the moon.

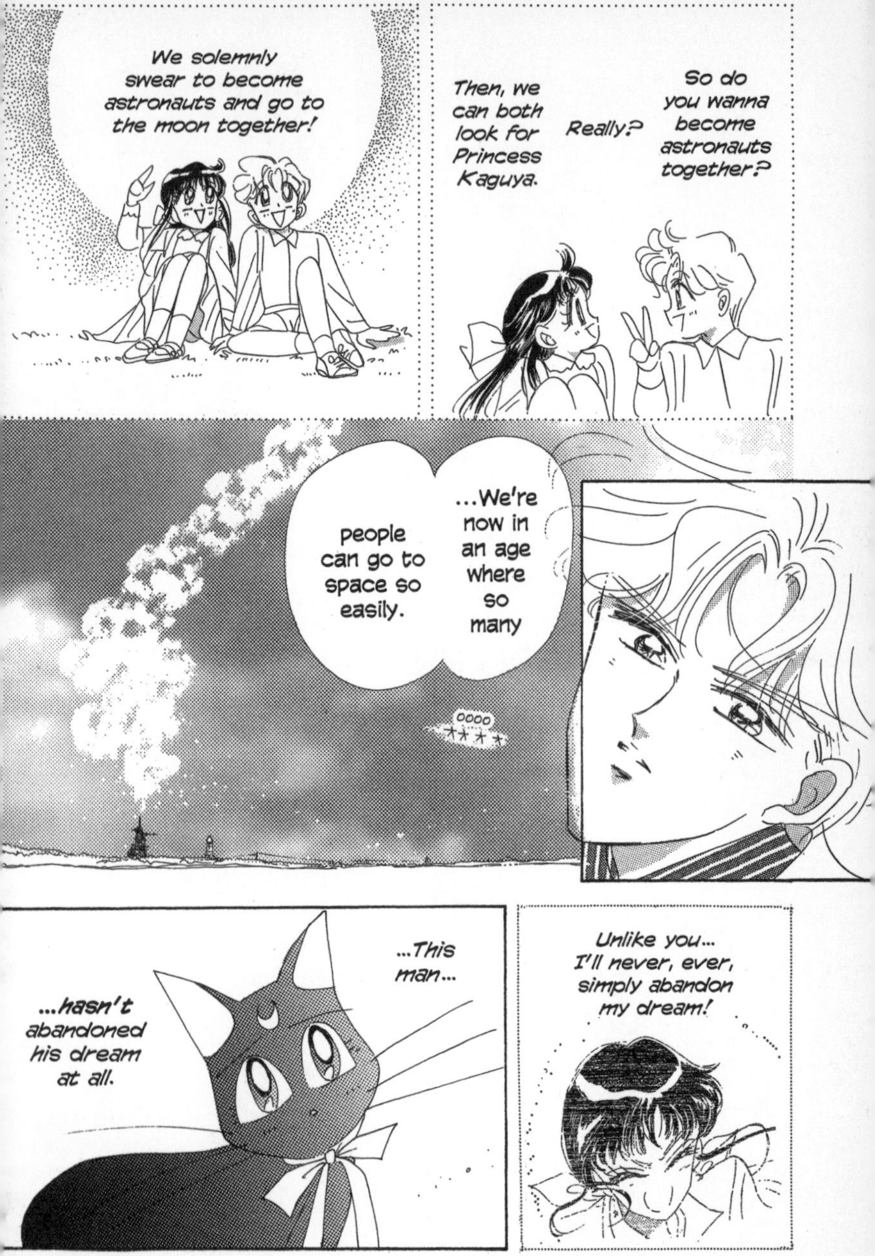
So do you wanna become astronauts together?
Really?
Then, we can both look for Princess Kaguya.
We solemnly swear to become astronauts and go to the moon together!
...We're now in an age where so many
people can go to space so easily.
Unlike you... I'll never, ever, simply abandon my dream!
...This man...
...hasn't abandoned his dream at all.

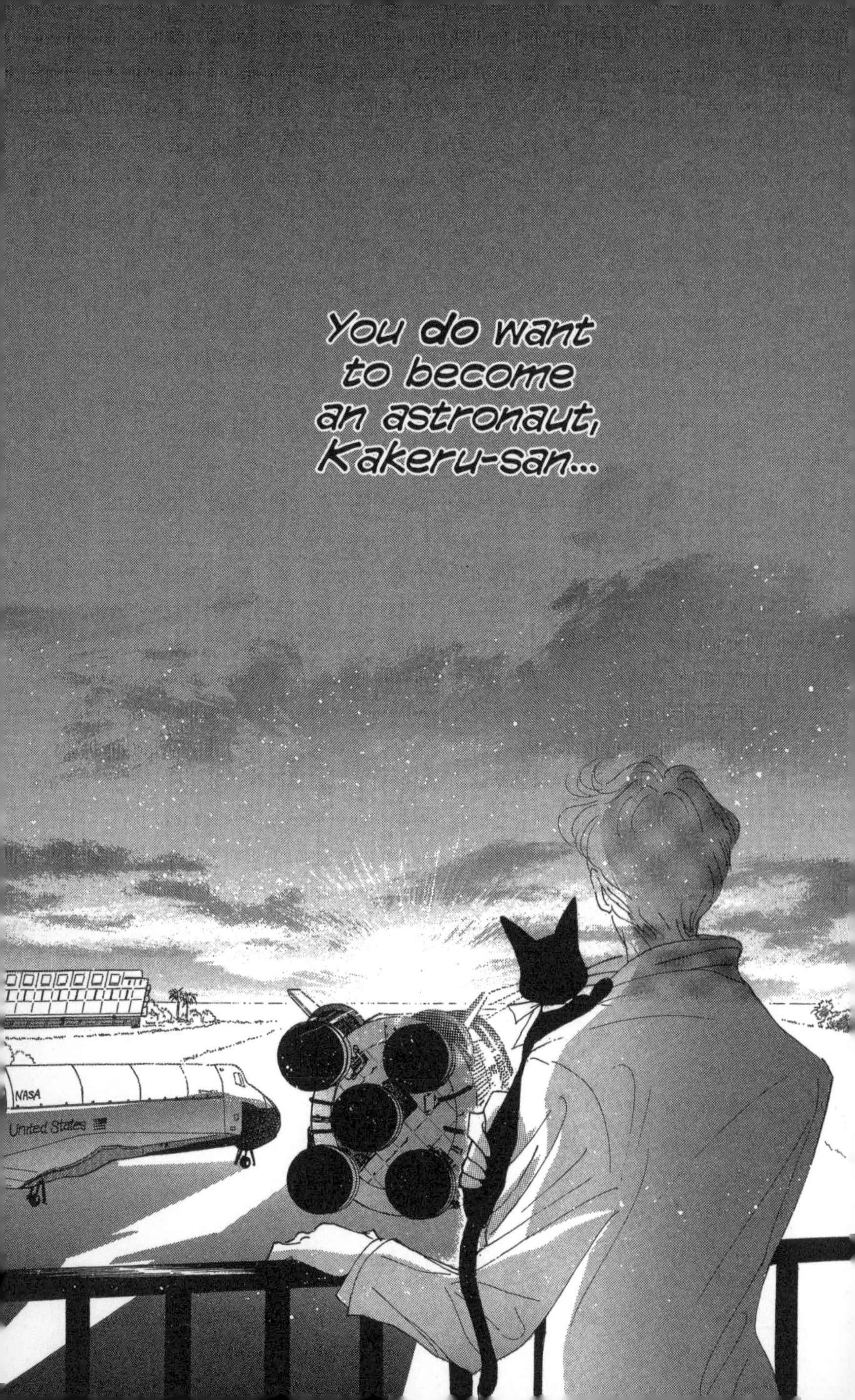
You do want to become an astronaut, Kakeru-san...
NASA
United States

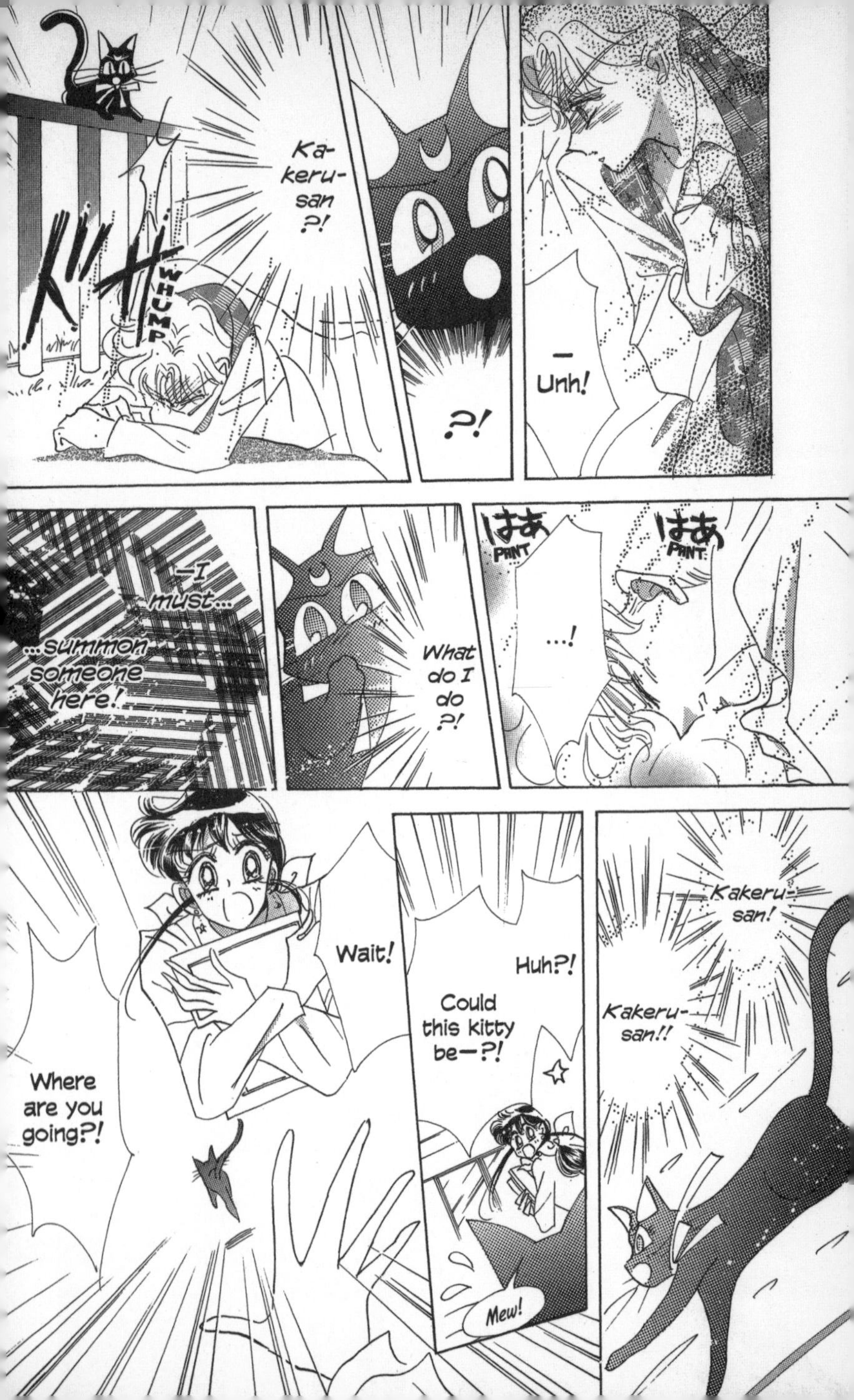
—Unh!
?!
Ka-keru-san?!
WHUMP
はあ PANT
はあ PANT
...!
What do I do?!
—I must...
...summon someone here!
Kakeru-san!
Kakeru-san!!
Huh?!
Could this kitty be—?!
Mew!
Wait!
Where are you going?!

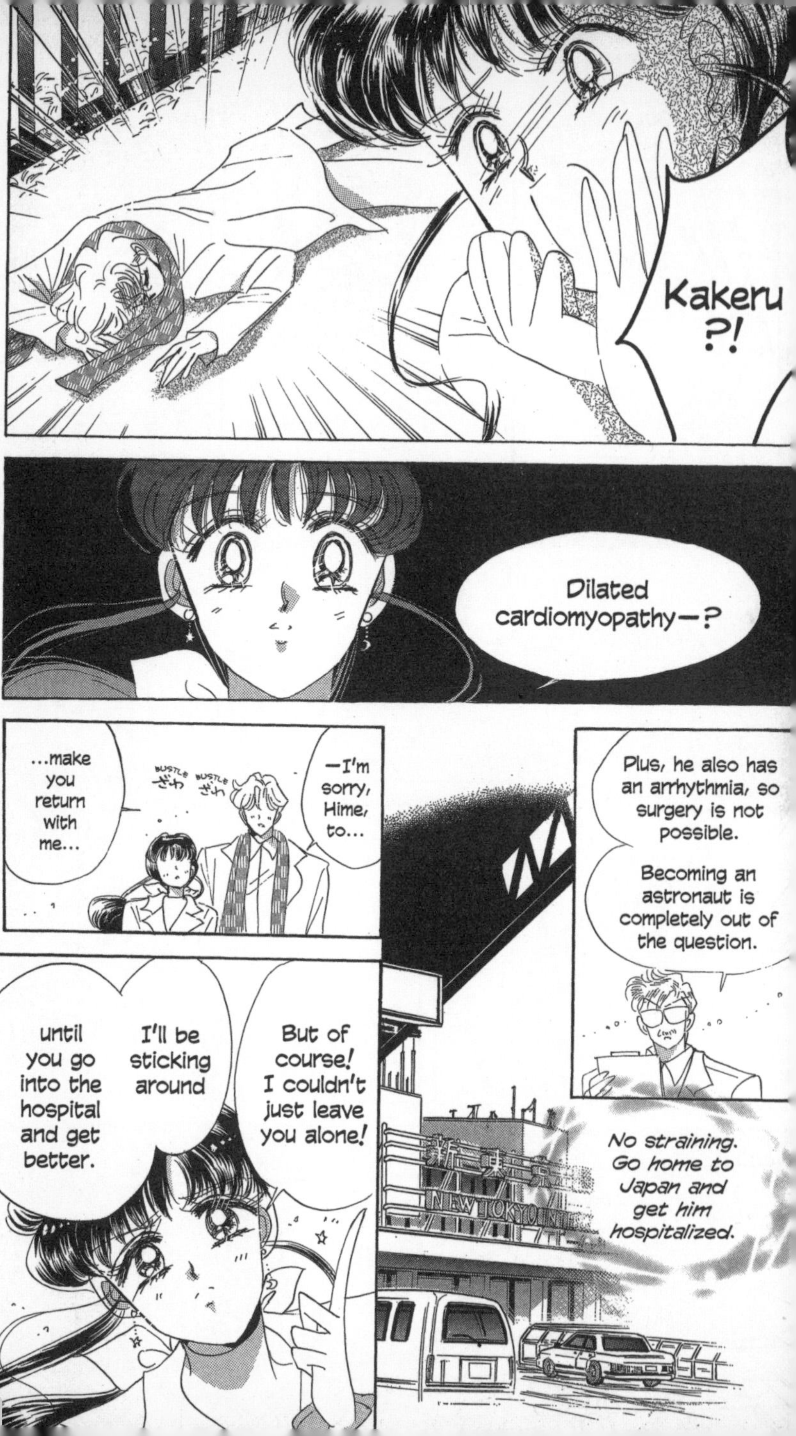
Kakeru ?!
Dilated cardiomyopathy—?
Plus, he also has an arrhythmia, so surgery is not possible.
Becoming an astronaut is completely out of the question.
No straining. Go home to Japan and get him hospitalized.
—I'm sorry, Hime, to...
...make you return with me...
BUSTLE ざわ BUSTLE ざわ
But of course! I couldn't just leave you alone!
I'll be sticking around
until you go into the hospital and get better.

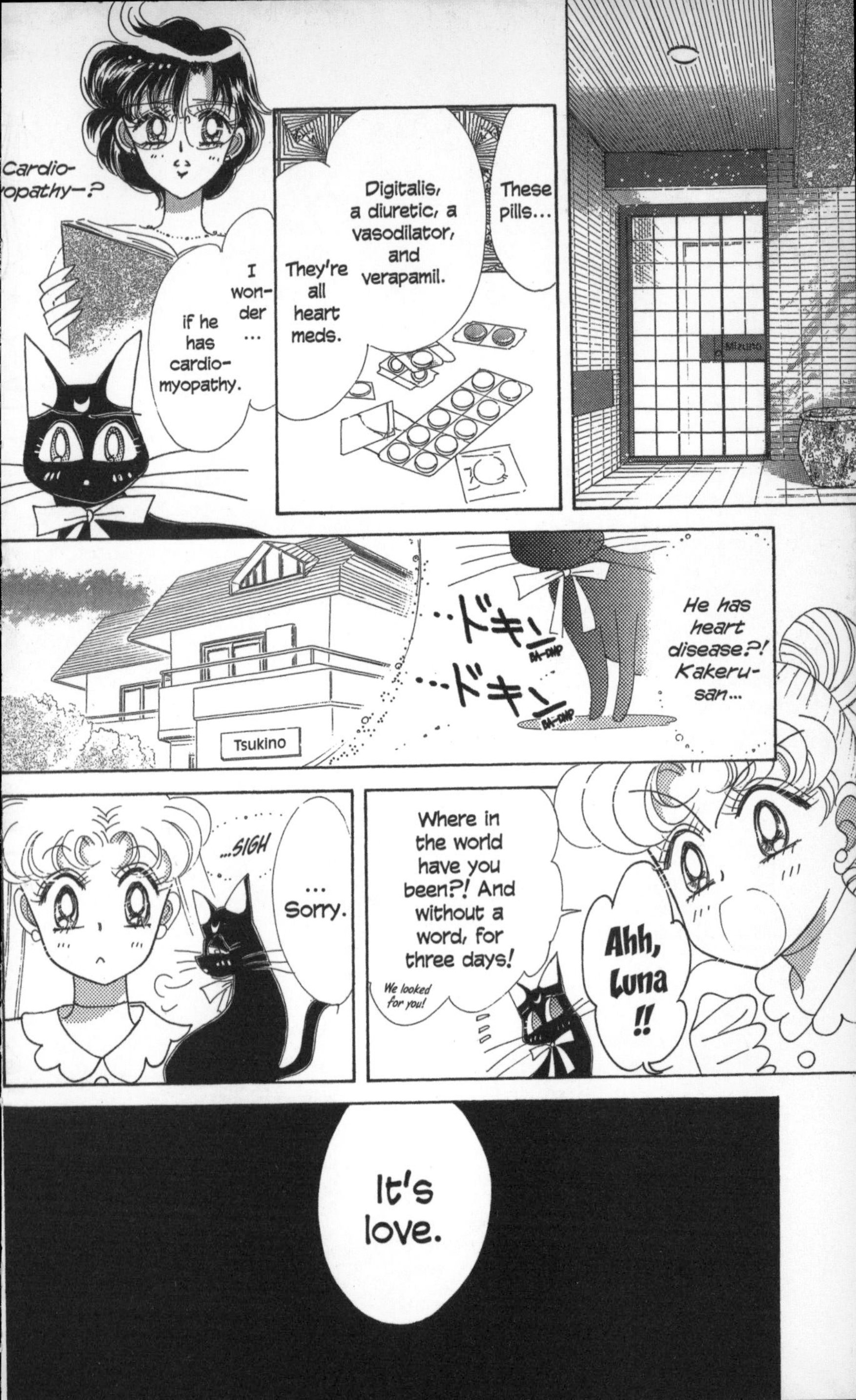
Mizuno
These pills...
Digitalis, a diuretic, a vasodilator, and verapamil.
They're all heart meds.
Cardio-myopathy—?
I won-der... if he has cardio-myopathy.
Tsukino
He has heart disease?! Kakeru-san...
...ドキン BA-DMP
...ドキン BA-DMP
Ahh, Luna!!
Where in the world have you been?! And without a word, for three days!
We looked for you!
...SIGH
... Sorry.
It's love.

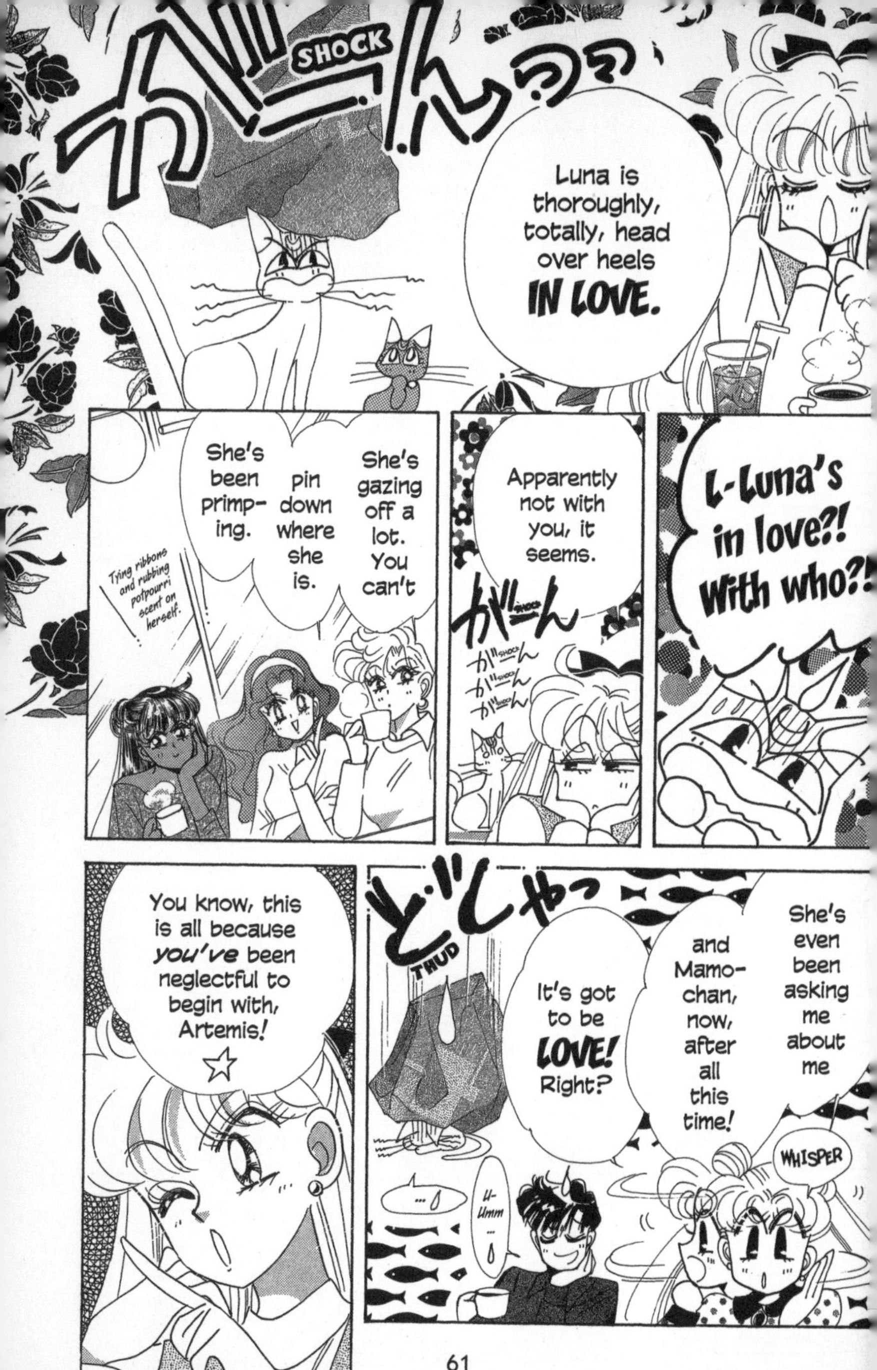
Luna is thoroughly, totally, head over heels IN LOVE.
がーんっ?? SHOCK
L-Luna's in love?! With who?!
Apparently not with you, it seems.
がーん SHOCK
がーん SHOCK
がーん SHOCK
がーん SHOCK
She's gazing off a lot. You can't
pin down where she is.
She's been primping.
Tying ribbons and rubbing potpourri scent on herself.
She's even been asking me about me
and Mamo-chan, now, after all this time!
It's got to be LOVE! Right?
WHISPER
U-Umm...
...
どしゃっ THUD
You know, this is all because *you've* been neglectful to begin with, Artemis! ☆

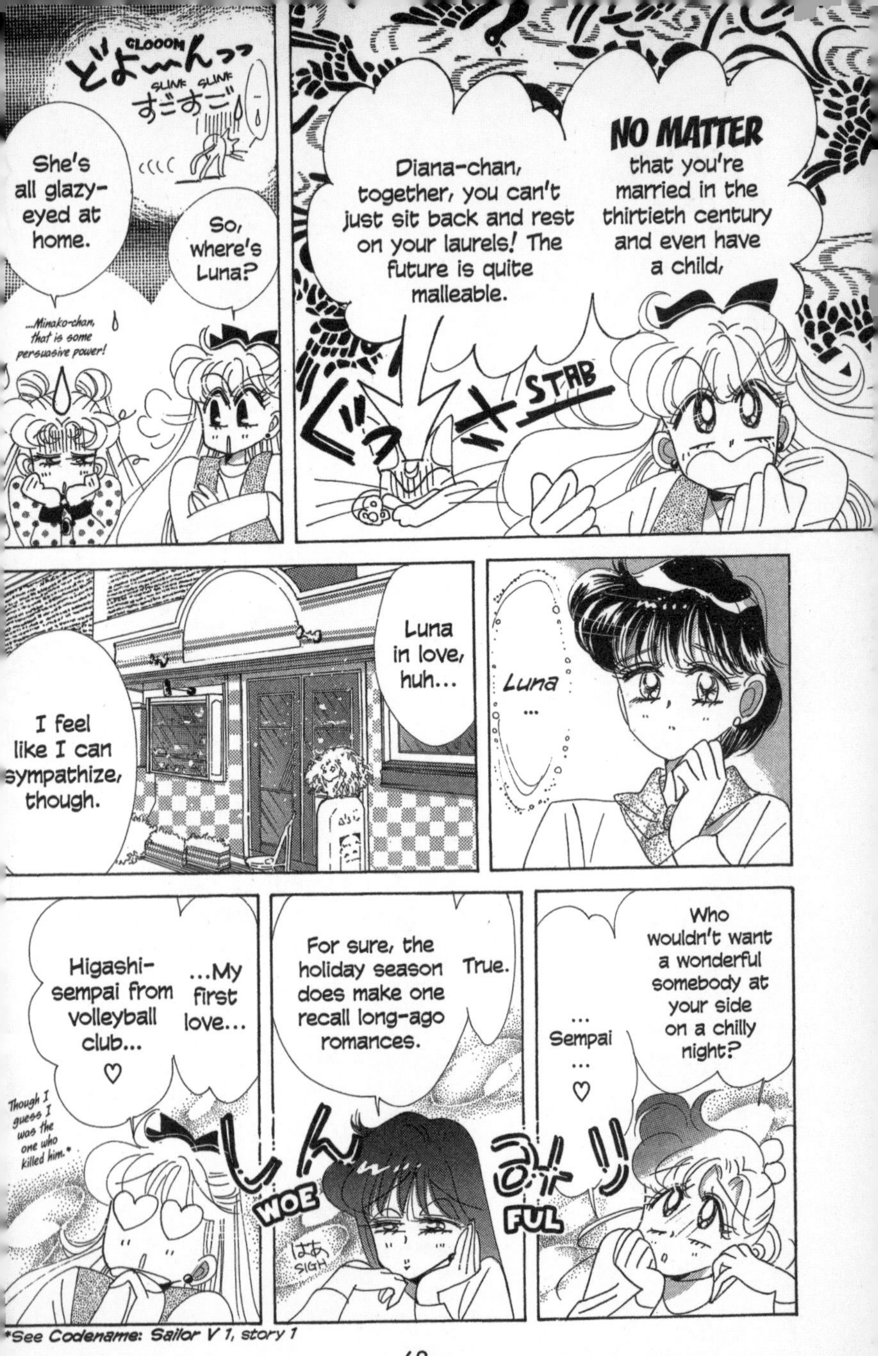
NO MATTER that you're married in the thirtieth century and even have a child,
Diana-chan, together, you can't just sit back and rest on your laurels! The future is quite malleable.
STAB
GLOOOM
SLINK SLINK
So, where's Luna?
She's all glazy-eyed at home.
...Minako-chan, that is some persuasive power!
Luna ...
Luna in love, huh...
I feel like I can sympathize, though.
Who wouldn't want a wonderful somebody at your side on a chilly night?
... Sempai ... ♡
True.
For sure, the holiday season does make one recall long-ago romances.
SIGH
WOE FUL
...My first love...
Higashi-sempai from volleyball club... ♡
Though I guess I was the one who killed him.*

*See *Codename: Sailor V* 1, story 1

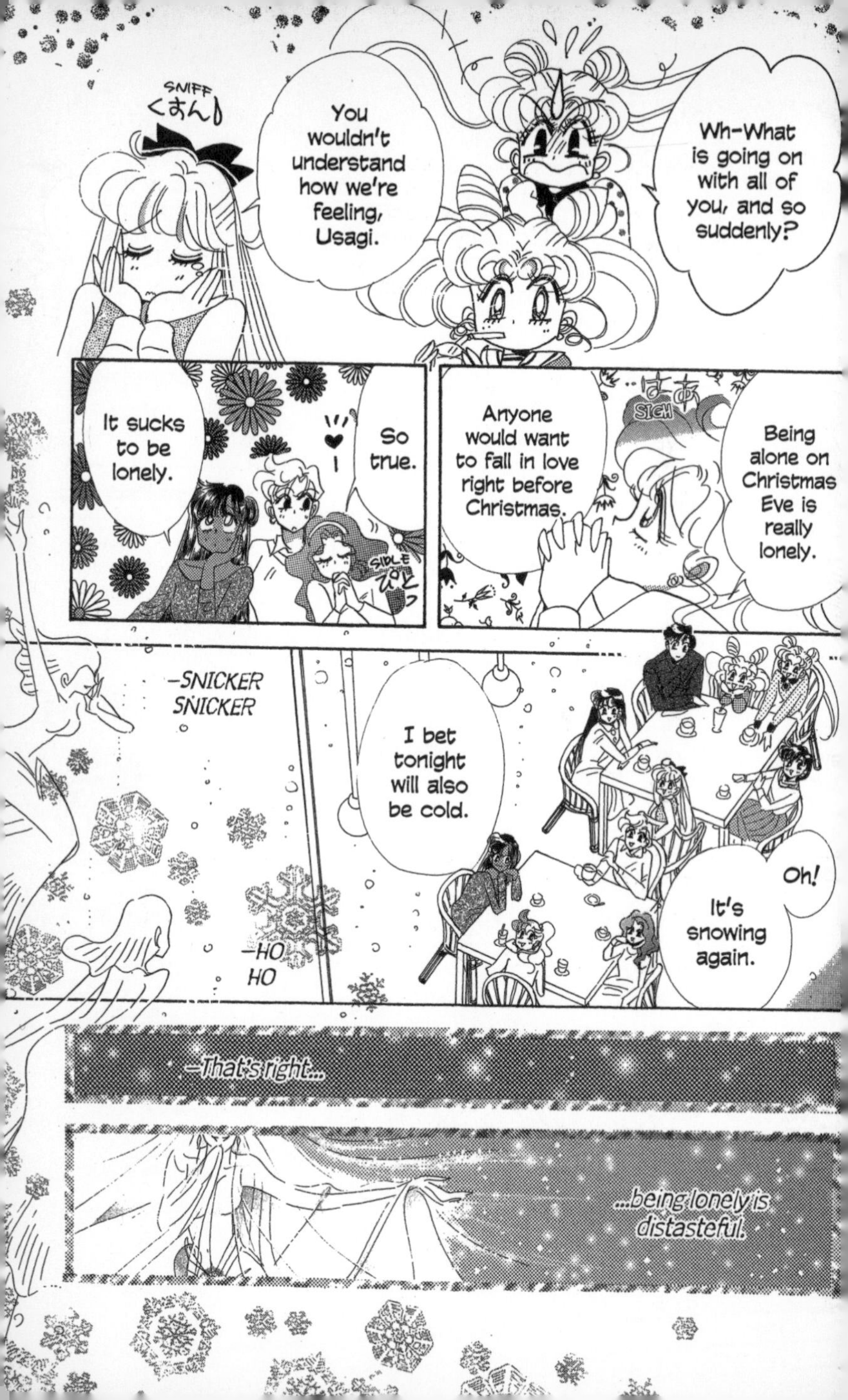
Wh-What is going on with all of you, and so suddenly?
You wouldn't understand how we're feeling, Usagi.
SNIFF
くすん
Being alone on Christmas Eve is really lonely.
...はぁ
SIGH
Anyone would want to fall in love right before Christmas.
So true.
It sucks to be lonely.
SIDLE
ぴと
Oh! It's snowing again.
I bet tonight will also be cold.
—SNICKER SNICKER
—HO HO
—That's right...
...being lonely is distasteful.

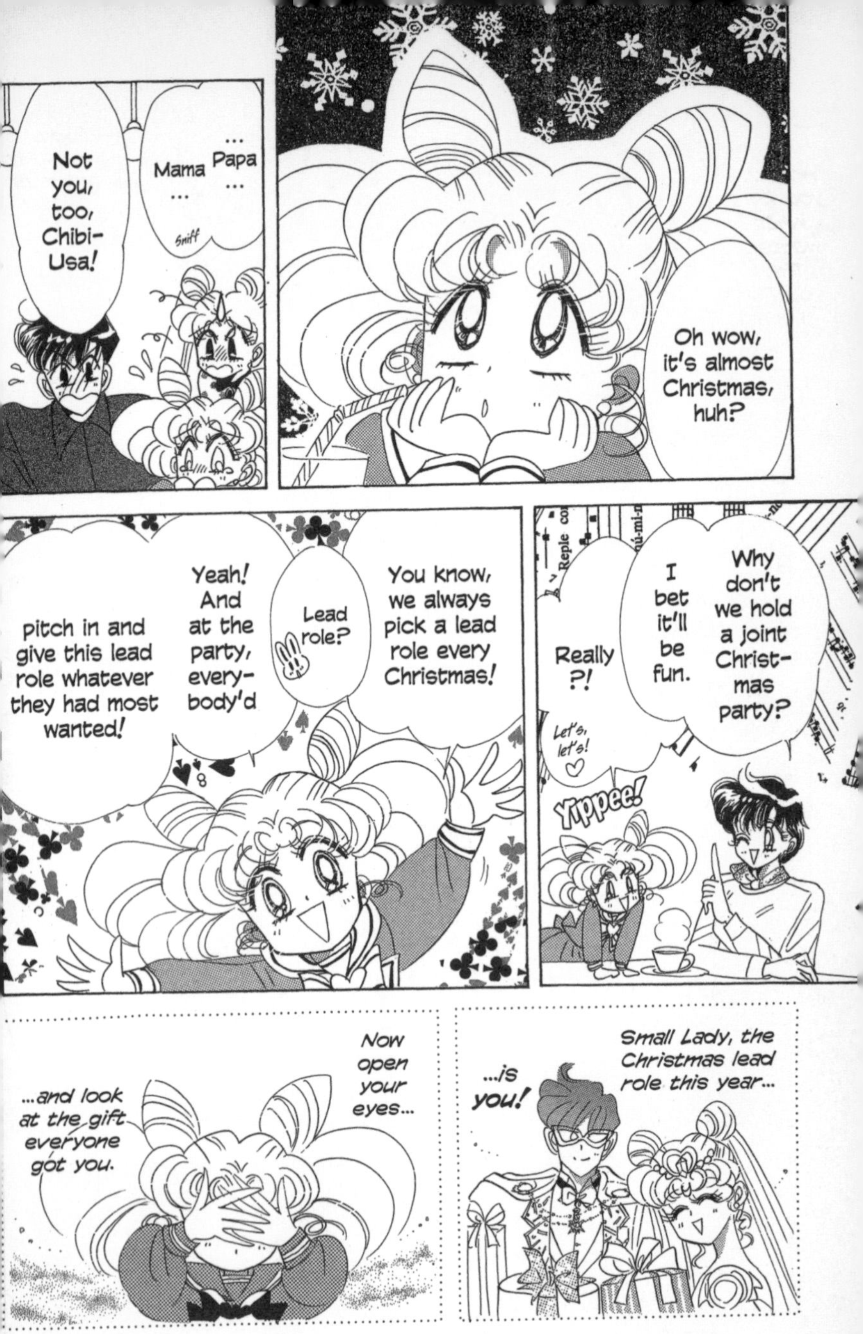
Oh wow, it's almost Christmas, huh?
... Papa ... Mama ...
Sniff
Not you, too, Chibi-Usa!
Why don't we hold a joint Christmas party?
I bet it'll be fun.
Really?!
Let's, let's! ♡
Yippee!
You know, we always pick a lead role every Christmas!
Lead role?
Yeah! And at the party, everybody'd
pitch in and give this lead role whatever they had most wanted!
Small Lady, the Christmas lead role this year...
...is you!
Now open your eyes...
...and look at the gift everyone got you.

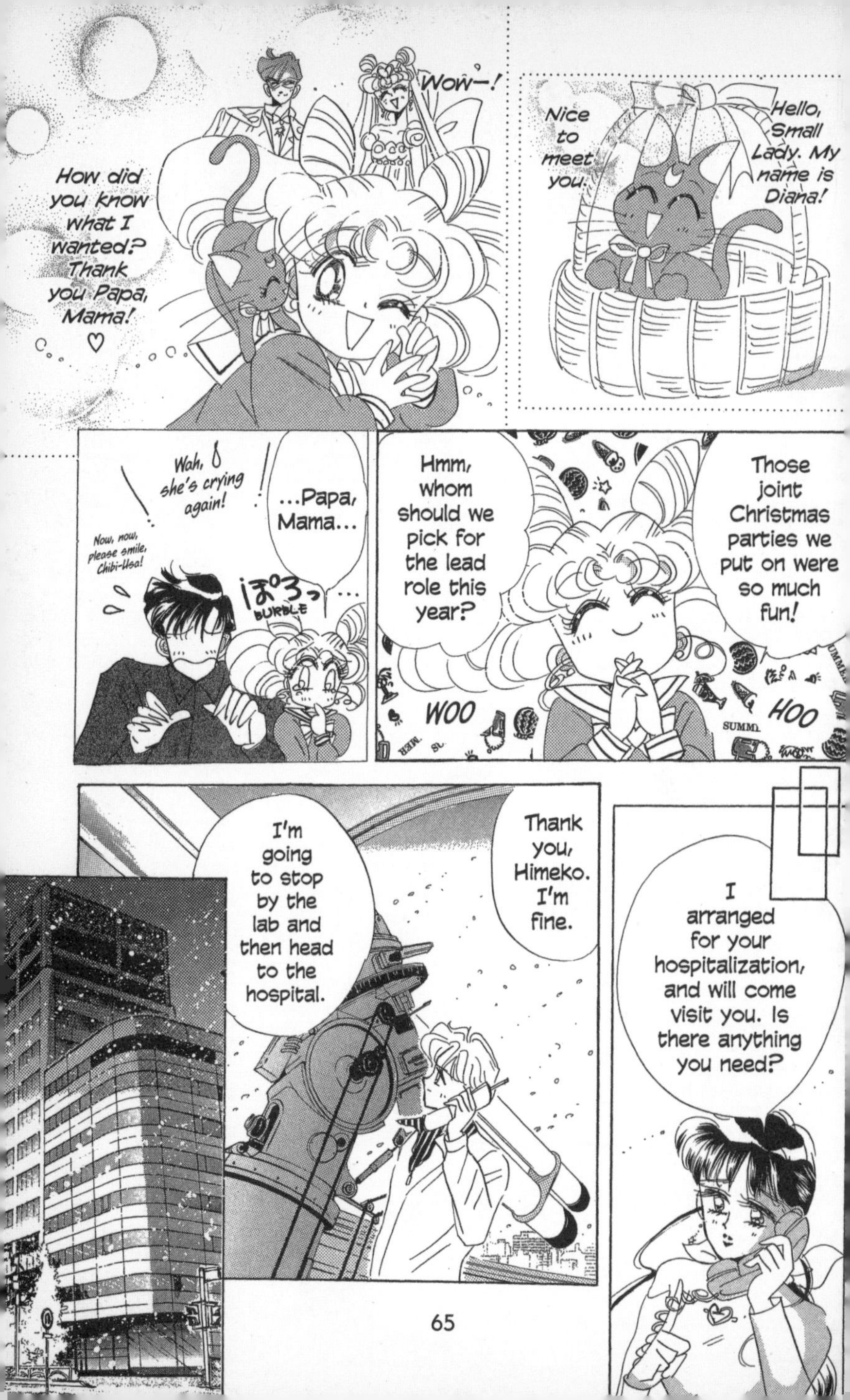
Hello, Small Lady. My name is Diana!
Nice to meet you.
Wow—!
How did you know what I wanted? Thank you Papa, Mama! ♡
Those joint Christmas parties we put on were so much fun!
Hmm, whom should we pick for the lead role this year?
WOO
HOO
...Papa, Mama...
Wah, she's crying again!
Now, now, please smile, Chibi-Usa!
ぽろっ
BURBLE
I arranged for your hospitalization, and will come visit you. Is there anything you need?
Thank you, Himeko. I'm fine.
I'm going to stop by the lab and then head to the hospital.

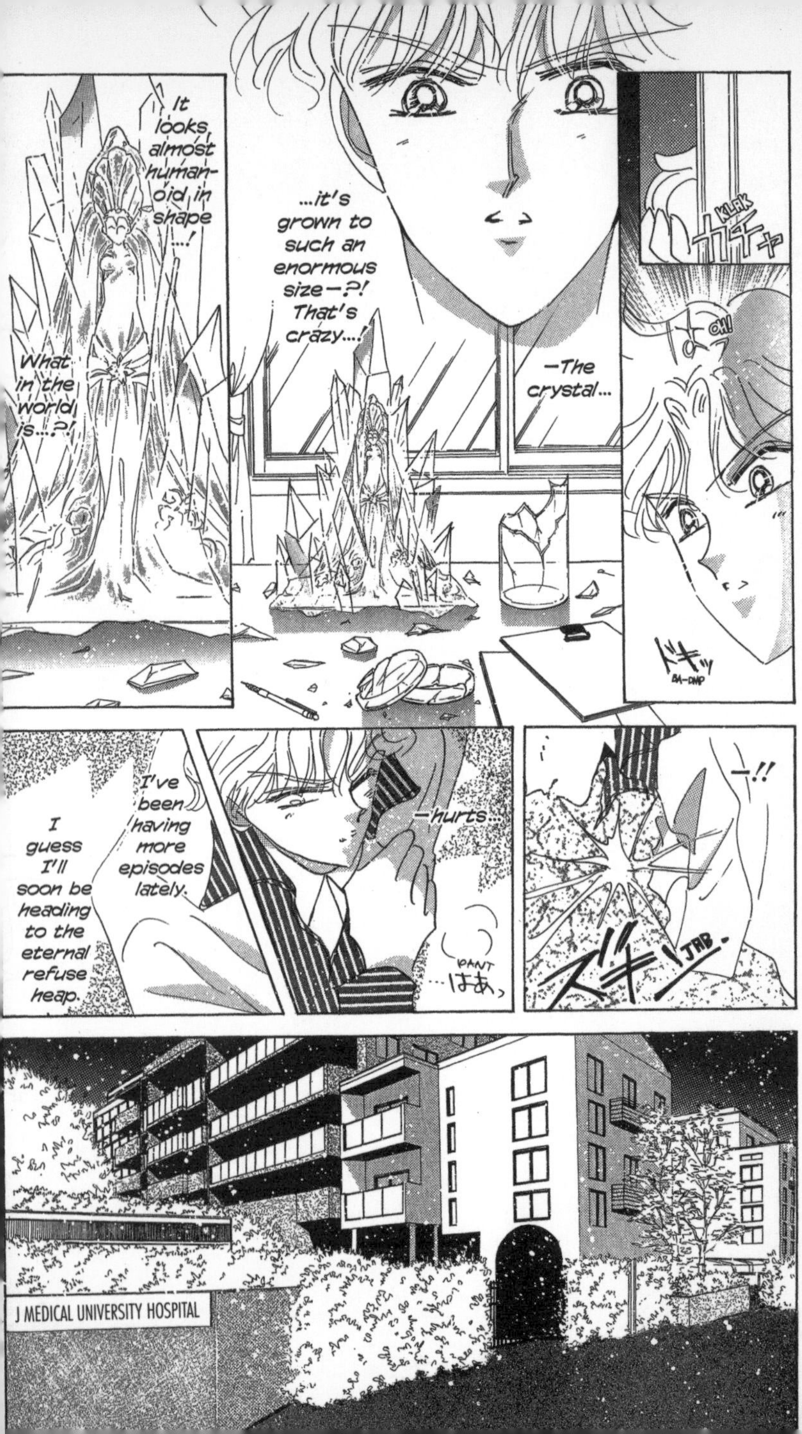
KLAK
カチャ
OH!
ドキッ
BA-DMP
—The crystal...
...it's grown to such an enormous size—?! That's crazy...!
It looks almost humanoid in shape...!
What in the world is...?!
—!!
JAB
ズキン
—hurts...
PANT
...はあっ
I've been having more episodes lately.
I guess I'll soon be heading to the eternal refuse heap.
J MEDICAL UNIVERSITY HOSPITAL

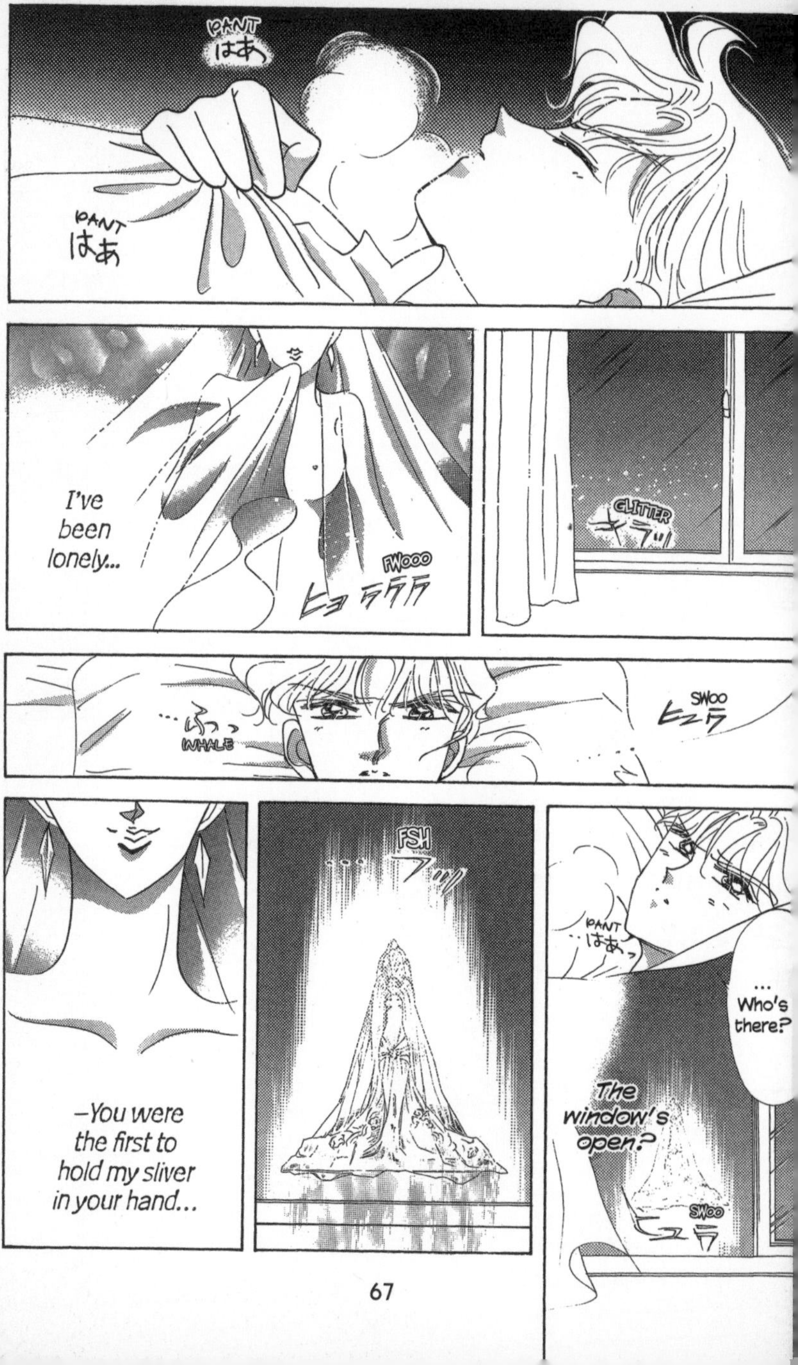
PANT
はあ
PANT
はあ
GLITTER
キラッ
I've been lonely...
FWOOO
ヒョラララ
SWOO
ヒュラ
...ふっ
INHALE
PANT
...はあっ
... Who's there?
The window's open?
SWOO
ヒュラ
FSH
フッ
–You were the first to hold my sliver in your hand...

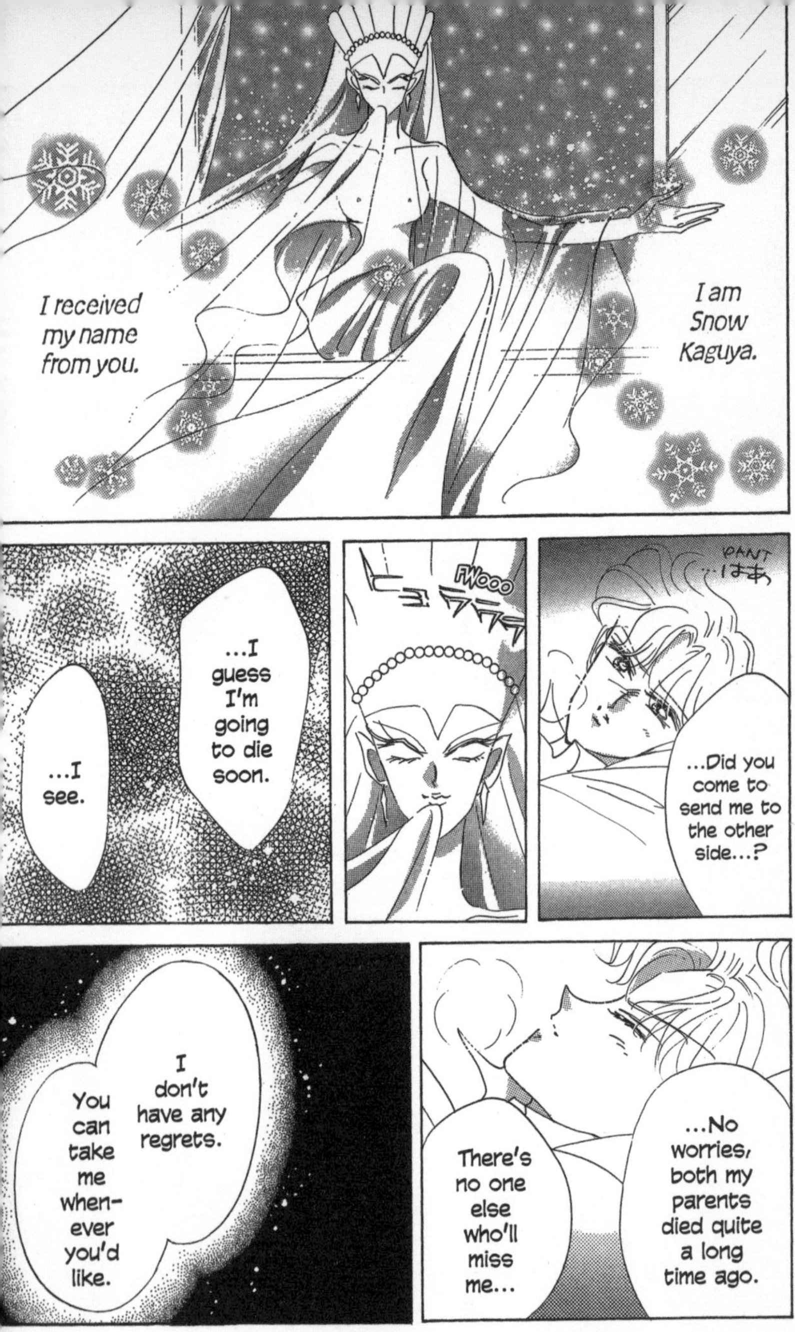
I am Snow Kaguya.
I received my name from you.
PANT
...はあ
...Did you come to send me to the other side...?
FWOOO
...I guess I'm going to die soon.
...I see.
...No worries, both my parents died quite a long time ago.
There's no one else who'll miss me...
I don't have any regrets.
You can take me whenever you'd like.

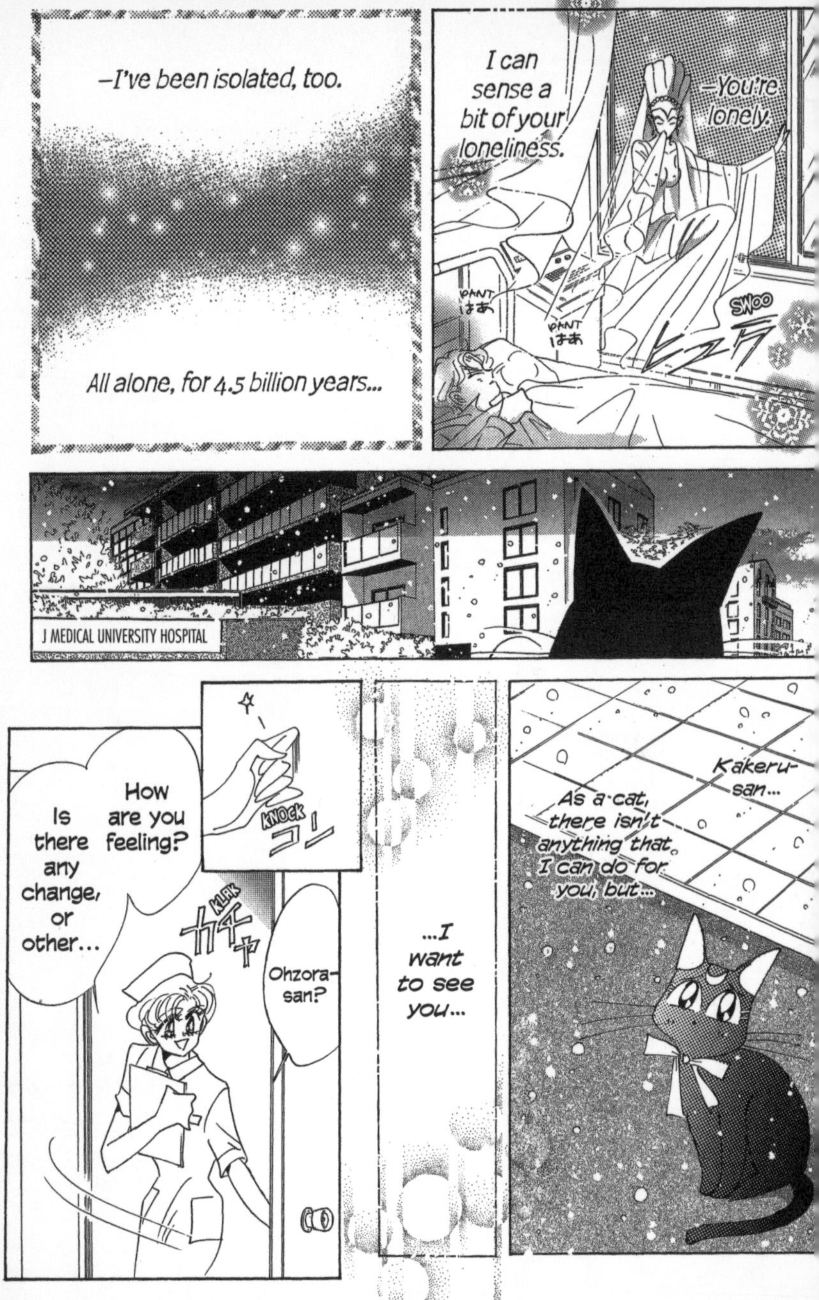
—You're lonely.
I can sense a bit of your loneliness.
PANT はあ
PANT はあ
SWOO ヒュラ
—I've been isolated, too.
All alone, for 4.5 billion years...
J MEDICAL UNIVERSITY HOSPITAL
Kakeru-san...
As a cat, there isn't anything that I can do for you, but...
...I want to see you...
KNOCK コン
KLAK カチャ
Ohzora-san?
How are you feeling?
Is there any change, or other...

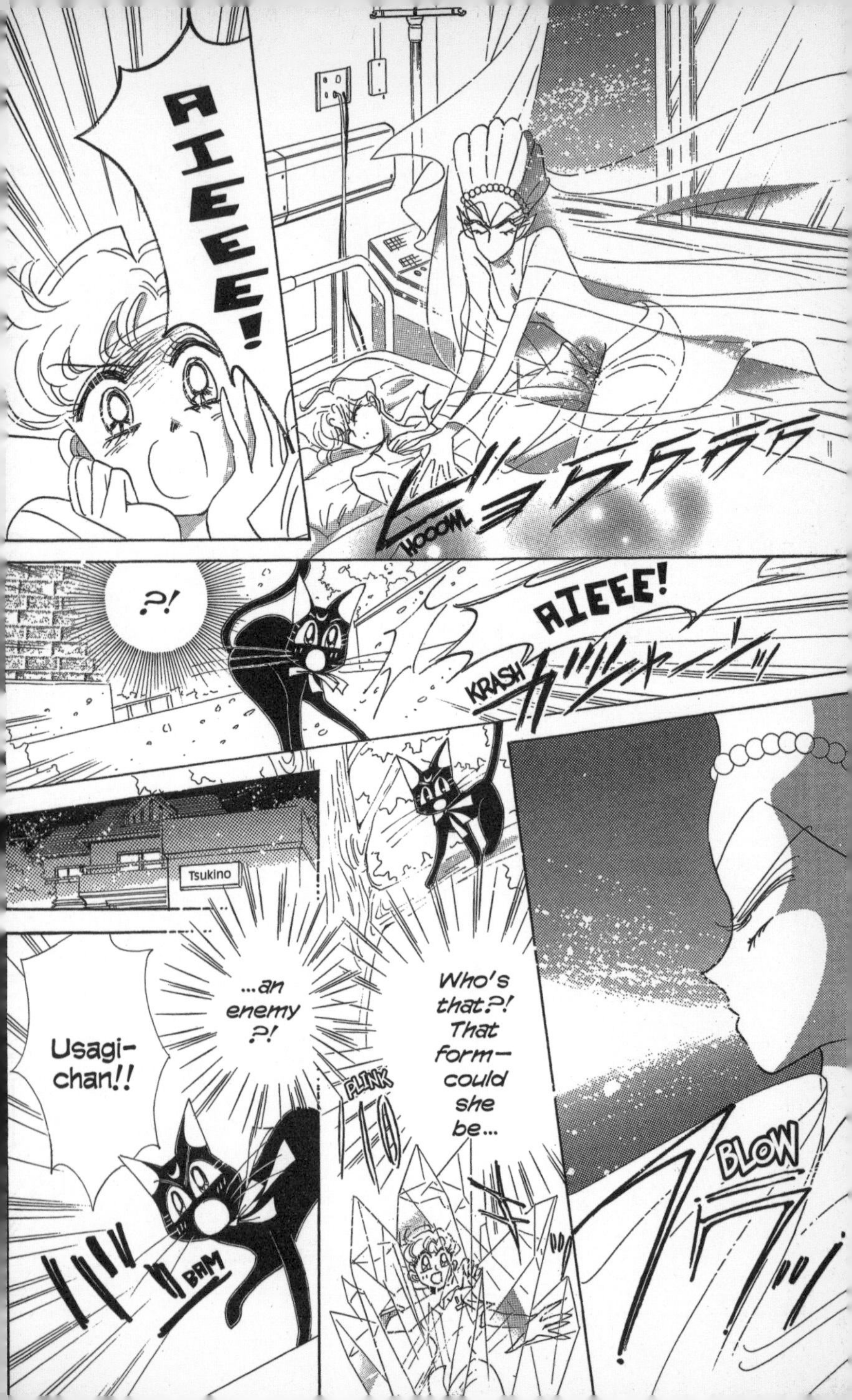
AIEEE!
HOOOWL
AIEEE!
KRASH
?!
BLOW
Tsukino
Who's that?! That form—could she be...
PLINK
...an enemy?!
Usagi-chan!!
BAM

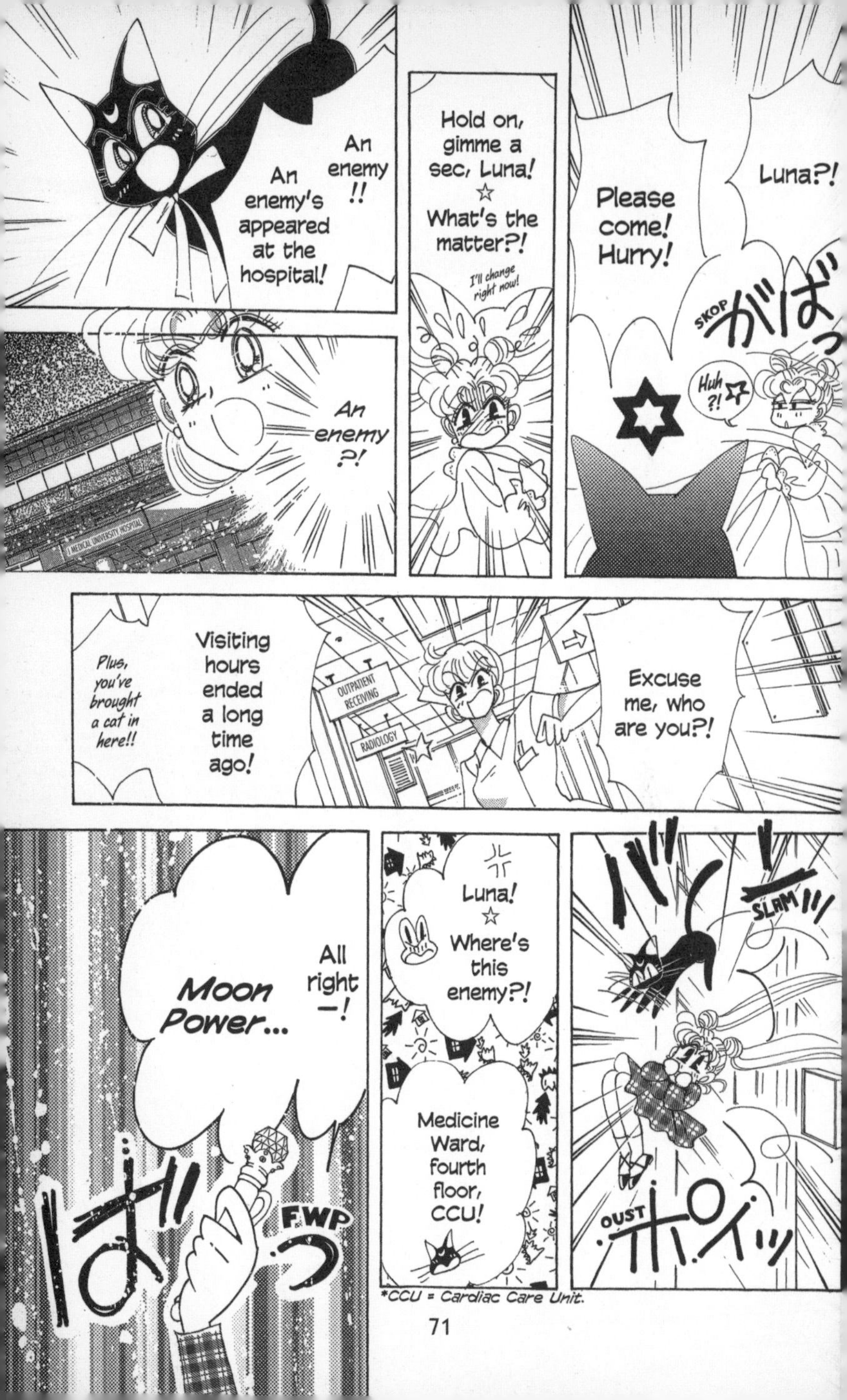
Luna?!
Please come! Hurry!
SKOP
Huh ?!
Hold on, gimme a sec, Luna! ☆ What's the matter?!
I'll change right now!
An enemy !!
An enemy's appeared at the hospital!
An enemy ?!
MEDICAL UNIVERSITY HOSPITAL
Excuse me, who are you?!
OUTPATIENT RECEIVING
RADIOLOGY
Visiting hours ended a long time ago!
Plus, you've brought a cat in here!!
SLAM
OUST
Luna! ☆ Where's this enemy?!
Medicine Ward, fourth floor, CCU!
All right—!
Moon Power...
FWP

*CCU = Cardiac Care Unit.

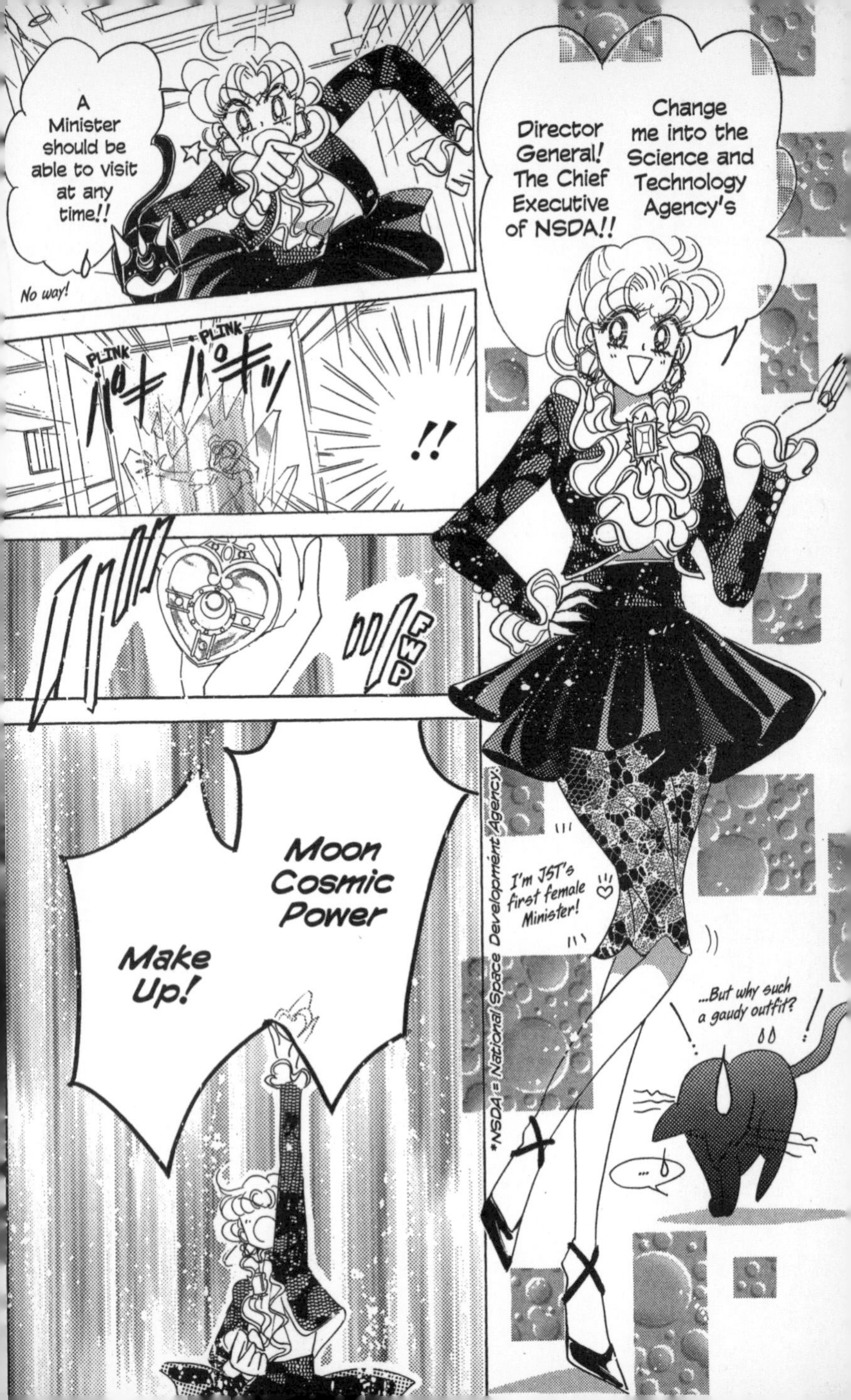

Change me into the Science and Technology Agency's
Director General! The Chief Executive of NSDA!!
I'm JST's first female Minister!
...But why such a gaudy outfit?
...
*NSDA = National Space Development Agency.
A Minister should be able to visit at any time!!
No way!
PLINK
PLINK
!!
FWP
Moon Cosmic Power
Make Up!

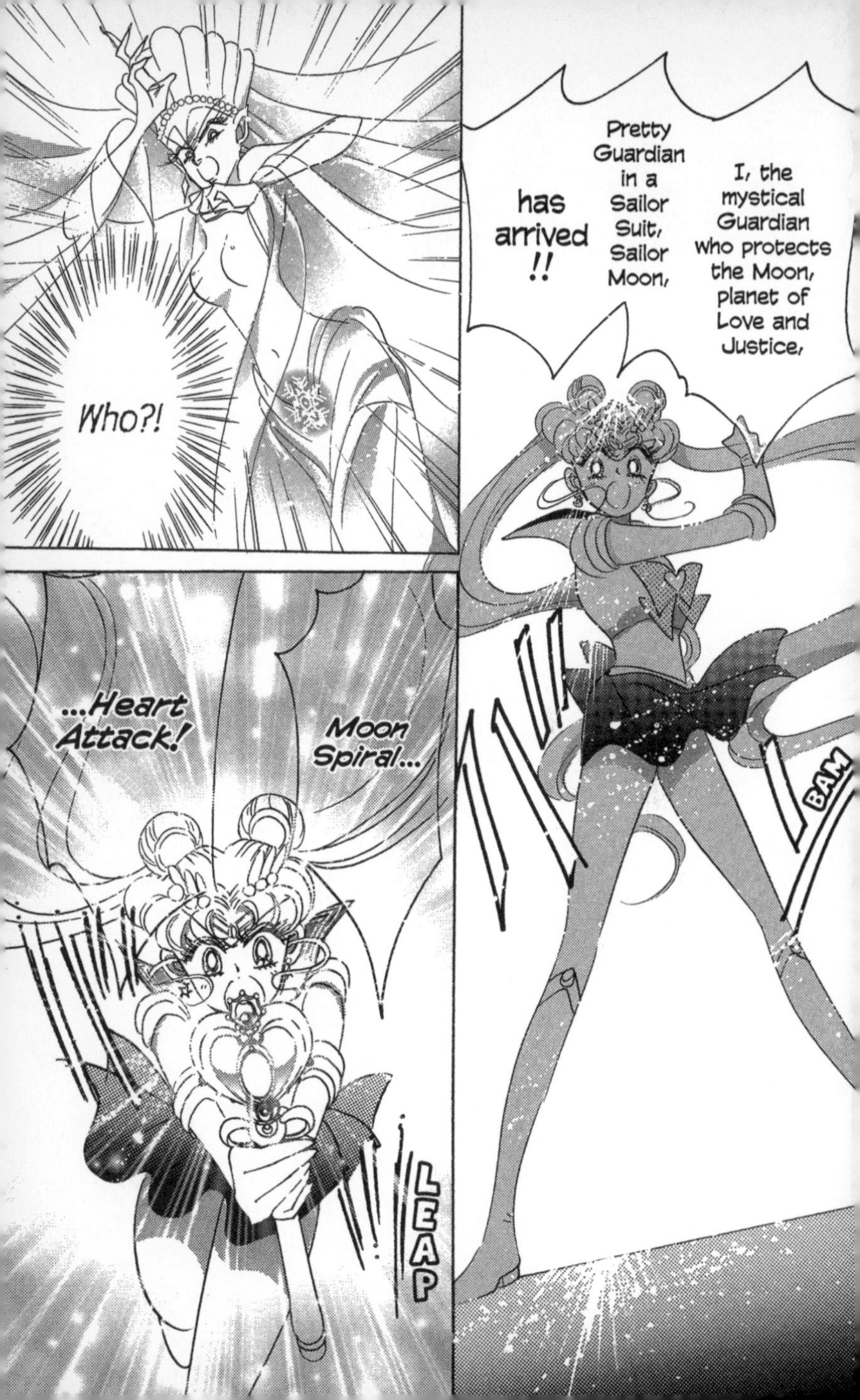
I, the mystical Guardian who protects the Moon, planet of Love and Justice, Pretty Guardian in a Sailor Suit, Sailor Moon, has arrived !!
BAM
Who?!
Moon Spiral...
...Heart Attack!
LEAP

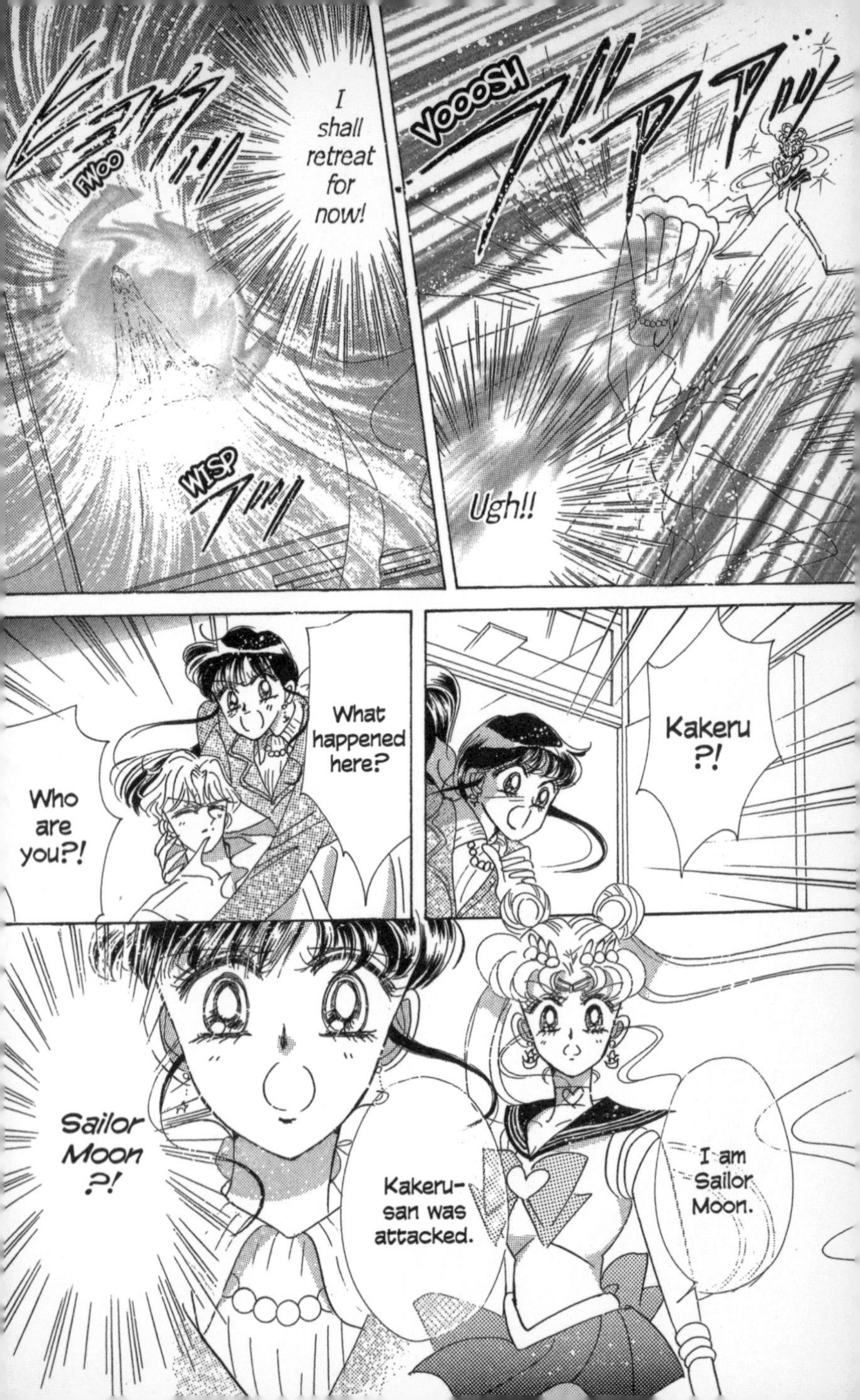
VOOOSH
Ugh!!
I shall retreat for now!
FWOO
WISP
Kakeru?!
What happened here?
Who are you?!
I am Sailor Moon.
Kakeru-san was attacked.
Sailor Moon?!

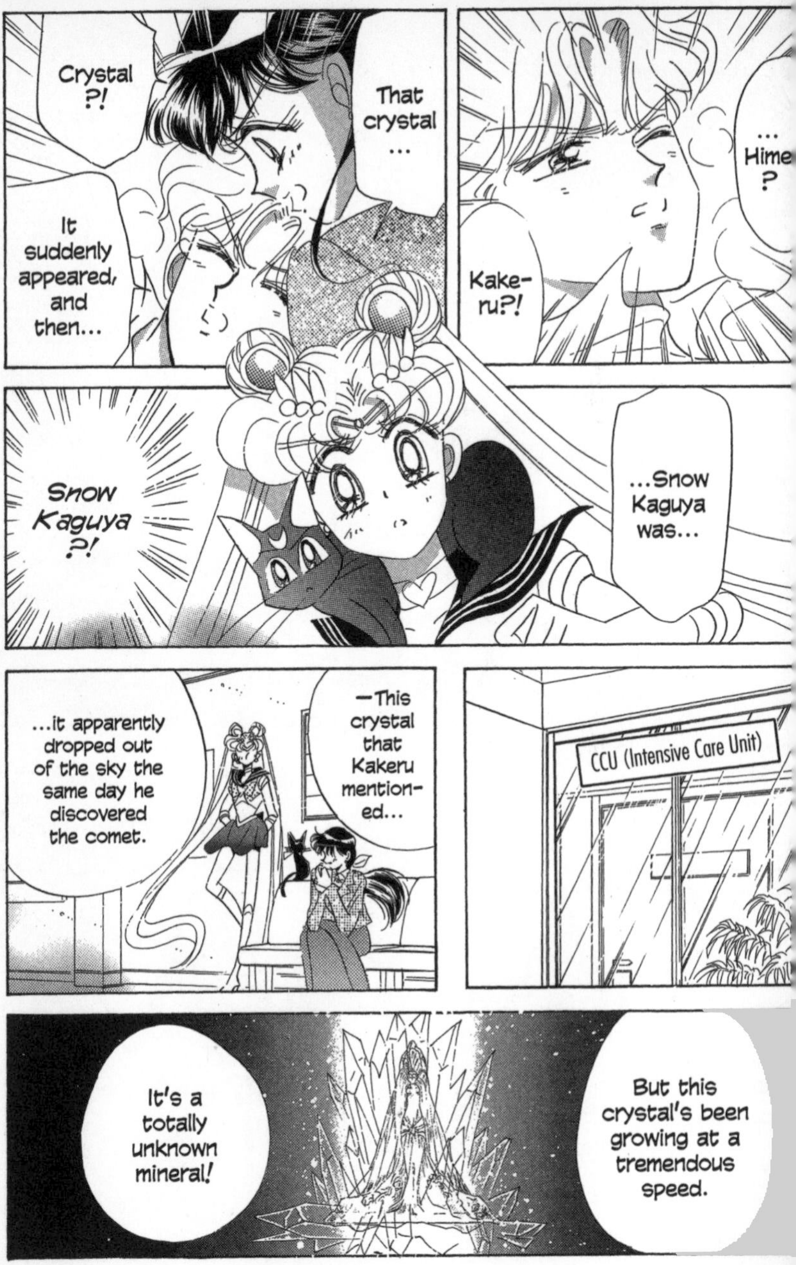
...Hime?
Kakeru?!
That crystal...
Crystal?!
It suddenly appeared, and then...
...Snow Kaguya was...
Snow Kaguya?!
CCU (Intensive Care Unit)
—This crystal that Kakeru mentioned...
...it apparently dropped out of the sky the same day he discovered the comet.
But this crystal's been growing at a tremendous speed.
It's a totally unknown mineral!

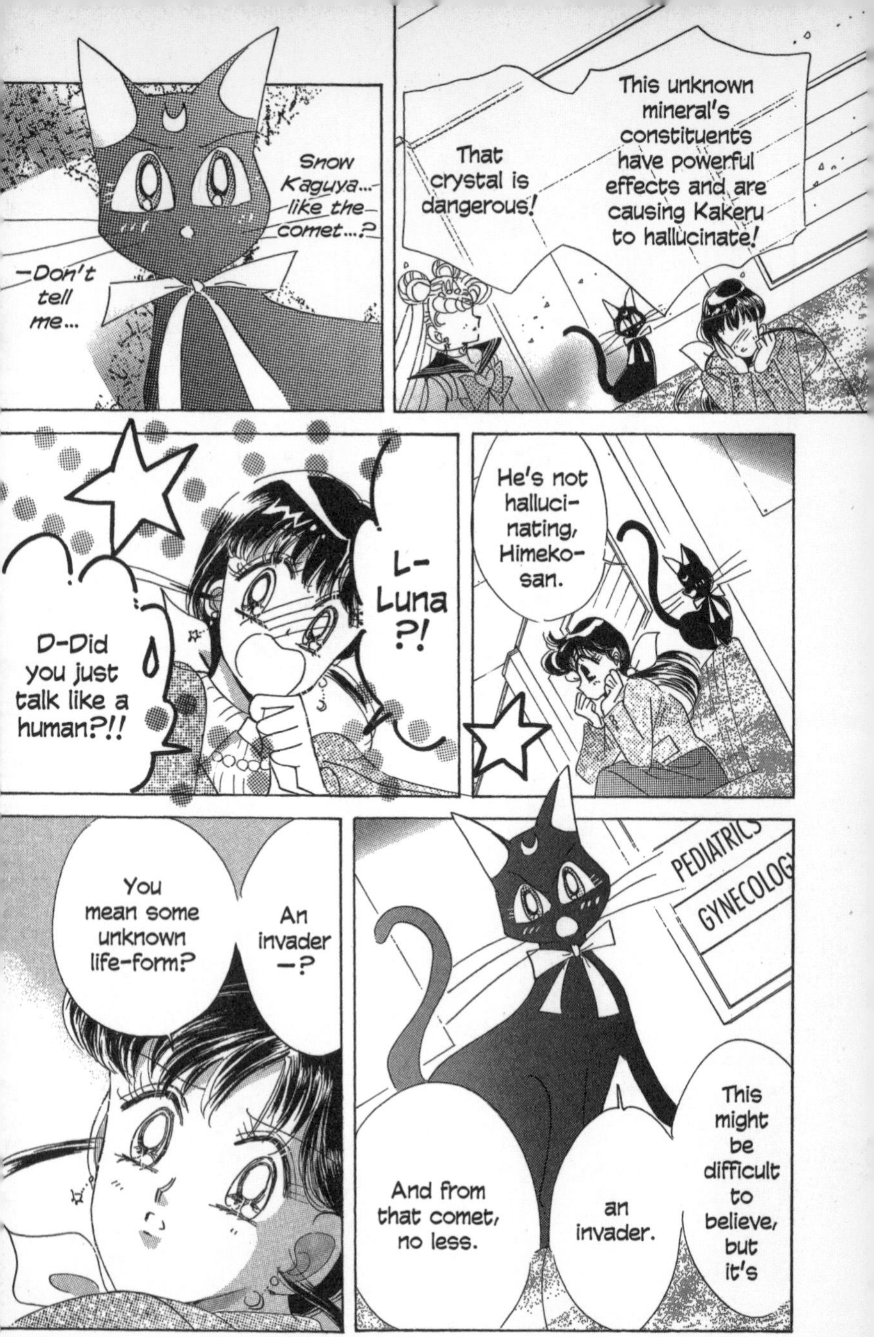
This unknown mineral's constituents have powerful effects and are causing Kakeru to hallucinate!
That crystal is dangerous!
Snow Kaguya... like the comet...?
—Don't tell me...
He's not halluci-nating, Himeko-san.
L-Luna?!
D-Did you just talk like a human?!!
PEDIATRICS
GYNECOLOGY
This might be difficult to believe, but it's
an invader.
And from that comet, no less.
An invader—?
You mean some unknown life-form?

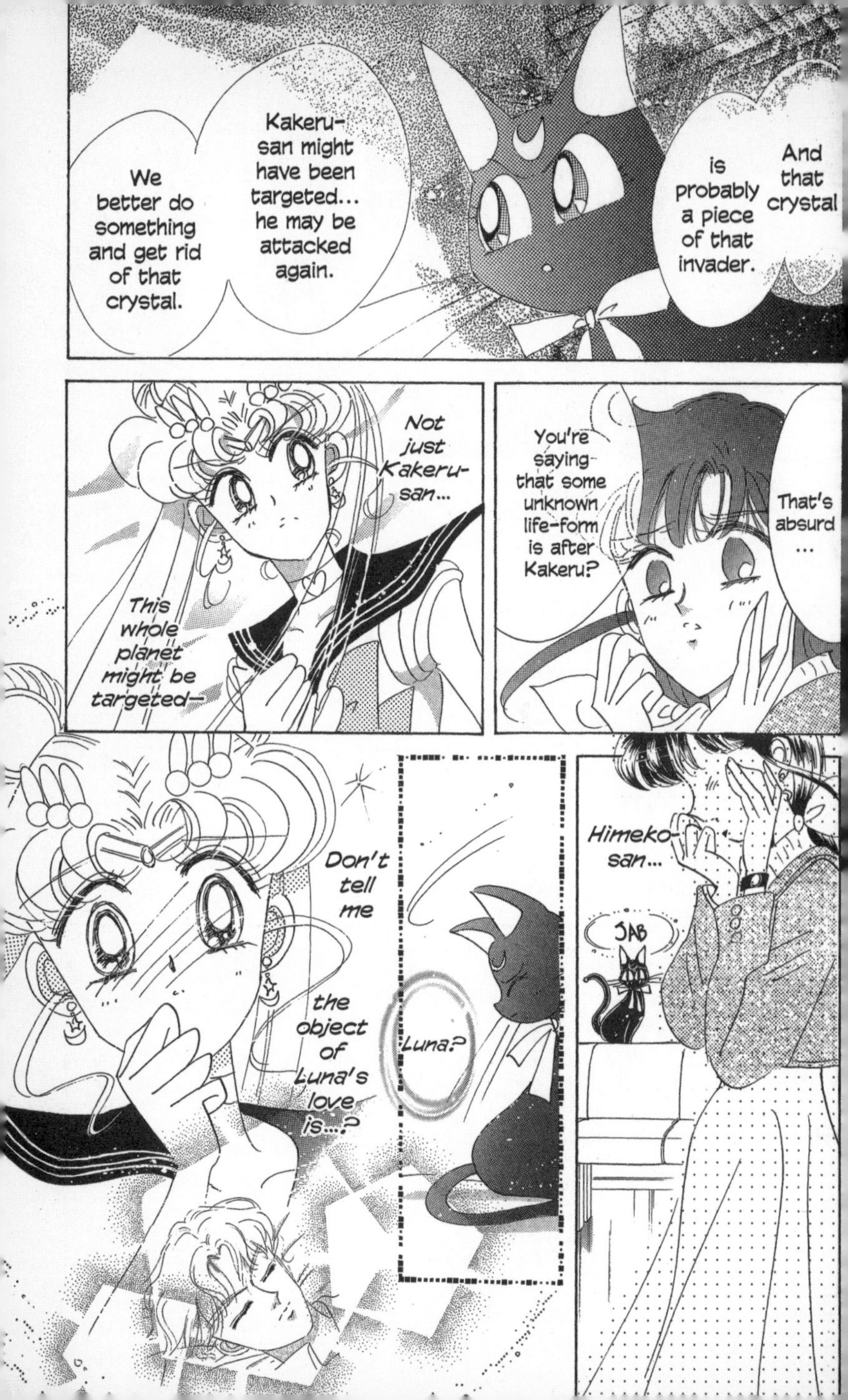
And that crystal
is probably a piece of that invader.
Kakeru-san might have been targeted... he may be attacked again.
We better do something and get rid of that crystal.
You're saying that some unknown life-form is after Kakeru?
That's absurd ...
Not just Kakeru-san...
This whole planet might be targeted—
Himeko-san...
JAB
Luna?
Don't tell me
the object of Luna's love is...?

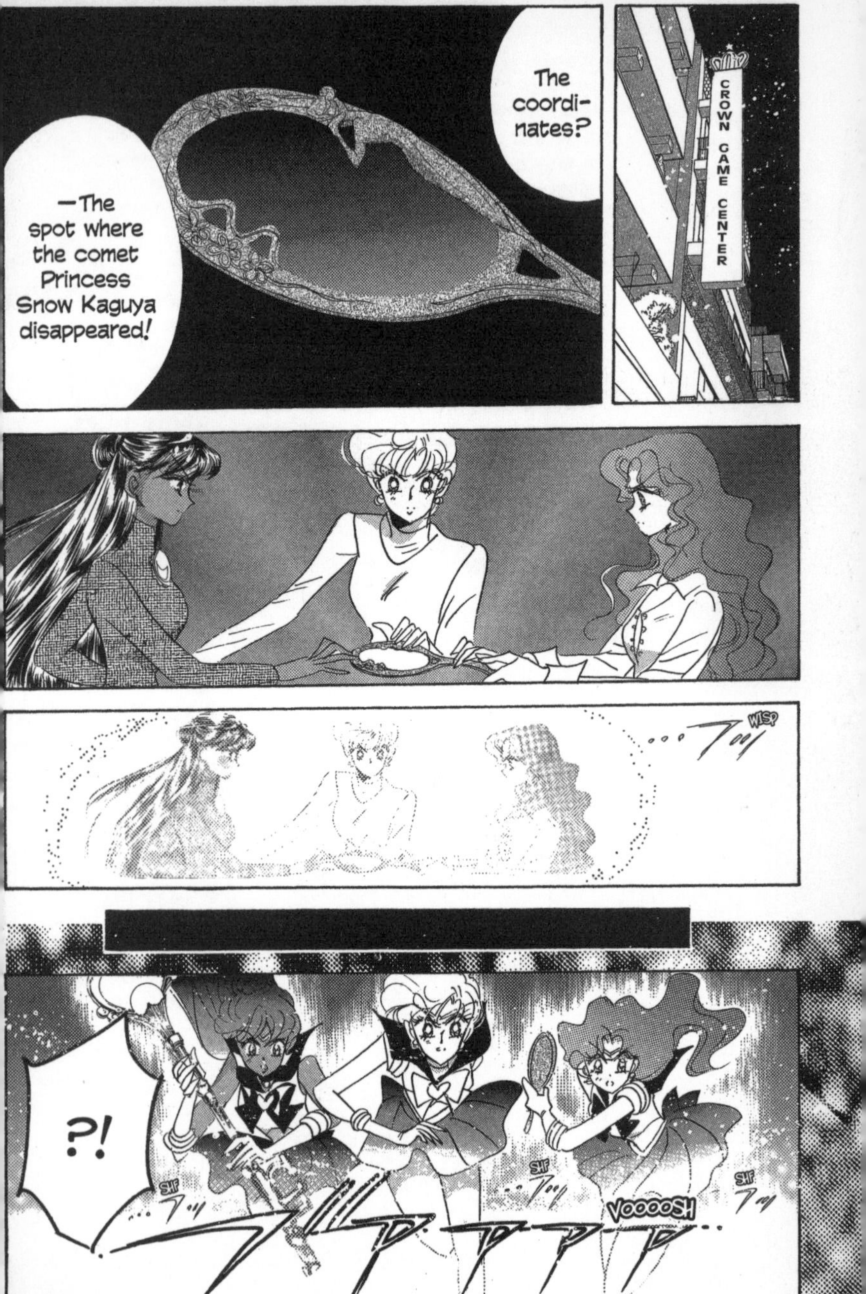
CROWN GAME CENTER
The coordinates?
—The spot where the comet Princess Snow Kaguya disappeared!
WISP
SHF
SHF
?!
VOOOOSH
SHF

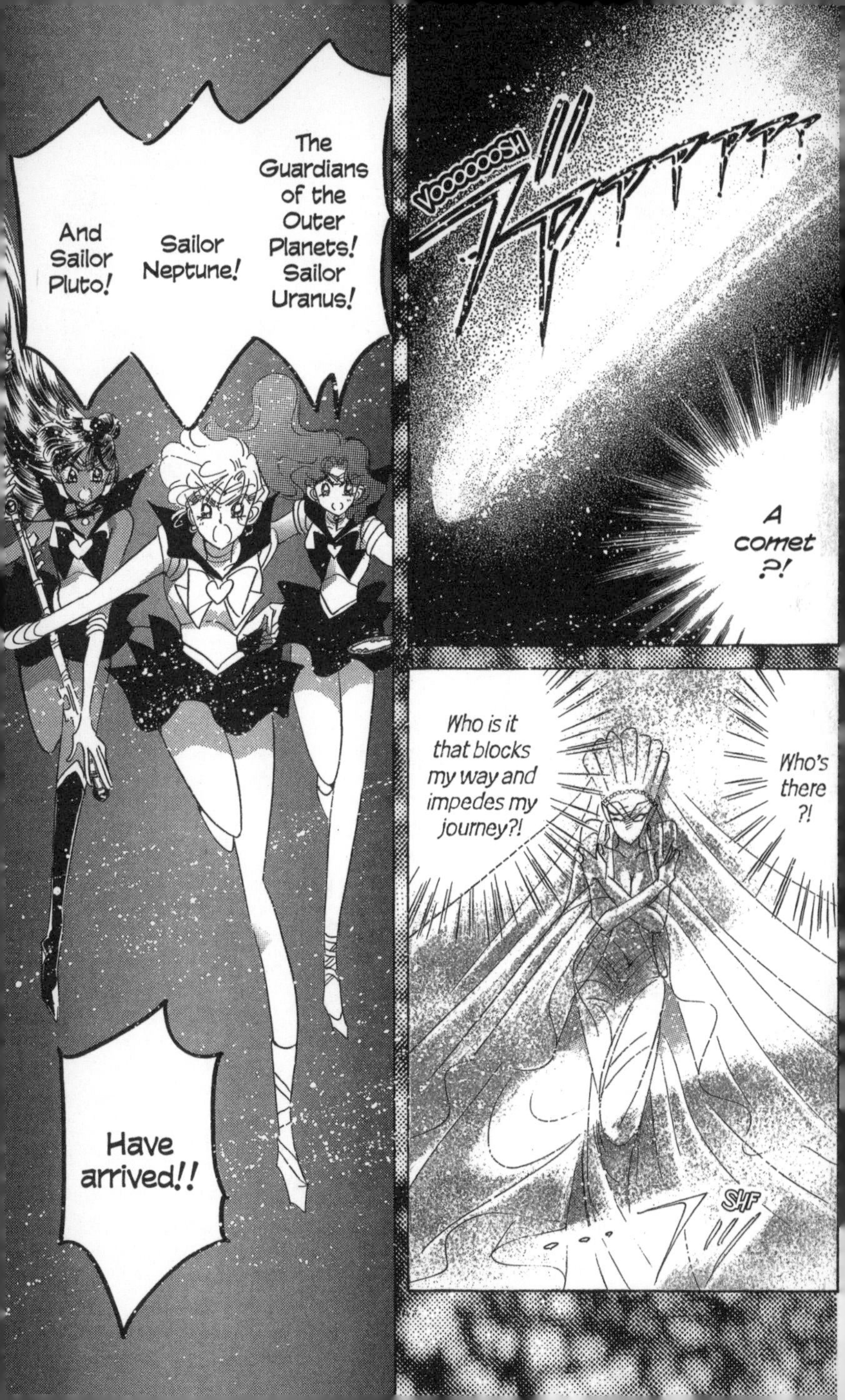
VOOOOOOOSH
A comet ?!
Who's there ?!
Who is it that blocks my way and impedes my journey?!
SHF
The Guardians of the Outer Planets! Sailor Uranus!
Sailor Neptune!
And Sailor Pluto!
Have arrived!!

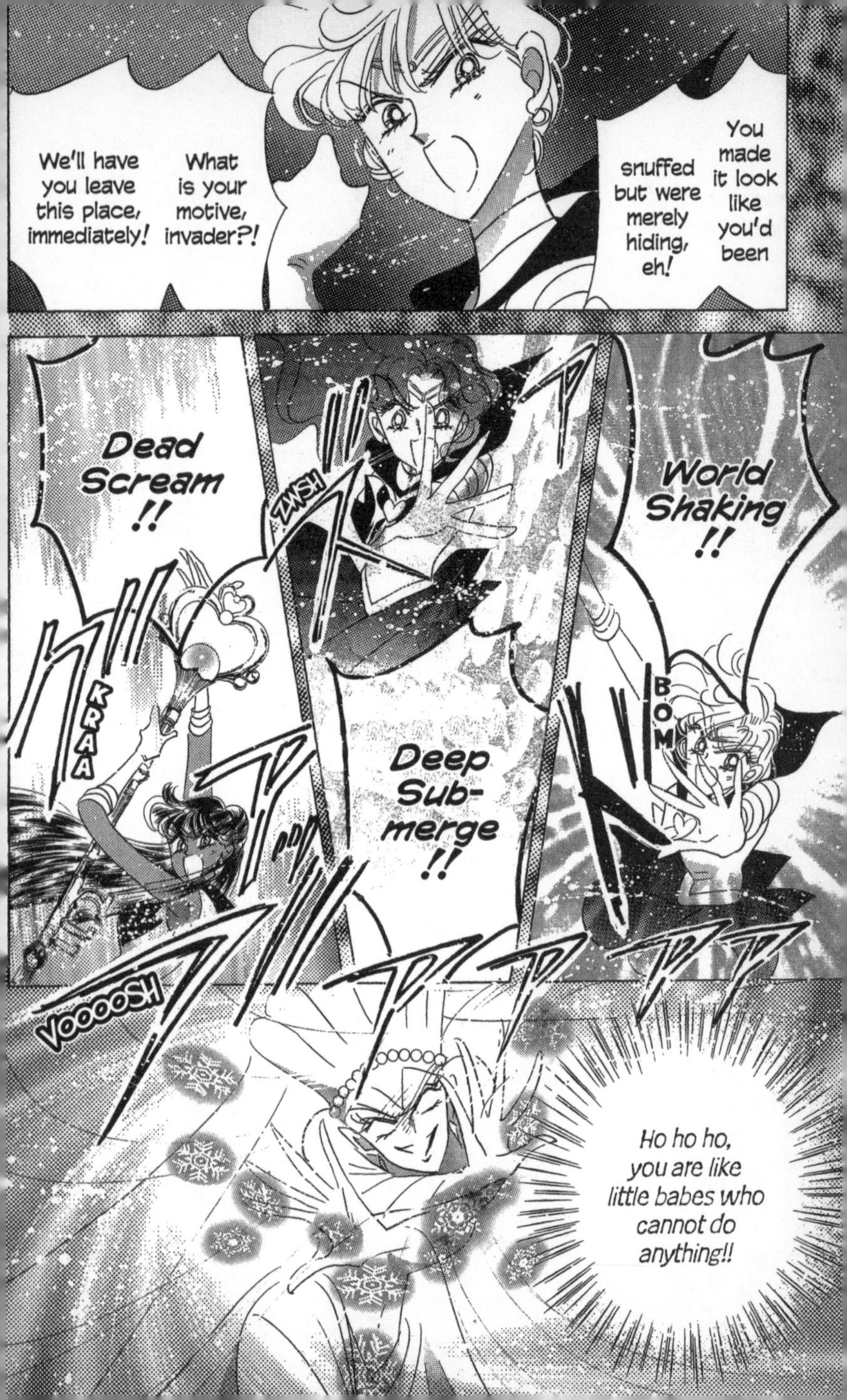
You made it look like you'd been snuffed but were merely hiding, eh!
What is your motive, invader?!
We'll have you leave this place, immediately!
World Shaking!!
BOOM
Deep Sub-merge!!
ZWSH
Dead Scream!!
KRAA
VOOOOSH
Ho ho ho, you are like little babes who cannot do anything!!

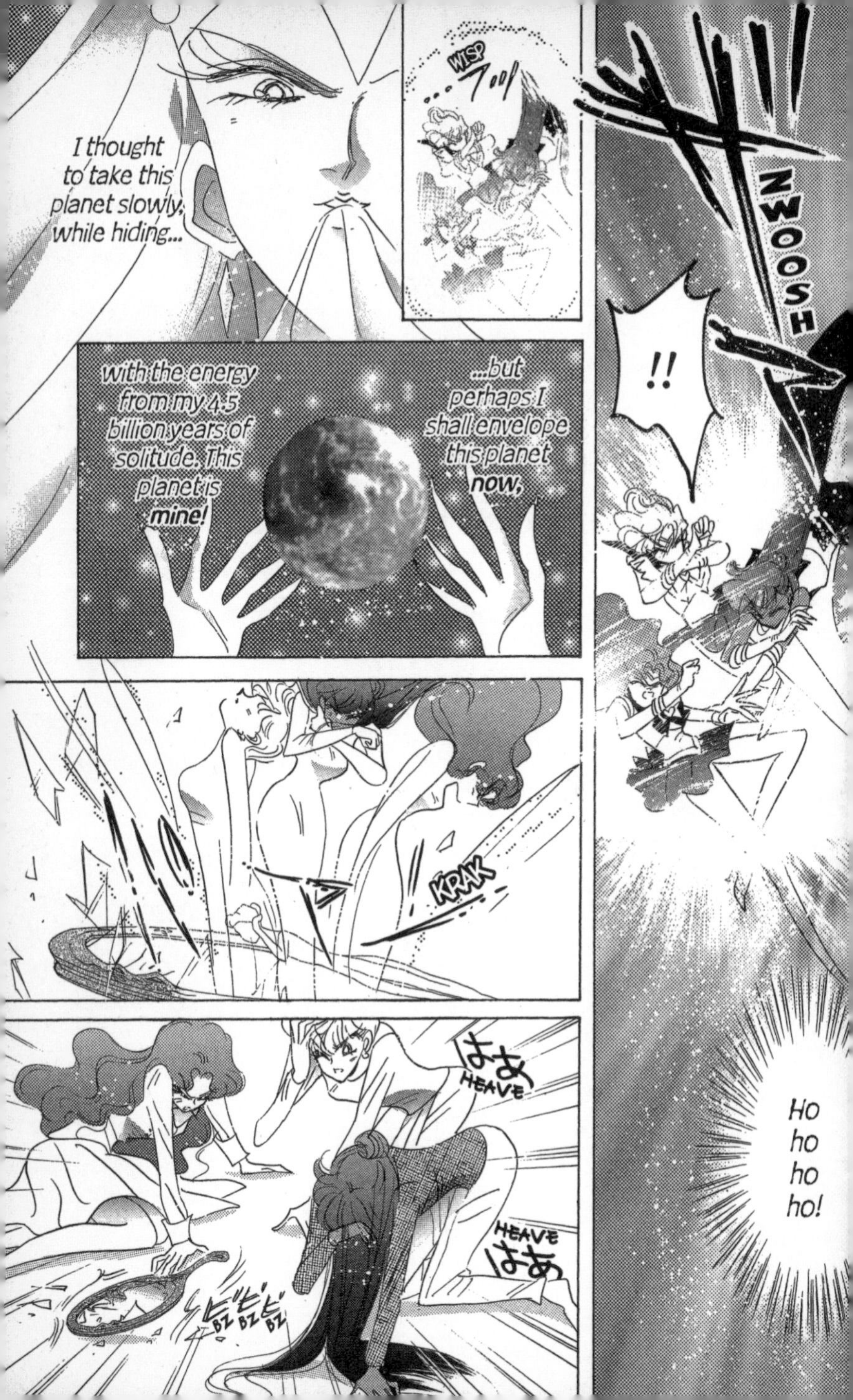
ZWOOSH
!!
Ho ho ho ho!
WISP
...
I thought to take this planet slowly, while hiding...
...but perhaps I shall envelope this planet now,
with the energy from my 4.5 billion years of solitude. This planet is **mine!**
KRAK
はあ HEAVE
HEAVE はあ
BZ BZ BZ

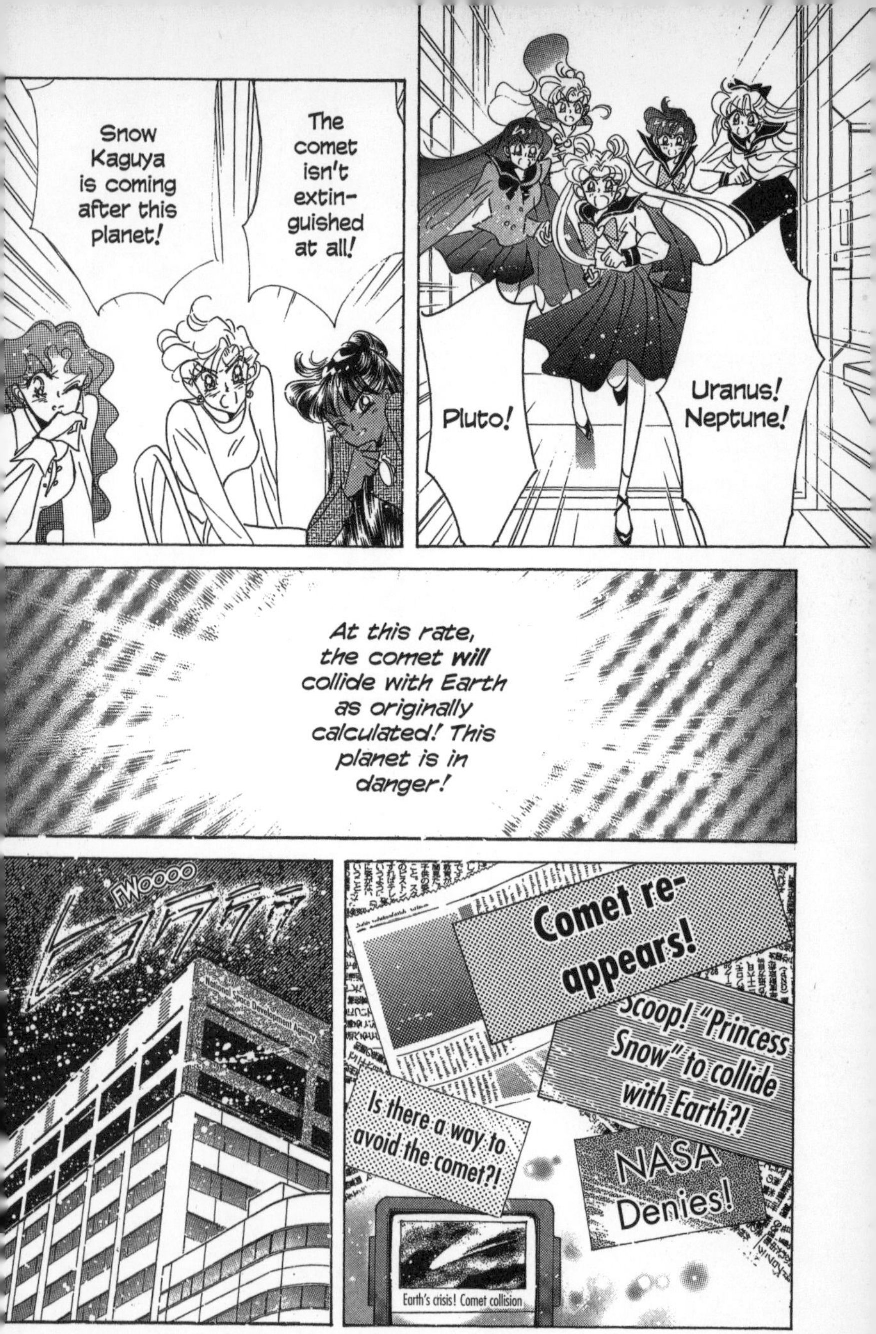
Uranus! Neptune!
Pluto!
The comet isn't extin-guished at all!
Snow Kaguya is coming after this planet!
At this rate, the comet will collide with Earth as originally calculated! This planet is in danger!
Comet re-appears!
Scoop! "Princess Snow" to collide with Earth?!
NASA Denies!
Is there a way to avoid the comet?!
Earth's crisis! Comet collision
FWOOOO
National Space Development Agency

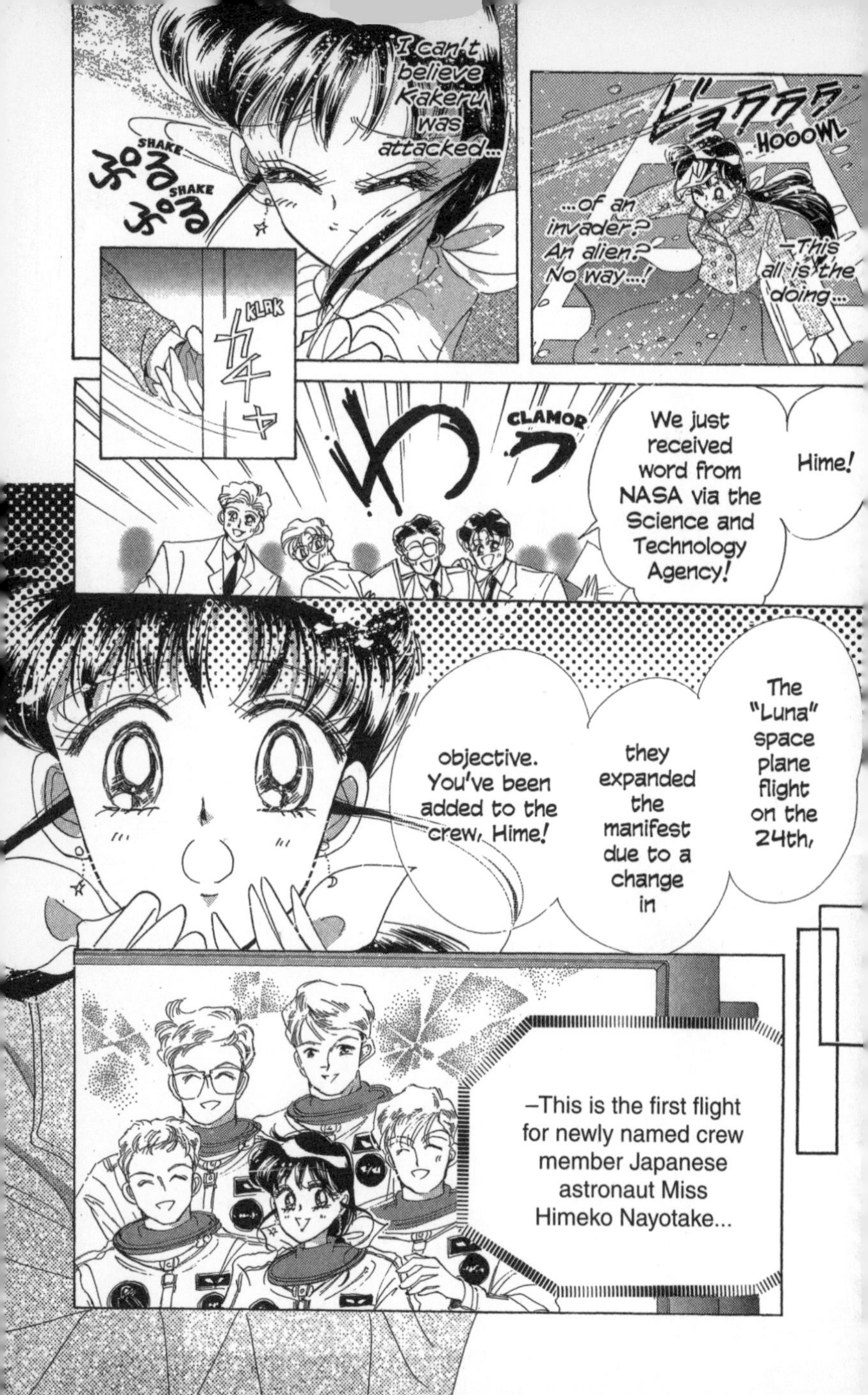
ビョウウウ
HOOOWL
—This all is the doing...
...of an invader? An alien? No way...!
I can't believe Kakeru was attacked...
SHAKE
ぷる
SHAKE
ぷる
KLAK
カチャ
Hime!
We just received word from NASA via the Science and Technology Agency!
CLAMOR
わっ
The "Luna" space plane flight on the 24th,
they expanded the manifest due to a change in
objective. You've been added to the crew, Hime!
—This is the first flight for newly named crew member Japanese astronaut Miss Himeko Nayotake...

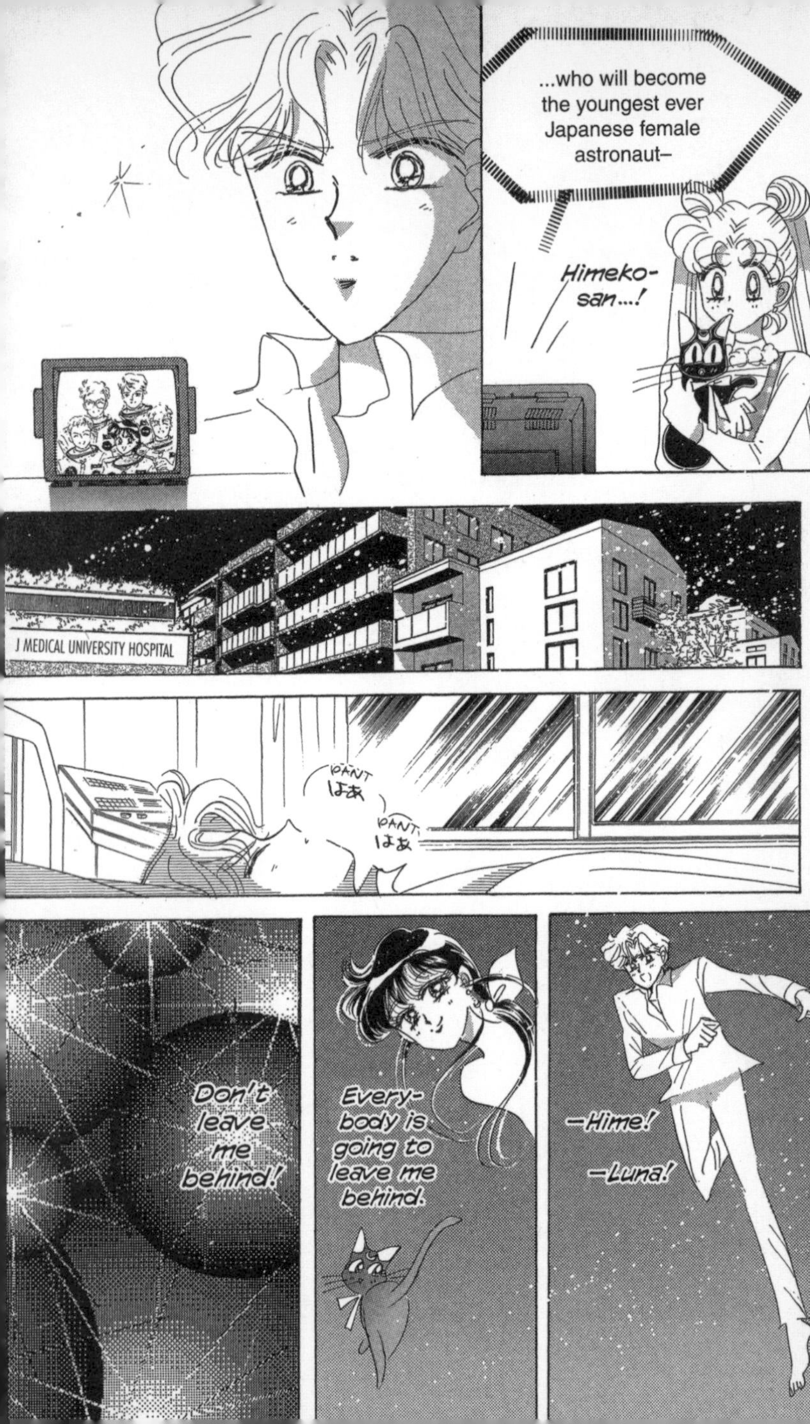
...who will become the youngest ever Japanese female astronaut–
Himeko-san...!
J MEDICAL UNIVERSITY HOSPITAL
PANT はあ
PANT はあ
–Hime!
–Luna!
Every-body is going to leave me behind.
Don't leave me behind!

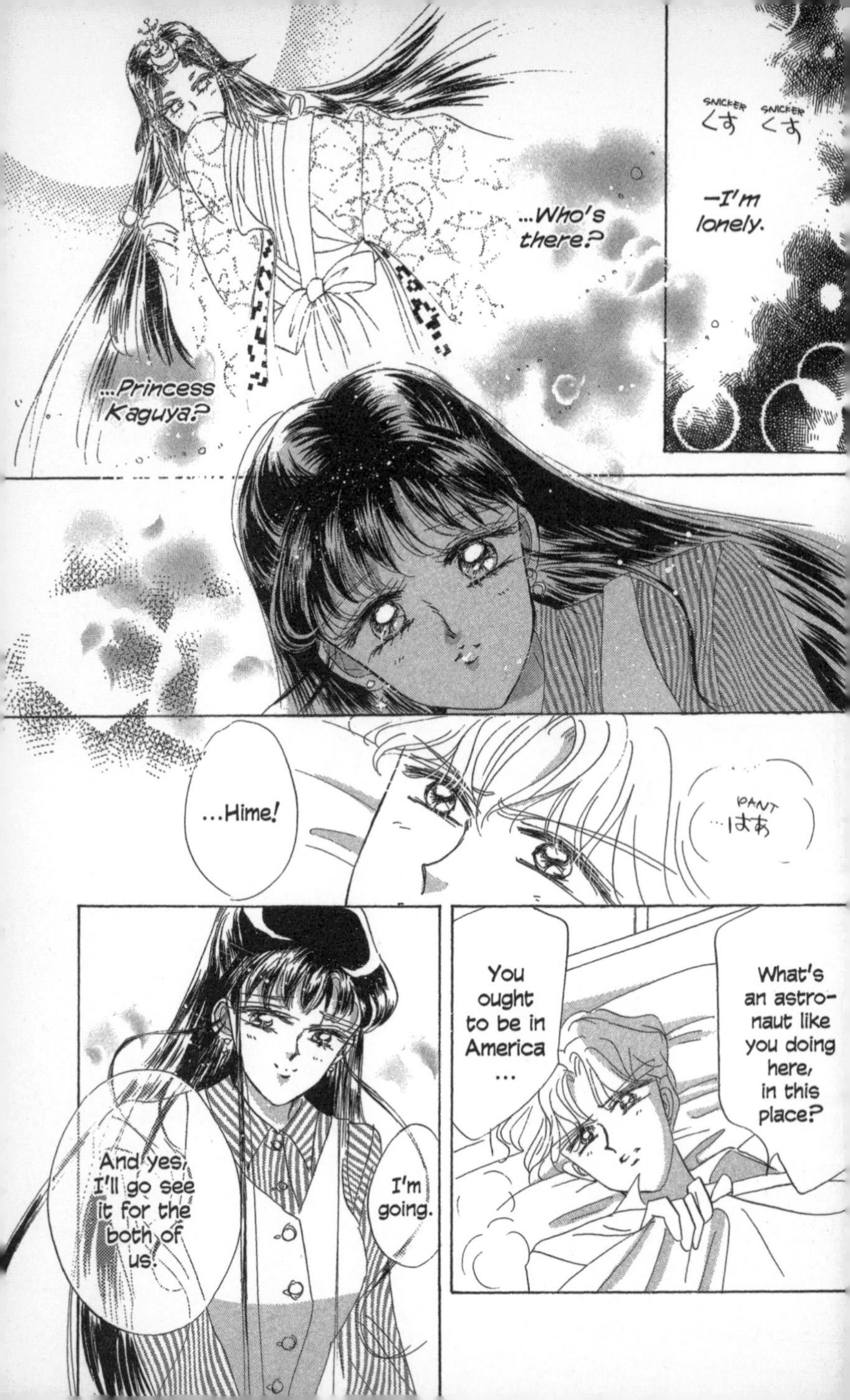
SNICKER SNICKER
くす くす
—I'm lonely.
...Who's there?
...Princess Kaguya?
PANT
...はあ
...Hime!
What's an astronaut like you doing here, in this place?
You ought to be in America ...
I'm going.
And yes, I'll go see it for the both of us.

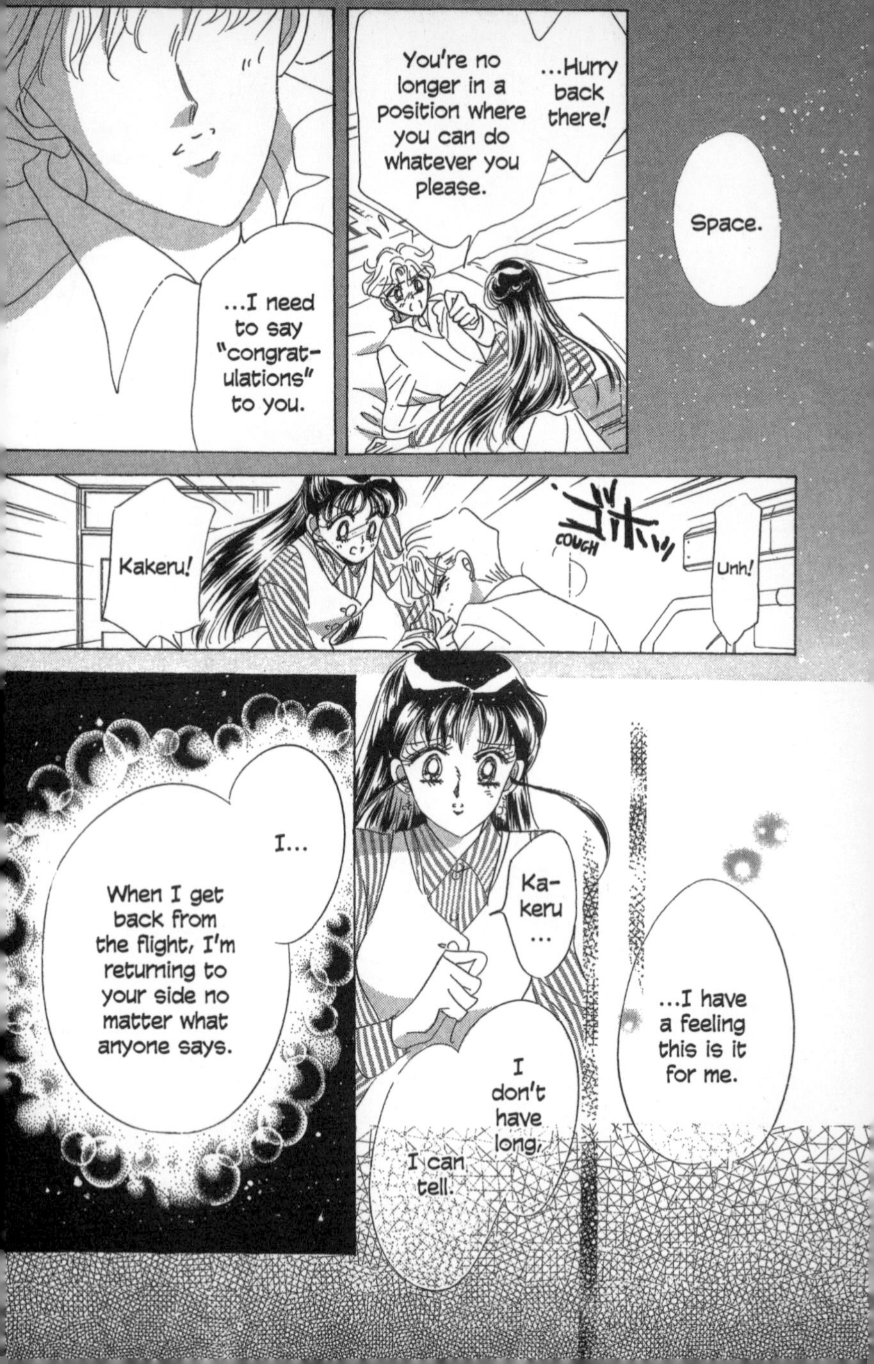
Space.
...Hurry back there!
You're no longer in a position where you can do whatever you please.
...I need to say "congratulations" to you.
Unh!
ゴホッ
COUGH
Kakeru!
Ka-keru...
...I have a feeling this is it for me.
I don't have long, I can tell.
I...
When I get back from the flight, I'm returning to your side no matter what anyone says.

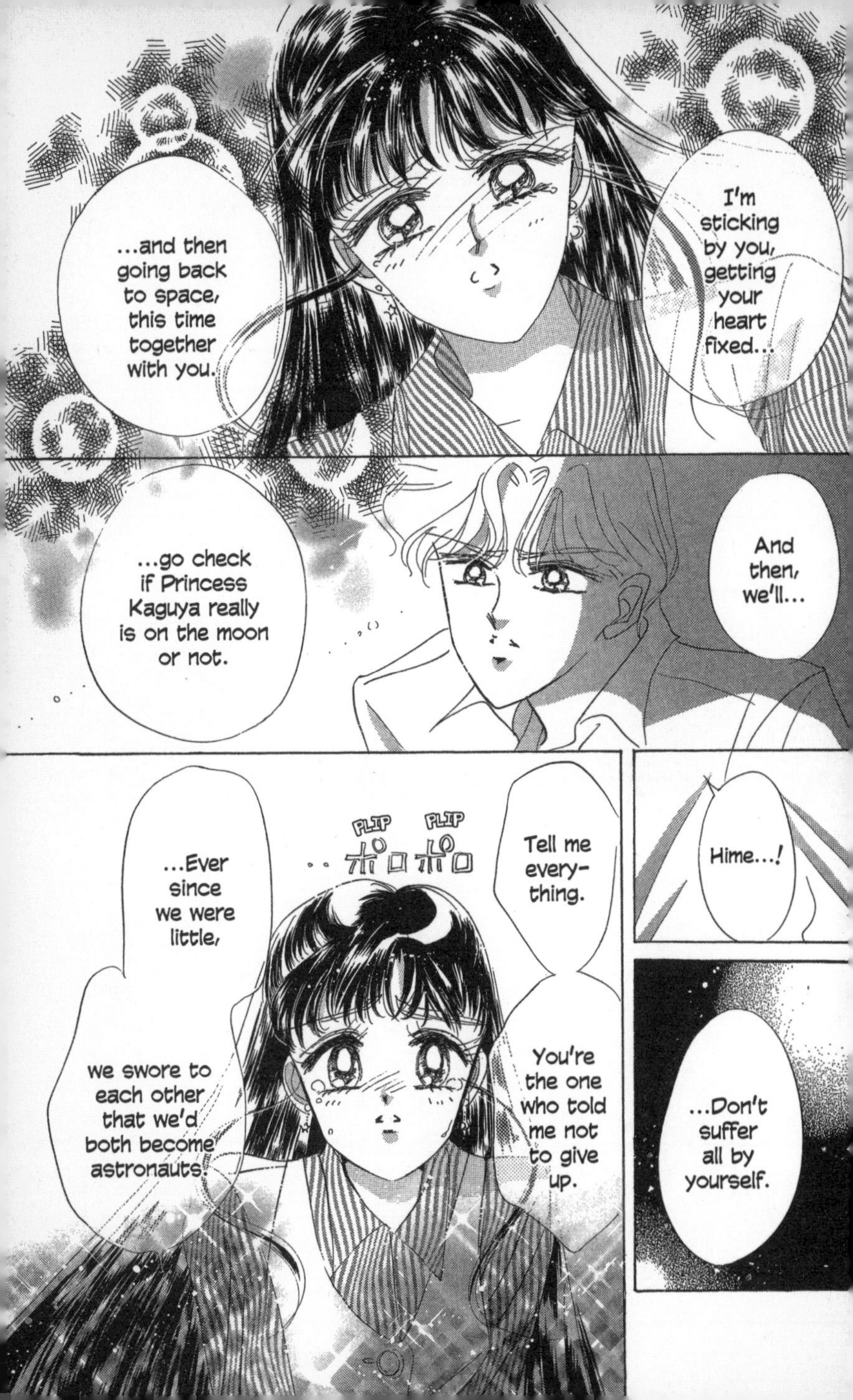
I'm sticking by you, getting your heart fixed...
...and then going back to space, this time together with you.
And then, we'll...
...go check if Princess Kaguya really is on the moon or not.
Hime...!
...Don't suffer all by yourself.
Tell me every-thing.
PLIP PLIP
..ポロポロ
You're the one who told me not to give up.
...Ever since we were little,
we swore to each other that we'd both become astronauts.

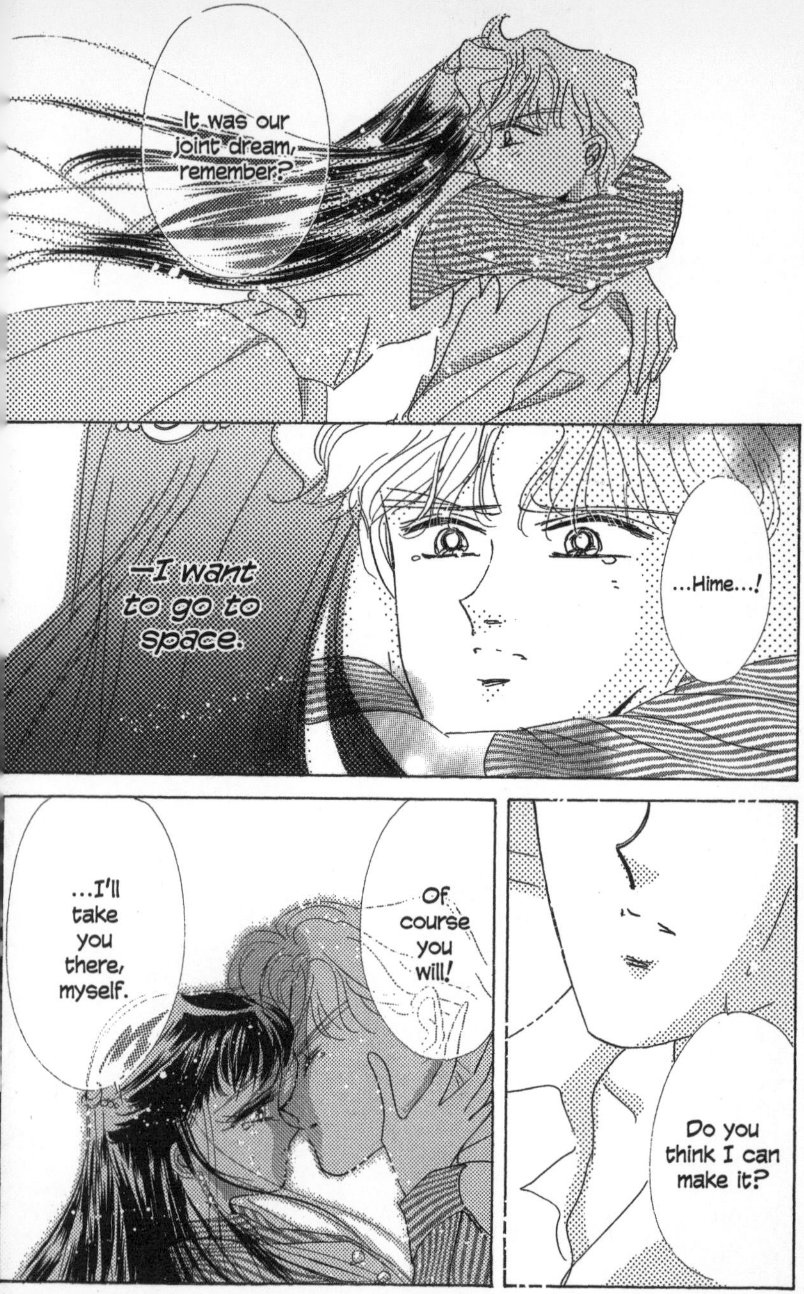
It was our joint dream, remember?
...Hime...!
—I want to go to space.
Do you think I can make it?
Of course you will!
...I'll take you there, myself.

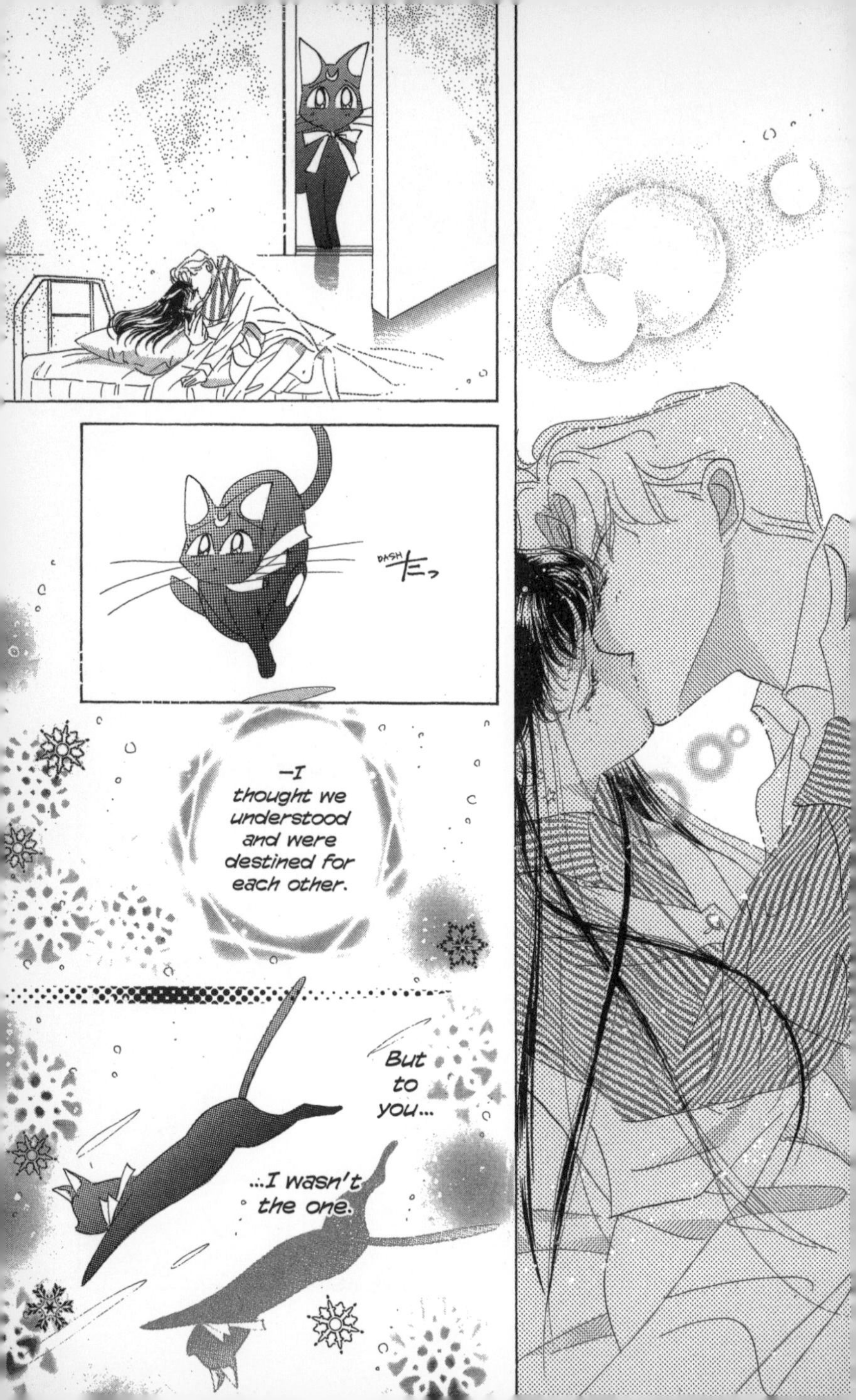
DASH たっ
—I thought we understood and were destined for each other.
But to you...
...I wasn't the one.

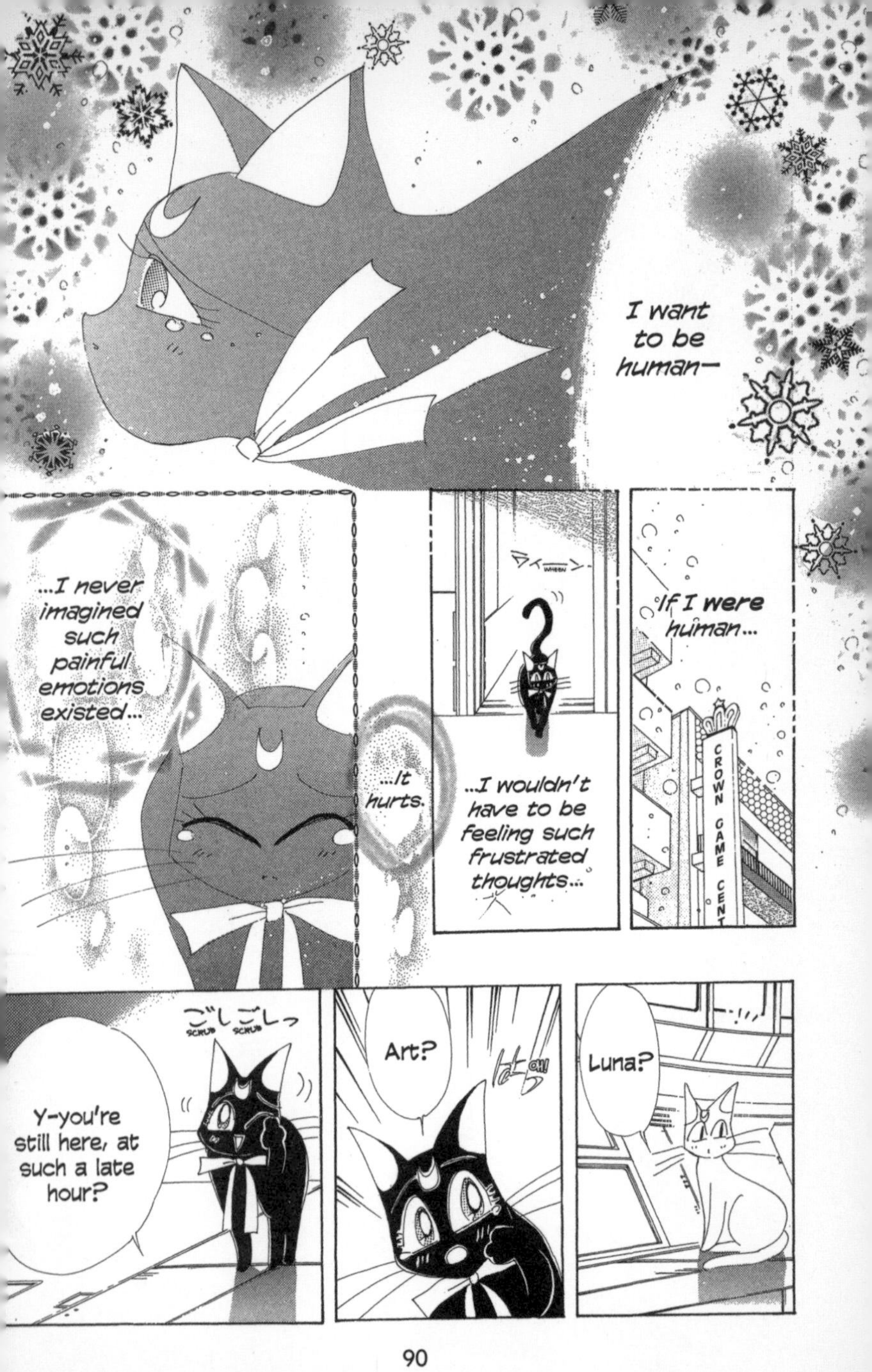
I want to be human—
If I were human...
CROWN GAME CENT
WHEEN
...I wouldn't have to be feeling such frustrated thoughts...
...It hurts.
...I never imagined such painful emotions existed...
Luna?
OH!
Art?
ごしごしっ
SCRUB SCRUB
Y-you're still here, at such a late hour?

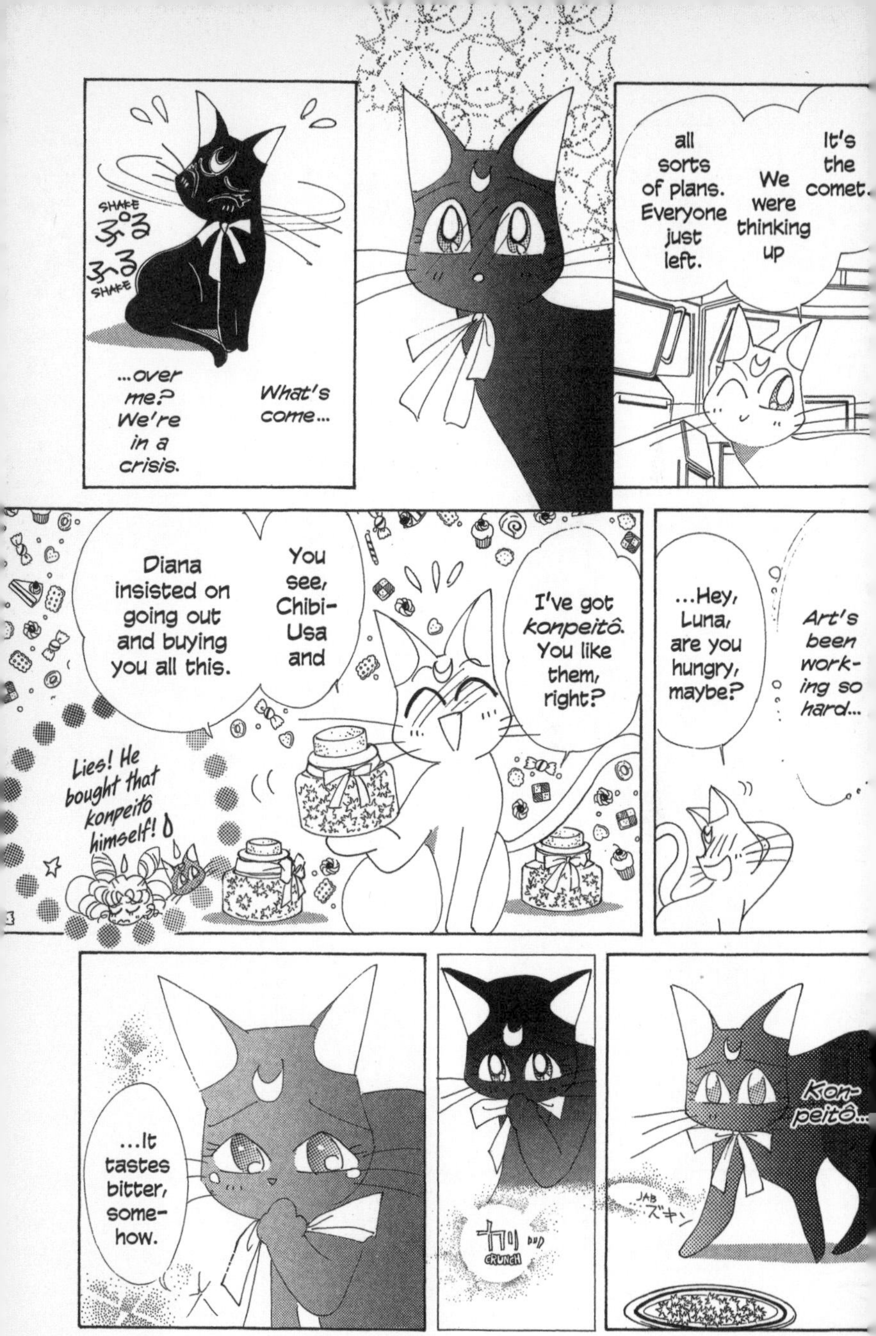
It's the comet.
We were thinking up
all sorts of plans. Everyone just left.
What's come...
...over me? We're in a crisis.
SHAKE ぷる
ぷる SHAKE
Art's been working so hard...
...Hey, Luna, are you hungry, maybe?
I've got *konpeitô*. You like them, right?
You see, Chibi-Usa and
Diana insisted on going out and buying you all this.
Lies! He bought that konpeitô himself!
Kon-peitô...
JAB ズキン
カリ CRUNCH
...It tastes bitter, somehow.

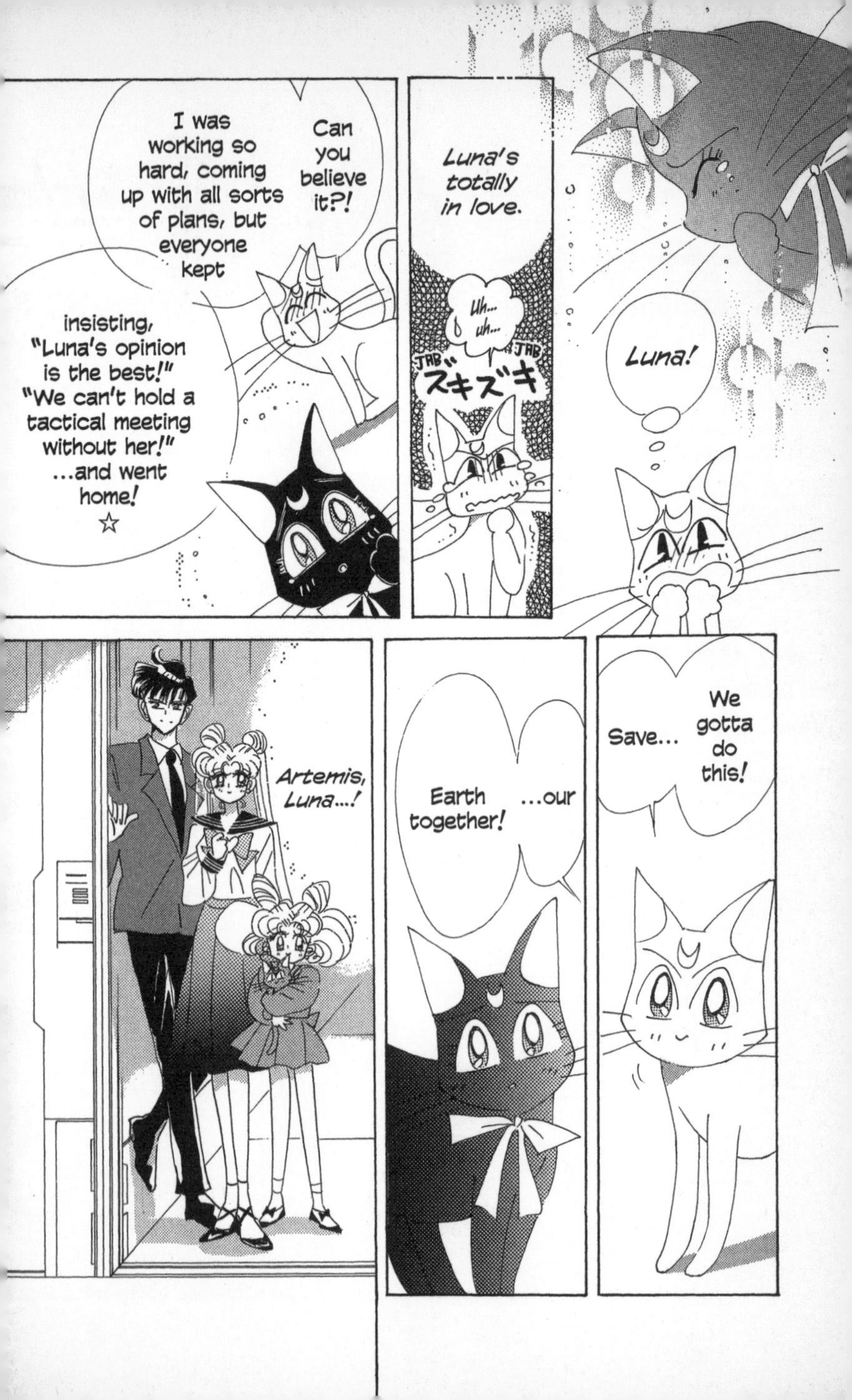
Luna!
Luna's totally in love.
uh... uh...
JAB ズキズキ JAB
Can you believe it?!
I was working so hard, coming up with all sorts of plans, but everyone kept
insisting, "Luna's opinion is the best!" "We can't hold a tactical meeting without her!" ...and went home! ☆
We gotta do this!
Save...
...our
Earth together!
Artemis, Luna...!

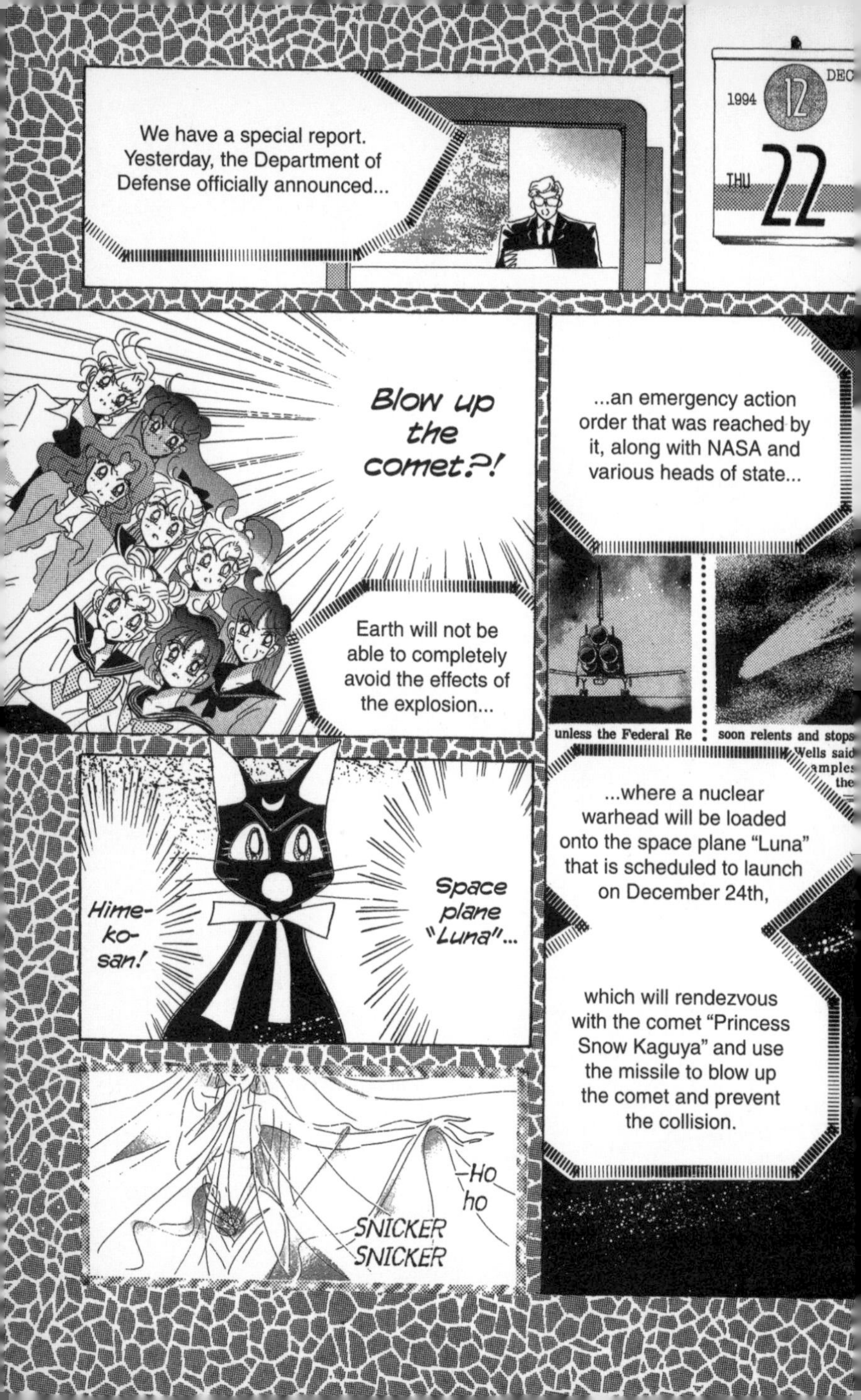
1994
12
DEC
THU
22
We have a special report. Yesterday, the Department of Defense officially announced...
...an emergency action order that was reached by it, along with NASA and various heads of state...
unless the Federal Re
soon relents and stops
Wells said
amples
the
...where a nuclear warhead will be loaded onto the space plane "Luna" that is scheduled to launch on December 24th,
which will rendezvous with the comet "Princess Snow Kaguya" and use the missile to blow up the comet and prevent the collision.
Blow up the comet?!
Earth will not be able to completely avoid the effects of the explosion...
Space plane "Luna"...
Hime-ko-san!
Ho ho
SNICKER SNICKER

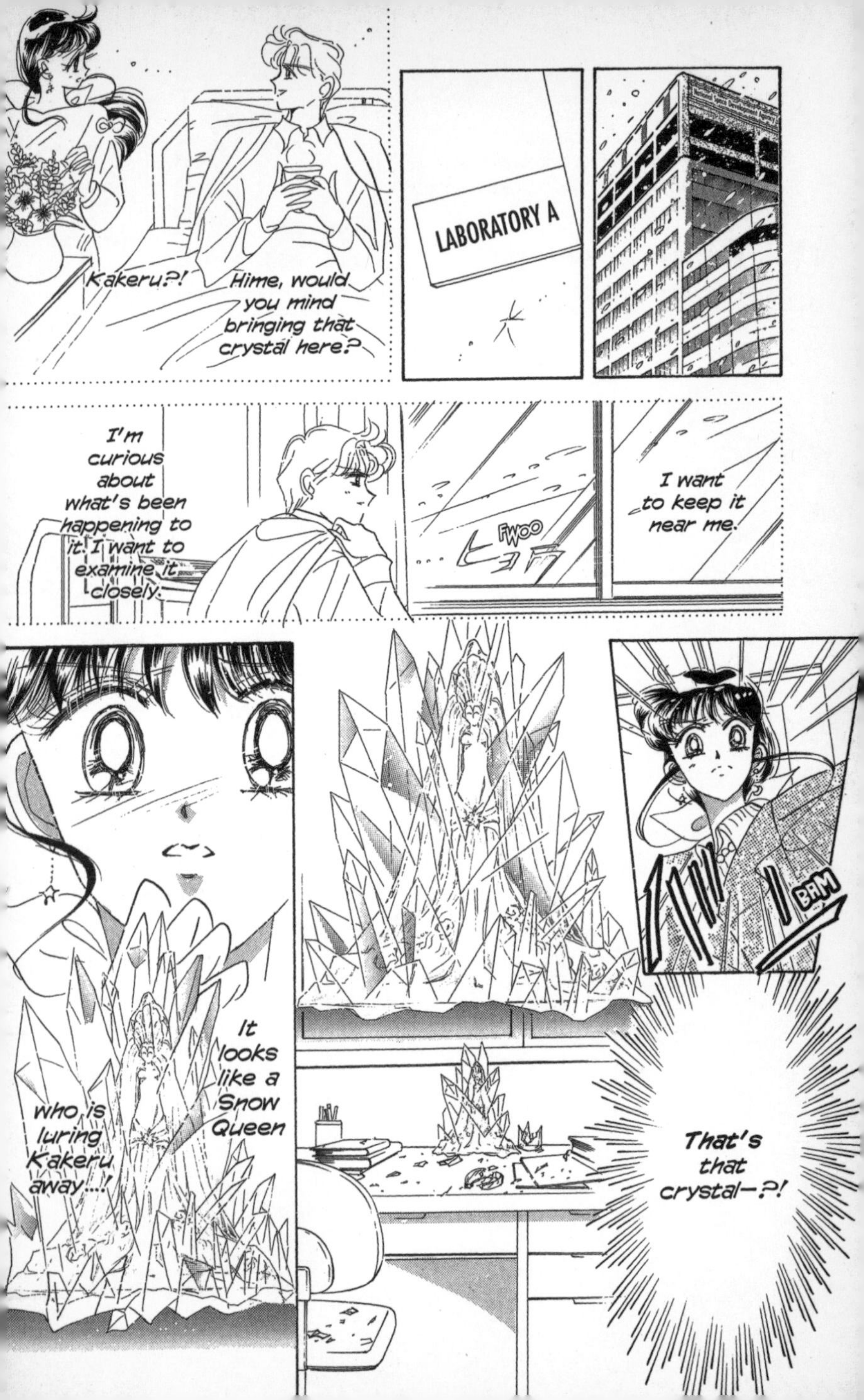

LABORATORY A
Hime, would you mind bringing that crystal here?
Kakeru?!
I want to keep it near me.
FWOO
I'm curious about what's been happening to it. I want to examine it closely.
BAM
That's that crystal—?!
It looks like a Snow Queen
who is luring Kakeru away...!

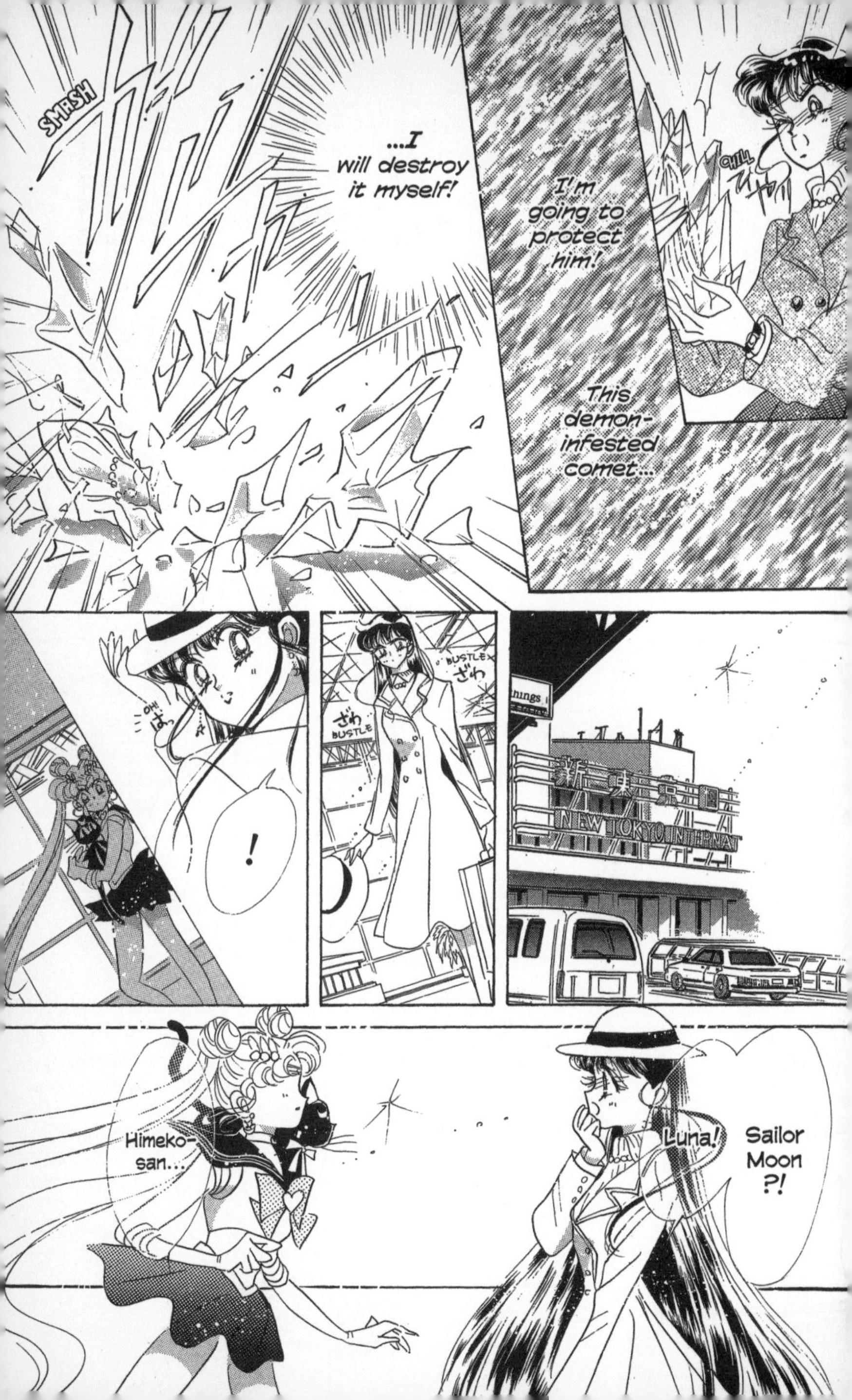
CHILL
I'm going to protect him!
This demon-infested comet...
...I will destroy it myself!
SMASH
NEW TOKYO INTERNAT
things
BUSTLE ざわ
ざわ BUSTLE
!
OH! はっ
Sailor Moon ?!
Luna!
Himeko-san...

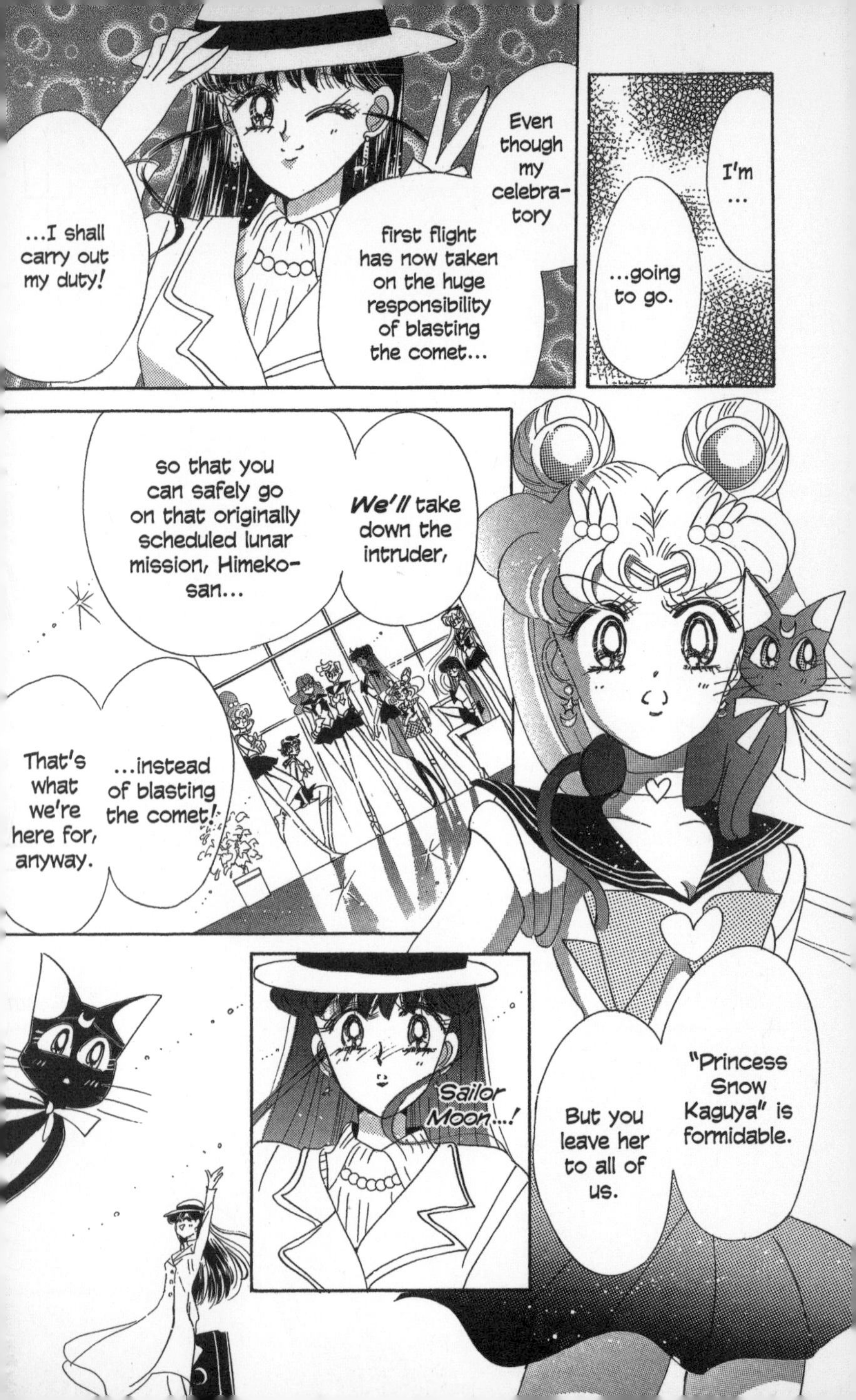
I'm ...
...going to go.
Even though my celebratory first flight has now taken on the huge responsibility of blasting the comet...
...I shall carry out my duty!
We'll take down the intruder,
so that you can safely go on that originally scheduled lunar mission, Himeko-san...
...instead of blasting the comet!
That's what we're here for, anyway.
"Princess Snow Kaguya" is formidable.
But you leave her to all of us.
Sailor Moon...!

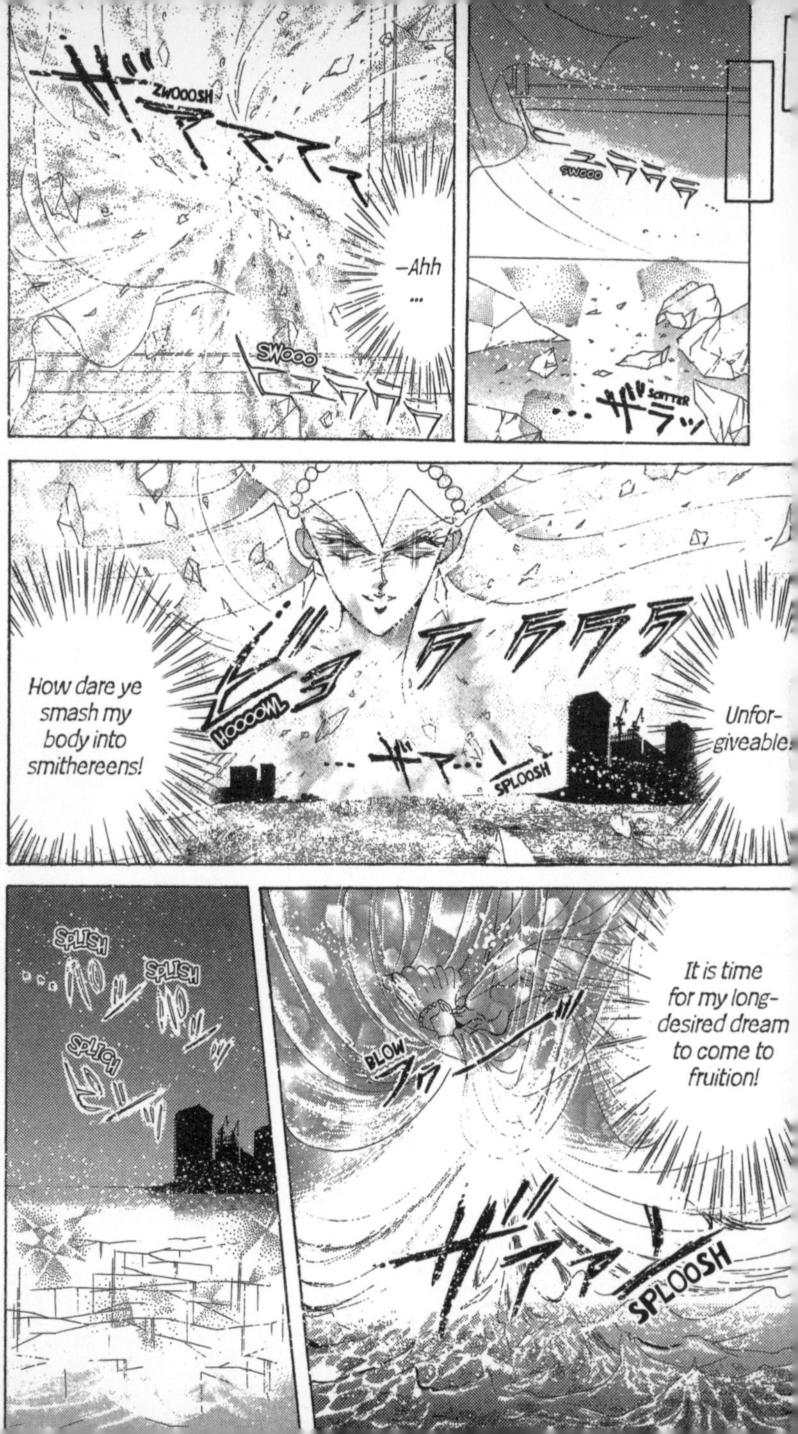
SWOOO
SCATTER
ZWOOOSH
—Ahh ...
SWOOO
Unfor-giveable!
HOOOOWL
How dare ye smash my body into smithereens!
SPLOOSH
It is time for my long-desired dream to come to fruition!
BLOW
SPLOOSH
SPLISH
SPLISH
SPLICH

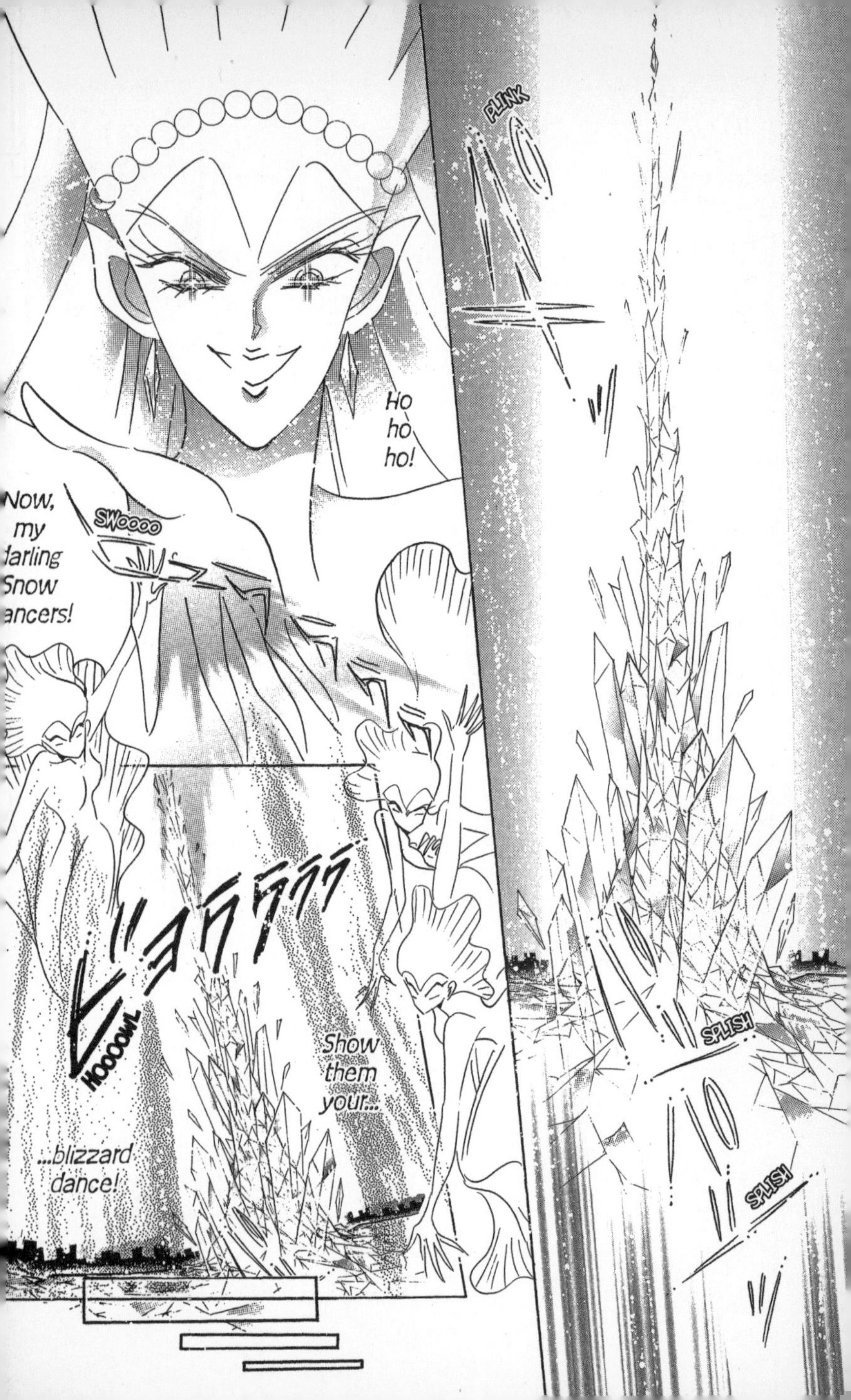
PLINK
SPLISH
SPLISH
Ho ho ho!
Now, my darling Snow ancers!
SWOOOO
Show them your...
...blizzard dance!
HOOOOWL

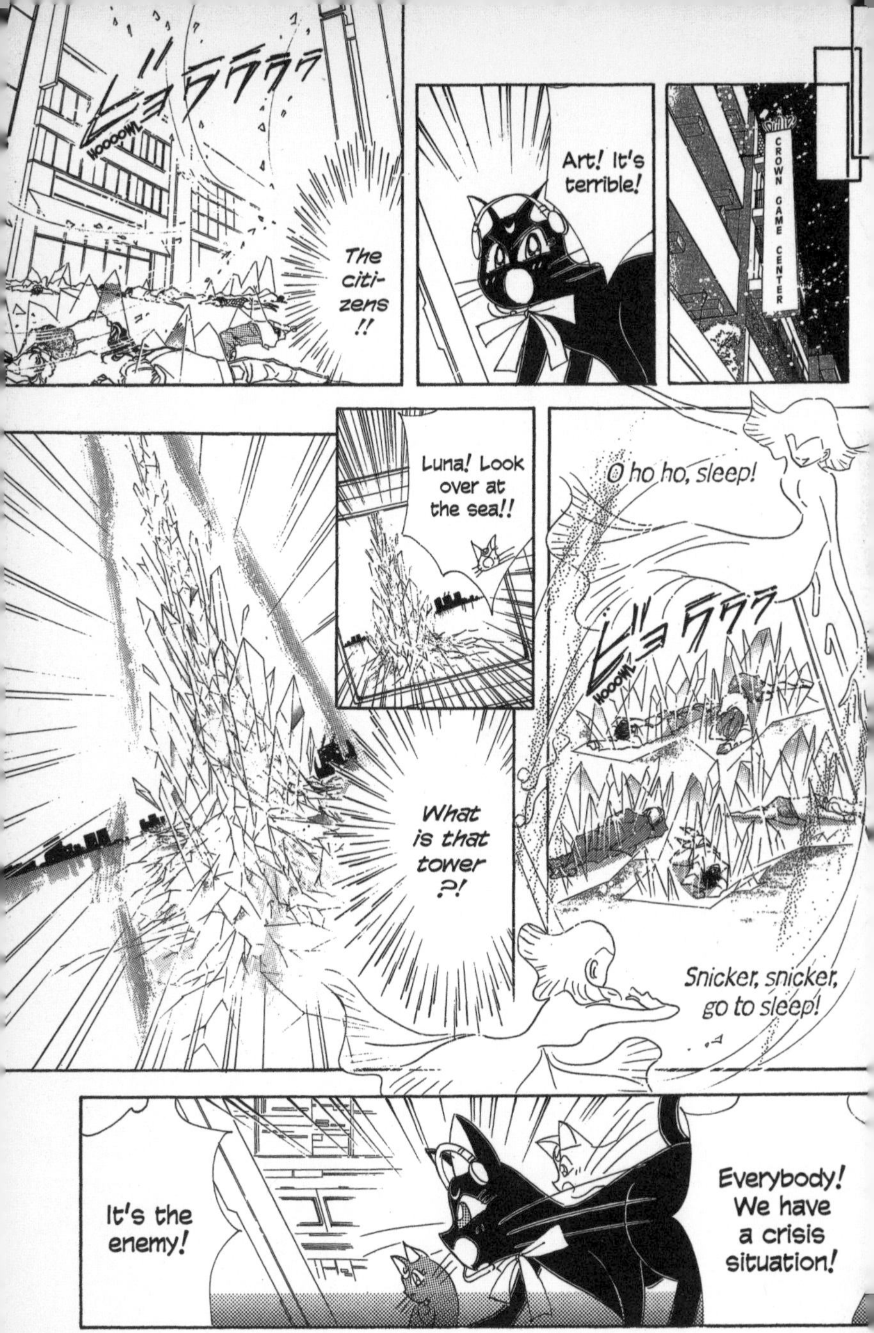
CROWN GAME CENTER
Art! It's terrible!
HOOOOWL
The citi-zens!!
O ho ho, sleep!
HOOOWL
Snicker, snicker, go to sleep!
Luna! Look over at the sea!!
What is that tower?!
Everybody! We have a crisis situation!
It's the enemy!

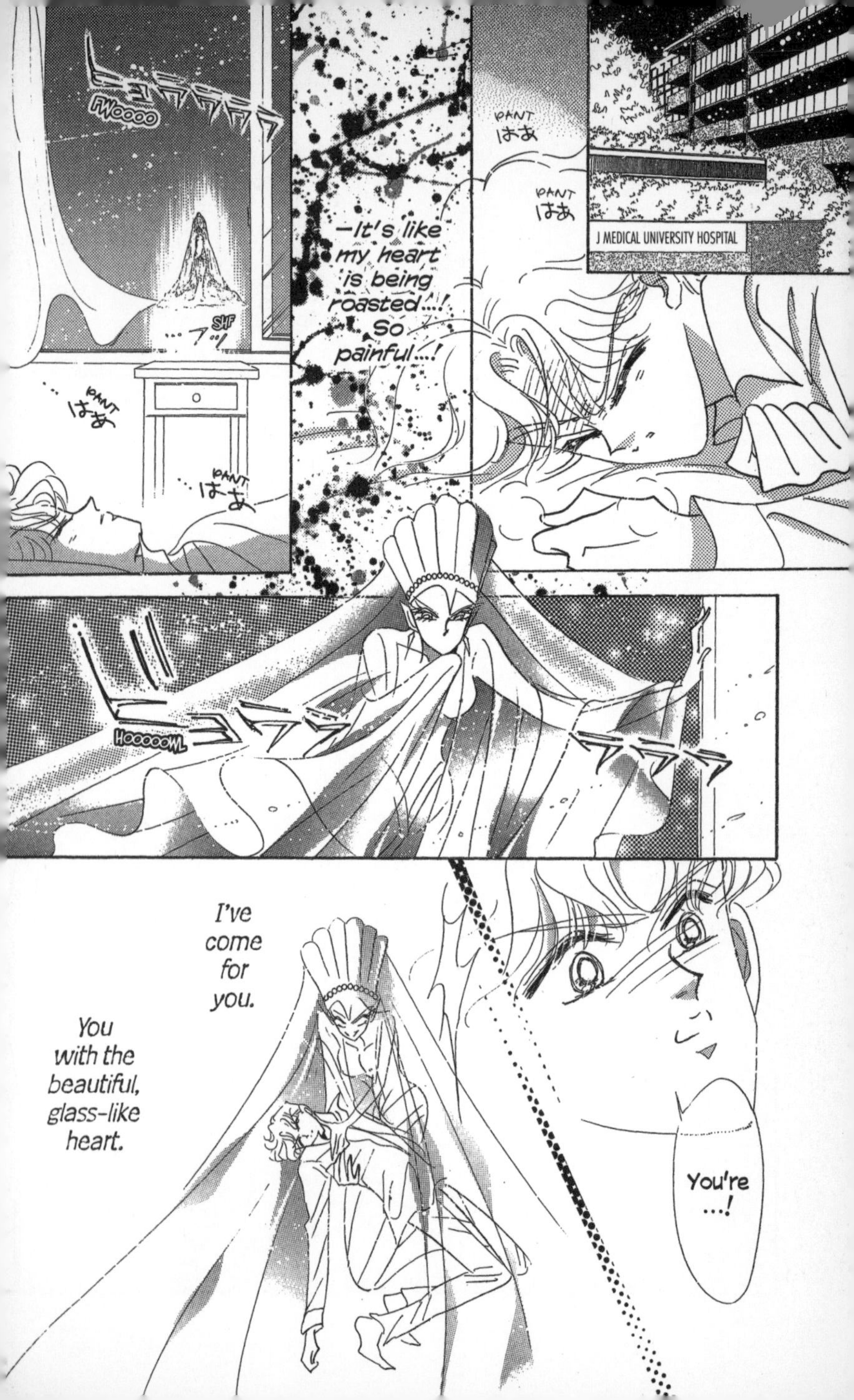
J MEDICAL UNIVERSITY HOSPITAL
PANT はあ
PANT はあ
—It's like my heart is being roasted...! So painful...!
FWOOOO
SHF …フッ
…PANT はあ
…PANT はあ
HOOOOOWL
You're ...!
I've come for you.
You with the beautiful, glass-like heart.

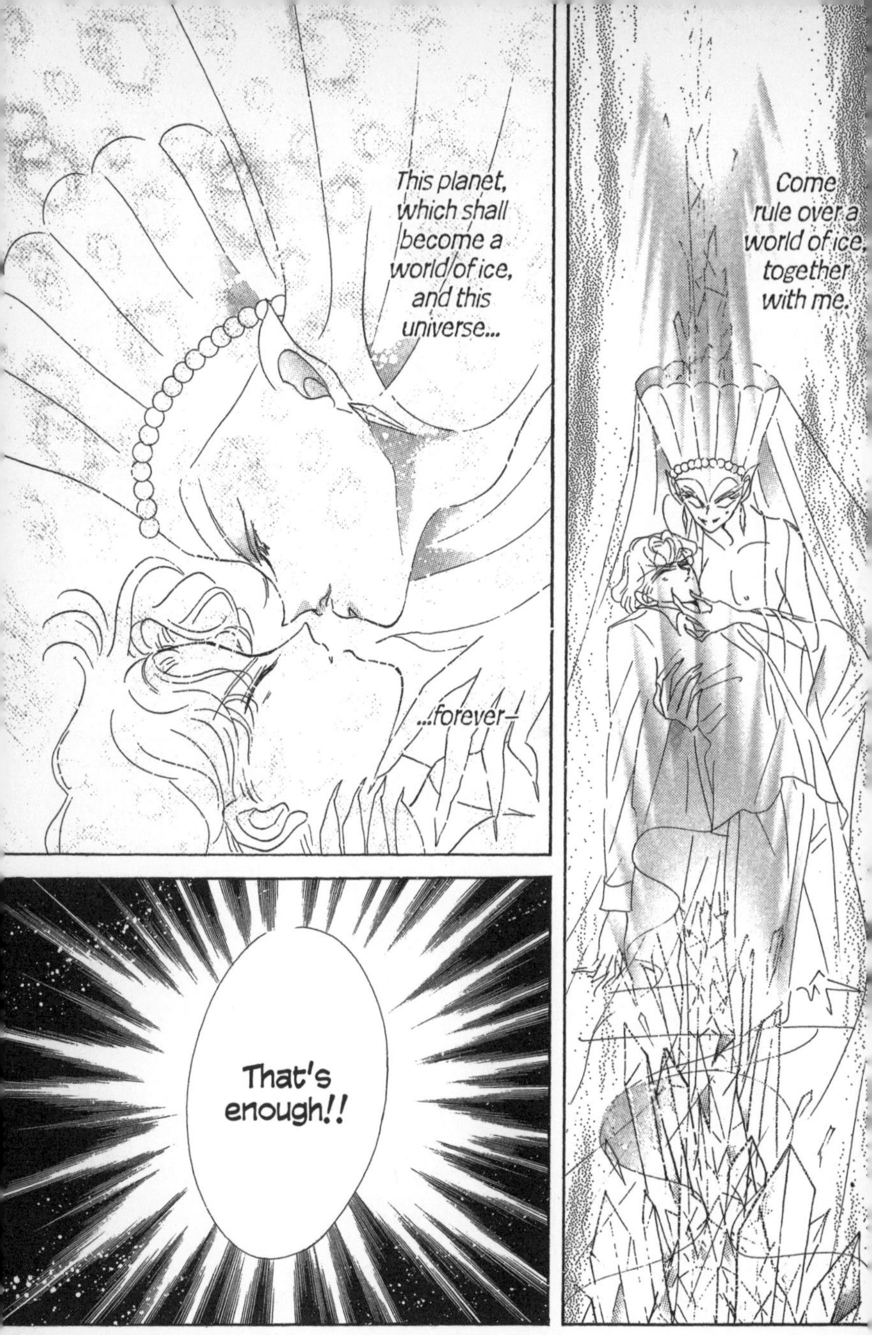
Come rule over a world of ice, together with me.
This planet, which shall become a world of ice, and this universe...
...forever—
That's enough!!

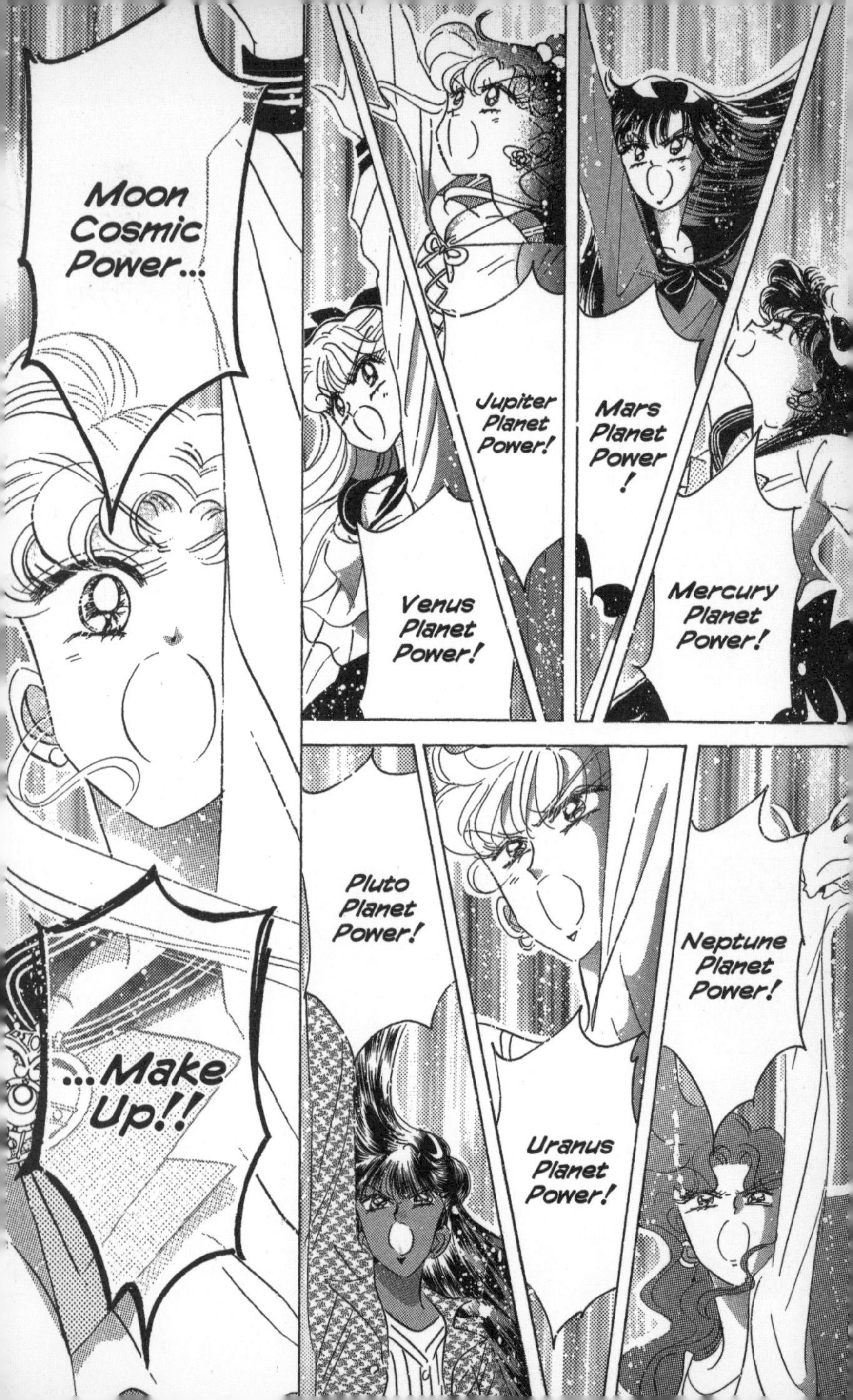

Mercury Planet Power!
Mars Planet Power!
Jupiter Planet Power!
Venus Planet Power!
Neptune Planet Power!
Uranus Planet Power!
Pluto Planet Power!
Moon Cosmic Power...
...Make Up!!

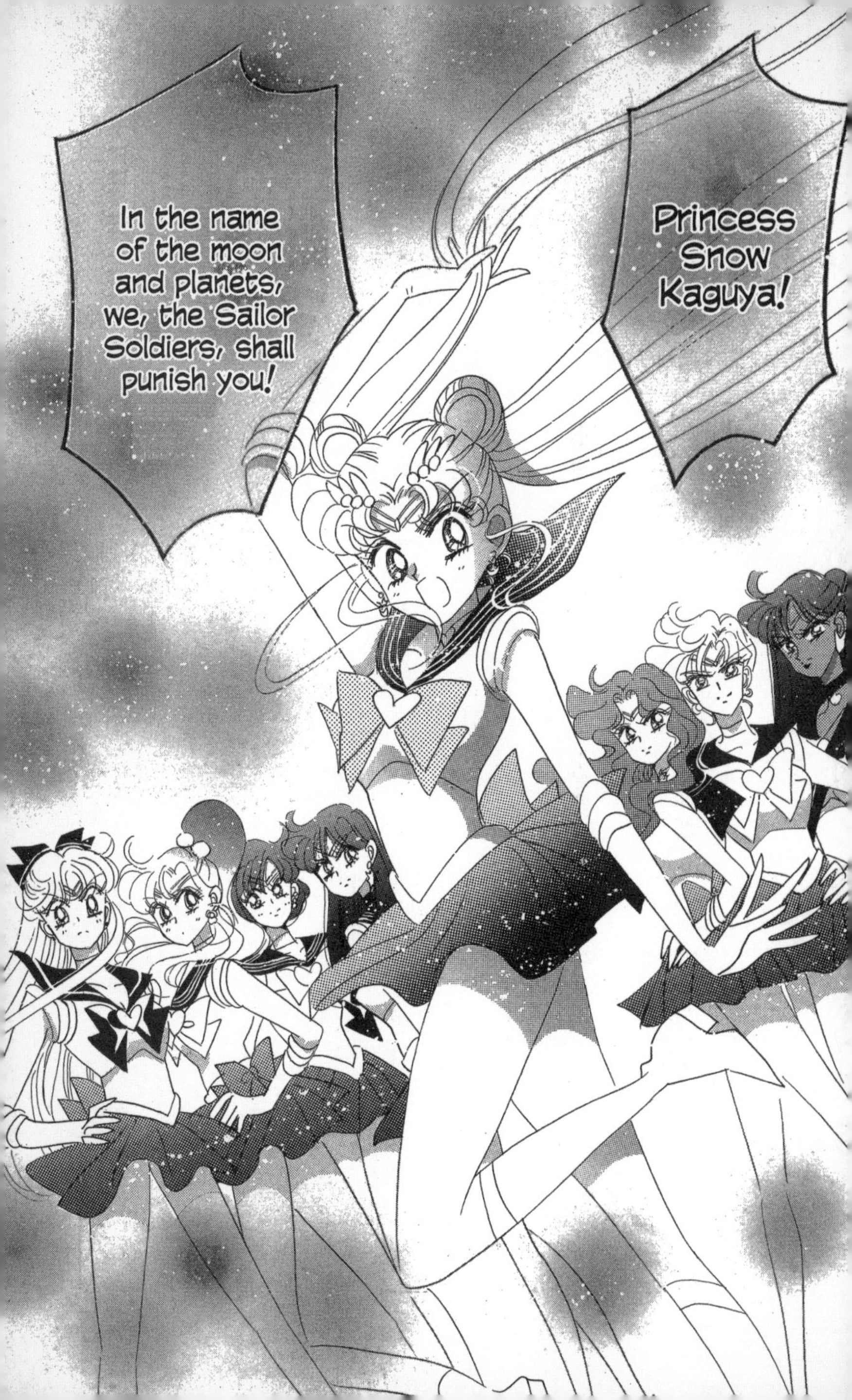
Princess Snow Kaguya!
In the name of the moon and planets, we, the Sailor Soldiers, shall punish you!

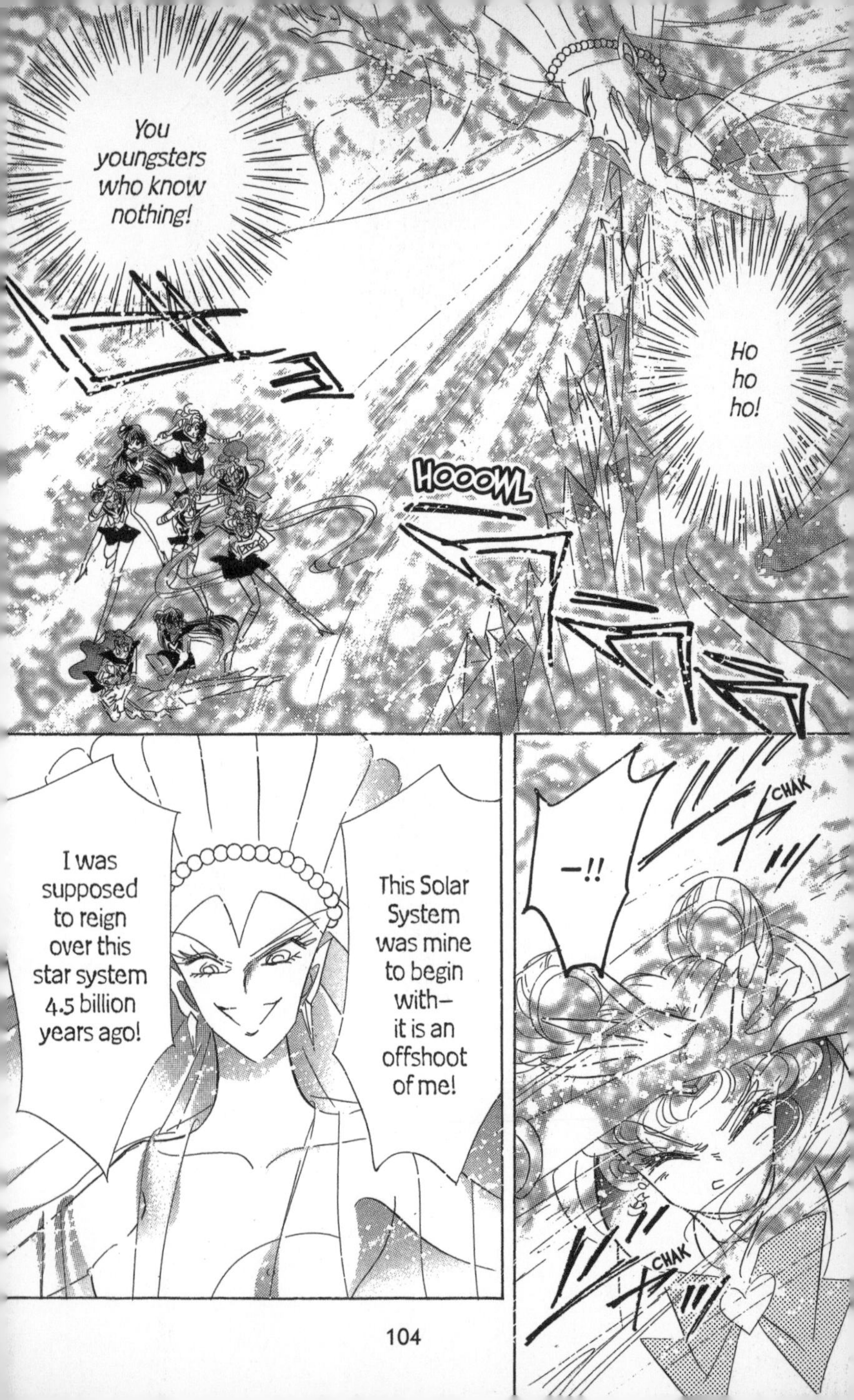
You youngsters who know nothing!
Ho ho ho!
HOOOWL
—!!
CHAK
CHAK
This Solar System was mine to begin with— it is an offshoot of me!
I was supposed to reign over this star system 4.5 billion years ago!

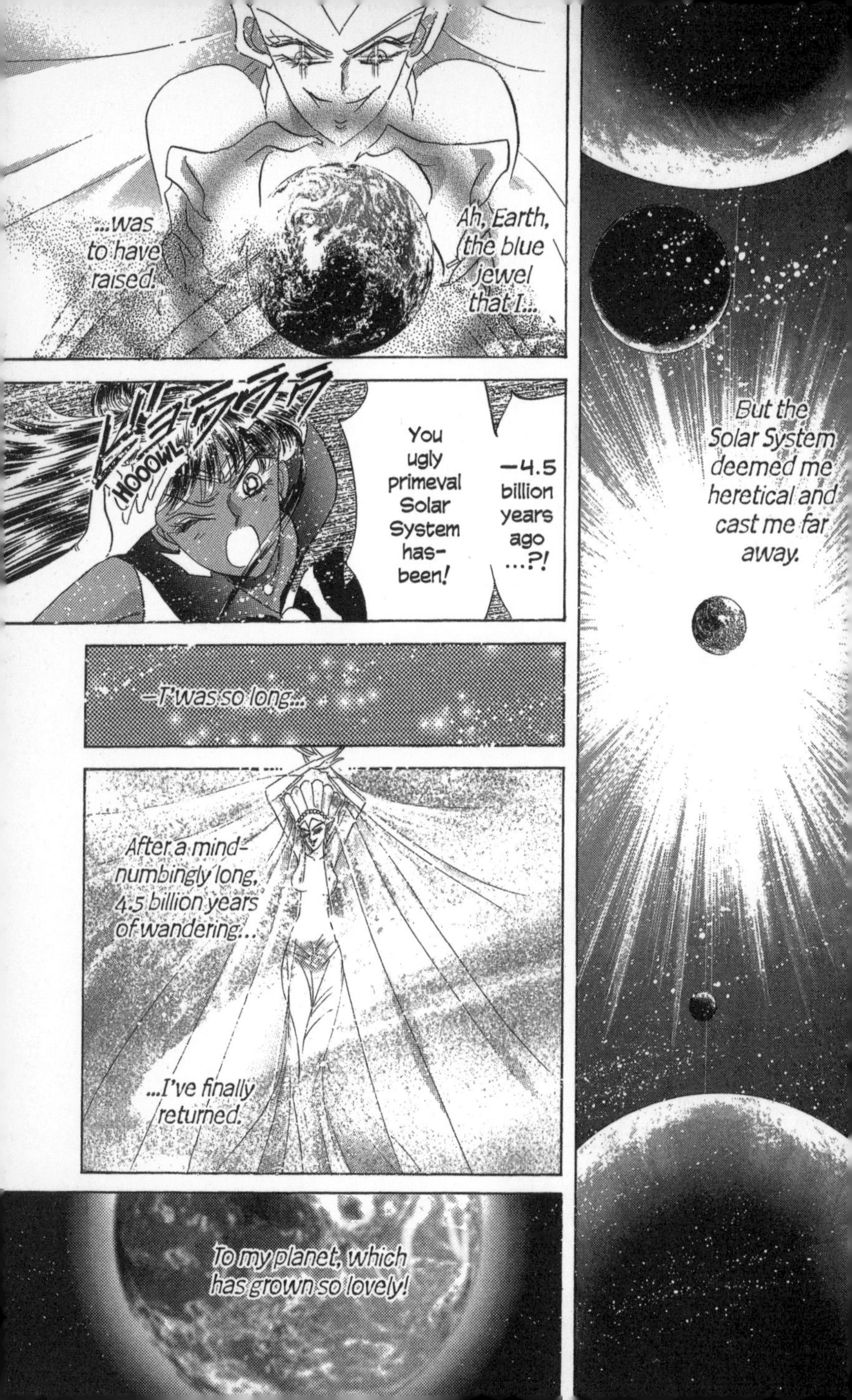
But the Solar System deemed me heretical and cast me far away.
Ah, Earth, the blue jewel that I...
...was to have raised.
—4.5 billion years ago ...?!
You ugly primeval Solar System has-been!
HOOOWL
—T'was so long...
After a mind-numbingly long, 4.5 billion years of wandering...
...I've finally returned.
To my planet, which has grown so lovely!

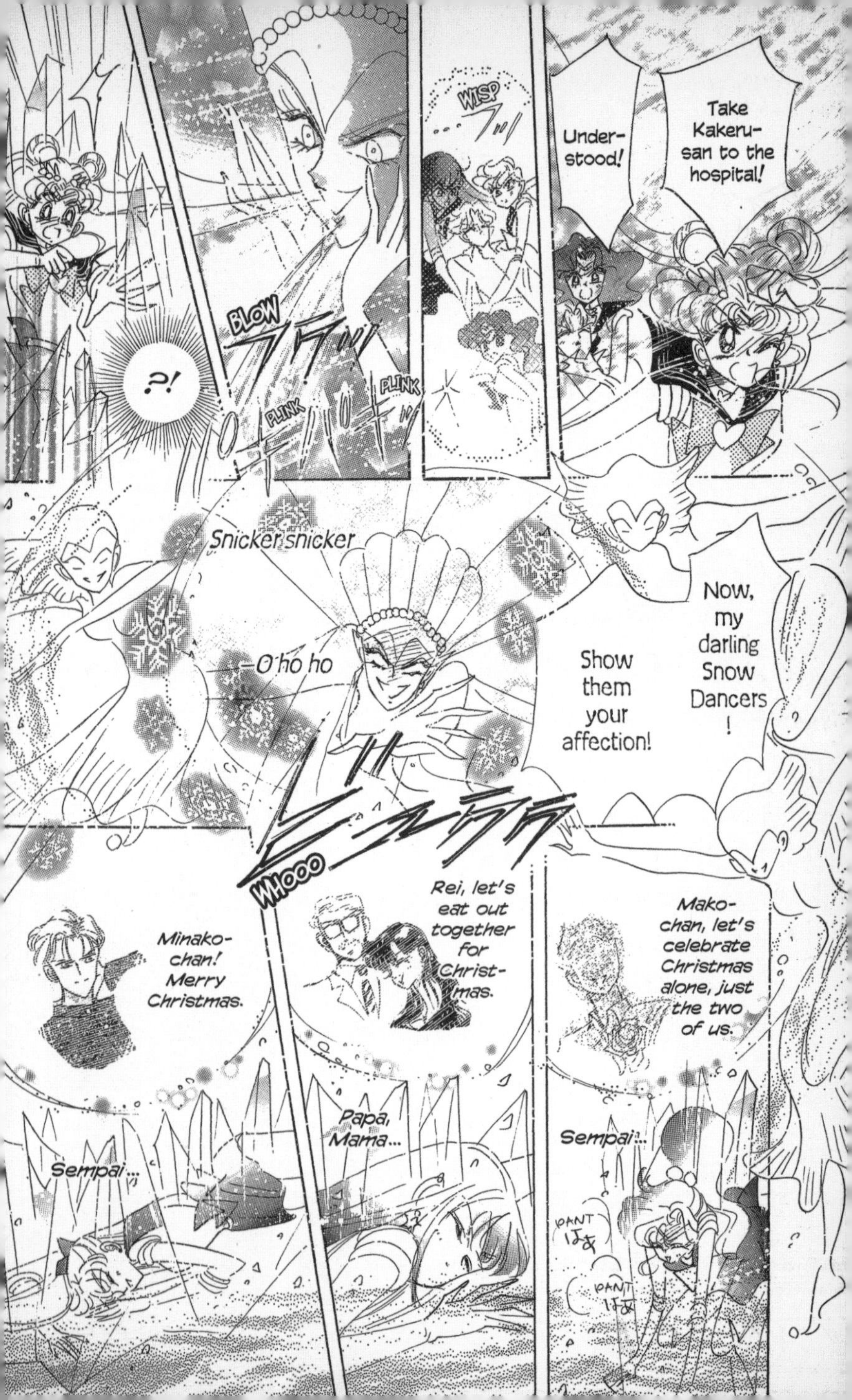
Take Kakeru-san to the hospital!
Under-stood!
WISP
BLOW
PLINK
PLINK
?!
Now, my darling Snow Dancers!
Show them your affection!
Snicker snicker
O ho ho
WHOOO
Mako-chan, let's celebrate Christmas alone, just the two of us.
Sempai...
PANT
PANT
Rei, let's eat out together for Christ-mas.
Papa, Mama...
Minako-chan! Merry Christmas.
Sempai...

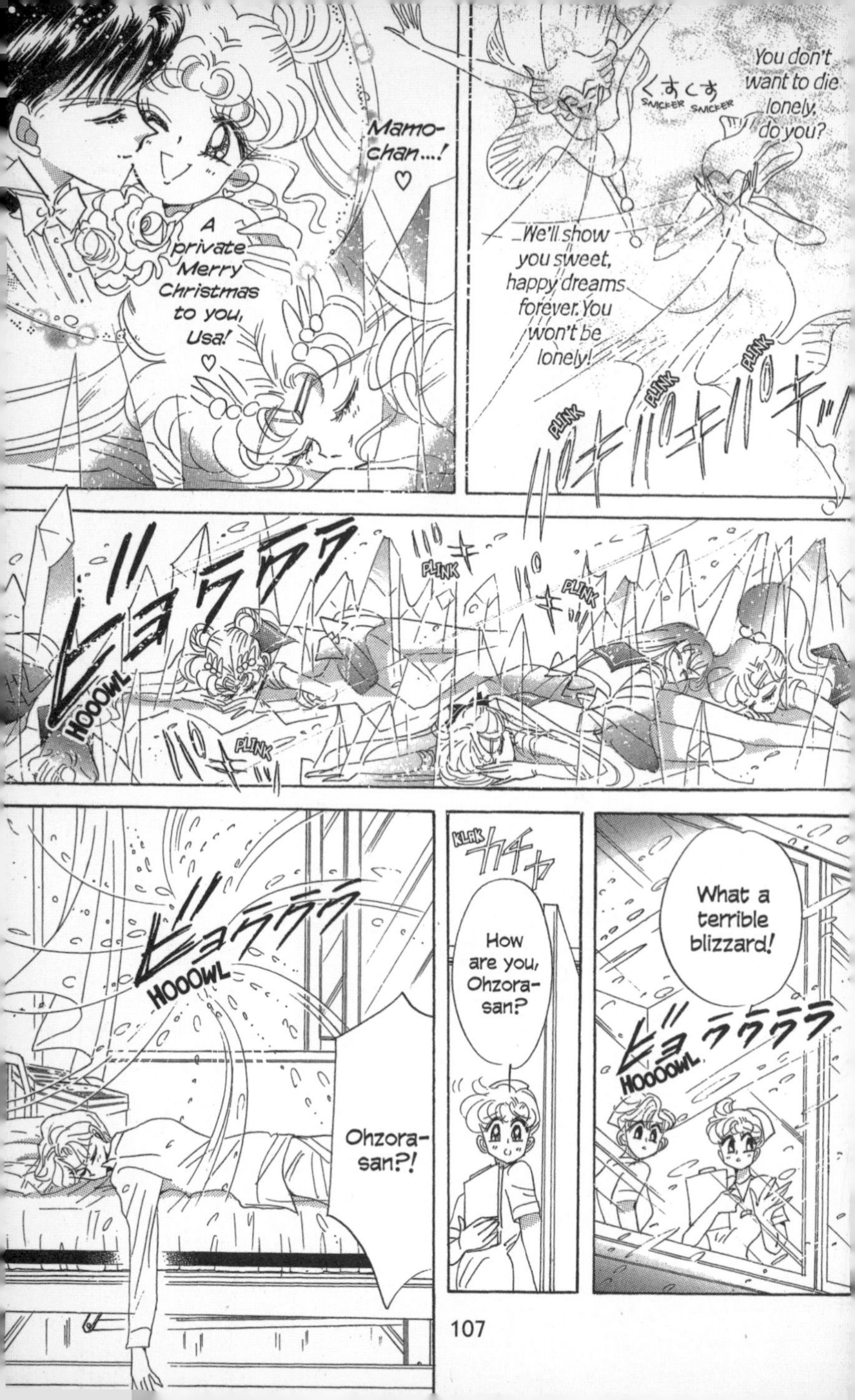

You don't want to die lonely, do you?
SNICKER SNICKER
We'll show you sweet, happy dreams forever. You won't be lonely!
PLINK
PLINK
PLINK
Mamo-chan...! ♡
A private Merry Christmas to you, Usa! ♡
PLINK
PLINK
HOOOWL
PLINK
What a terrible blizzard!
HOOOWL
KLAK
How are you, Ohzora-san?
HOOOWL
Ohzora-san?!

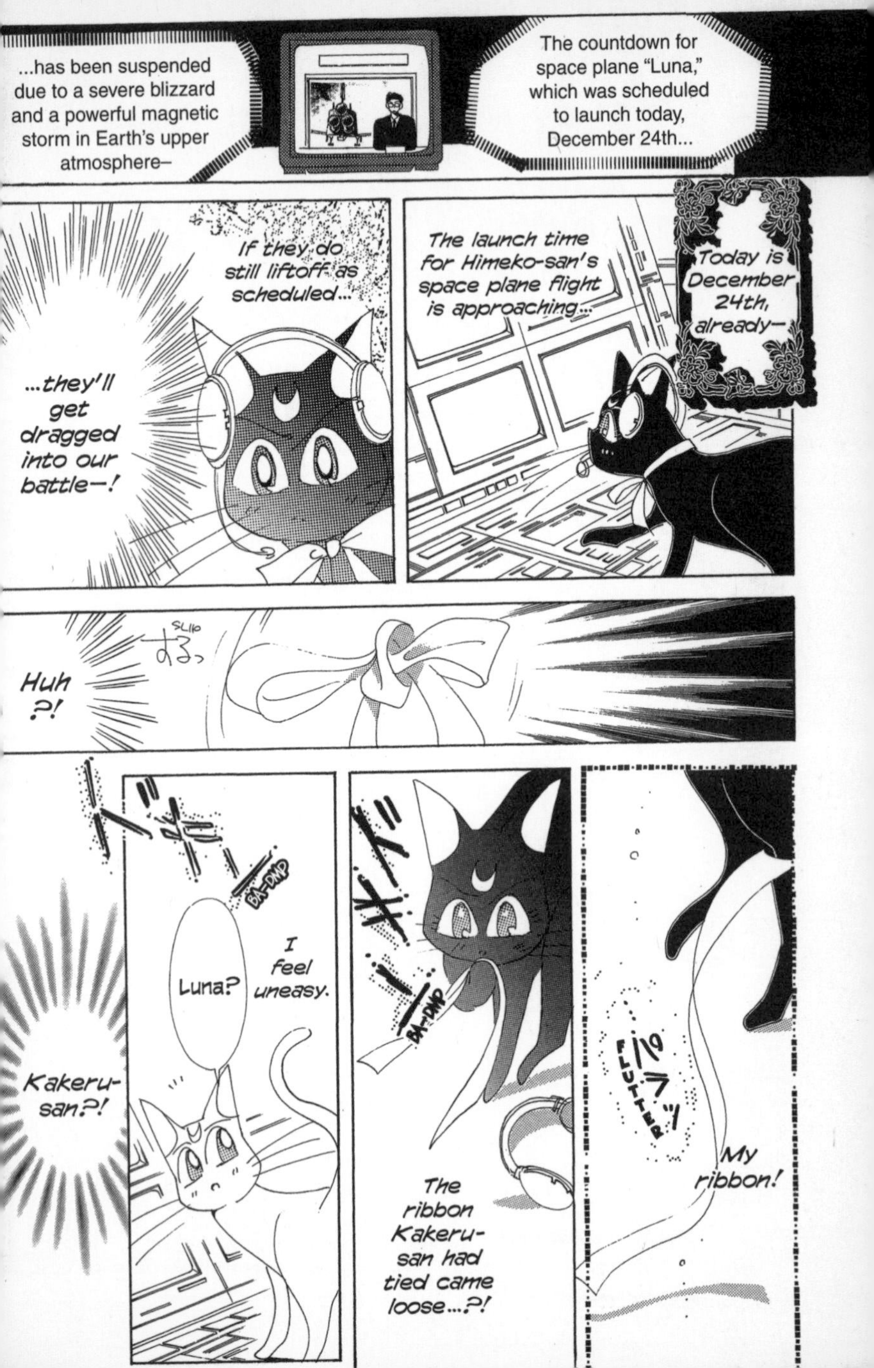
The countdown for space plane "Luna," which was scheduled to launch today, December 24th...
...has been suspended due to a severe blizzard and a powerful magnetic storm in Earth's upper atmosphere–
Today is December 24th, already–
The launch time for Himeko-san's space plane flight is approaching...
If they do still liftoff as scheduled...
...they'll get dragged into our battle–!
SLIP
Huh ?!
FLUTTER
My ribbon!
BA-DMP
The ribbon Kakeru-san had tied came loose...?!
BA-DMP
I feel uneasy.
Luna?
Kakeru-san?!

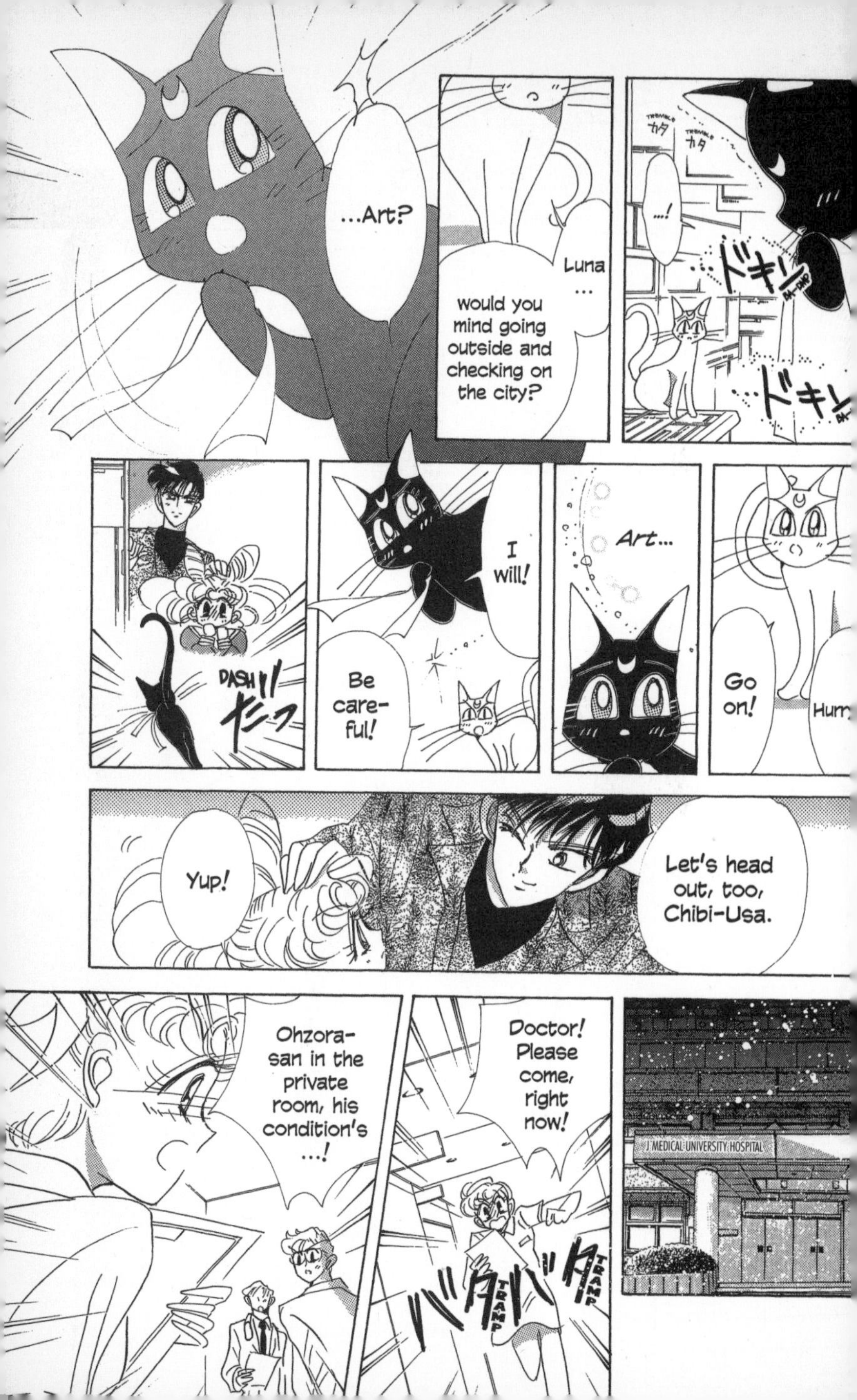
TREMBLE カタ
TREMBLE カタ
...!
ドキン BA-DMP
ドキン
Luna ...
would you mind going outside and checking on the city?
...Art?
Go on!
Art...
I will!
Be care-ful!
DASH ダッ
Let's head out, too, Chibi-Usa.
Yup!
J. MEDICAL UNIVERSITY HOSPITAL
Doctor! Please come, right now!
TRAMP TRAMP
Ohzora-san in the private room, his condition's ...!

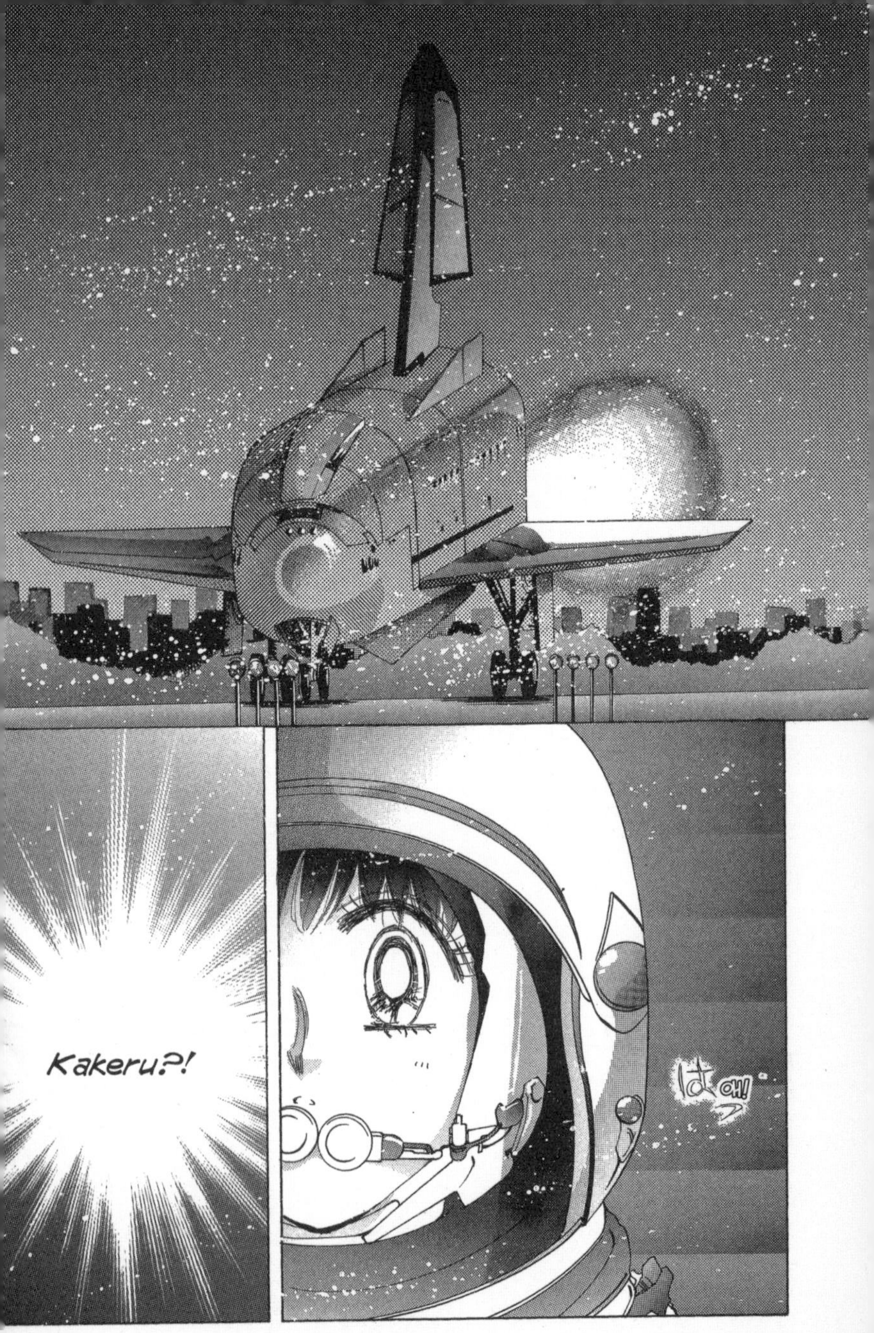
OH!
Kakeru?!

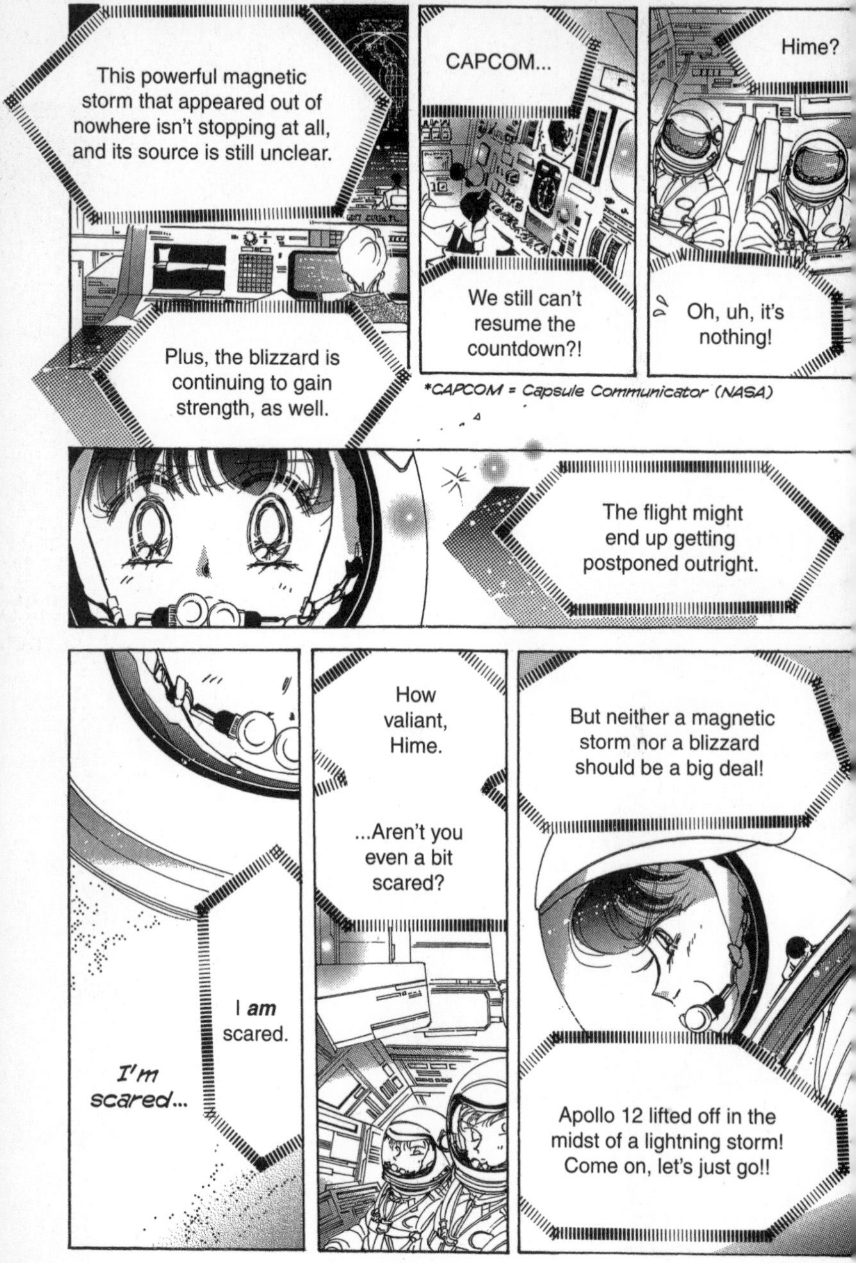
Hime?
Oh, uh, it's nothing!
CAPCOM...
We still can't resume the countdown?!
This powerful magnetic storm that appeared out of nowhere isn't stopping at all, and its source is still unclear.
Plus, the blizzard is continuing to gain strength, as well.
*CAPCOM = Capsule Communicator (NASA)
The flight might end up getting postponed outright.
But neither a magnetic storm nor a blizzard should be a big deal!
Apollo 12 lifted off in the midst of a lightning storm! Come on, let's just go!!
How valiant, Hime.
...Aren't you even a bit scared?
I *am* scared.
I'm scared...

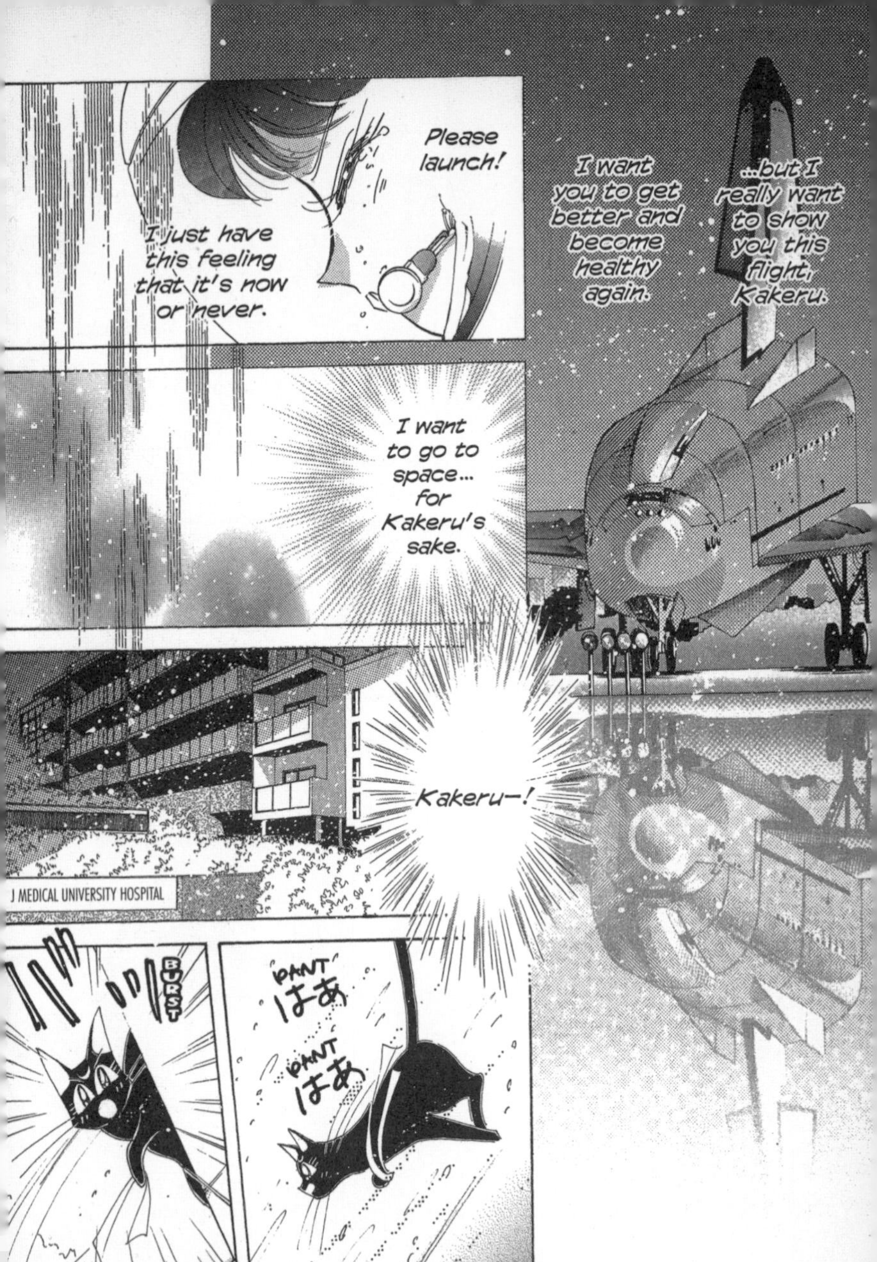
I want you to get better and become healthy again.
...but I really want to show you this flight, Kakeru.
Please launch!
I just have this feeling that it's now or never.
I want to go to space... for Kakeru's sake.
Kakeru—!
J MEDICAL UNIVERSITY HOSPITAL
PANT はあ
PANT はあ
BURST

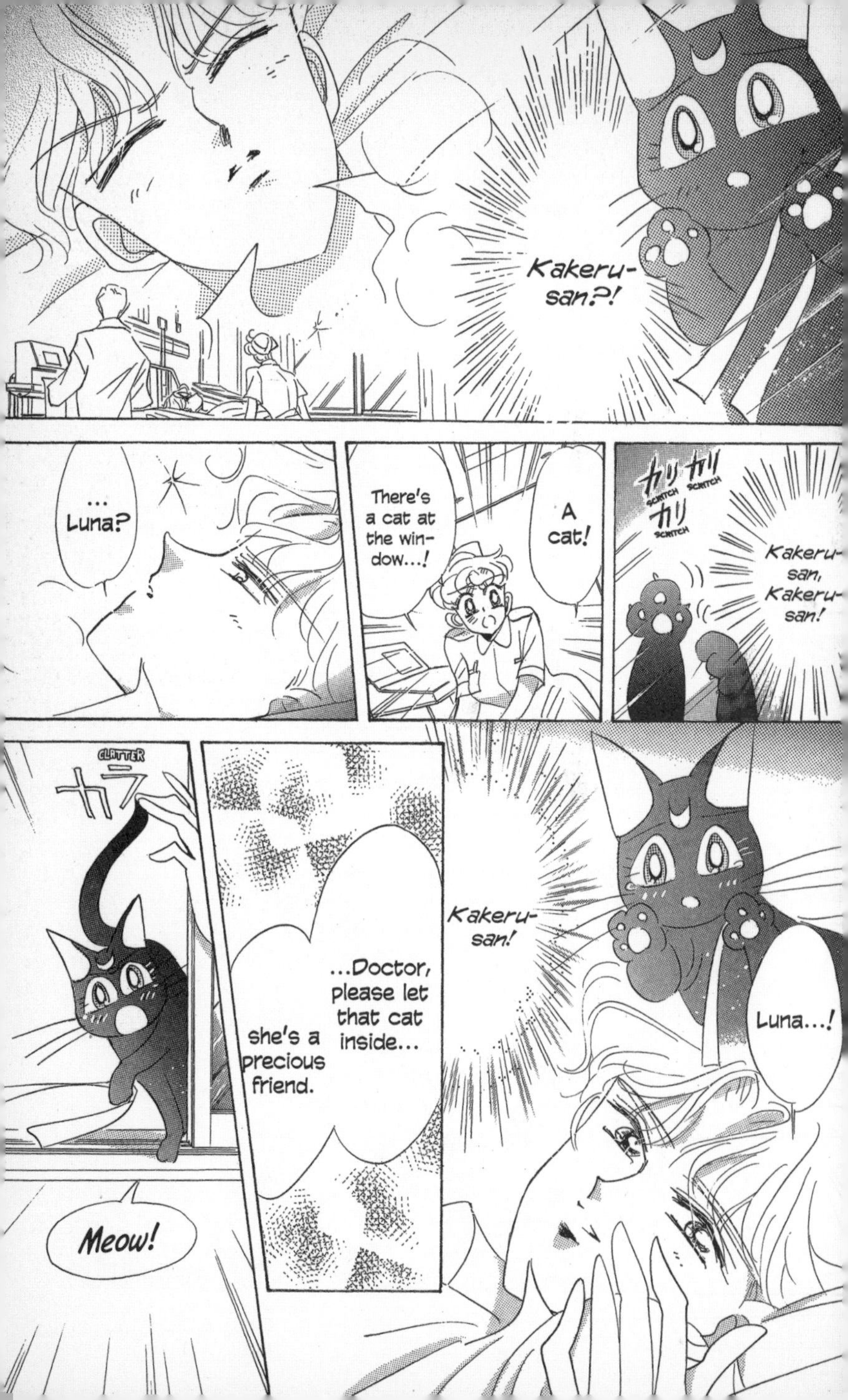

Kakeru-san?!
カリカリ SCRITCH SCRITCH
カリ SCRITCH
Kakeru-san, Kakeru-san!
A cat!
There's a cat at the window...!
...Luna?
Kakeru-san!
Luna...!
...Doctor, please let that cat inside...
she's a precious friend.
カラ CLATTER
Meow!

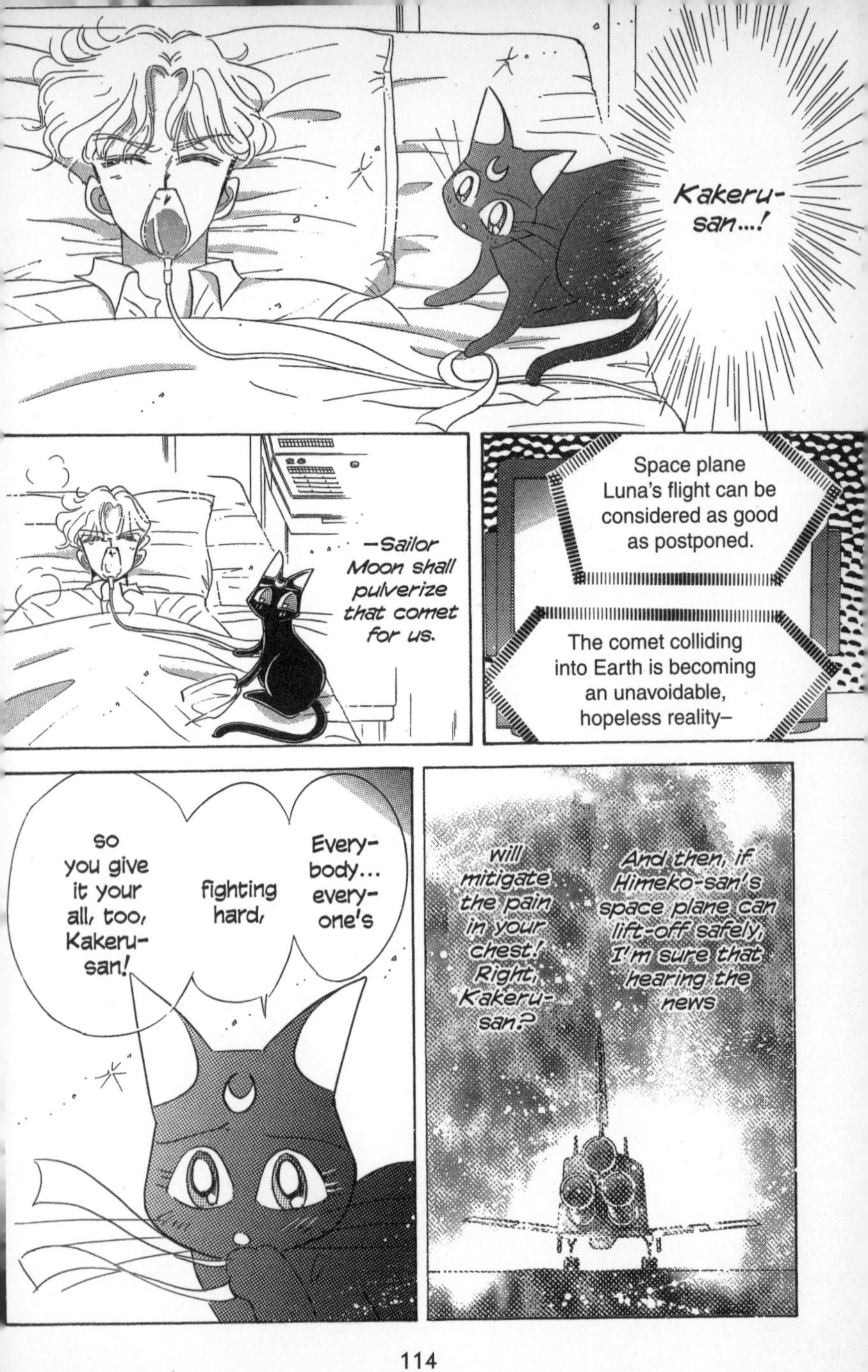
Kakeru-san...!
Space plane Luna's flight can be considered as good as postponed.
The comet colliding into Earth is becoming an unavoidable, hopeless reality–
—Sailor Moon shall pulverize that comet for us.
And then, if Himeko-san's space plane can lift-off safely, I'm sure that hearing the news
will mitigate the pain in your chest! Right, Kakeru-san?
Every-body... every-one's
fighting hard,
so you give it your all, too, Kakeru-san!

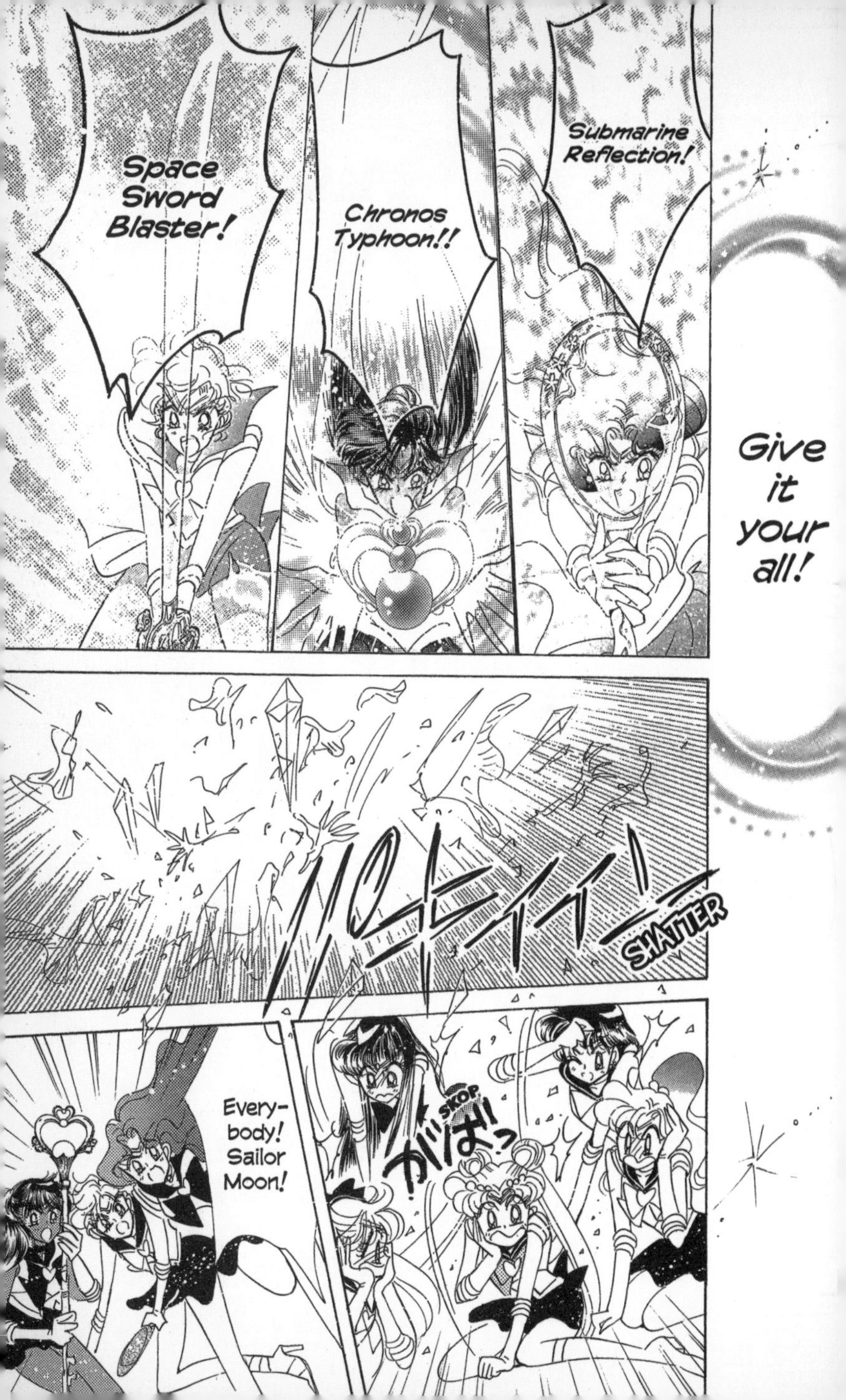
Give it your all!
Submarine Reflection!
Chronos Typhoon!!
Space Sword Blaster!
SHATTER
SKOP
がばっ
Every-body! Sailor Moon!

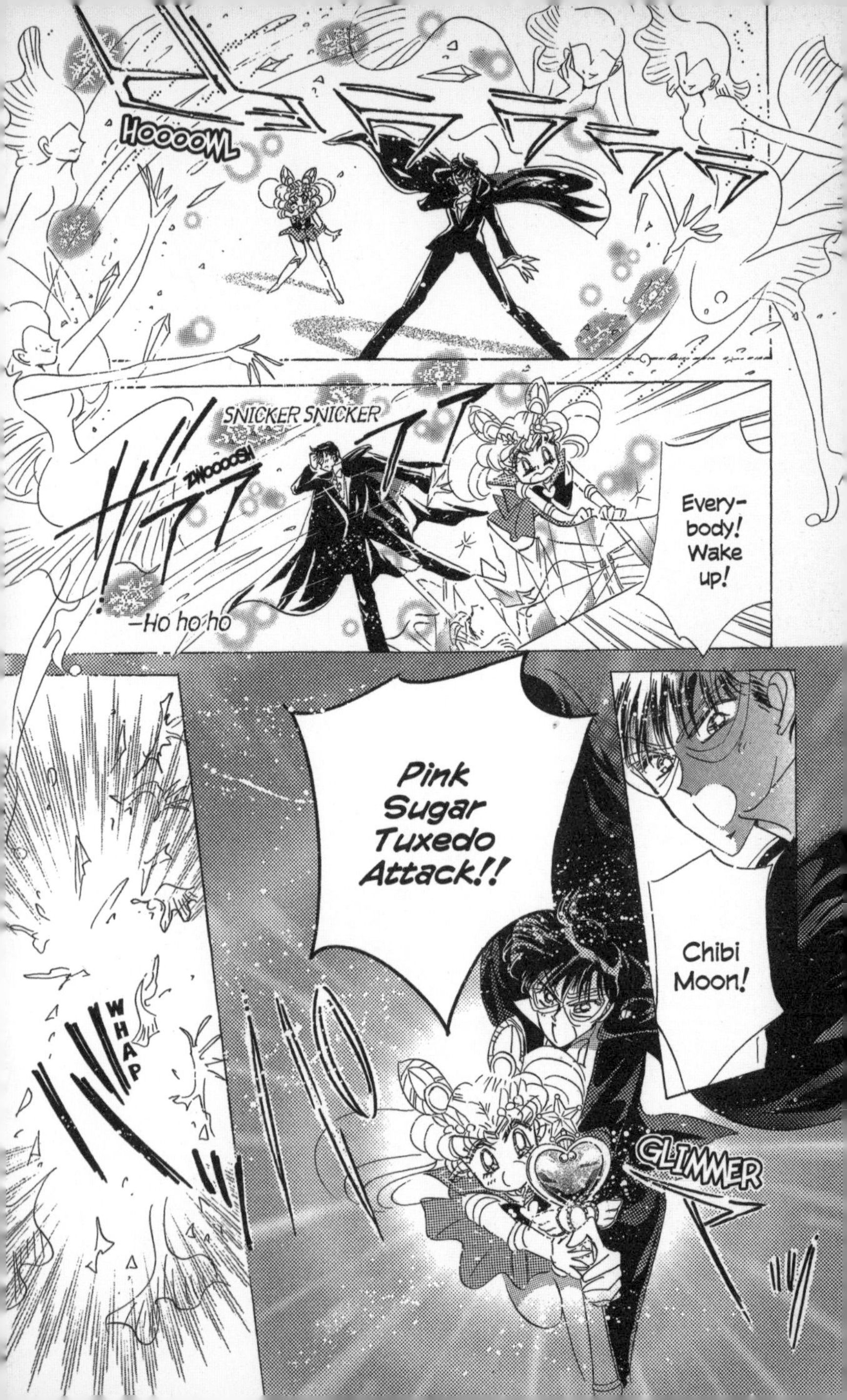
HOOOOWL
Every-body! Wake up!
SNICKER SNICKER
ZWOOOOSH
—Ho ho ho
Chibi Moon!
Pink Sugar Tuxedo Attack!!
GLIMMER
WHAP

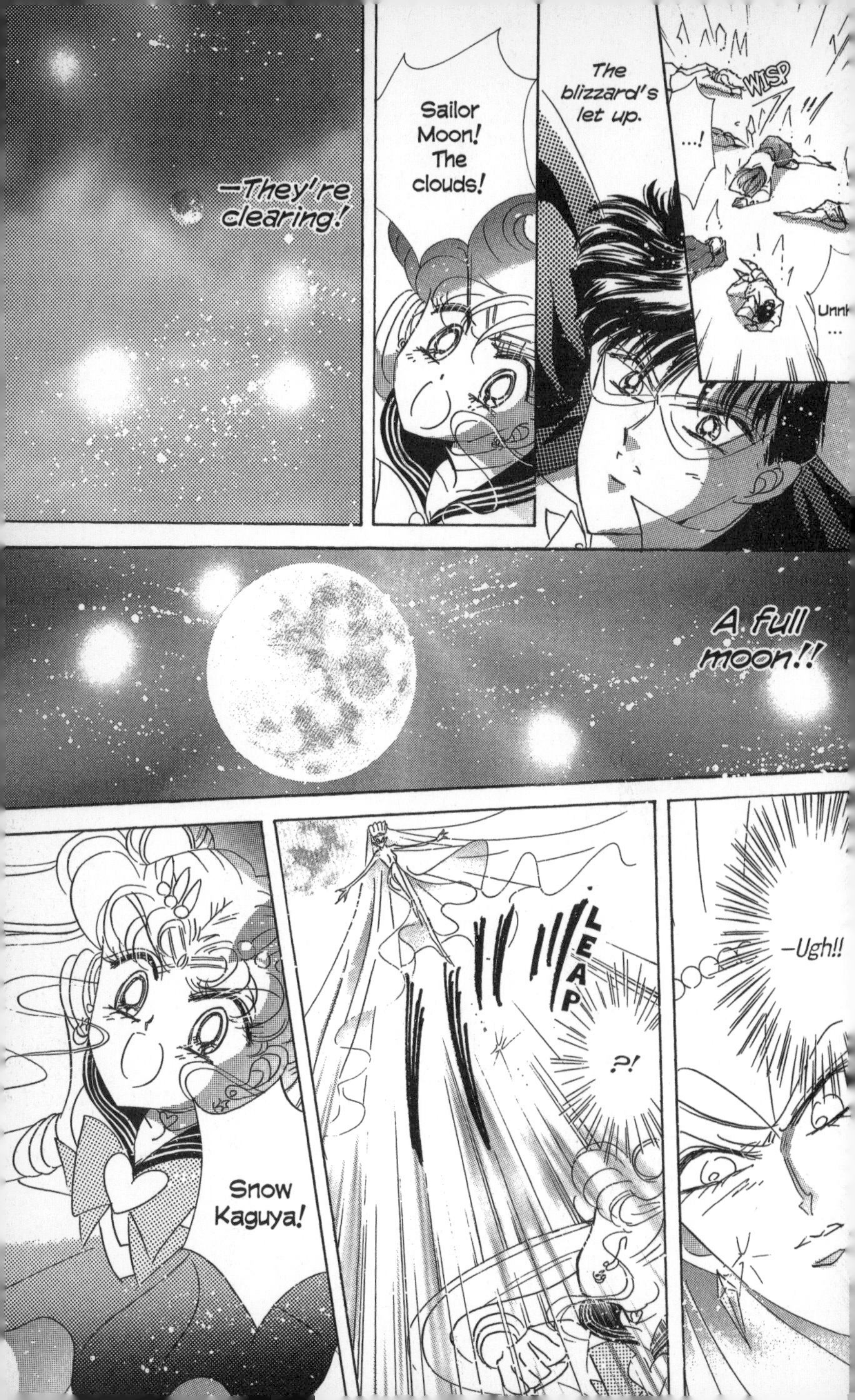
WISP
...!
Unnh ...
The blizzard's let up.
Sailor Moon! The clouds!
—They're clearing!
A full moon!!
—Ugh!!
LEAP
?!
Snow Kaguya!

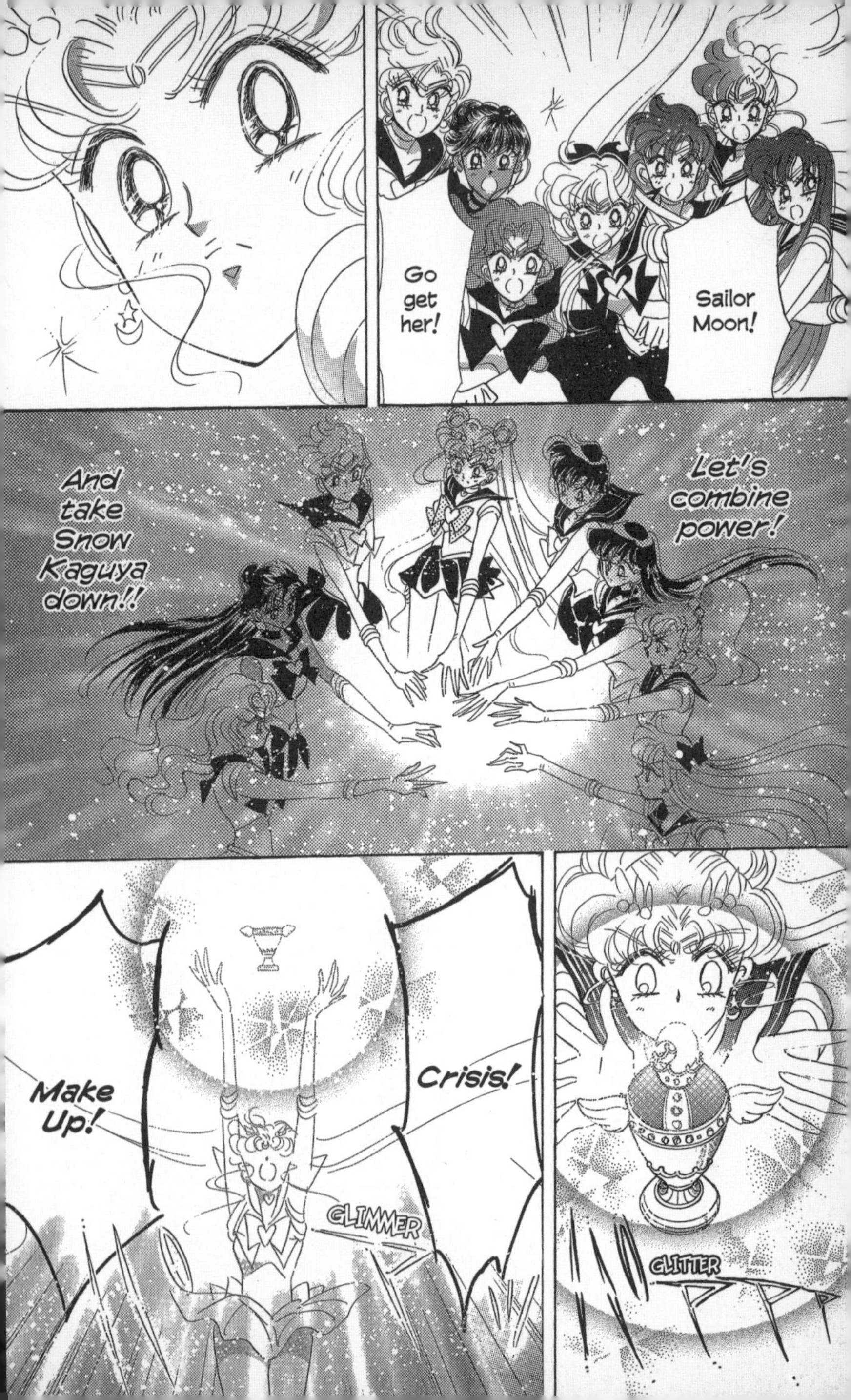
Sailor Moon!
Go get her!
Let's combine power!
And take Snow Kaguya down!!
GLITTER
Crisis!
Make Up!
GLIMMER

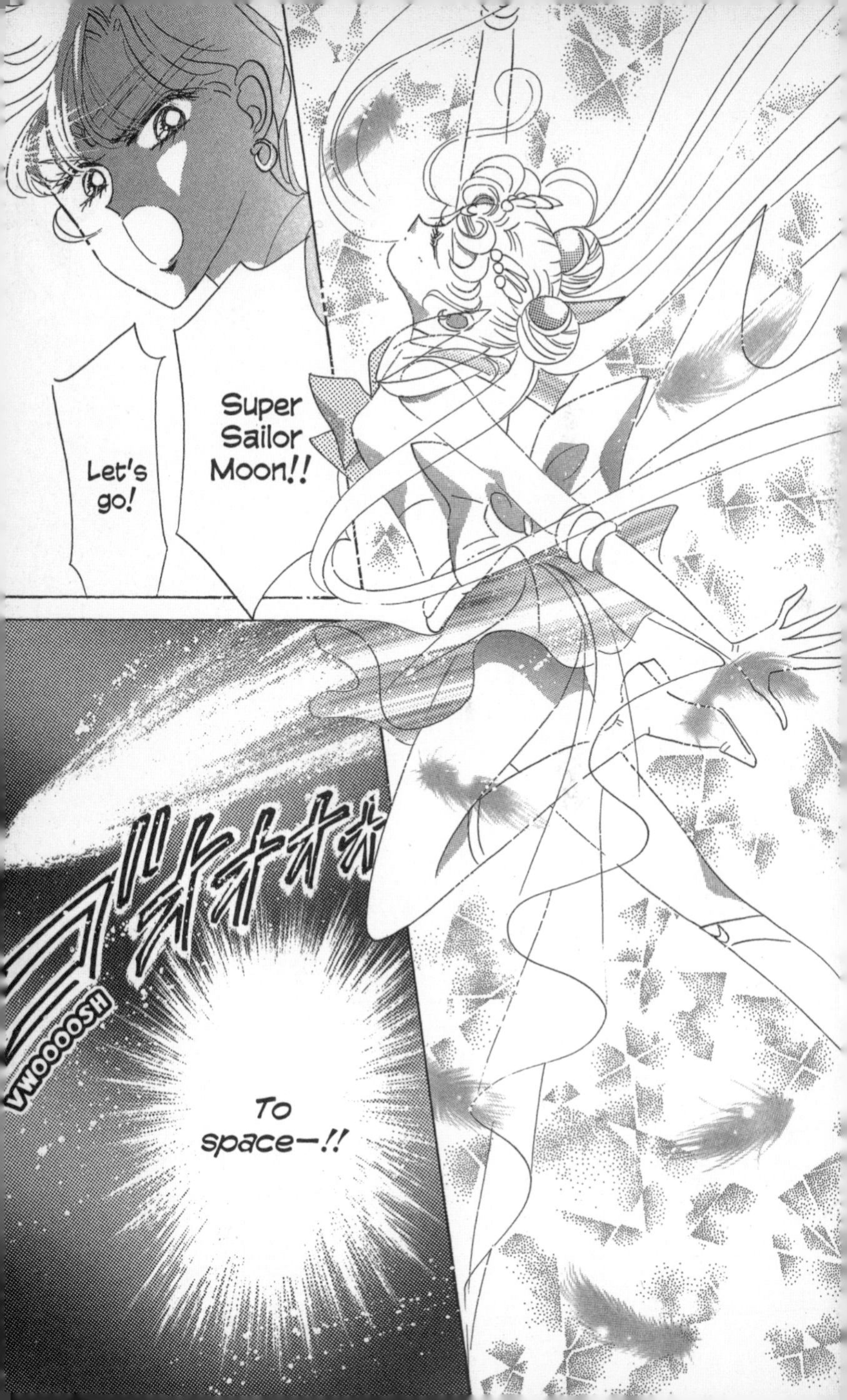
Super Sailor Moon!!
Let's go!
VWOOOOSH
To space—!!

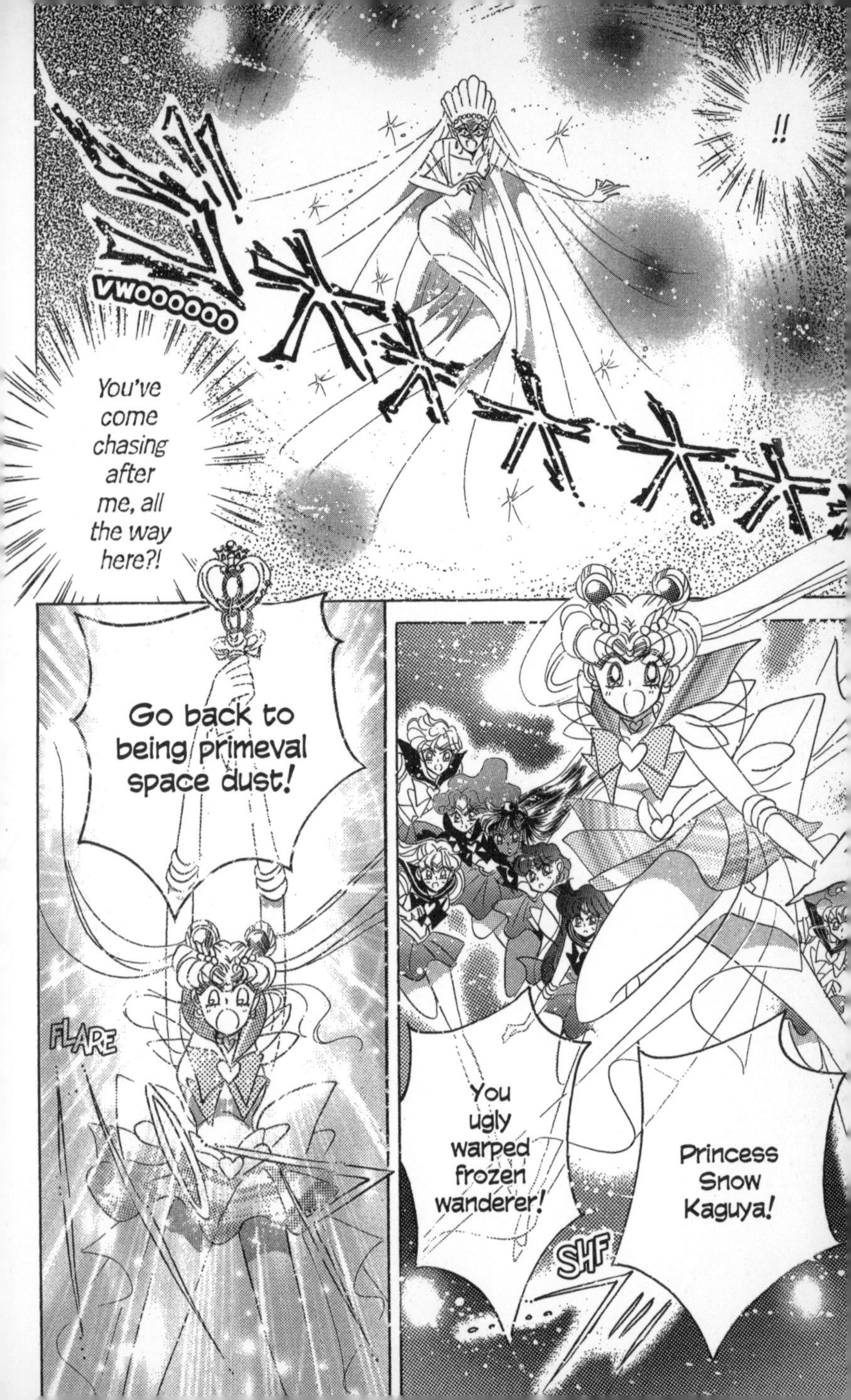
!!
VWOOOOOO
You've come chasing after me, all the way here?!
Princess Snow Kaguya!
You ugly warped frozen wanderer!
SHF
Go back to being primeval space dust!
FLARE

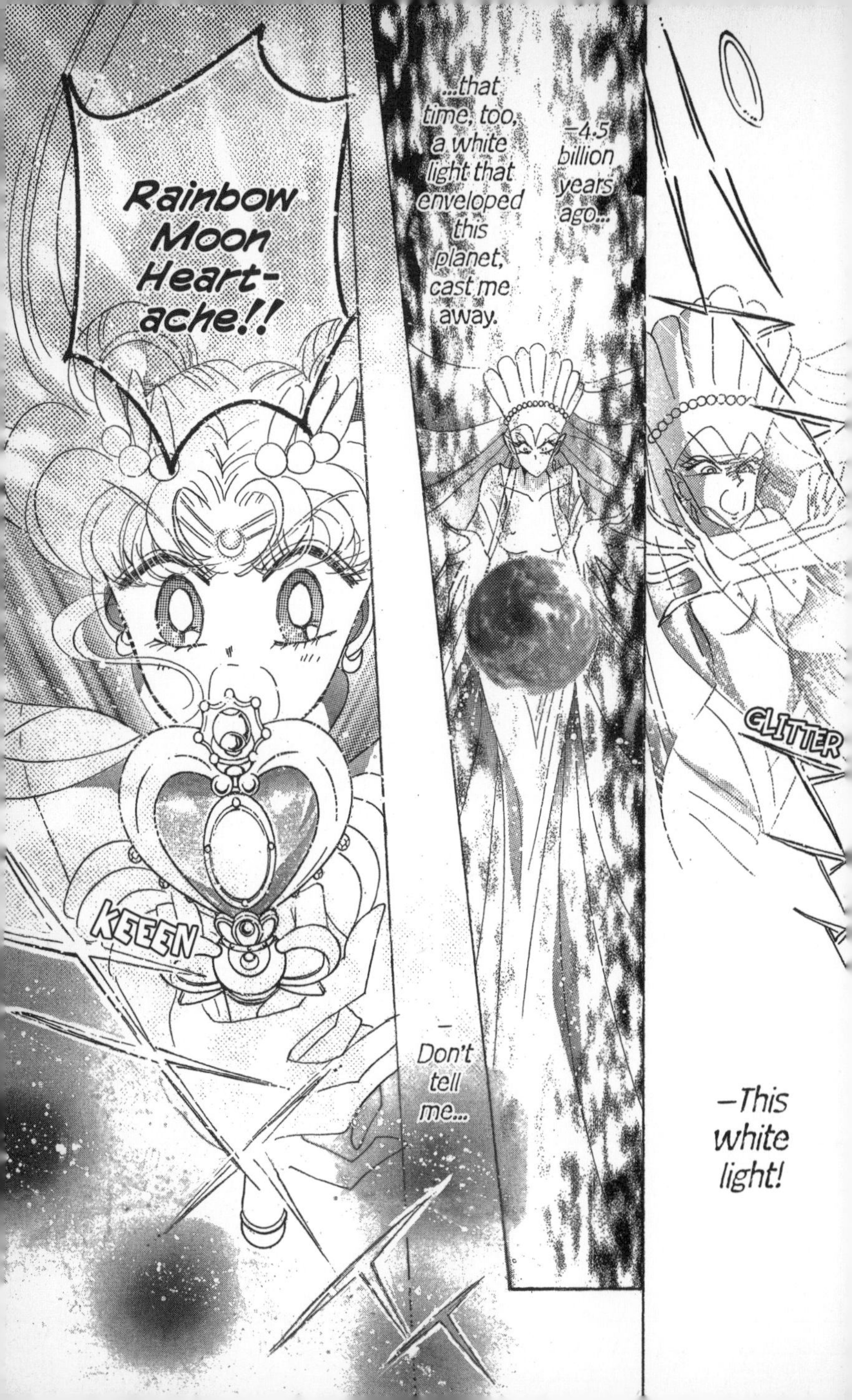
GLITTER
—This white light!
—4.5 billion years ago...
...that time, too, a white light that enveloped this planet, cast me away.
—Don't tell me...
Rainbow Moon Heart-ache!!
KEEEN

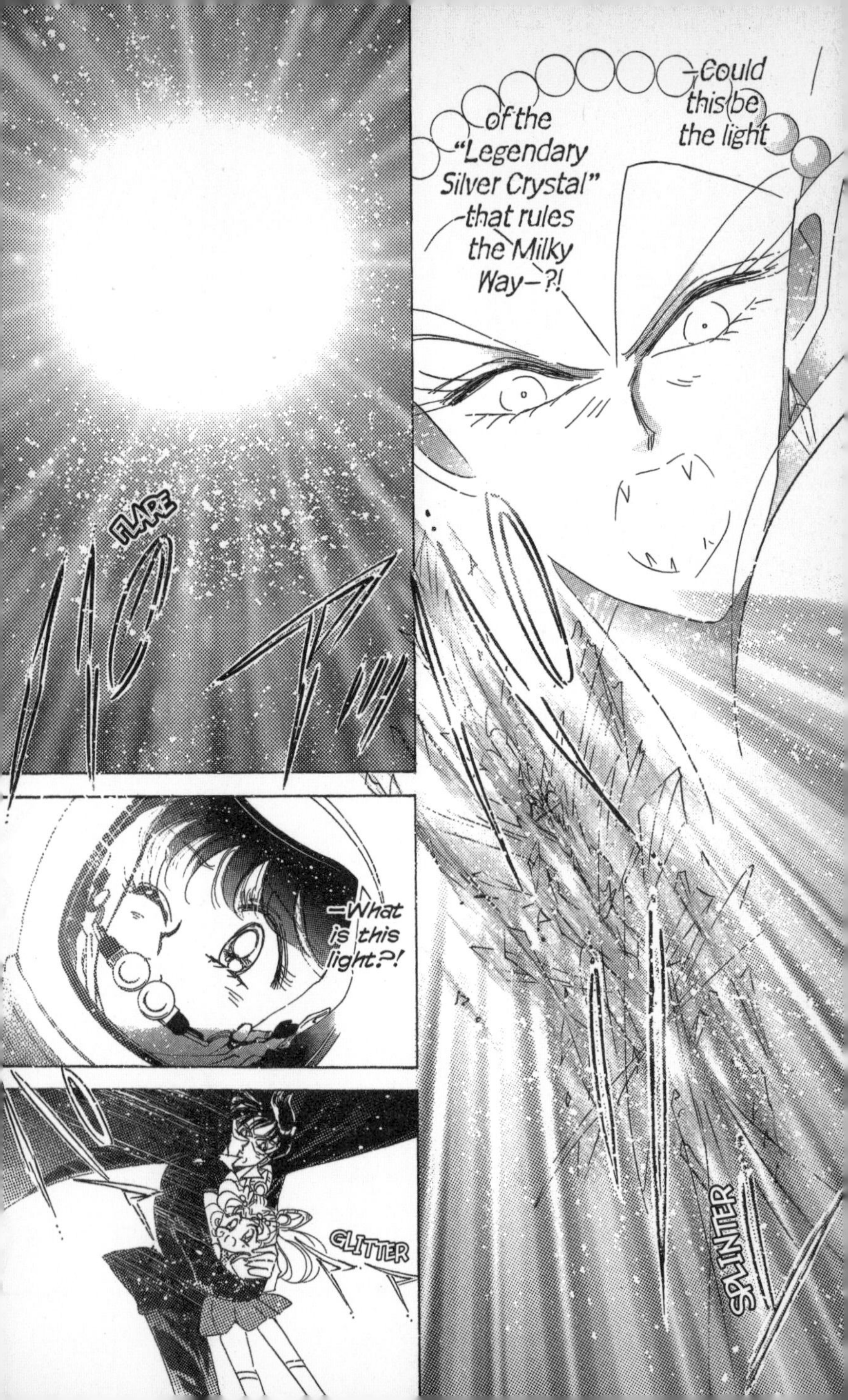
—Could this be the light of the "Legendary Silver Crystal" that rules the Milky Way—?!
SPLINTER
FLARE
—What is this light?!
GLITTER

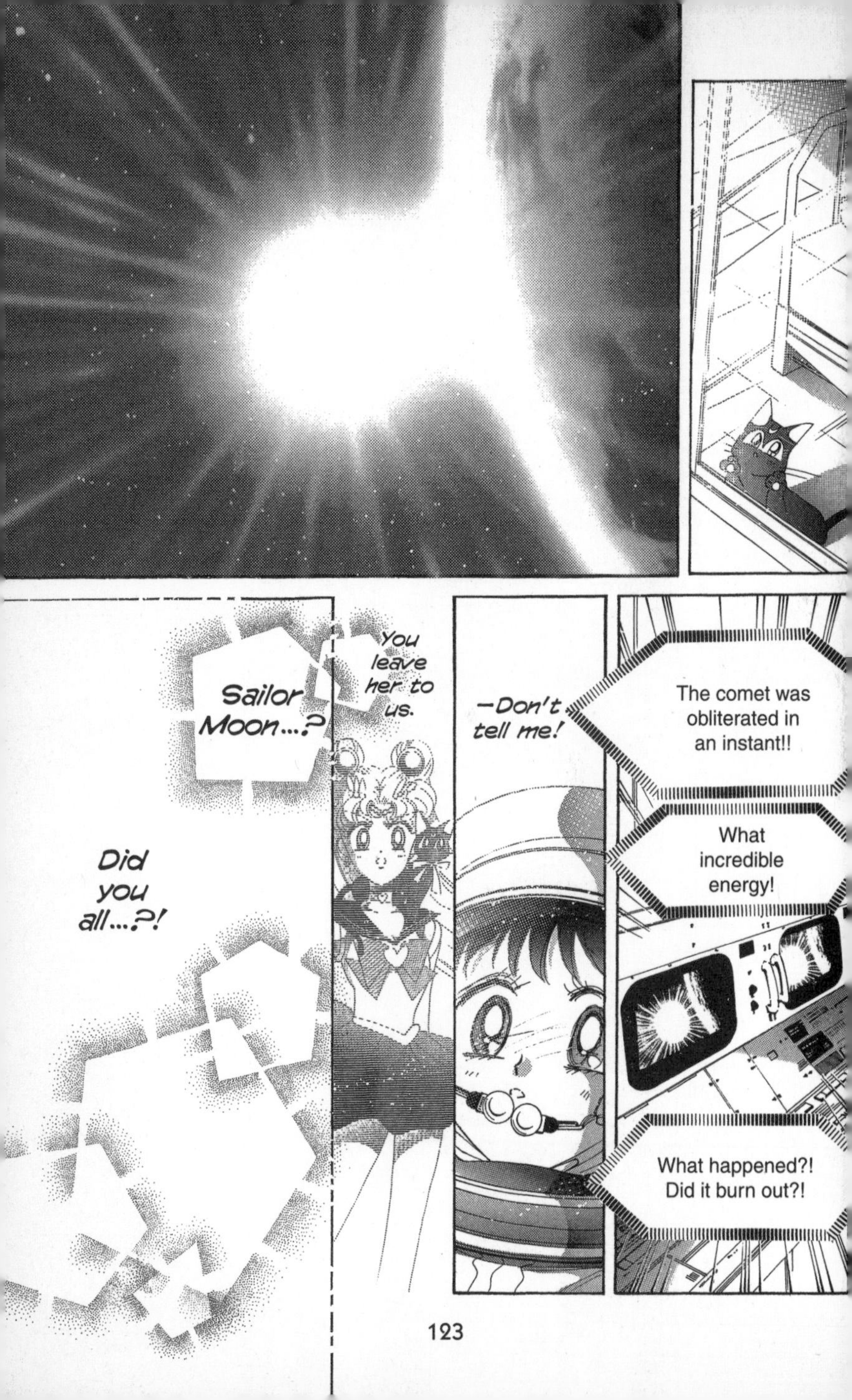
The comet was obliterated in an instant!!
What incredible energy!
What happened?! Did it burn out?!
—Don't tell me!
You leave her to us.
Sailor Moon...?
Did you all...?!

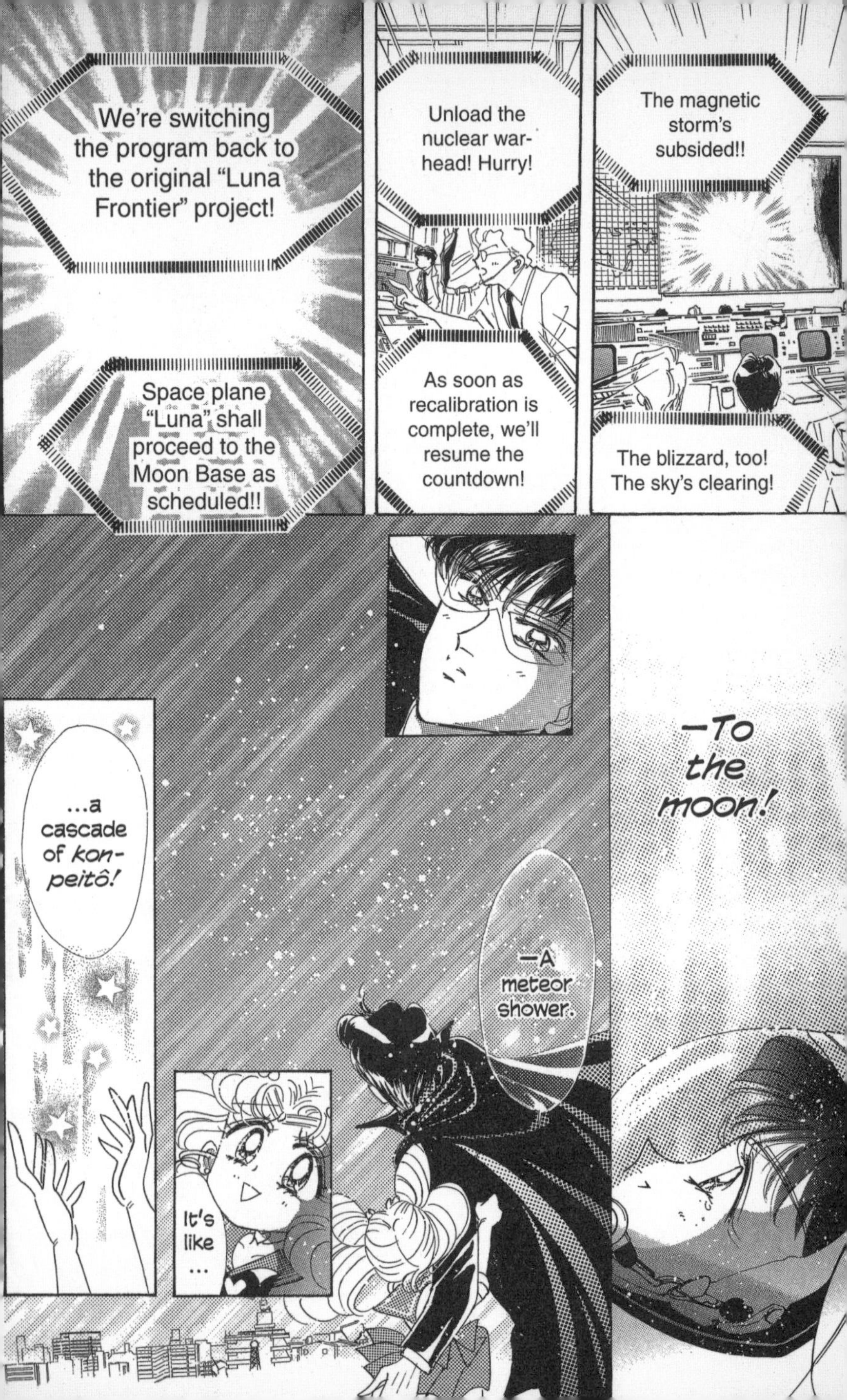
The magnetic storm's subsided!!
The blizzard, too! The sky's clearing!
Unload the nuclear war-head! Hurry!
As soon as recalibration is complete, we'll resume the countdown!
We're switching the program back to the original "Luna Frontier" project!
Space plane "Luna" shall proceed to the Moon Base as scheduled!!
—To the moon!
—A meteor shower.
It's like...
...a cascade of *kon-peitô!*

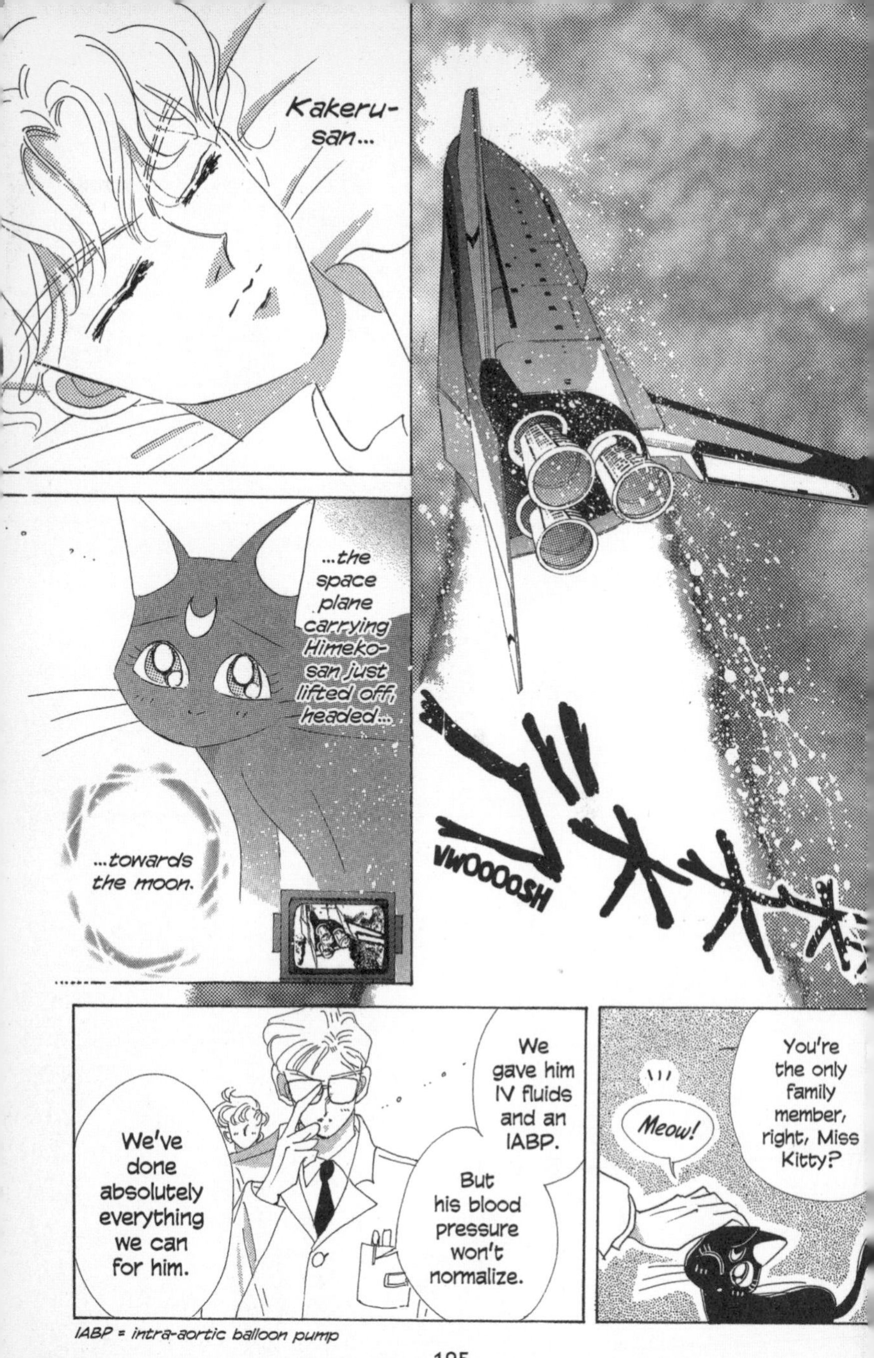
VWOOOOSH
Kakeru-san...
...the space plane carrying Himeko-san just lifted off, headed...
...towards the moon.
You're the only family member, right, Miss Kitty?
Meow!
We gave him IV fluids and an IABP.
But his blood pressure won't normalize.
We've done absolutely everything we can for him.

IABP = intra-aortic balloon pump

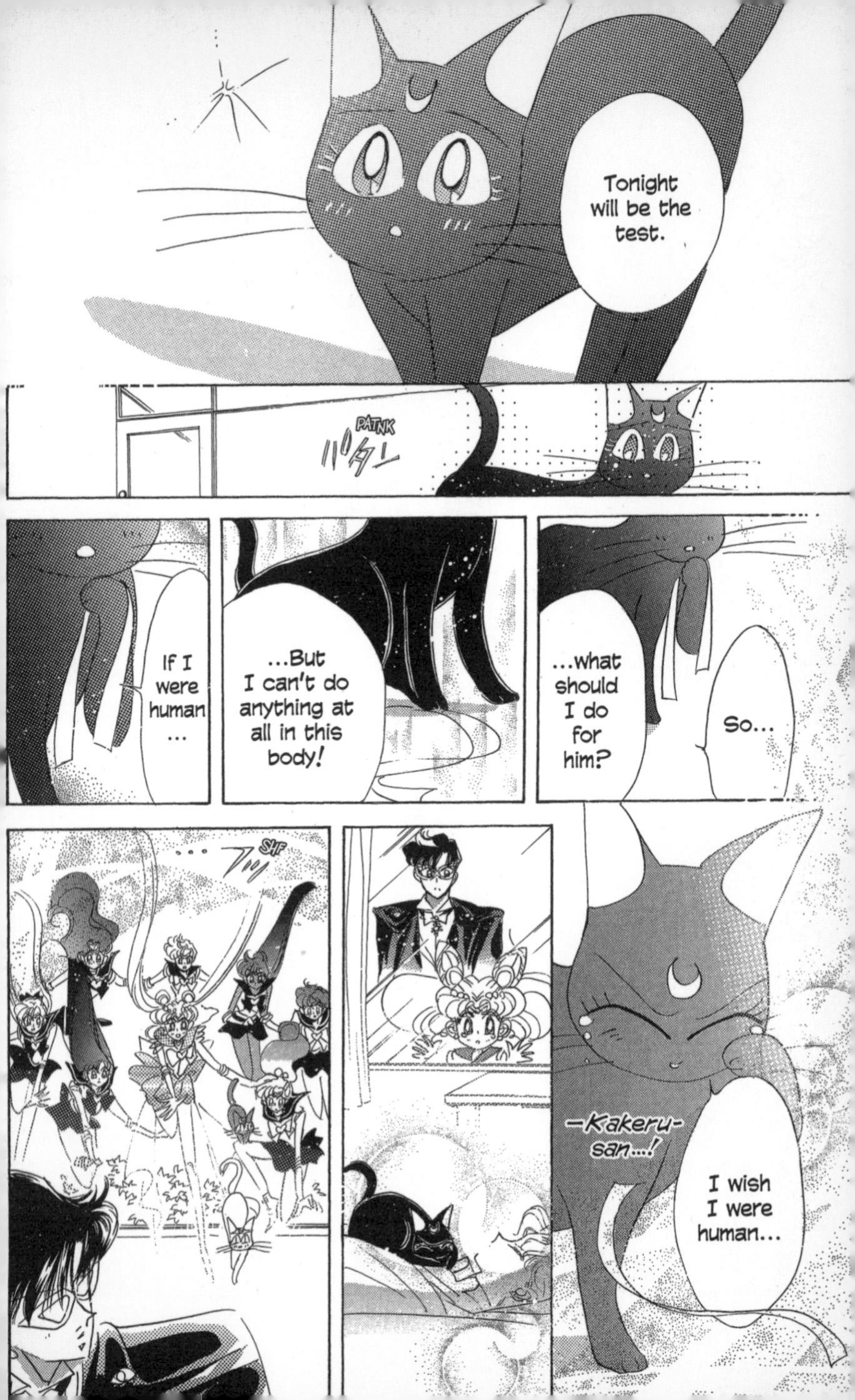
Tonight will be the test.
PATNK
So...
...what should I do for him?
...But I can't do anything at all in this body!
If I were human...
I wish I were human...
—Kakeru-san...!
SHF
...

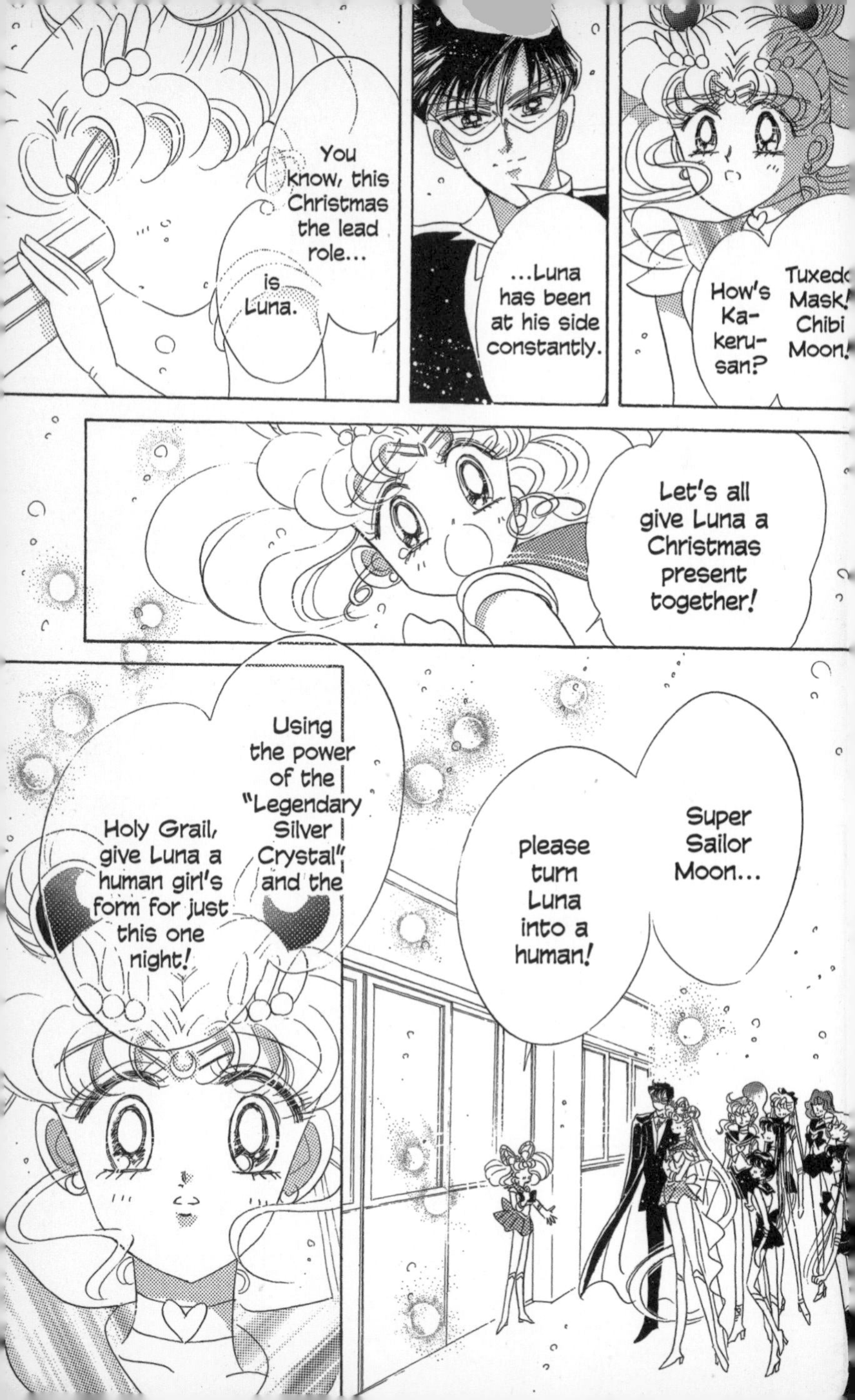
Tuxedo Mask! Chibi Moon!
How's Ka-keru-san?
...Luna has been at his side constantly.
You know, this Christmas the lead role...
is Luna.
Let's all give Luna a Christmas present together!
Super Sailor Moon...
please turn Luna into a human!
Using the power of the "Legendary Silver Crystal" and the
Holy Grail, give Luna a human girl's form for just this one night!

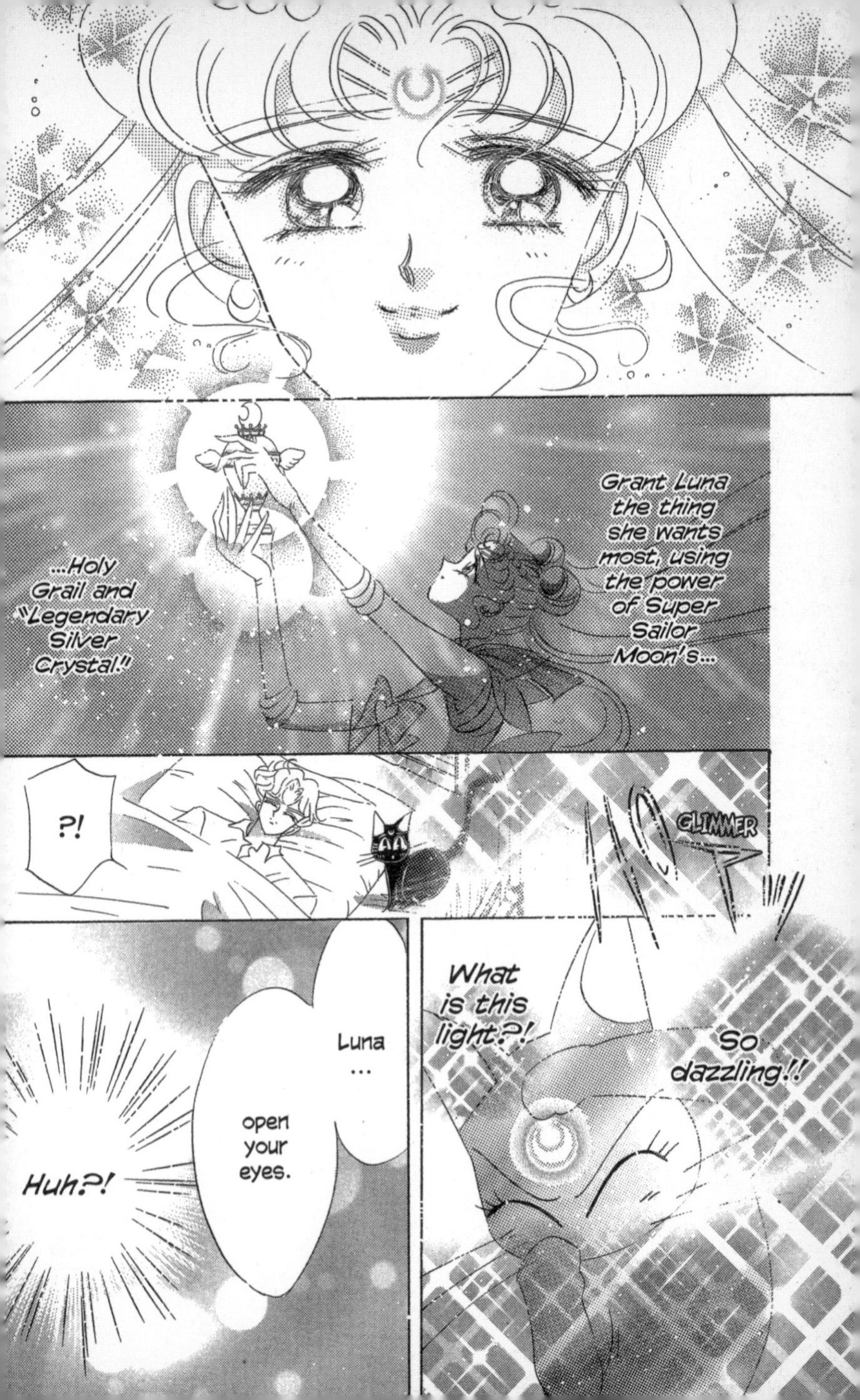
Grant Luna the thing she wants most, using the power of Super Sailor Moon's...
...Holy Grail and "Legendary Silver Crystal."
GLIMMER
?!
What is this light?!
So dazzling!!
Luna ... open your eyes.
Huh?!

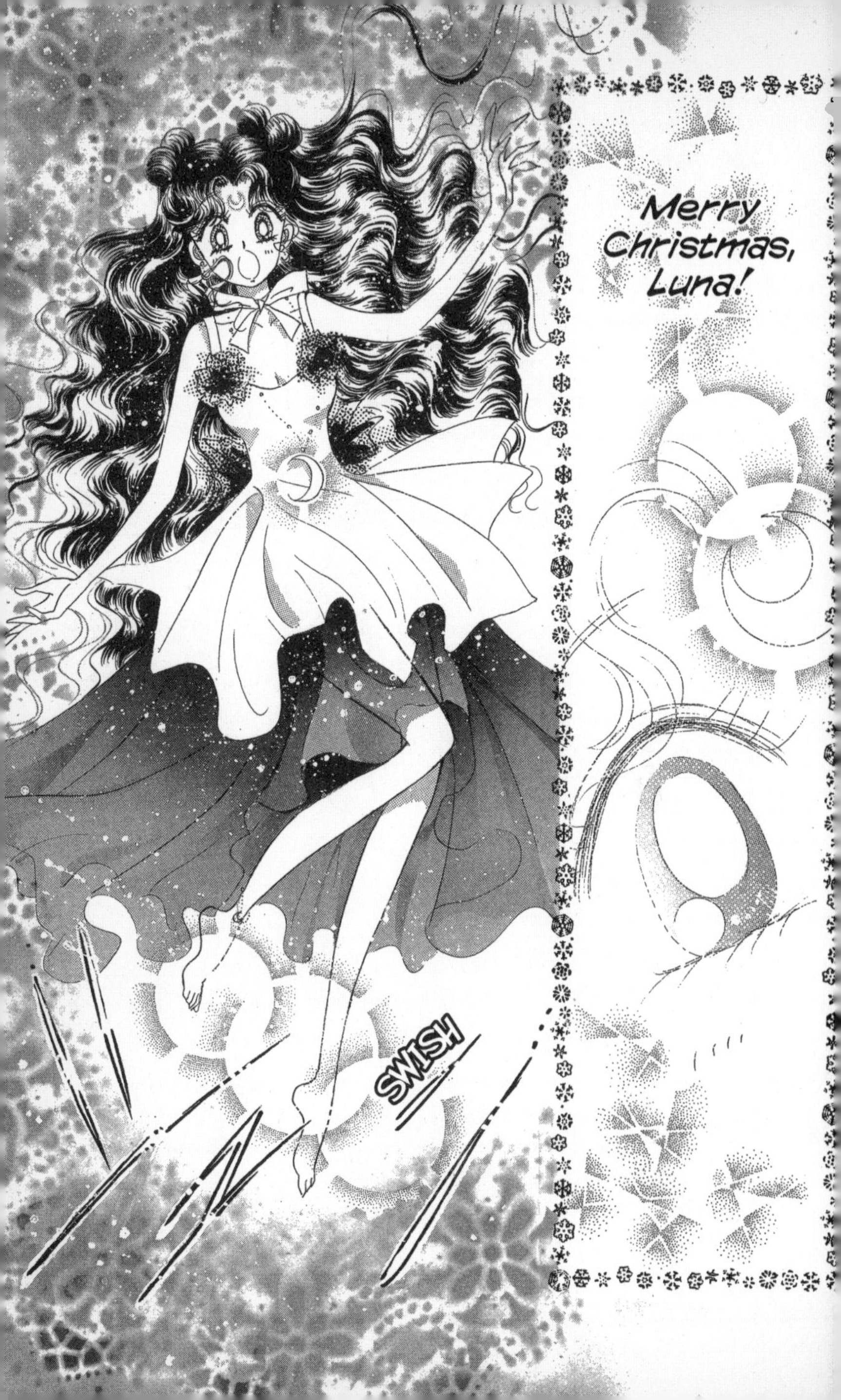
Merry Christmas, Luna!
SWISH

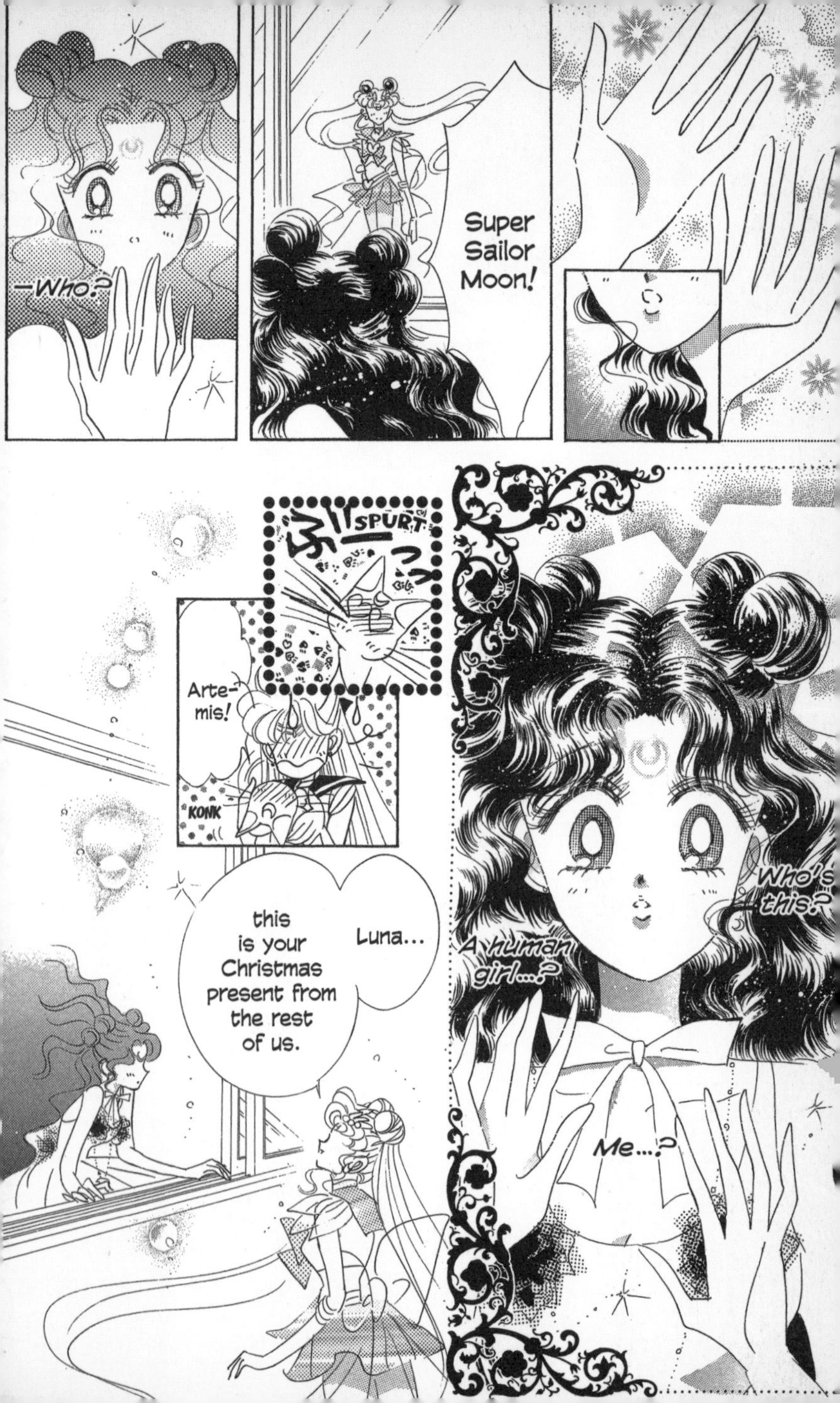
Super Sailor Moon!
—Who?
Who's this?
A human girl...?
Me...?
SPURT
Artemis!
KONK
Luna...
this is your Christmas present from the rest of us.

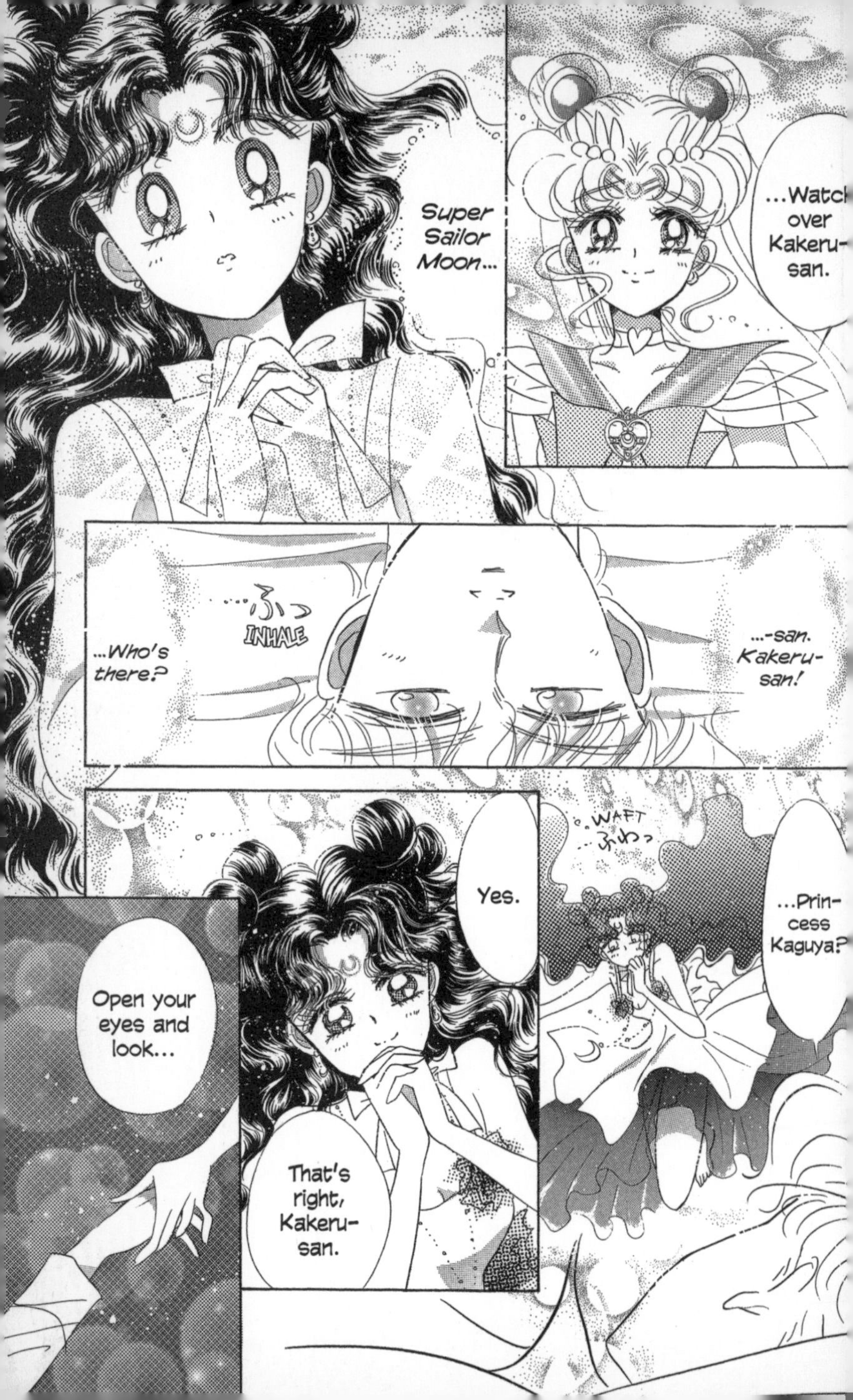

...Watc over Kakeru-san.
Super Sailor Moon...
...-san. Kakeru-san!
INHALE
...Who's there?
WAFT
...Princess Kaguya?
Yes.
That's right, Kakeru-san.
Open your eyes and look...

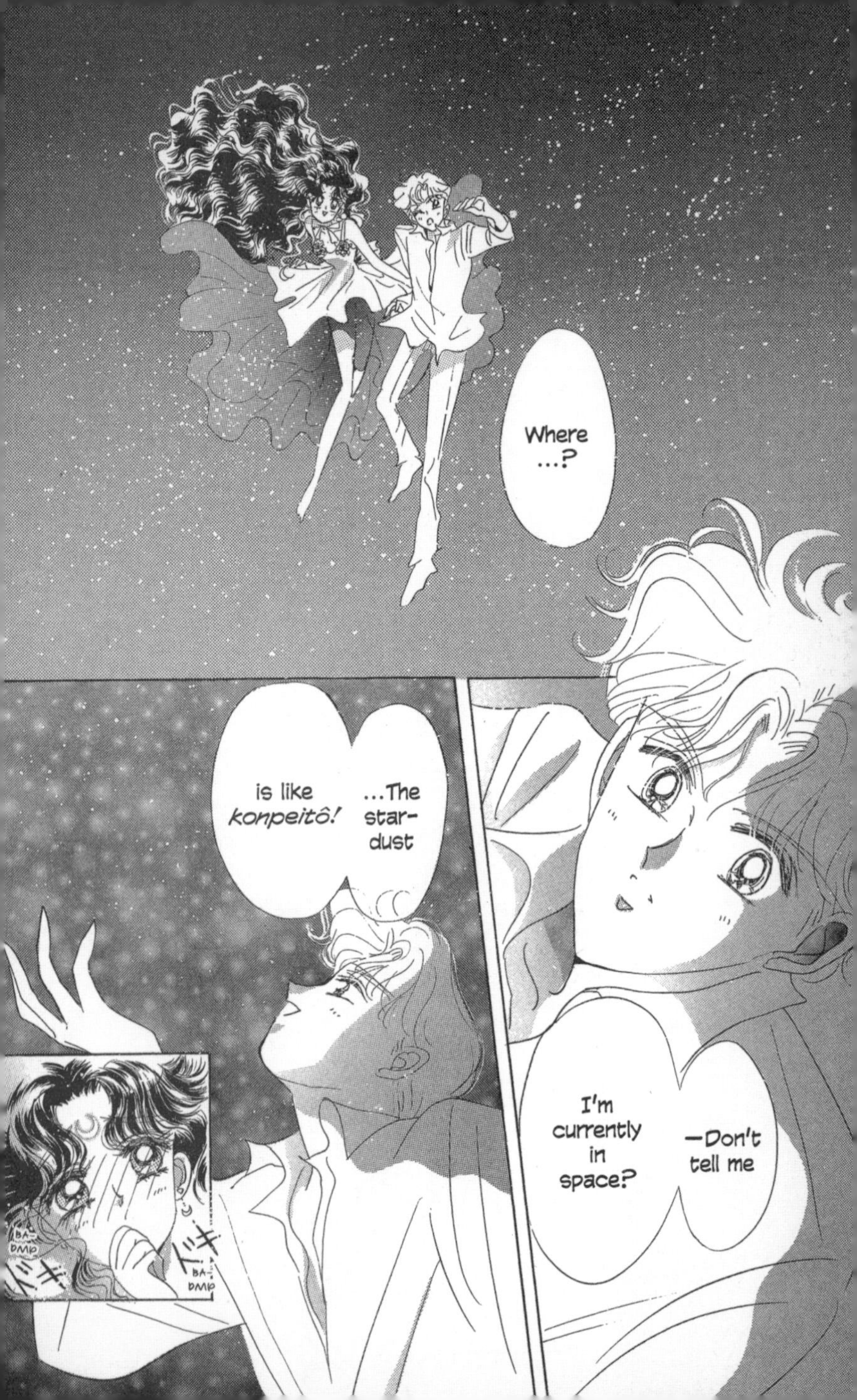
Where ...?
—Don't tell me I'm currently in space?
...The stardust is like konpeitô!
BA-DMP
BA-DMP

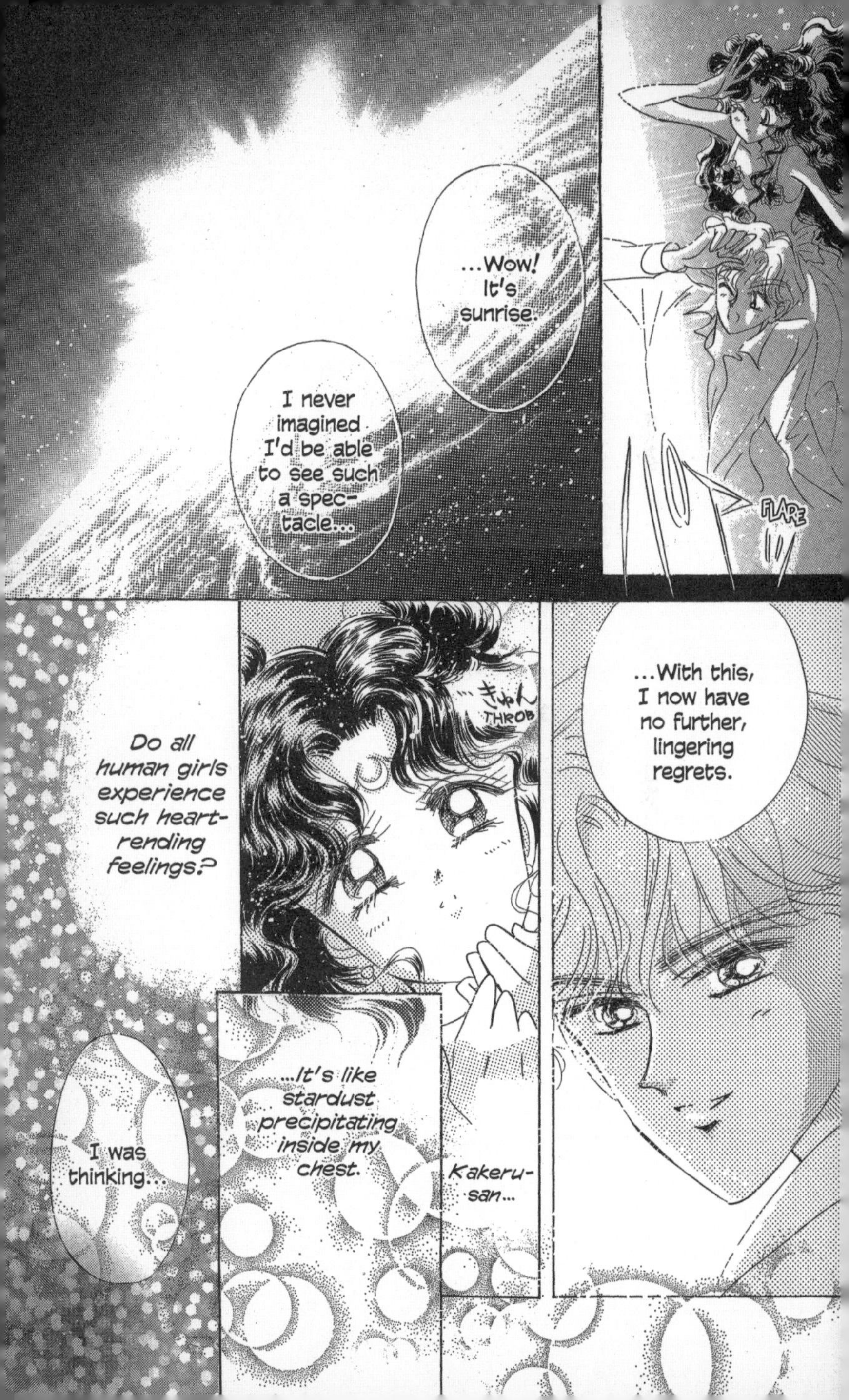
FLARE
...Wow! It's sunrise.
I never imagined I'd be able to see such a spectacle...
...With this, I now have no further, lingering regrets.
きゅん THROB
Kakeru-san...
...It's like stardust precipitating inside my chest.
Do all human girls experience such heart-rending feelings?
I was thinking...

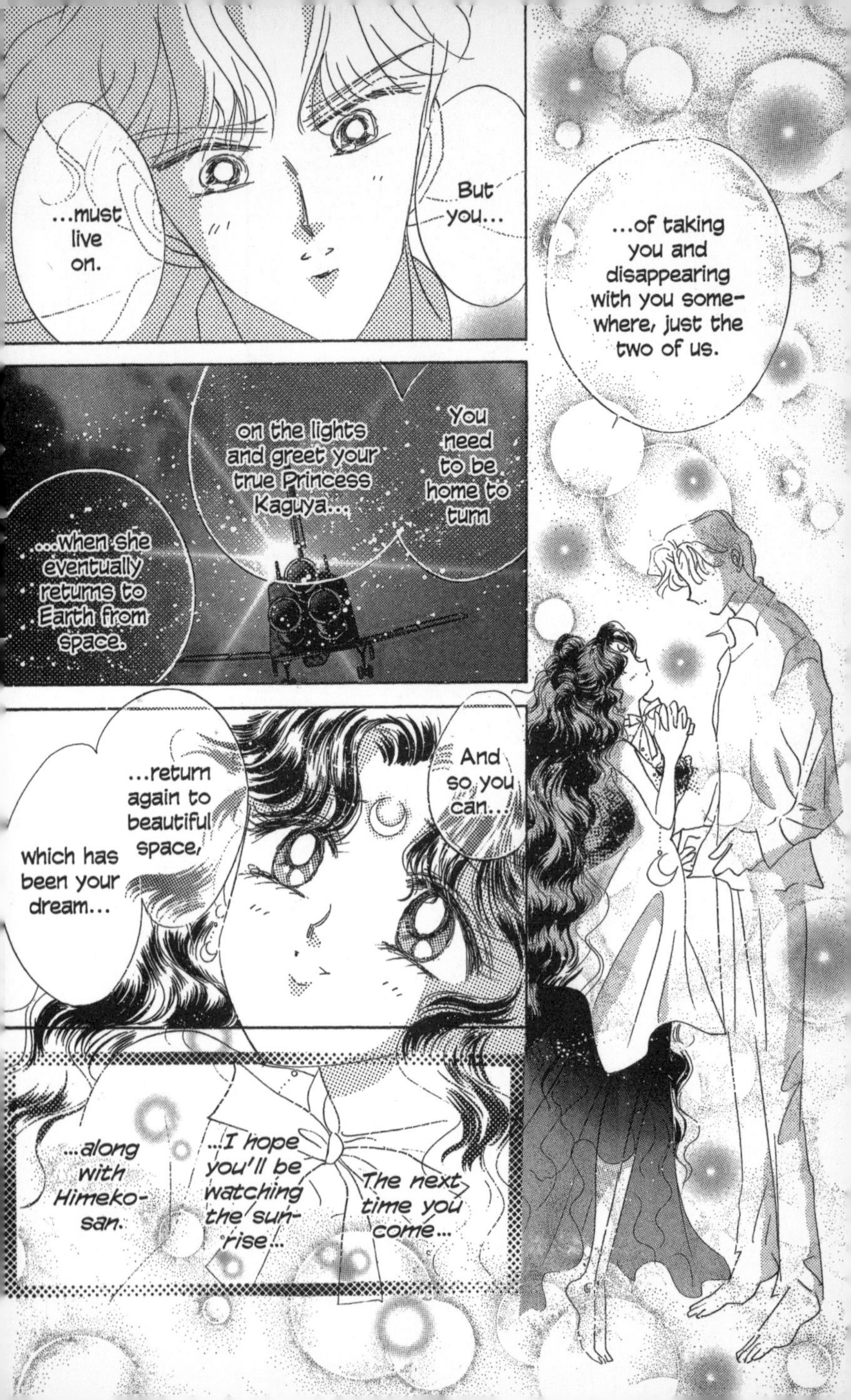

...of taking you and disappearing with you some-where, just the two of us.
But you...
...must live on.
You need to be home to turn
on the lights and greet your true Princess Kaguya...
...when she eventually returns to Earth from space.
And so you can...
...return again to beautiful space,
which has been your dream...
The next time you come...
...I hope you'll be watching the sun-rise...
...along with Himeko-san.

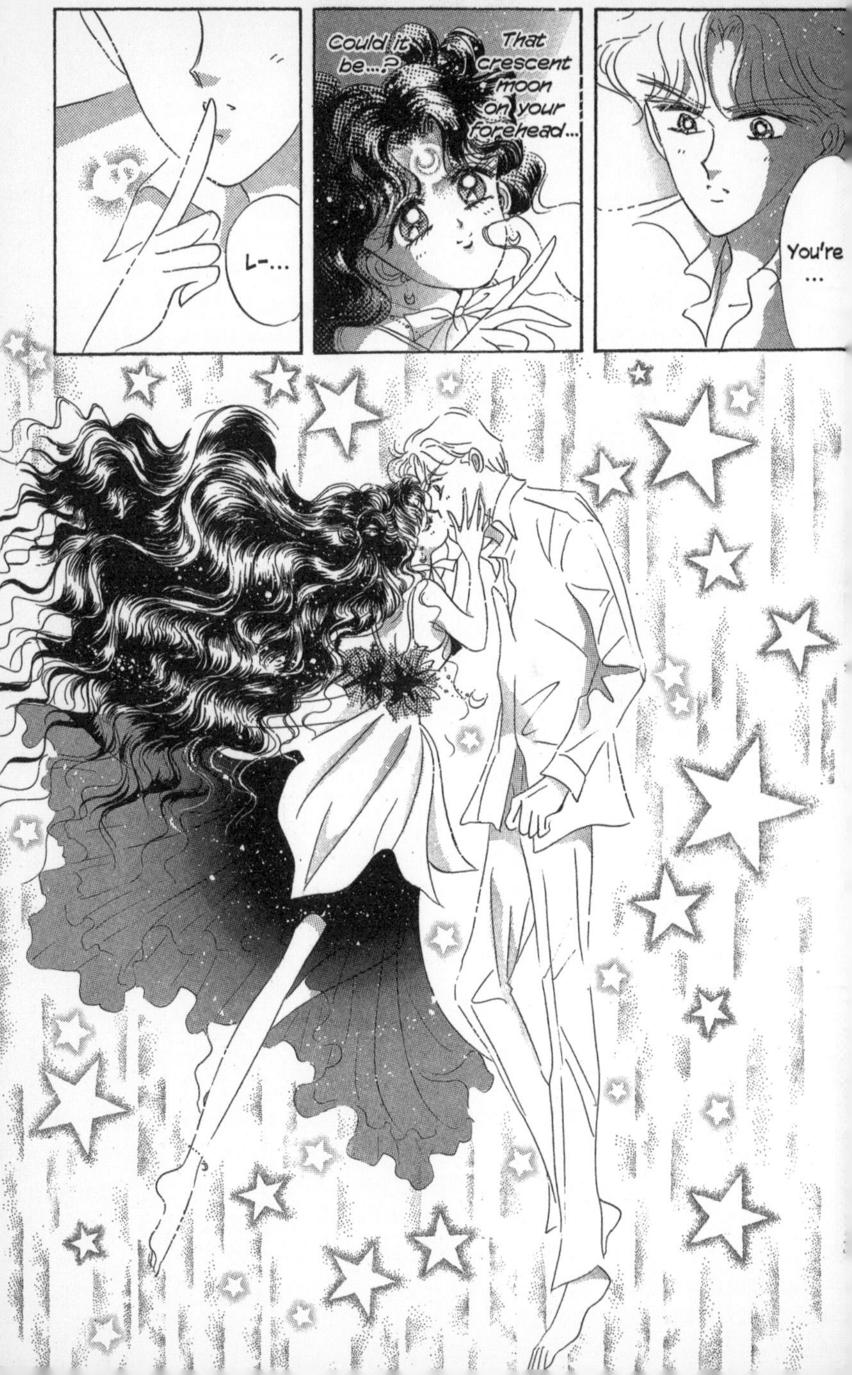
You're ...
That crescent moon on your forehead...
Could it be...?
L-...

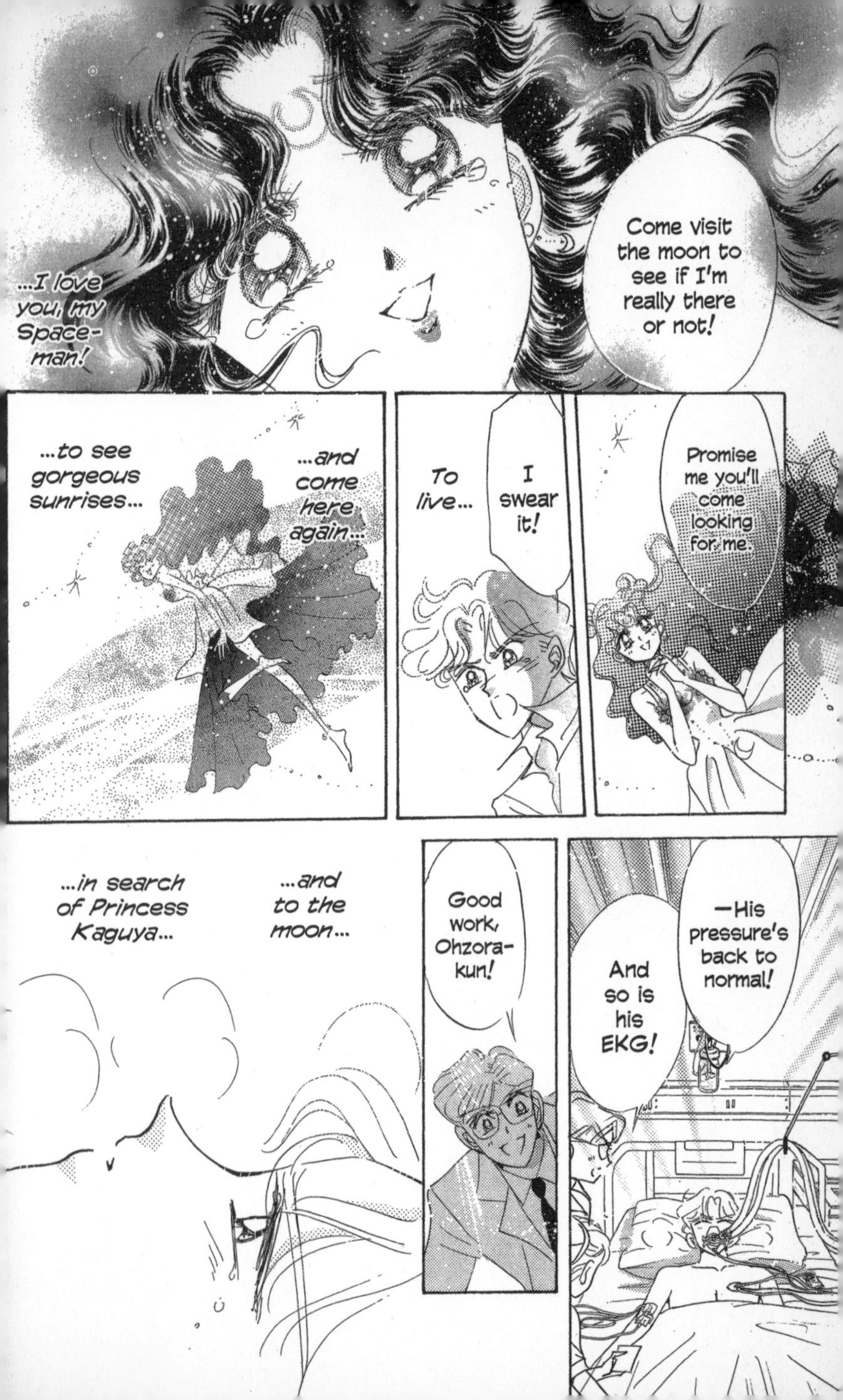
Come visit the moon to see if I'm really there or not!
...I love you, my Space-man!
Promise me you'll come looking for me.
I swear it!
To live...
...and come here again...
...to see gorgeous sunrises...
—His pressure's back to normal!
And so is his EKG!
Good work, Ohzora-kun!
...and to the moon...
...in search of Princess Kaguya...

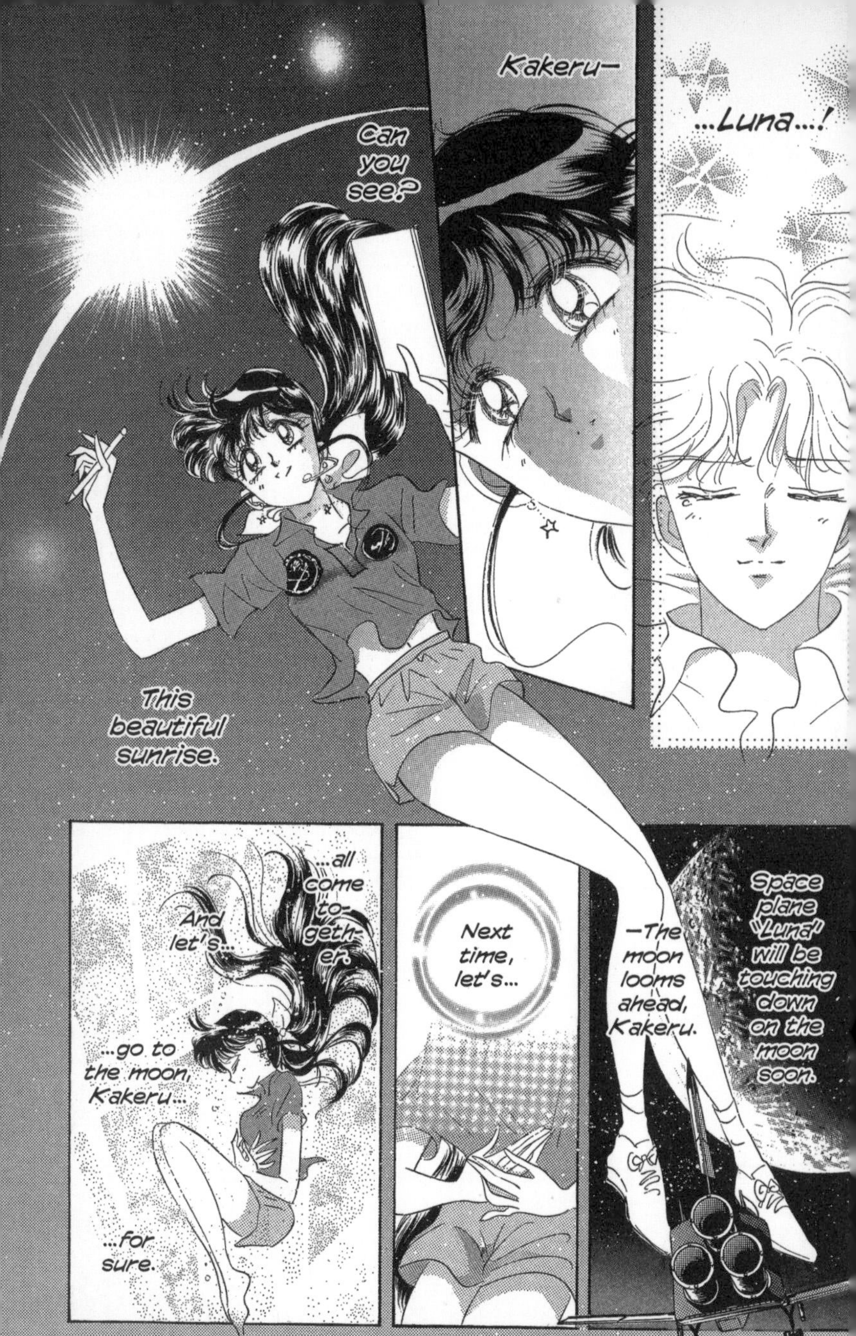
...Luna...!
Kakeru—
Can you see?
This beautiful sunrise.
Space plane "Luna" will be touching down on the moon soon.
—The moon looms ahead, Kakeru.
Next time, let's...
...all come together.
And let's...
...go to the moon, Kakeru...
...for sure.

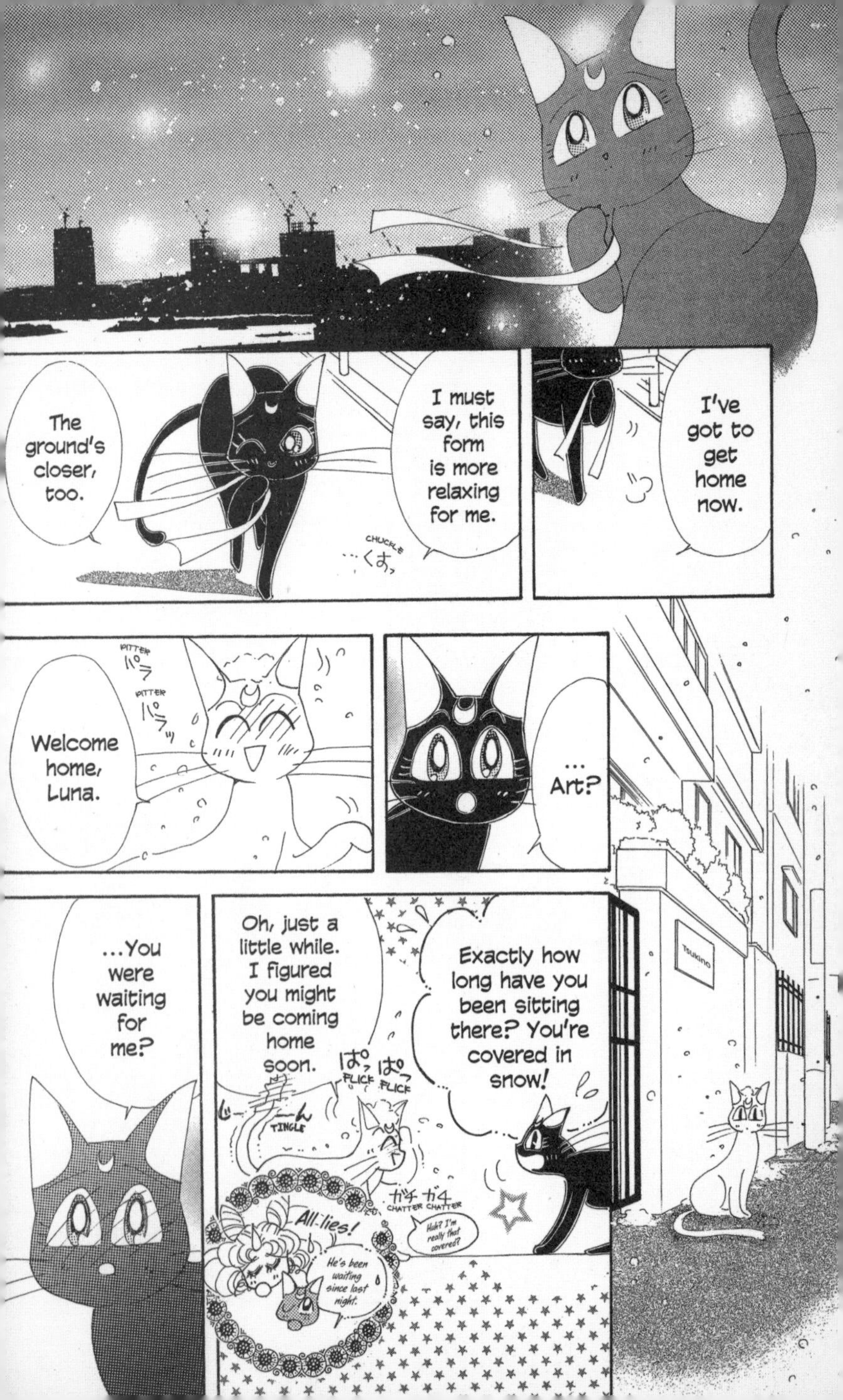
I've got to get home now.
I must say, this form is more relaxing for me.
The ground's closer, too.
...くすっ CHUCKLE
...Art?
パラ PITTER
パラッ PITTER
Welcome home, Luna.
Tsukino
Exactly how long have you been sitting there? You're covered in snow!
Oh, just a little while. I figured you might be coming home soon.
ぱっ FLICK ぱっ FLICK
じーーん TINGLE
ガチガチ CHATTER CHATTER
Huh? I'm really that covered?
All-lies!
He's been waiting since last night.
...You were waiting for me?

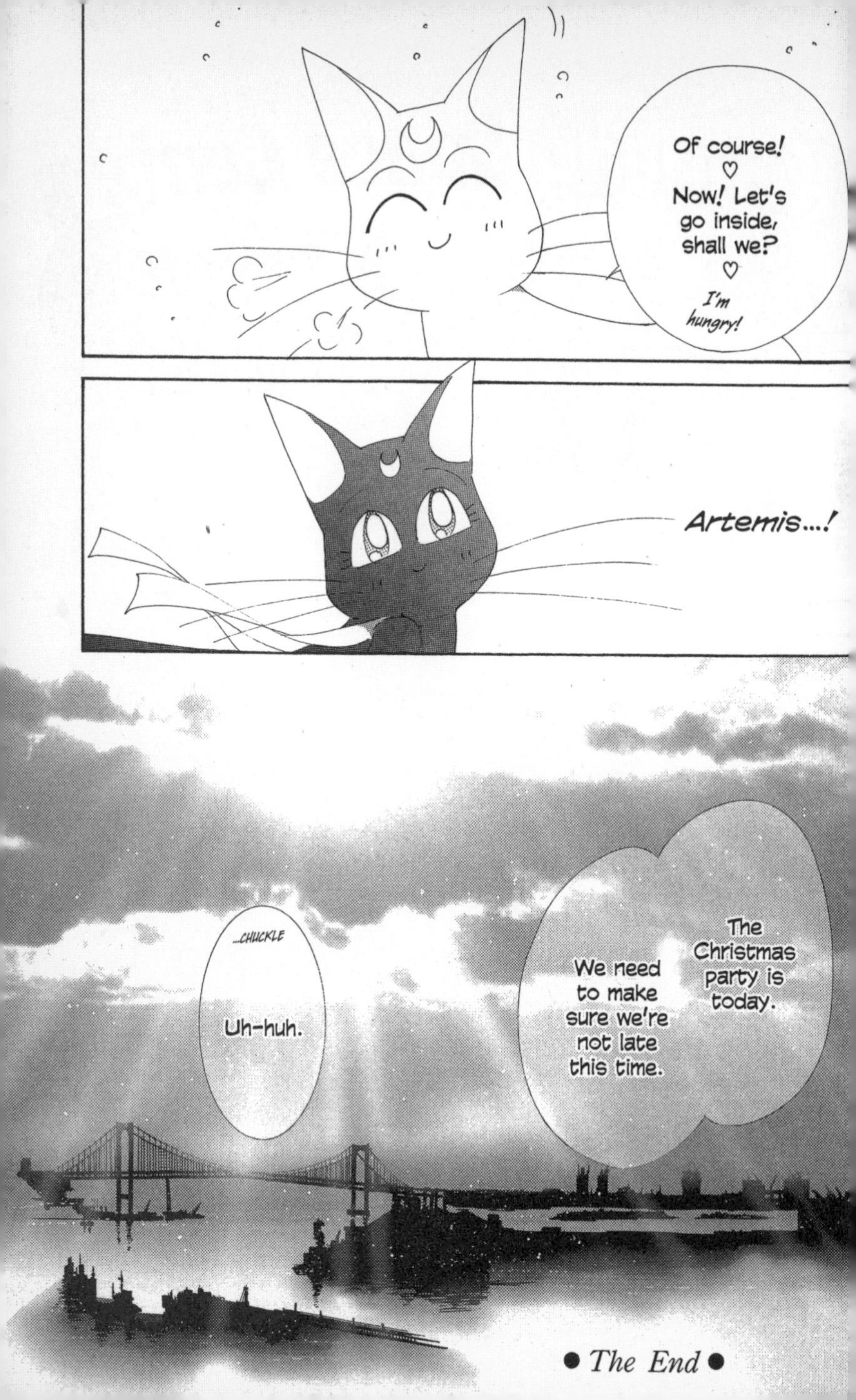
Of course! ♡ Now! Let's go inside, shall we? ♡
I'm hungry!
Artemis...!
The Christmas party is today.
We need to make sure we're not late this time.
...CHUCKLE
Uh-huh.
• The End •

Kennedy Space Center

Travel journal

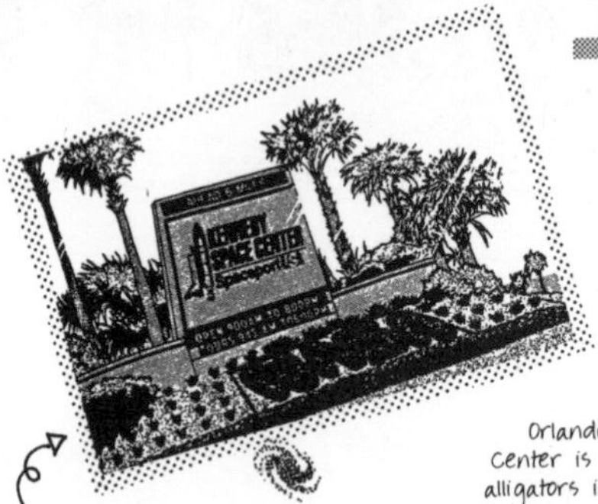
KENNEDY SPACE CENTER
Spaceport USA

July 8th, '94. I went to Kennedy Space Center in America to collect data. My goal was to witness the launch of the Space Shuttle "Columbia," which had (Dr.) Chiaki Mukai-san on board.

The weather that day was spectacular! ♡Lucky me! ♡

The Kennedy Space Center is sprawling! Its grounds are triple the size of the area encompassed by the Yamanote Line! (The famous Walt Disney World is (only) 1.5 times as large!)

Orlando, Florida, where the Kennedy Space Center is located, is a wetland region. There are alligators in area ponds and lakes! (And squirrels in grassy spots! ♡) You can even eat alligator meat in restaurants! (From farm-raised alligators, that is.) There are alligators in the ponds and rivers within the Space Center's grounds as well, of course! The Kennedy Space Center is a designated nature preserve, where dolphins, raccoons, armadillos, wild rats, alligators, bald eagles (I saw some! They were huge!), manatees (they apparently were in the pond), and other species are said to live freely.

Now, "Columbia"'s scheduled launch time is 12:43pm. Its launch site, Launch Pad 39A. It's the very same one that the ought-to-be-memorialized Apollo 11 lifted off from. ♡

Starting around 9am, I spread a picnic blanket, planted a beach umbrella, and leisurely awaited the shuttle launch from the opposite shore, at an inlet on Space Center grounds where dolphins live, with a bunch of Americans. There are plenty of bathing suit-clad sunbathing folks, too (although you can't swim there).

I knew ahead of time, but the launch pad is atop an island that is quite a distance away! It only looks about 1cm big! Sob sob! It's so far off! Let me watch from up close!

Surprisingly, the transmissions between the crew and the Center are openly broadcast over speakers mounted along roads within Center grounds. Partway through, I caught Mukai-san replying "clear," upon checking the comm equipment! ♡ That was at exactly 12:00 noon! Let me share with you some of the later transmissions. ♡

12:15pm. It is reported that there were thunderstorms this morning around the emergency runways (in Morocco and southern Africa).

12:25pm. The countdown is stopped for 10 minutes. (This is apparently a built-in thing to allow any operations lags to catch up)

12:43pm. Lift-off!!

12:51pm. 500 miles off the Atlantic coast, over the open sea. 6300 Km/h.

12:52pm. External tank off. Main engines off.

And so, Columbia set off on its 13-day, 18-hour journey.

This is the pass to enter Kennedy Space Center on a shuttle launch day. They'll issue you one if you apply for it in advance.

It's fluorescent yellow!

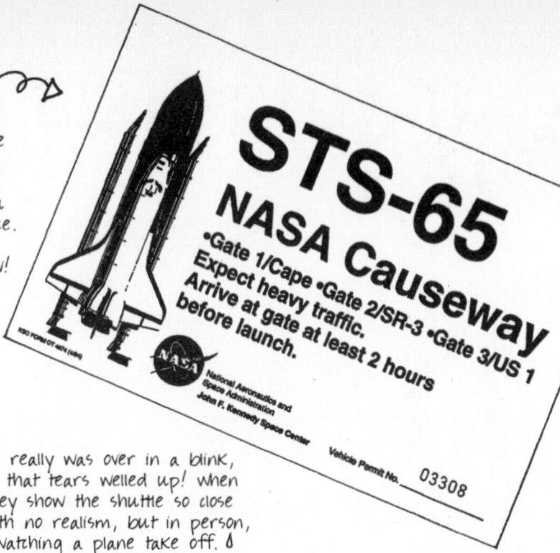

STS-65
NASA Causeway
•Gate 1/Cape •Gate 2/SR-3 •Gate 3/US 1
Expect heavy traffic.
Arrive at gate at least 2 hours
before launch.

National Aeronautics and
Space Administration
John F. Kennedy Space Center

Vehicle Permit No.   03308

Ah! The shuttle launch really was over in a blink, but I got so emotional that tears welled up! When you watch it on TV, they show the shuttle so close up, it's like a movie, with no realism, but in person, it was also sort of like watching a plane take off. ◊
(Sorry ◊ for the unexciting metaphor ◊)

Now! Immediately after watching the launch, I went on a bus tour of the grounds. It goes right near the still-piping-hot Launch Pad 39A. (Though they don't let you off. ◊) There are lots of news cameras set up around the launch pad, but perhaps due to the blast (?), they've all fallen over. ◊

(Incidentally, that giant plume of smoke you see during lift-off is water vapor.)

The centerpiece of the grounds! ♡

Ta-daa! The Saturn Rocket that launched the moon-landing Apollo 11 is displayed conspicuously on one side of the employee parking lot.

In addition, there is the Vehicle Assembly Building that the Space Shuttle can fit into vertically. (They apparently transport the shuttle on a Mobile Launcher Platform via Crawler-Transporters. What a tale of incredibly giant proportions!)

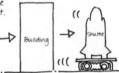

→ Building → Shuttle

Ahh! It was a truly thrilling data collection trip! ♡

I would so love to live in Orlando and make Space Shuttle launch events a regular thing. ♡

What I thought is lovely is that I heard when the Space Shuttle returns to Earth at night, Floridians turn on their house and yard lights and await it. It's apparently their way of saying, "Welcome home." This!!! I want to do this, too!! ♡

And of course, I'd put shuttle specialty plates on my car! ♡
(In Florida, you can get fundraising license plates with a drawing of a manatee, panther, or the Space Shuttle.)

FLORIDA
HDA 387

This is a manatee specialty plate

All right! I'm gonna do data collection again some day!
(I love covering things/events! ♡)
I'm gonna go to America again, too! ♡

(written exclusively for the graphic novel in November 199

Antique

Talking about antiques

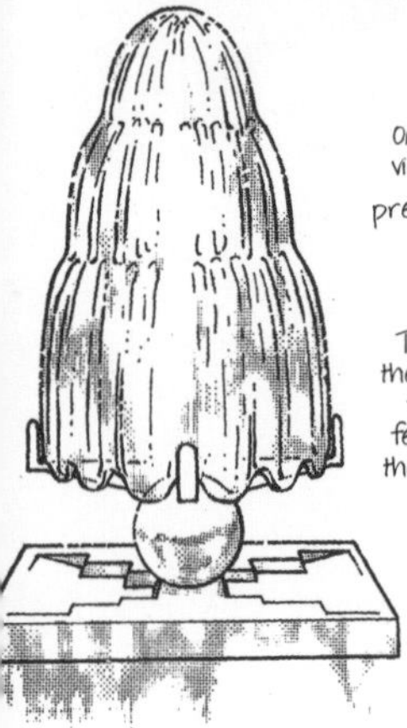

One of my hobbies is reading books about antiques and visiting antique shops. I'll introduce you to some of my precious possessions that I've presented in my manga too.

This Art Deco glass bedside lamp that I arbitrarily call the "Rain Tree." It's patterned after a fountain, but my first impression was that it looked like falling rain! I fell so in love with it that I ended up collecting four of them. So when the light is turned on in the entryway of my home, a silent, tiny rain is quietly precipitating.

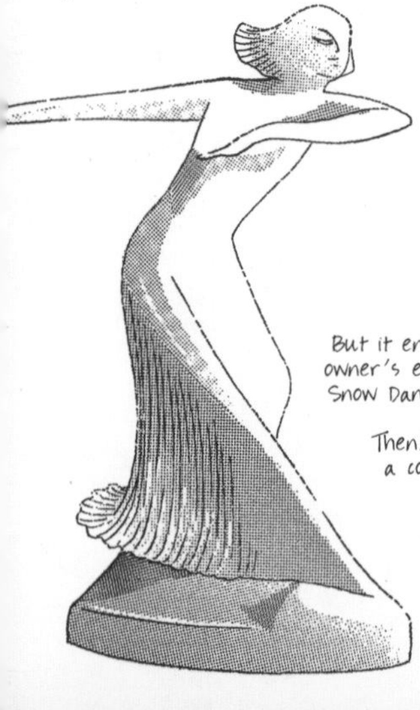

The model for the Snow Dancers in "Princess Kaguya's Lover" is this German ceramic and porcelain maker's ornamental piece, the "Dancer." It is a white, smooth ceramic figurine. I felt it was the very image of a creature dancing in the midst of a blizzard.

But it ended up betrothed to another (the antique shop owner's euphemism for "got sold"). Each time I drew a Snow Dancer in the manuscript, I got sad. Sob sob

Then! Unbelievably, the shop managed to acquire a completely identical item! So, finally, one got betrothed to me. ♡ Yippee! ♡

I mentioned this briefly in the brochure for the '94 theatrical film, but the model for Snow Kaguya in "Princess Kaguya's Lover" is an Art Deco ornamental piece called "Salome." She is indeed made from cold, delicious-seeming milk-colored (with just a hint of blue) glass.

I came up with the story by putting this "Salome" on my desk and gazing at her all day long.

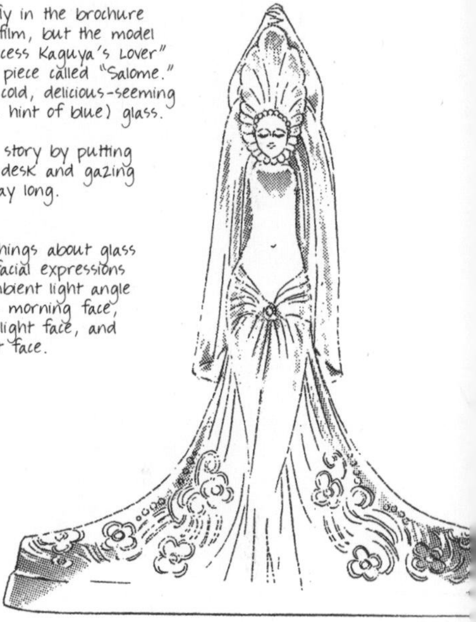

One of the alluring things about glass is that (figures'~) facial expressions change based on ambient light angle and level. There is morning face, afternoon face, twilight face, and then night face.

But whenever I look up at a time that work is reaching a critical point, they are usually glaring at me with an incredibly severe expression (this is their late night face).

Saying, "Hurry up and finish the manuscript!"

Sob sob

The other day, while riding a taxi, I was speaking on my cell phone with the owner of an antique shop that I frequent. The eavesdropping cab driver said "Passenger! Bonsai and antiques are the hobbies of the elderly!" Is that so?! I had a revelation and decided not to go to the antique shop that day. Sob sob

Later! ♡ Naoko ♡ Takeuchi '95

(written exclusively for the graphic novel in July 199

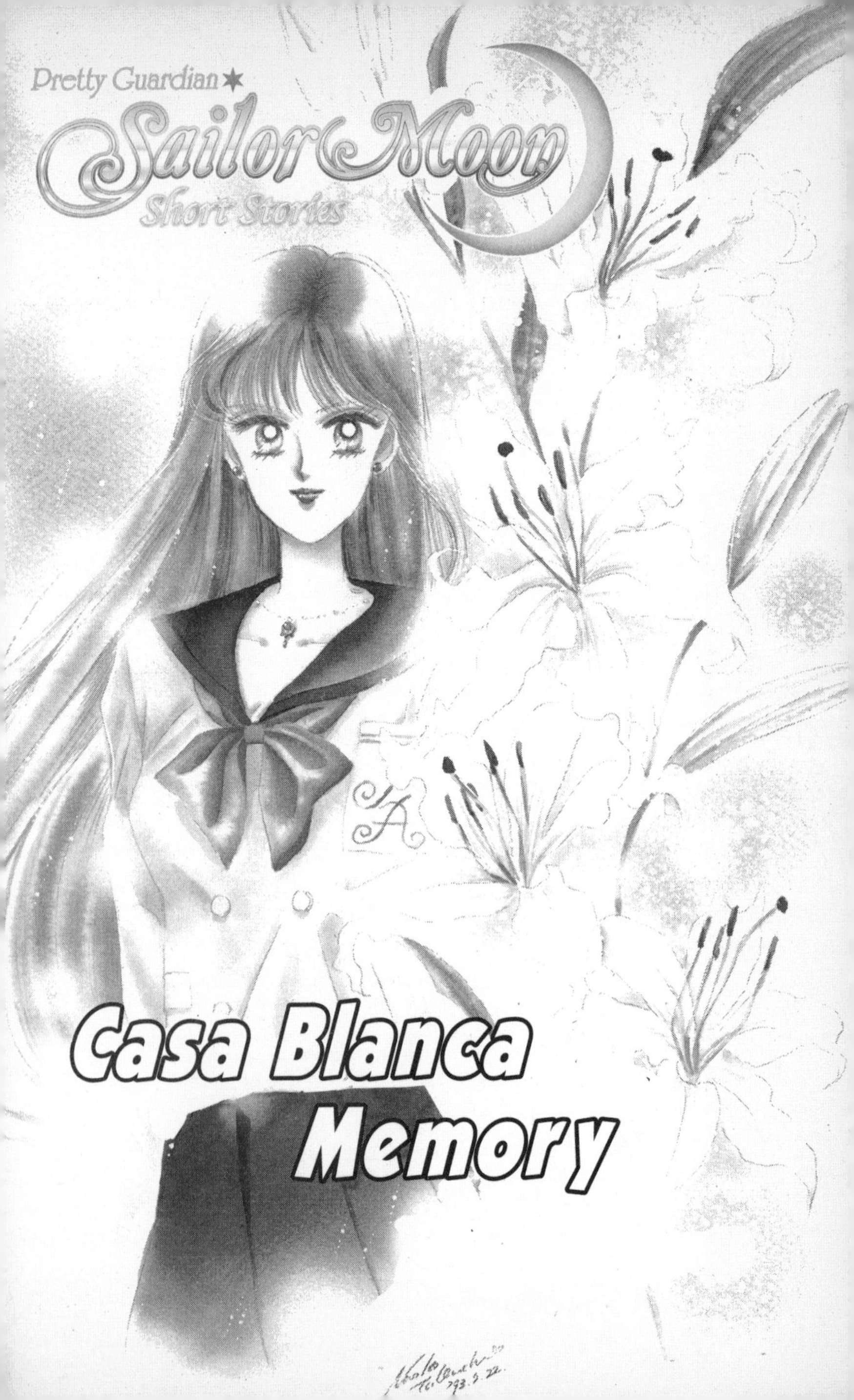
Pretty Guardian
Sailor Moon
Short Stories
Casa Blanca
Memory

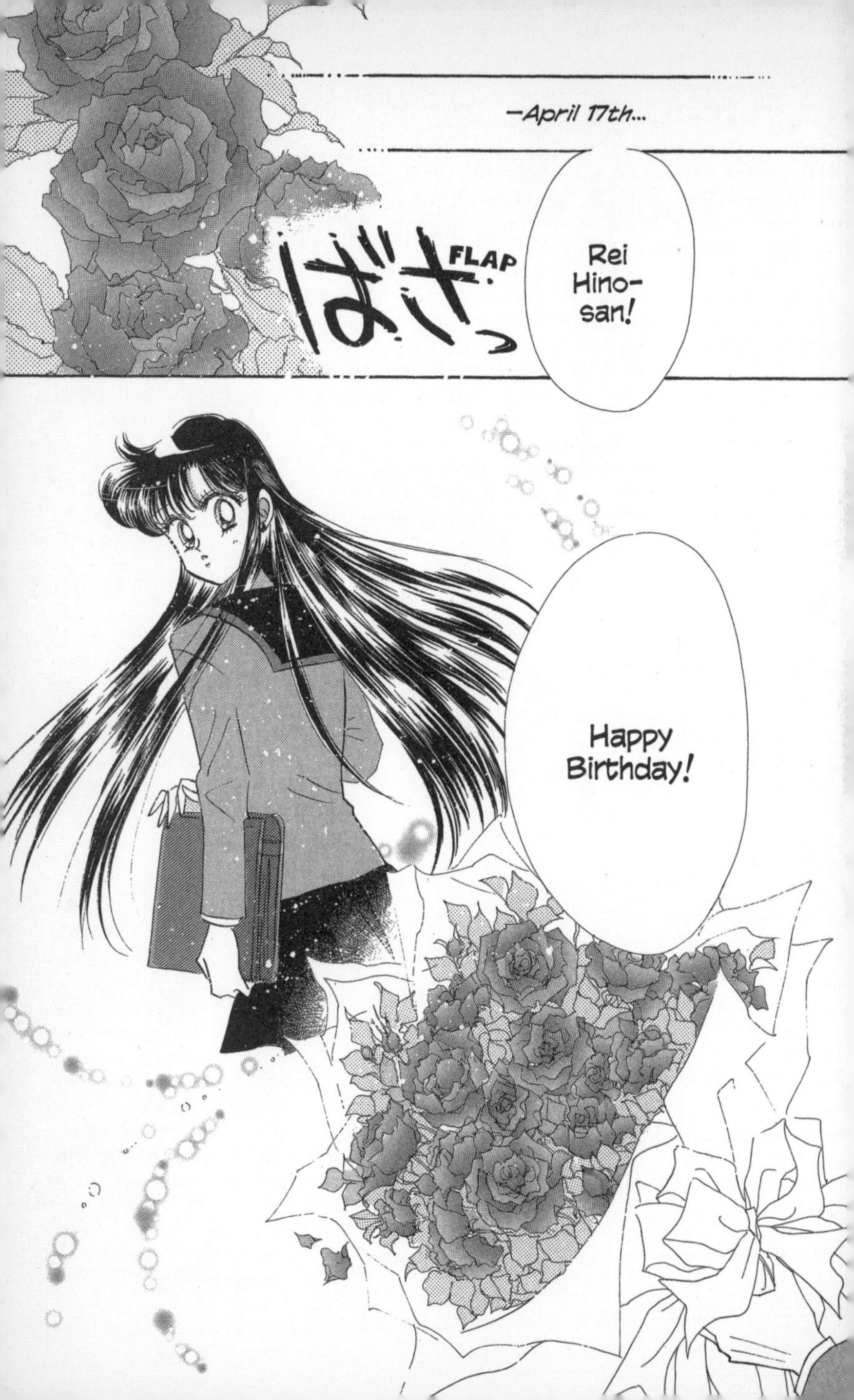
—April 17th...
ばさっ
FLAP
Rei Hino-san!
Happy Birthday!

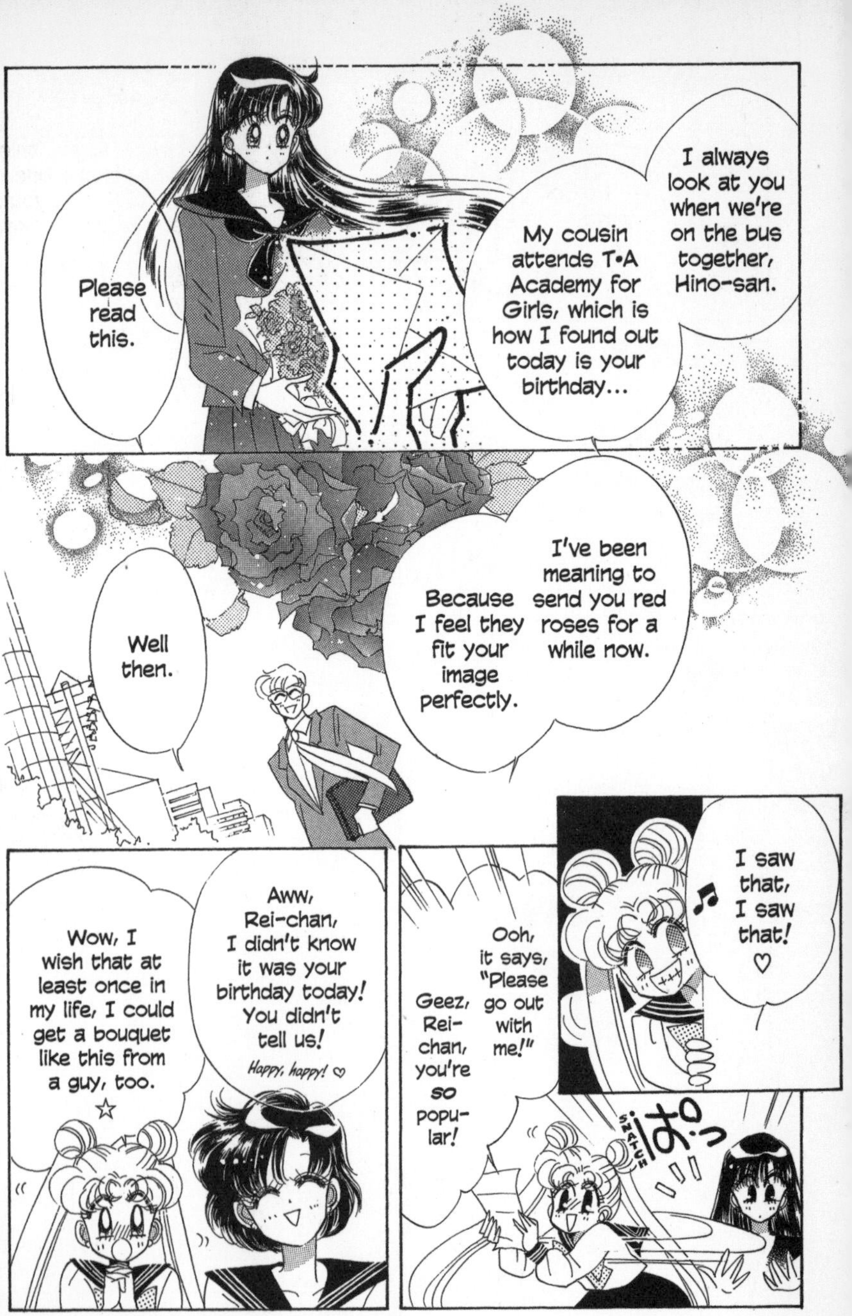
I always look at you when we're on the bus together, Hino-san.
My cousin attends T•A Academy for Girls, which is how I found out today is your birthday...
Please read this.
I've been meaning to send you red roses for a while now.
Because I feel they fit your image perfectly.
Well then.
I saw that, I saw that! ♡
Ooh, it says, "Please go out with me!"
Geez, Rei-chan, you're *so* popular!
SNATCH
Aww, Rei-chan, I didn't know it was your birthday today! You didn't tell us!
Happy, happy! ♡
Wow, I wish that at least once in my life, I could get a bouquet like this from a guy, too. ☆

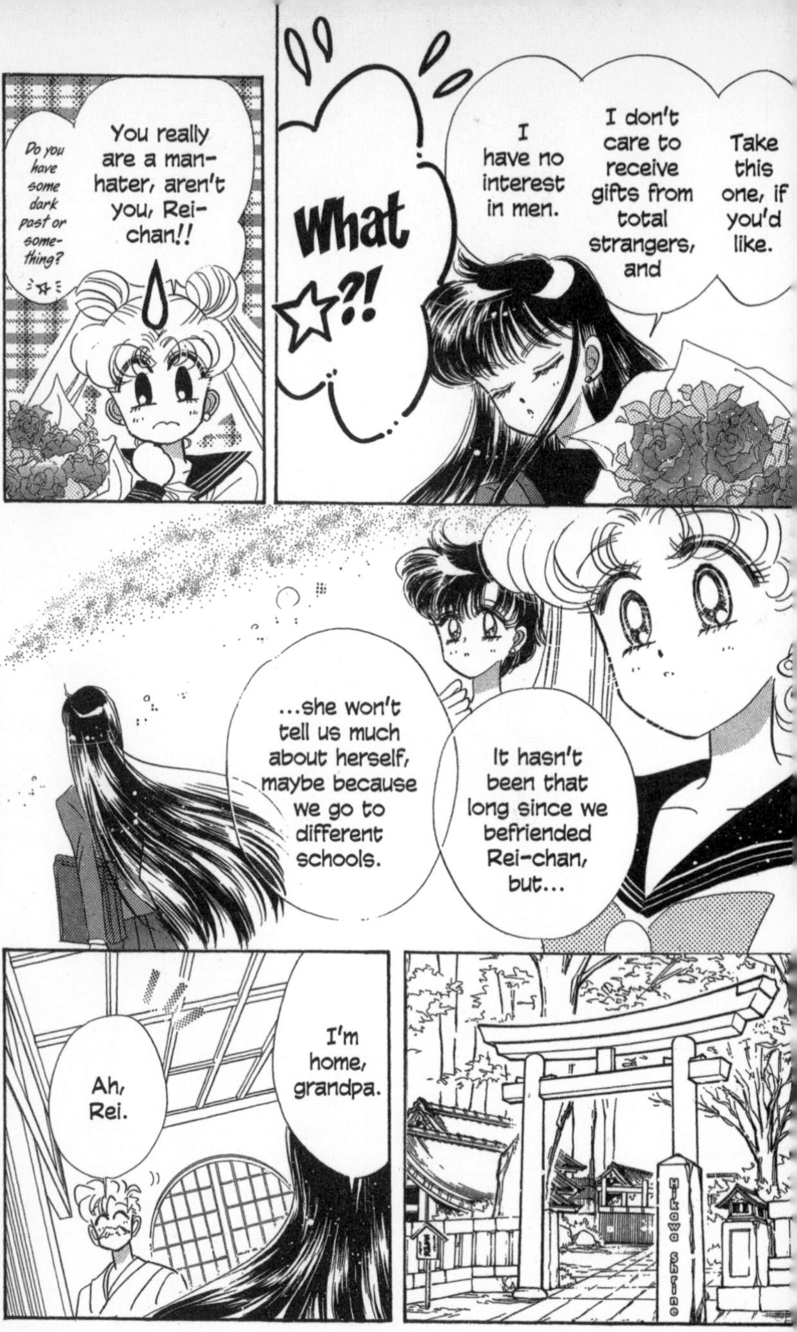
Take this one, if you'd like.
I don't care to receive gifts from total strangers, and
I have no interest in men.
What☆?!
You really are a man-hater, aren't you, Rei-chan!!
Do you have some dark past or something?
It hasn't been that long since we befriended Rei-chan, but...
...she won't tell us much about herself, maybe because we go to different schools.
Hikawa Shrine
I'm home, grandpa.
Ah, Rei.

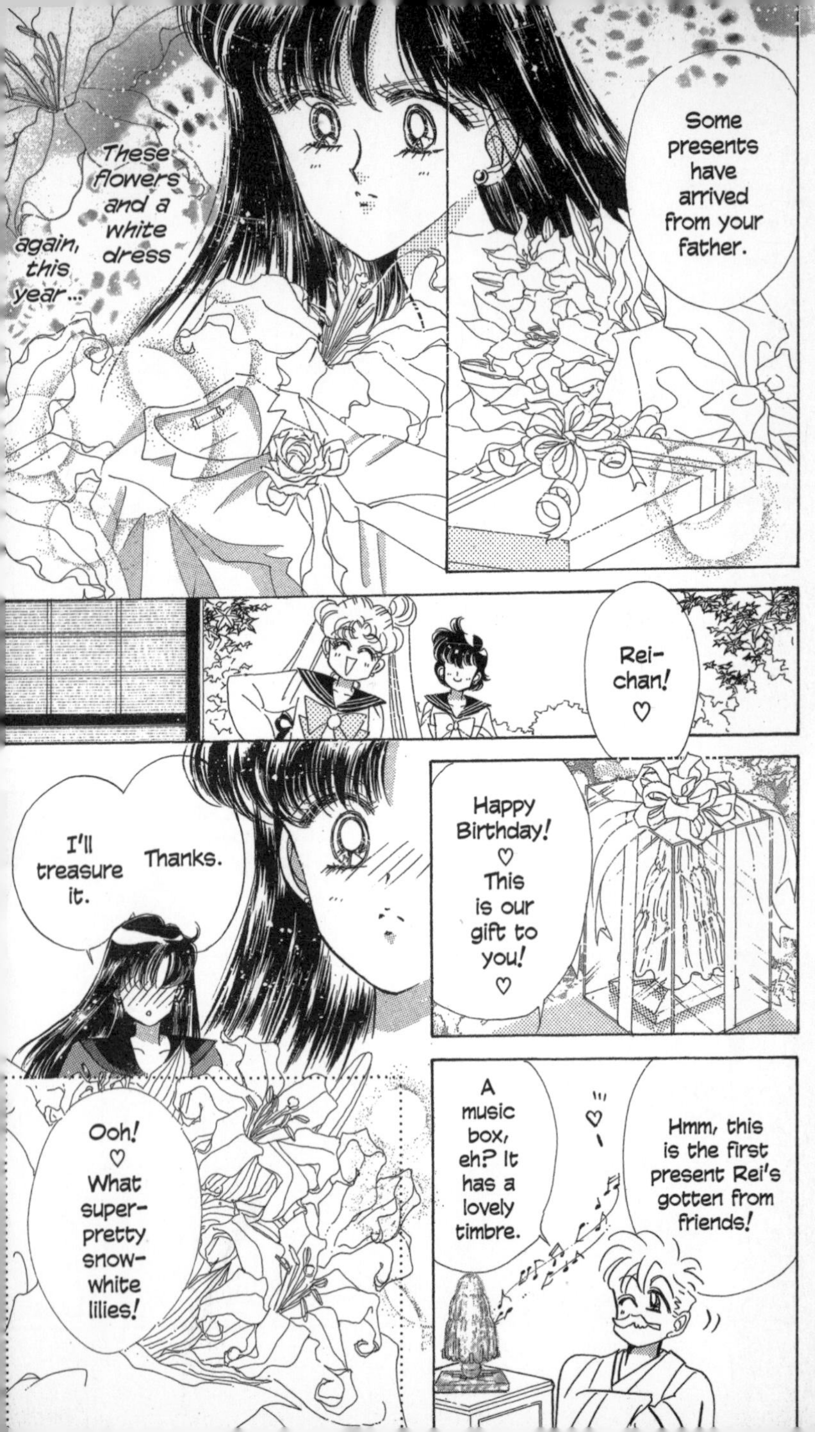
Some presents have arrived from your father.
These flowers and a white dress again, this year...
Rei-chan! ♡
Happy Birthday! ♡ This is our gift to you! ♡
Thanks.
I'll treasure it.
Hmm, this is the first present Rei's gotten from friends!
A music box, eh? It has a lovely timbre.
Ooh! ♡ What super-pretty snow-white lilies!

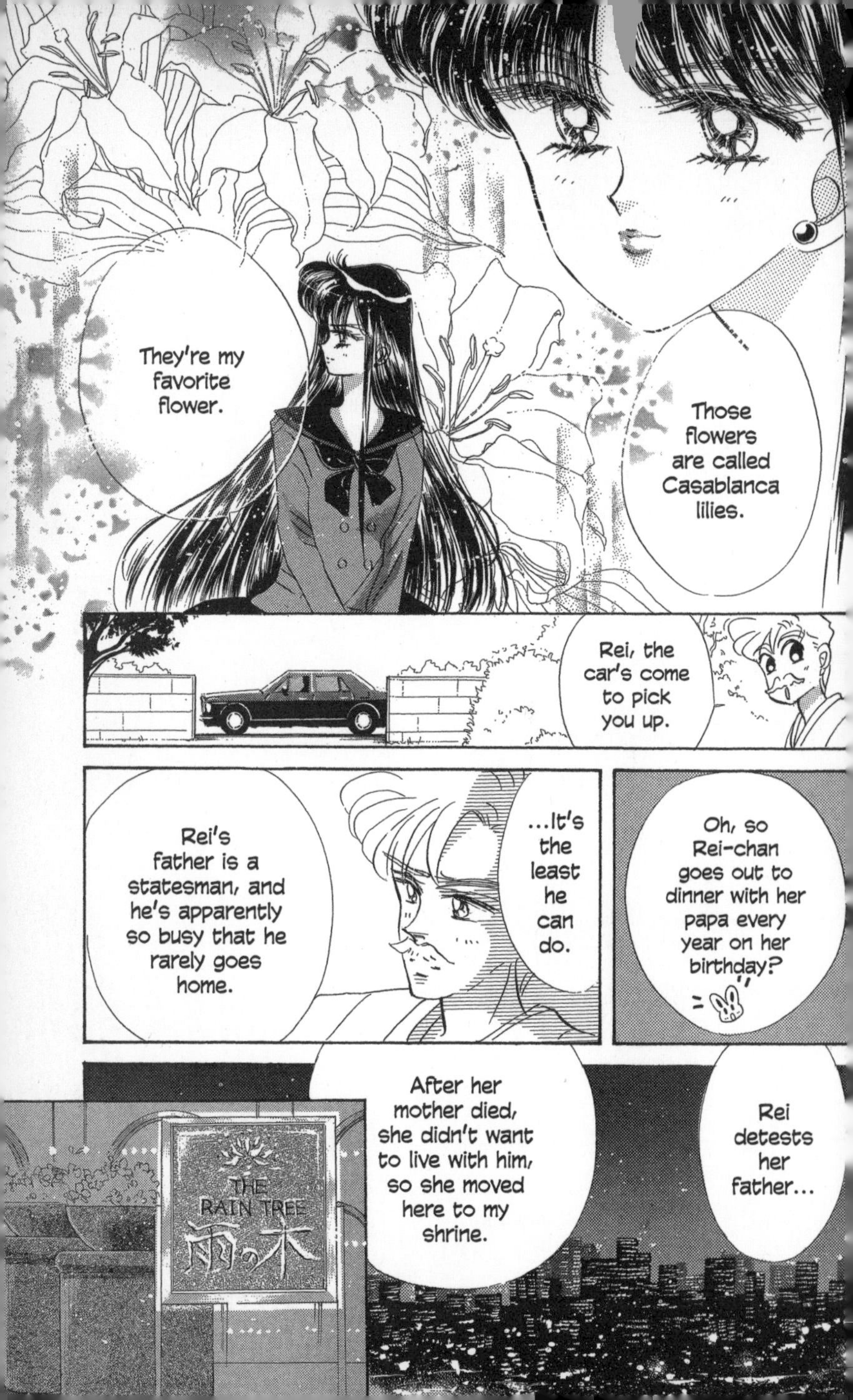
Those flowers are called Casablanca lilies.
They're my favorite flower.
Rei, the car's come to pick you up.
Oh, so Rei-chan goes out to dinner with her papa every year on her birthday?
...It's the least he can do.
Rei's father is a statesman, and he's apparently so busy that he rarely goes home.
Rei detests her father...
After her mother died, she didn't want to live with him, so she moved here to my shrine.
THE RAIN TREE
雨の木

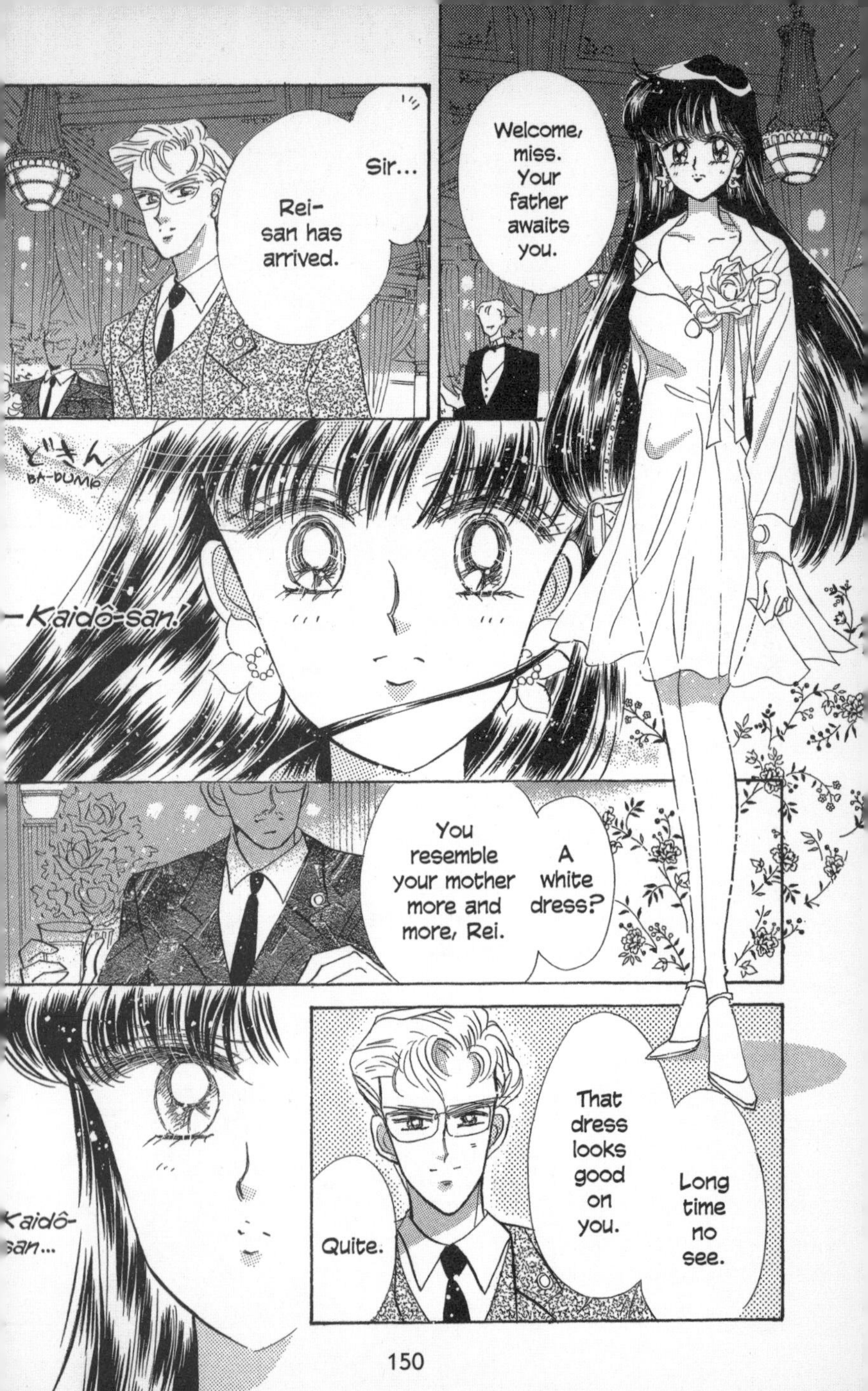
Welcome, miss. Your father awaits you.
Sir...
Rei-san has arrived.
どきん
BA-DUMP
—Kaidô-san!
A white dress?
You resemble your mother more and more, Rei.
Long time no see.
That dress looks good on you.
Quite.
Kaidô-san...

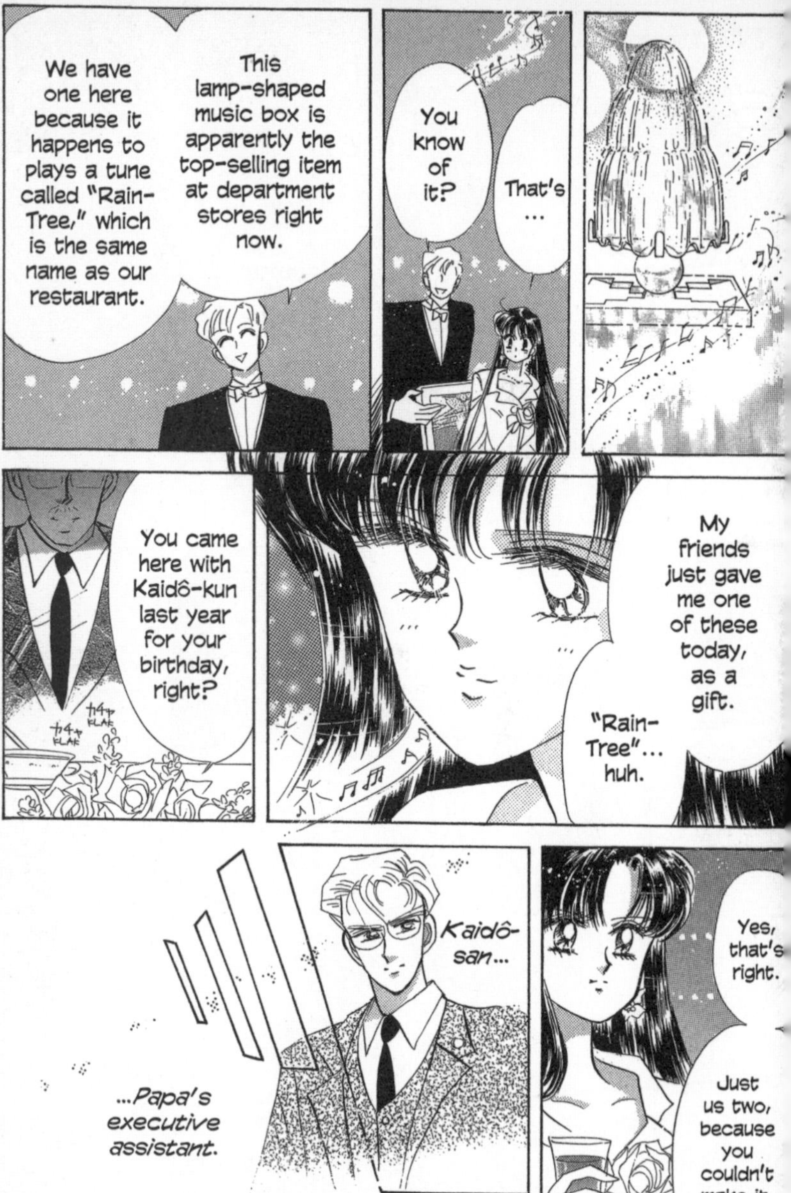
That's...
You know of it?
This lamp-shaped music box is apparently the top-selling item at department stores right now.
We have one here because it happens to plays a tune called "Rain-Tree," which is the same name as our restaurant.
My friends just gave me one of these today, as a gift.
"Rain-Tree"... huh.
You came here with Kaidô-kun last year for your birthday, right?
KLAK
KLAK
Yes, that's right.
Just us two, because you couldn't make it, Papa.
Kaidô-san...
...Papa's executive assistant.

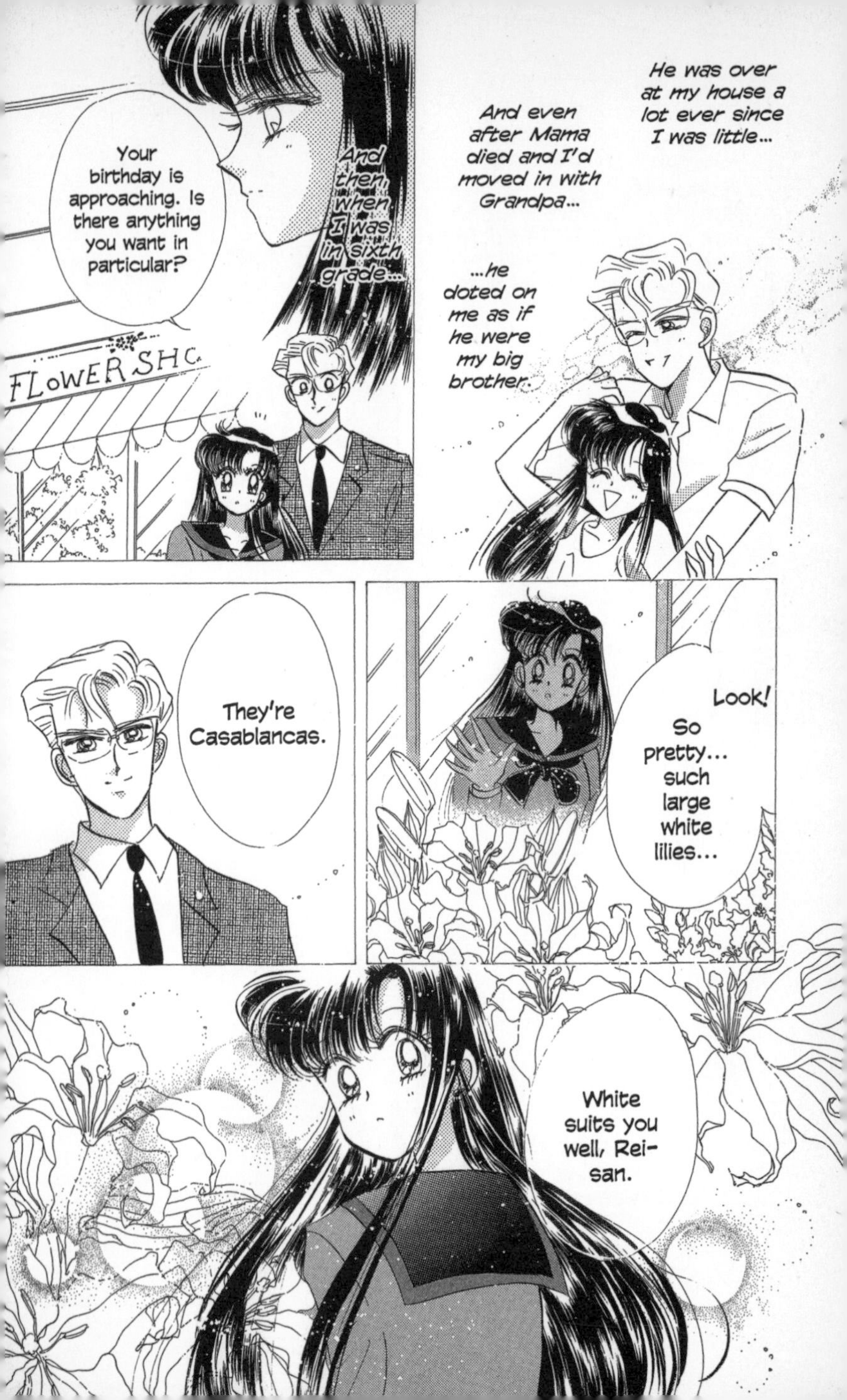
He was over at my house a lot ever since I was little...
And even after Mama died and I'd moved in with Grandpa...
...he doted on me as if he were my big brother.
And then, when I was in sixth grade...
Your birthday is approaching. Is there anything you want in particular?
FLOWER SH
Look! So pretty... such large white lilies...
They're Casablancas.
White suits you well, Rei-san.

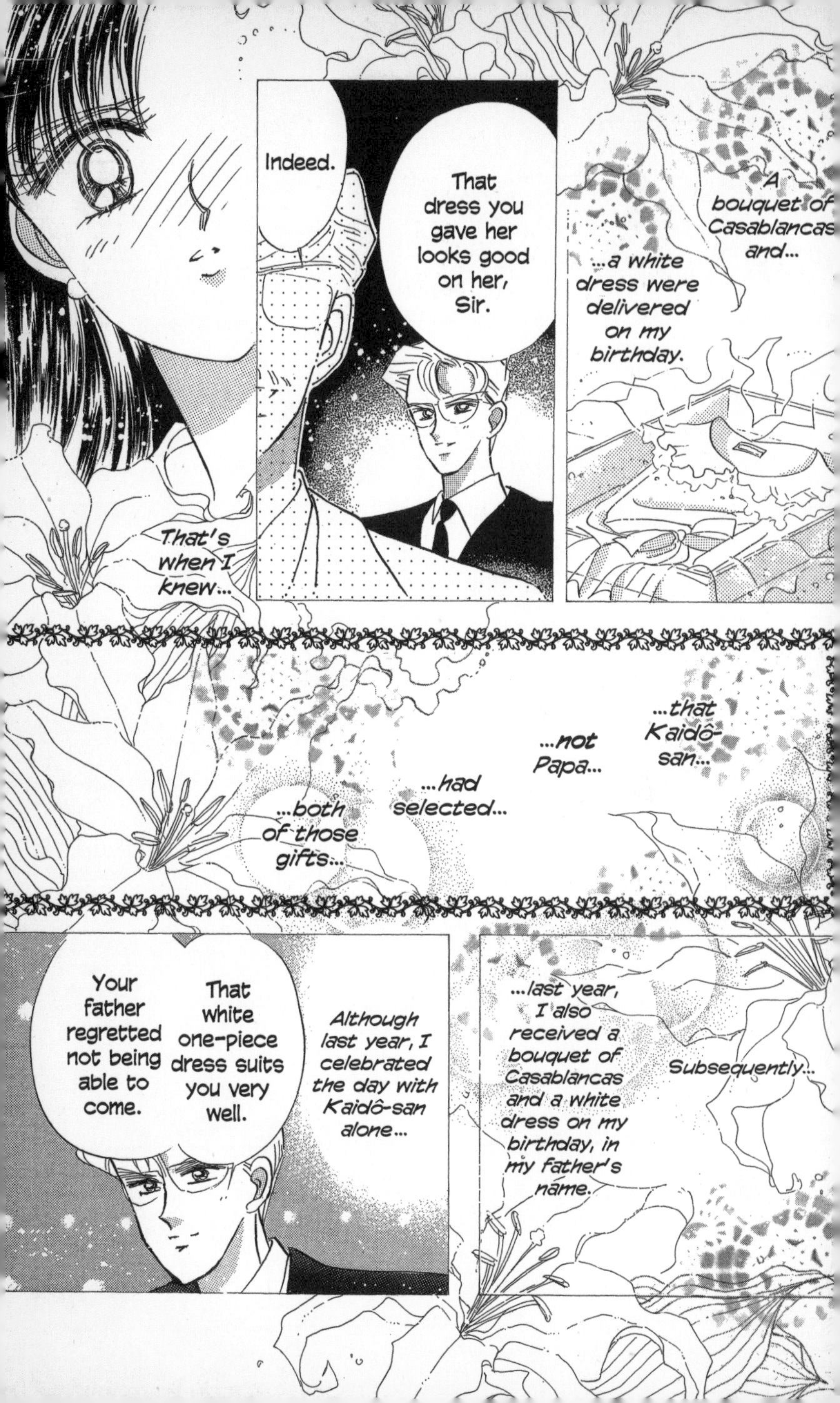
A bouquet of Casablancas and...
...a white dress were delivered on my birthday.
That dress you gave her looks good on her, Sir.
Indeed.
That's when I knew...
...that Kaidô-san...
...not Papa...
...had selected...
...both of those gifts...
Subsequently...
...last year, I also received a bouquet of Casablancas and a white dress on my birthday, in my father's name.
Although last year, I celebrated the day with Kaidô-san alone...
That white one-piece dress suits you very well.
Your father regretted not being able to come.

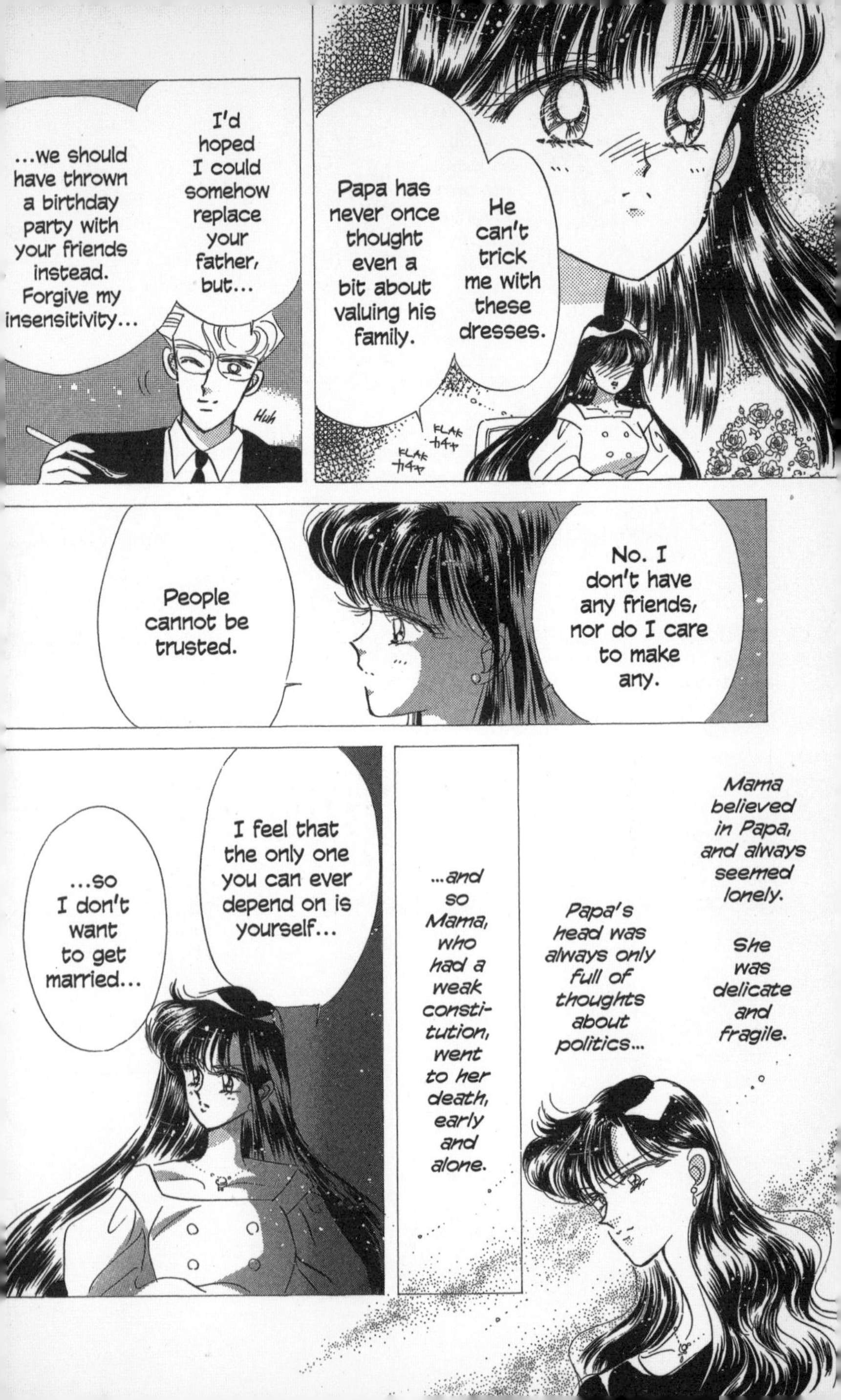
...
Papa has never once thought even a bit about valuing his family.
He can't trick me with these dresses.
FLAK
FLAK
I'd hoped I could somehow replace your father, but...
...we should have thrown a birthday party with your friends instead. Forgive my insensitivity...
Huh
No. I don't have any friends, nor do I care to make any.
People cannot be trusted.
Mama believed in Papa, and always seemed lonely.
She was delicate and fragile.
Papa's head was always only full of thoughts about politics...
...and so Mama, who had a weak constitution, went to her death, early and alone.
I feel that the only one you can ever depend on is yourself...
...so I don't want to get married...

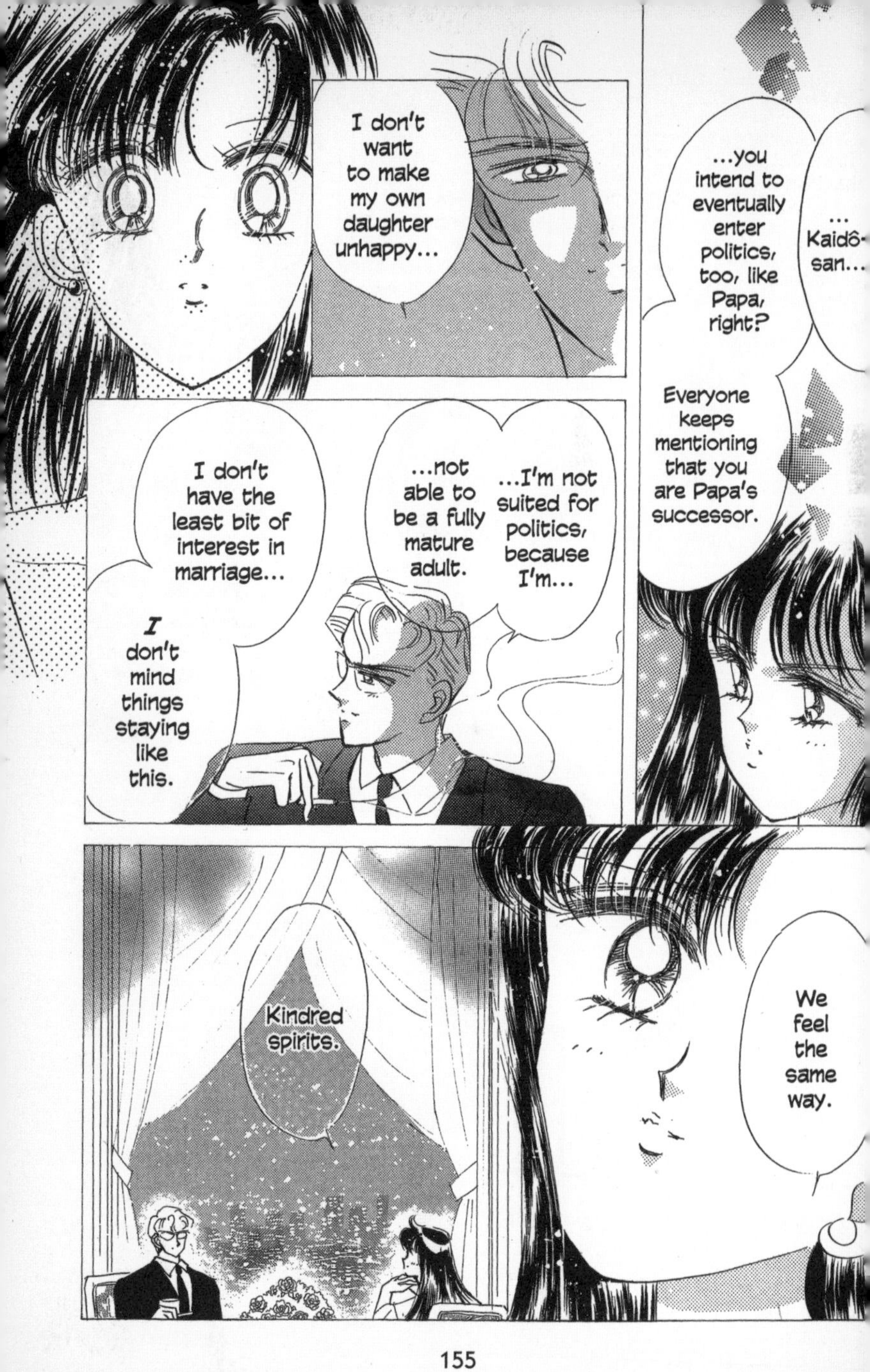

... Kaidô-san...
...you intend to eventually enter politics, too, like Papa, right?
Everyone keeps mentioning that you are Papa's successor.
I don't want to make my own daughter unhappy...
...I'm not suited for politics, because I'm...
...not able to be a fully mature adult.
I don't have the least bit of interest in marriage...
I don't mind things staying like this.
We feel the same way.
Kindred spirits.

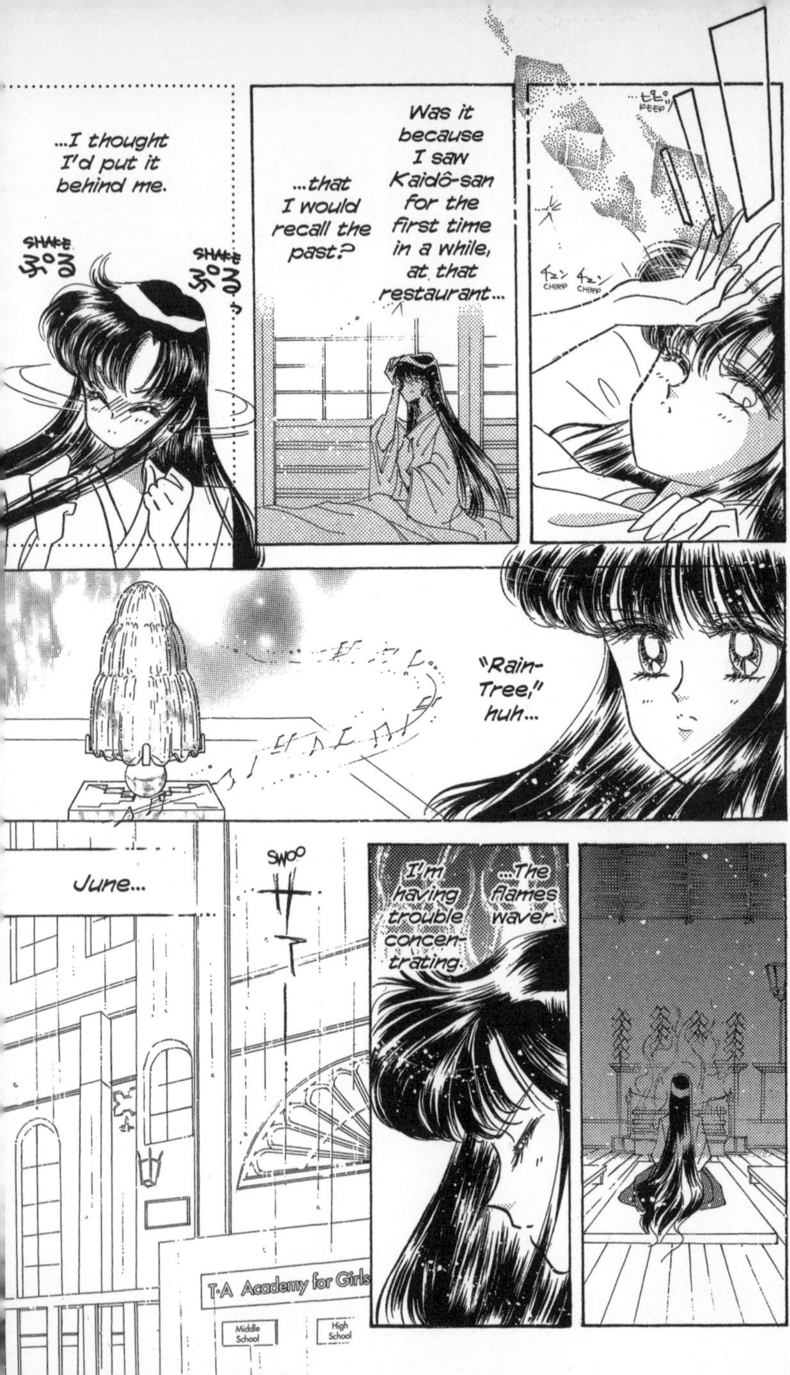

...ピピ
PEEP
チュン CHIRP
チュン CHIRP
Was it because I saw Kaidô-san for the first time in a while, at that restaurant...
...that I would recall the past?
...I thought I'd put it behind me.
SHAKE ぷる
SHAKE ぷる
"Rain-Tree," huh...
...The flames waver.
I'm having trouble concentrating.
SWOO サー
June...
T·A Academy for Girls
Middle School
High School

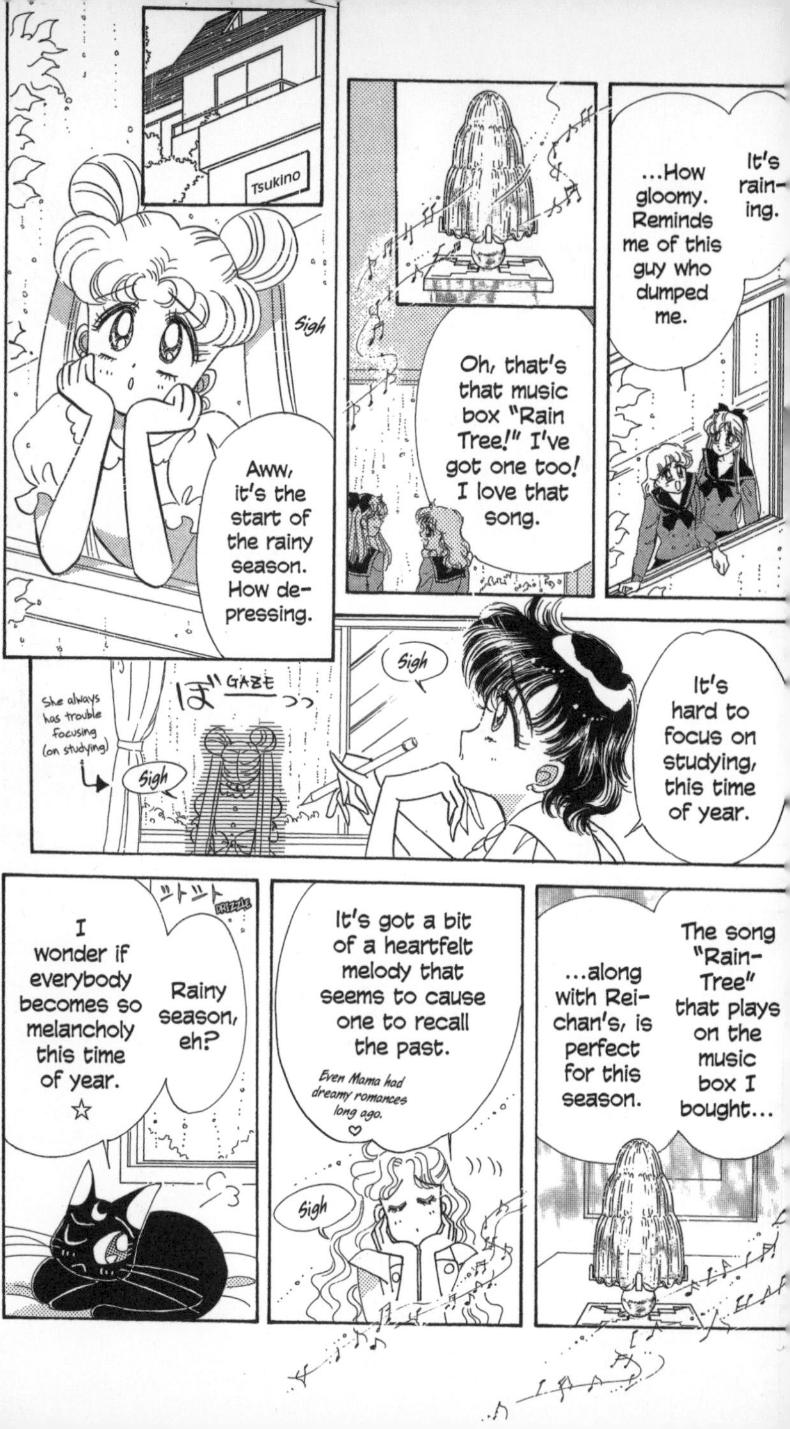

It's rain-ing.
...How gloomy. Reminds me of this guy who dumped me.
Oh, that's that music box "Rain Tree!" I've got one too! I love that song.
Tsukino
Sigh
Aww, it's the start of the rainy season. How de-pressing.
It's hard to focus on studying, this time of year.
Sigh
ぼ" GAZE っっ
Sigh
She always has trouble focusing (on studying)
The song "Rain-Tree" that plays on the music box I bought...
...along with Rei-chan's, is perfect for this season.
It's got a bit of a heartfelt melody that seems to cause one to recall the past.
Even Mama had dreamy romances long ago. ♡
Sigh
ツトツト DRIZZLE
Rainy season, eh?
I wonder if everybody becomes so melancholy this time of year. ☆

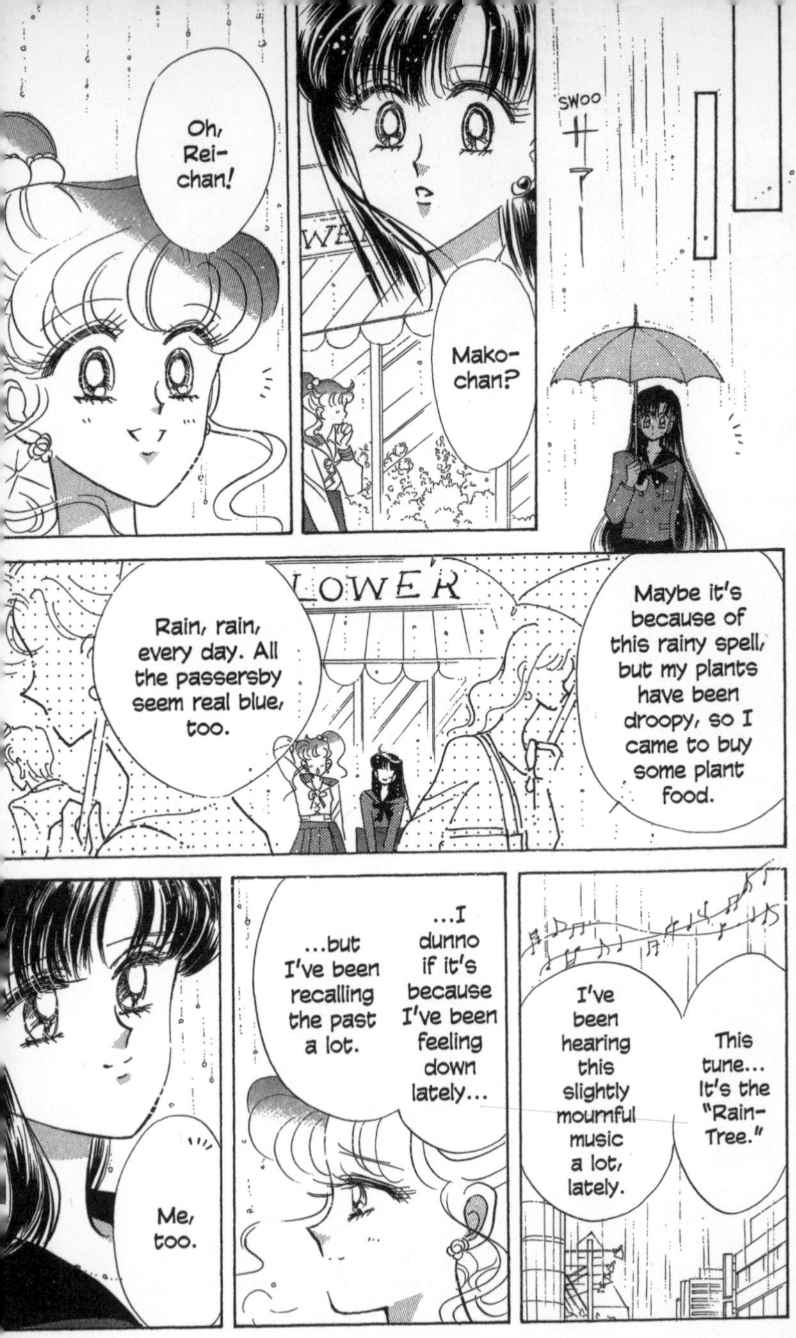
SWOO
Mako-chan?
Oh, Rei-chan!
Maybe it's because of this rainy spell, but my plants have been droopy, so I came to buy some plant food.
LOWER
Rain, rain, every day. All the passersby seem real blue, too.
This tune... It's the "Rain-Tree."
I've been hearing this slightly mournful music a lot, lately.
...I dunno if it's because I've been feeling down lately...
...but I've been recalling the past a lot.
Me, too.

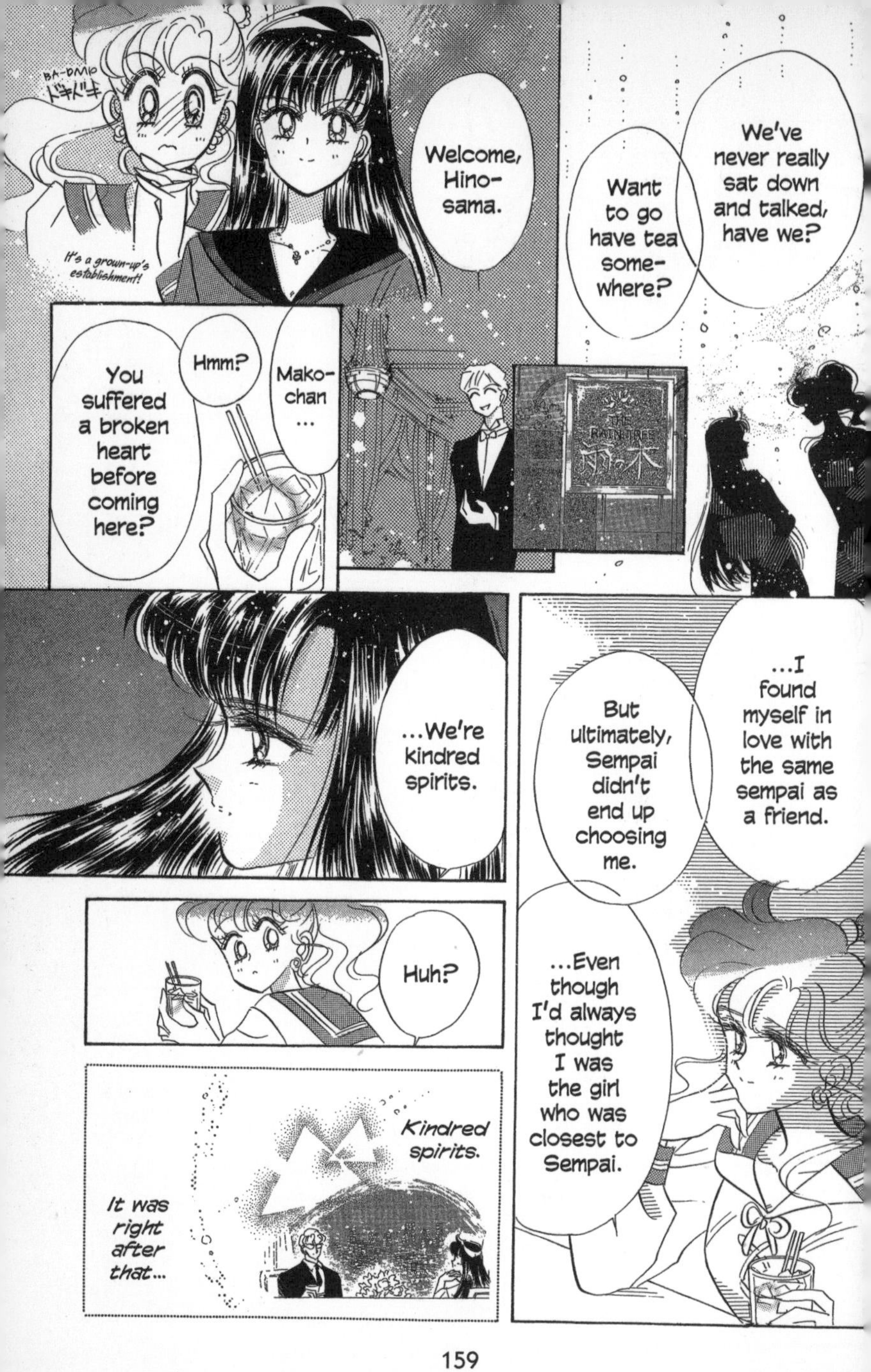
We've never really sat down and talked, have we?
Want to go have tea somewhere?
THE RAIN TREE
雨の木
Welcome, Hino-sama.
BA-DMP
ドキドキ
It's a grown-up's establishment!
Mako-chan...
Hmm?
You suffered a broken heart before coming here?
...I found myself in love with the same sempai as a friend.
But ultimately, Sempai didn't end up choosing me.
...Even though I'd always thought I was the girl who was closest to Sempai.
...We're kindred spirits.
Huh?
Kindred spirits.
It was right after that...

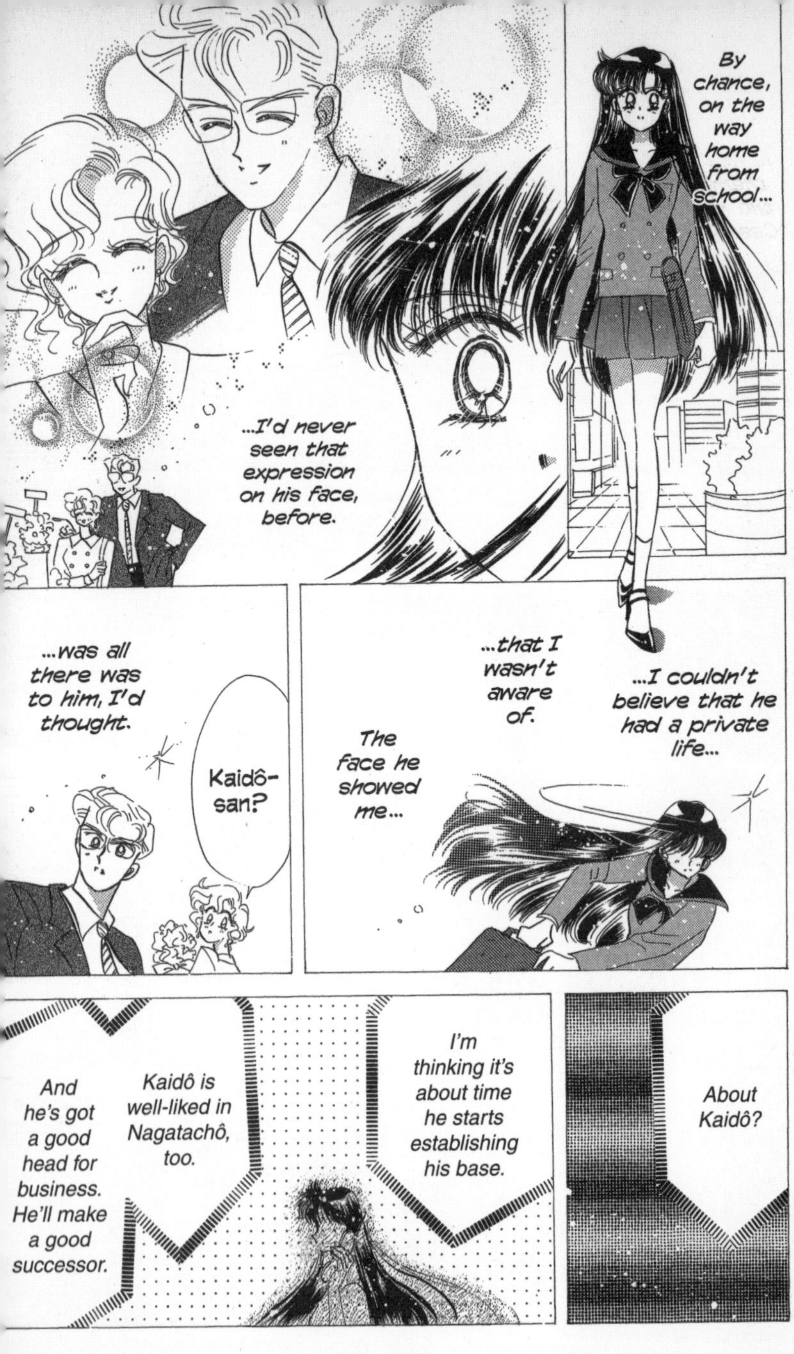
By chance, on the way home from school...
...I'd never seen that expression on his face, before.
...I couldn't believe that he had a private life...
...that I wasn't aware of.
The face he showed me...
...was all there was to him, I'd thought.
Kaidô-san?
About Kaidô?
I'm thinking it's about time he starts establishing his base.
Kaidô is well-liked in Nagatachô, too.
And he's got a good head for business. He'll make a good successor.

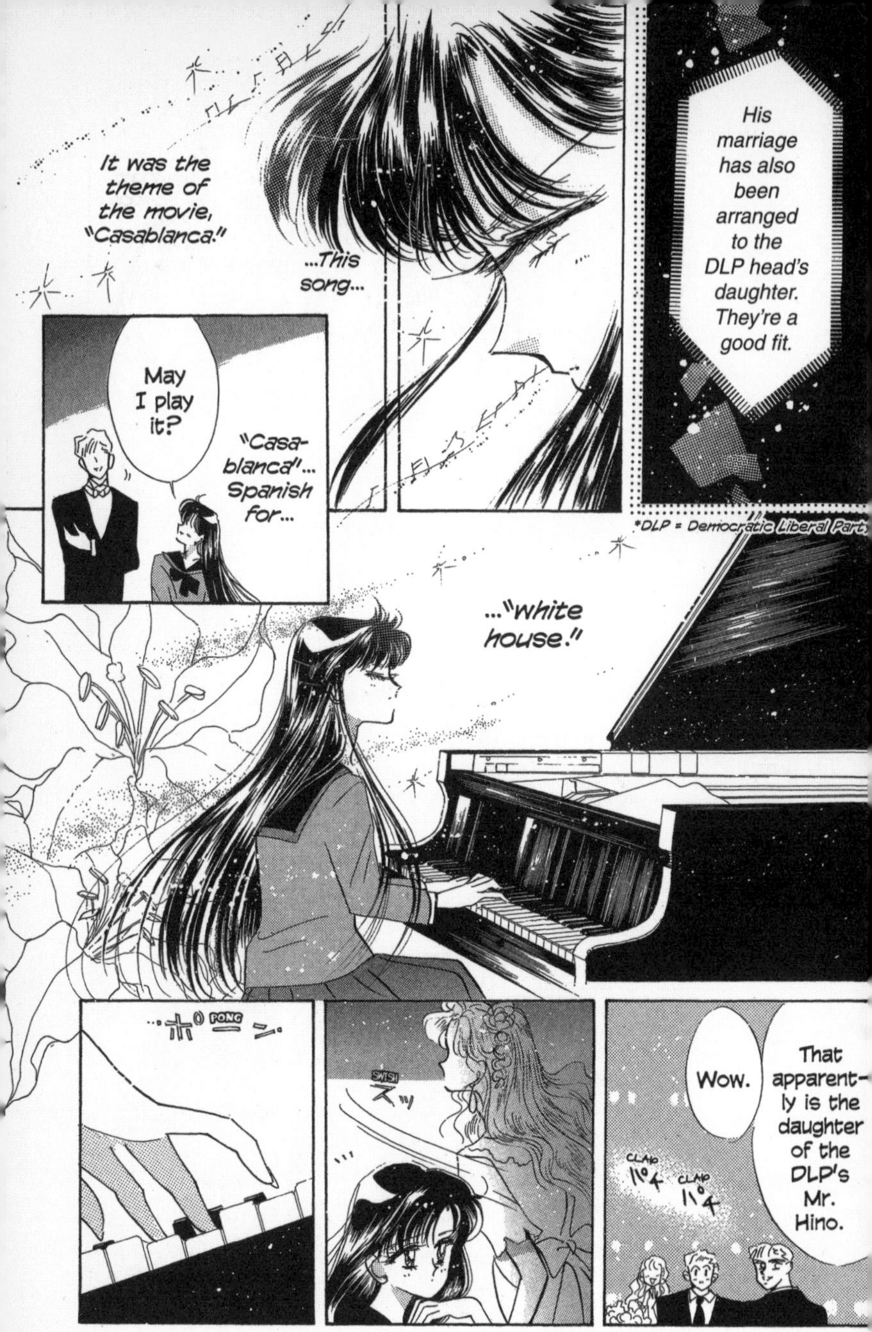
His marriage has also been arranged to the DLP head's daughter. They're a good fit.
...This song...
It was the theme of the movie, "Casablanca."
May I play it?
"Casablanca"... Spanish for...
*DLP = Democratic Liberal Part
..."white house."
That apparently is the daughter of the DLP's Mr. Hino.
Wow.
CLAP
CLAP
SWISH
PONG

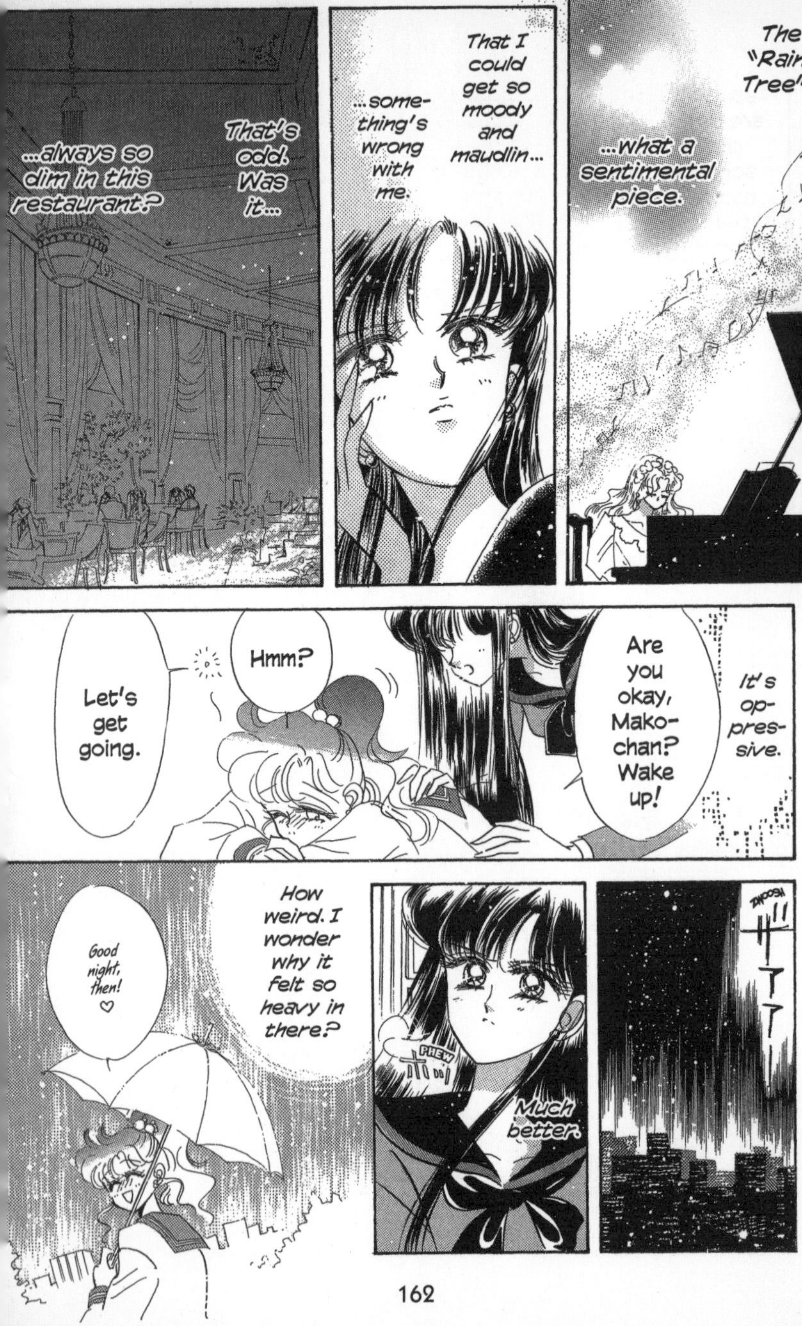
The "Rain-Tree"...
...what a sentimental piece.
That I could get so moody and maudlin...
...some-thing's wrong with me.
That's odd. Was it...
...always so dim in this restaurant?
It's op-pres-sive.
Are you okay, Mako-chan? Wake up!
Hmm?
Let's get going.
ZWOOSH
PHEW
Much better.
How weird. I wonder why it felt so heavy in there?
Good night, then! ♡

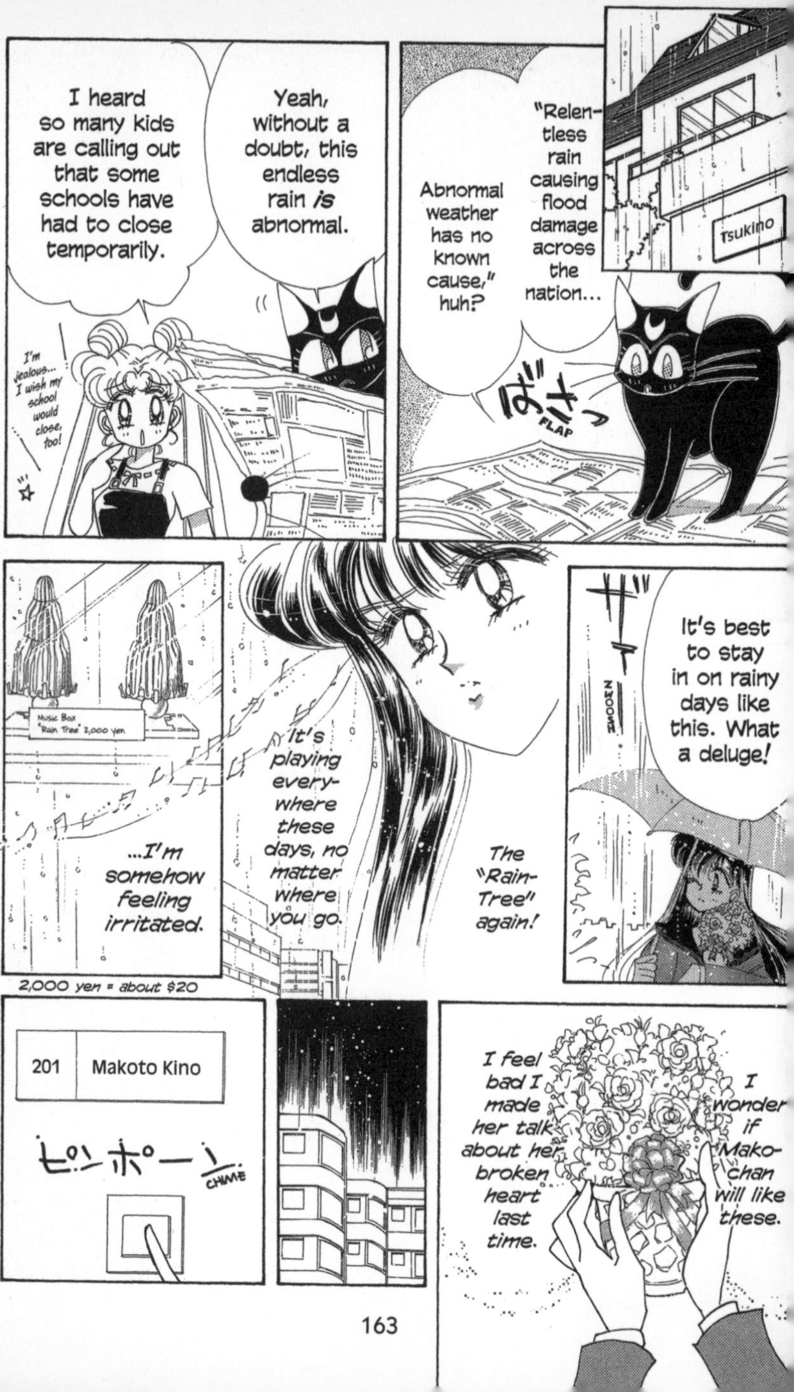
Tsukino
"Relentless rain causing flood damage across the nation...
Abnormal weather has no known cause," huh?
ばさっ
FLAP
Yeah, without a doubt, this endless rain *is* abnormal.
I heard so many kids are calling out that some schools have had to close temporarily.
I'm jealous... I wish my school would close, too!
ザー
ZWOOSH
It's best to stay in on rainy days like this. What a deluge!
The "Rain-Tree" again!
It's playing everywhere these days, no matter where you go.
...I'm somehow feeling irritated.
Music Box "Rain Tree" 2,000 yen
2,000 yen = about $20
I wonder if Mako-chan will like these.
I feel bad I made her talk about her broken heart last time.
201 Makoto Kino
ピンポーン
CHIME

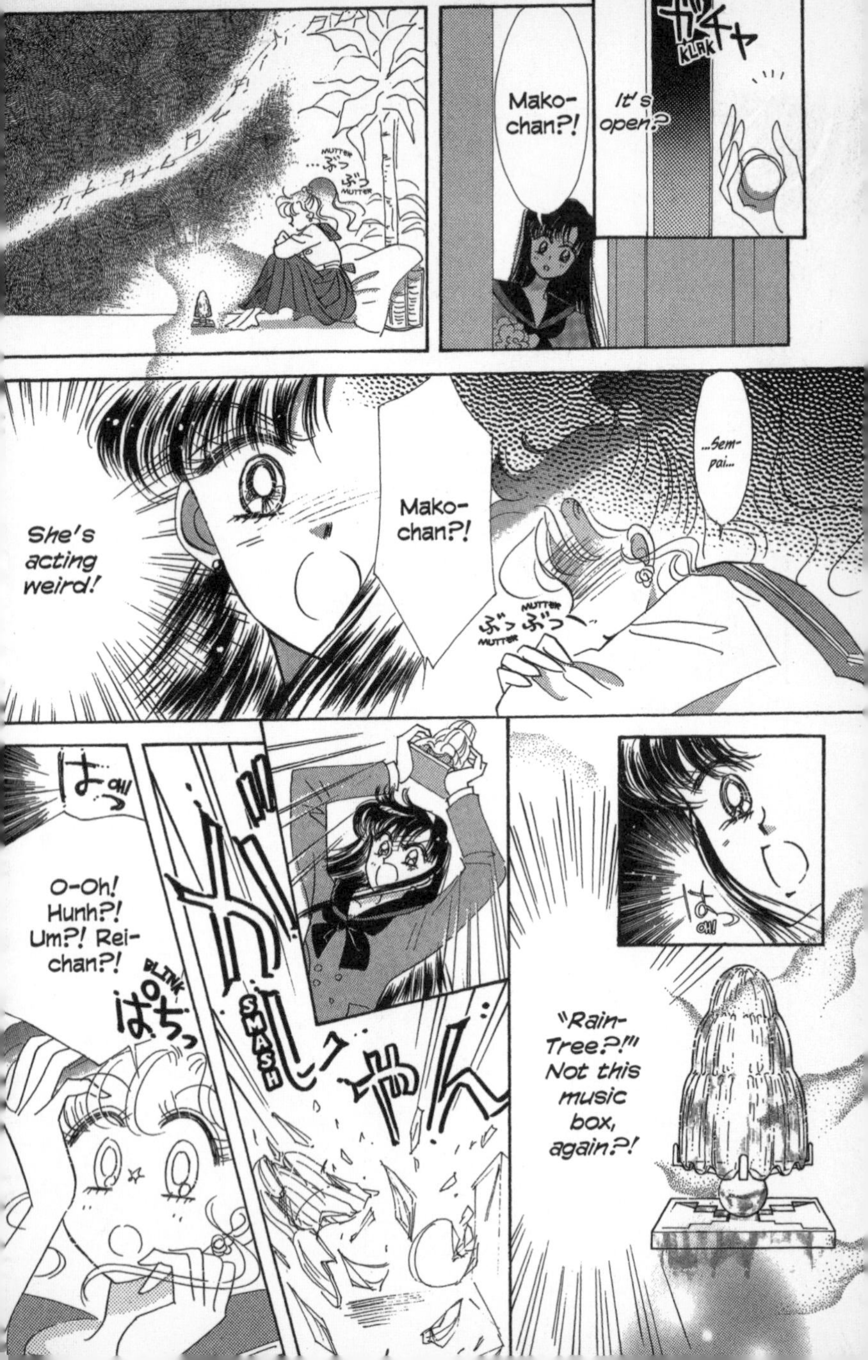
ガチャ
KLAK
It's open?
Mako-chan?!
MUTTER
...ぶつ ぶつ
MUTTER
...Sem-pai...
MUTTER
ぶつぶつ
MUTTER
Mako-chan?!
She's acting weird!
はっ
OH!
"Rain-Tree?!" Not this music box, again?!
SMASH
はっ
OH!
O-Oh! Hunh?! Um?! Rei-chan?!
BLINK
ぱちっ

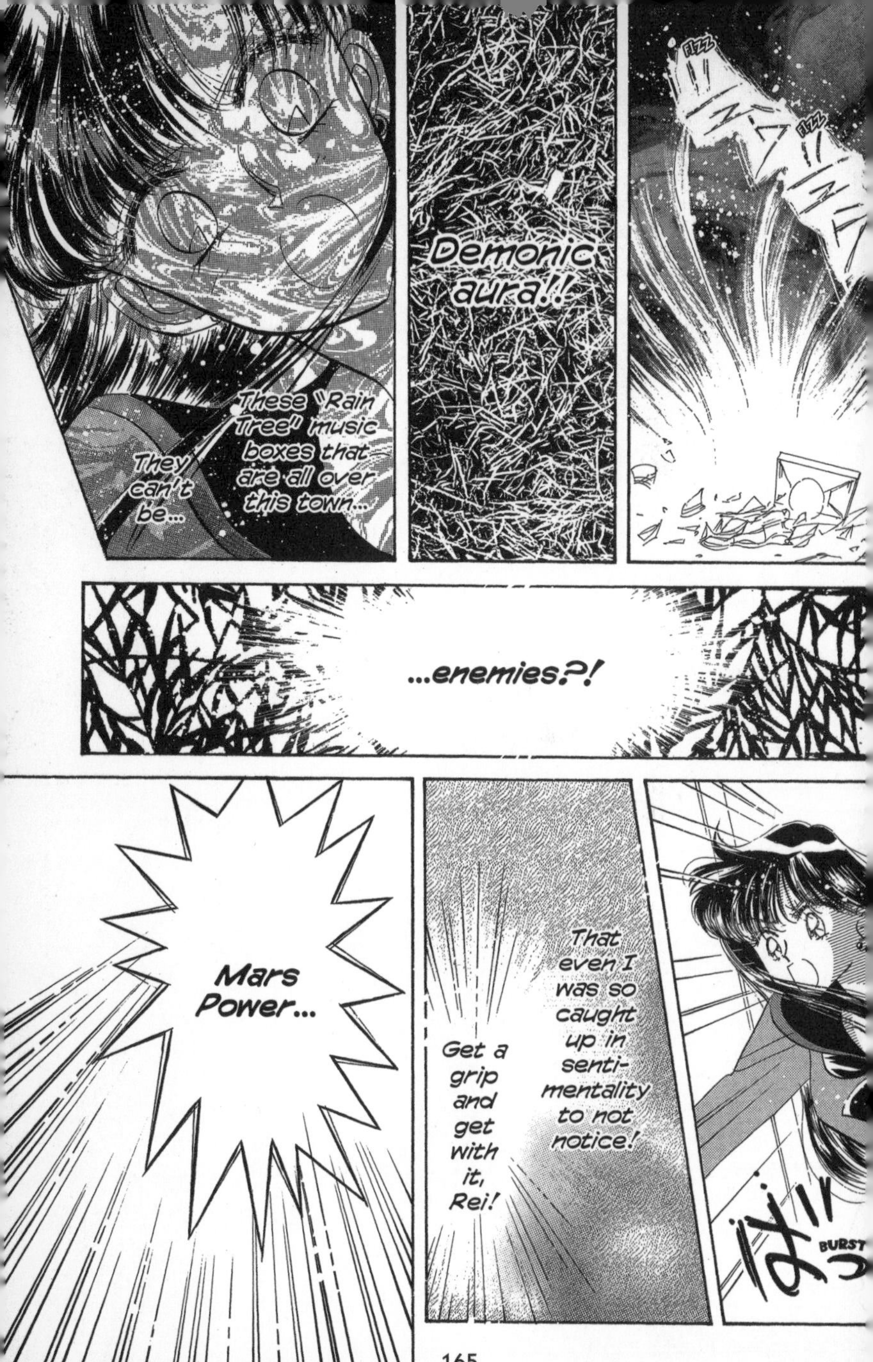
FIZZ
FIZZ
Demonic aura!!
These "Rain Tree" music boxes that are all over this town...
They can't be...
...enemies?!
BURST
That even I was so caught up in senti-mentality to not notice!
Get a grip and get with it, Rei!
Mars Power...

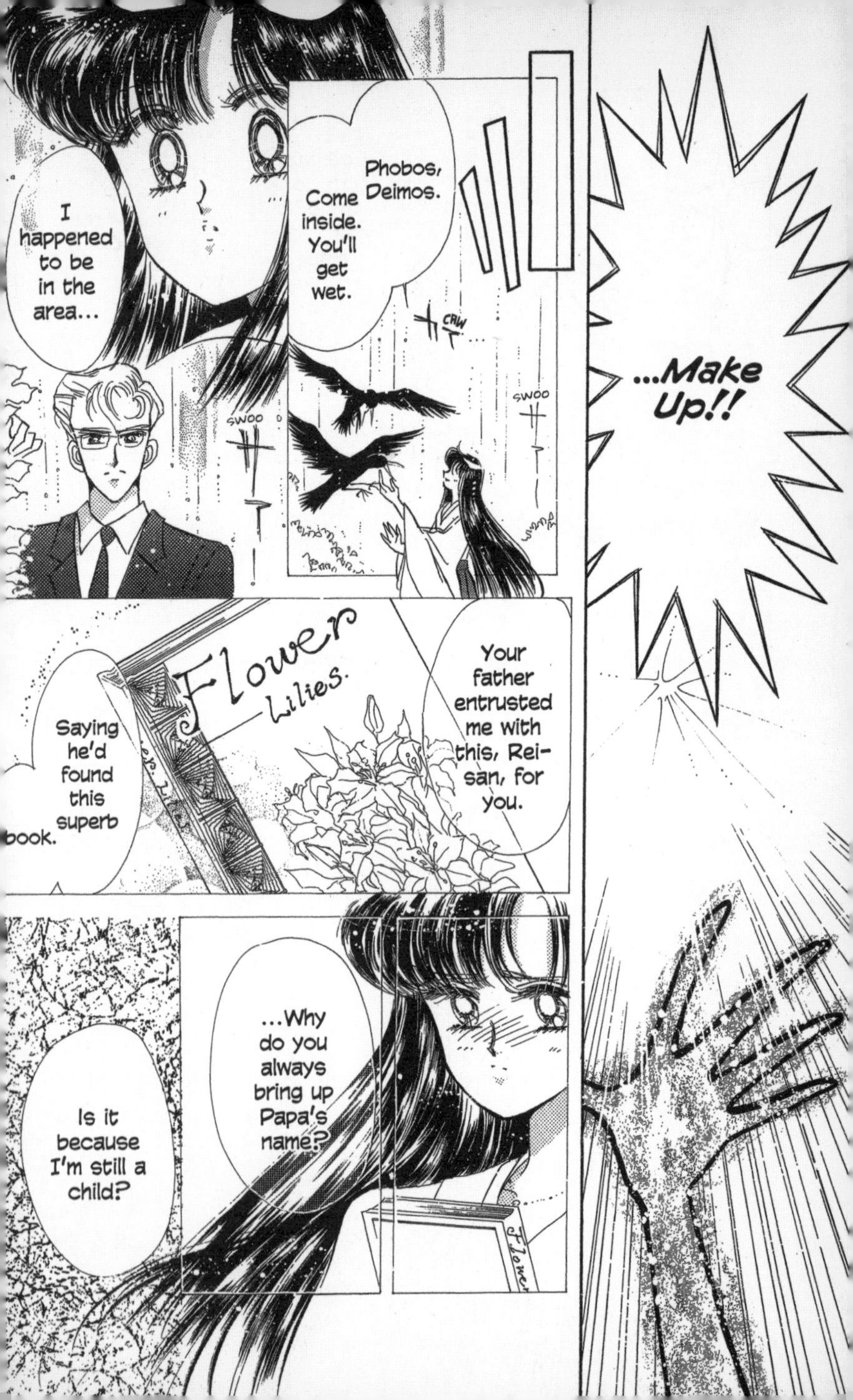
...Make Up!!
Phobos, Deimos.
Come inside. You'll get wet.
CAW
SWOO
I happened to be in the area...
SWOO
Your father entrusted me with this, Rei-san, for you.
Flower
Lilies.
Saying he'd found this superb book.
...Why do you always bring up Papa's name?
Is it because I'm still a child?

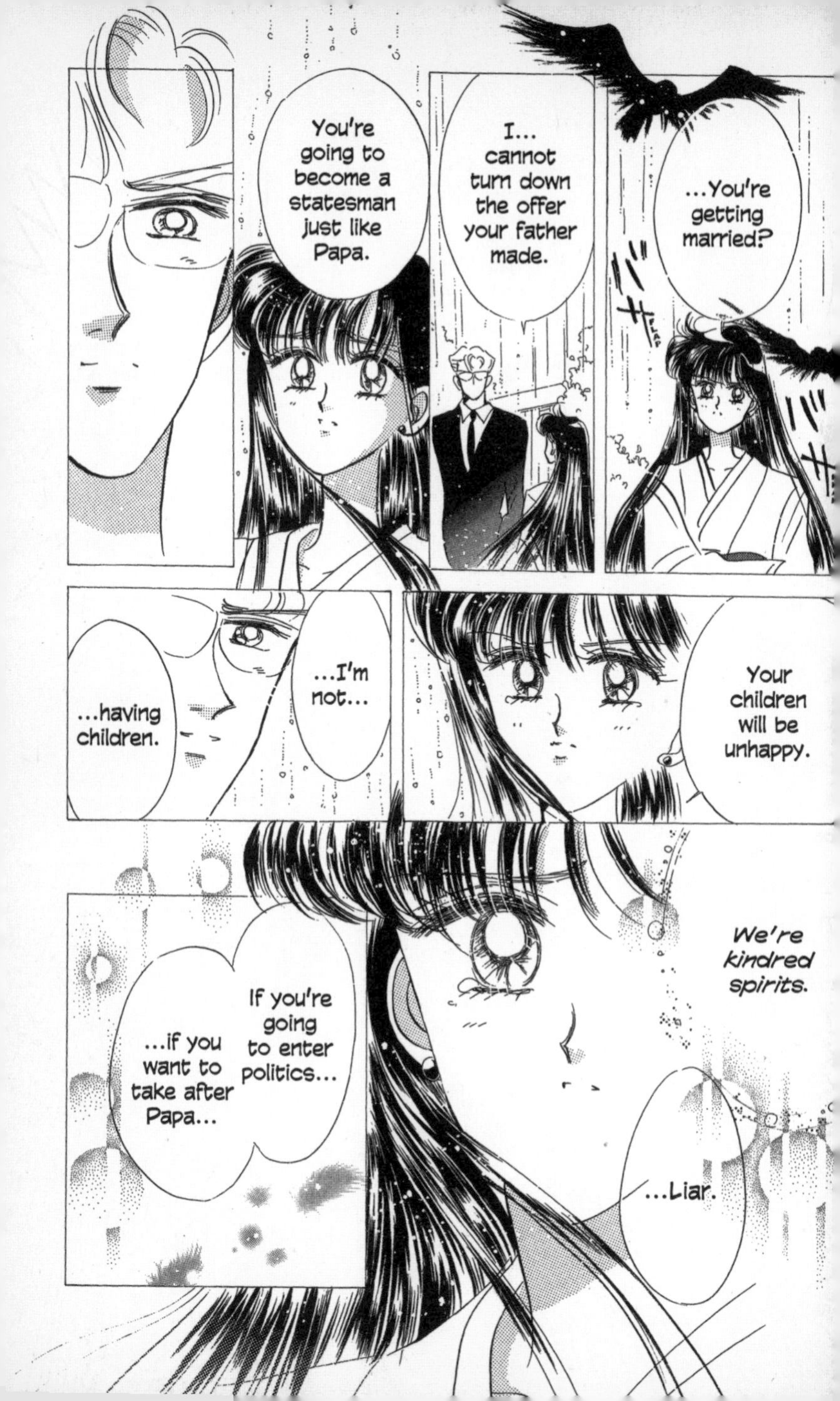
...You're getting married?
バサ
FLAP
バサ
I... cannot turn down the offer your father made.
You're going to become a statesman just like Papa.
Your children will be unhappy.
...I'm not...
...having children.
We're kindred spirits.
If you're going to enter politics...
...if you want to take after Papa...
...Liar.

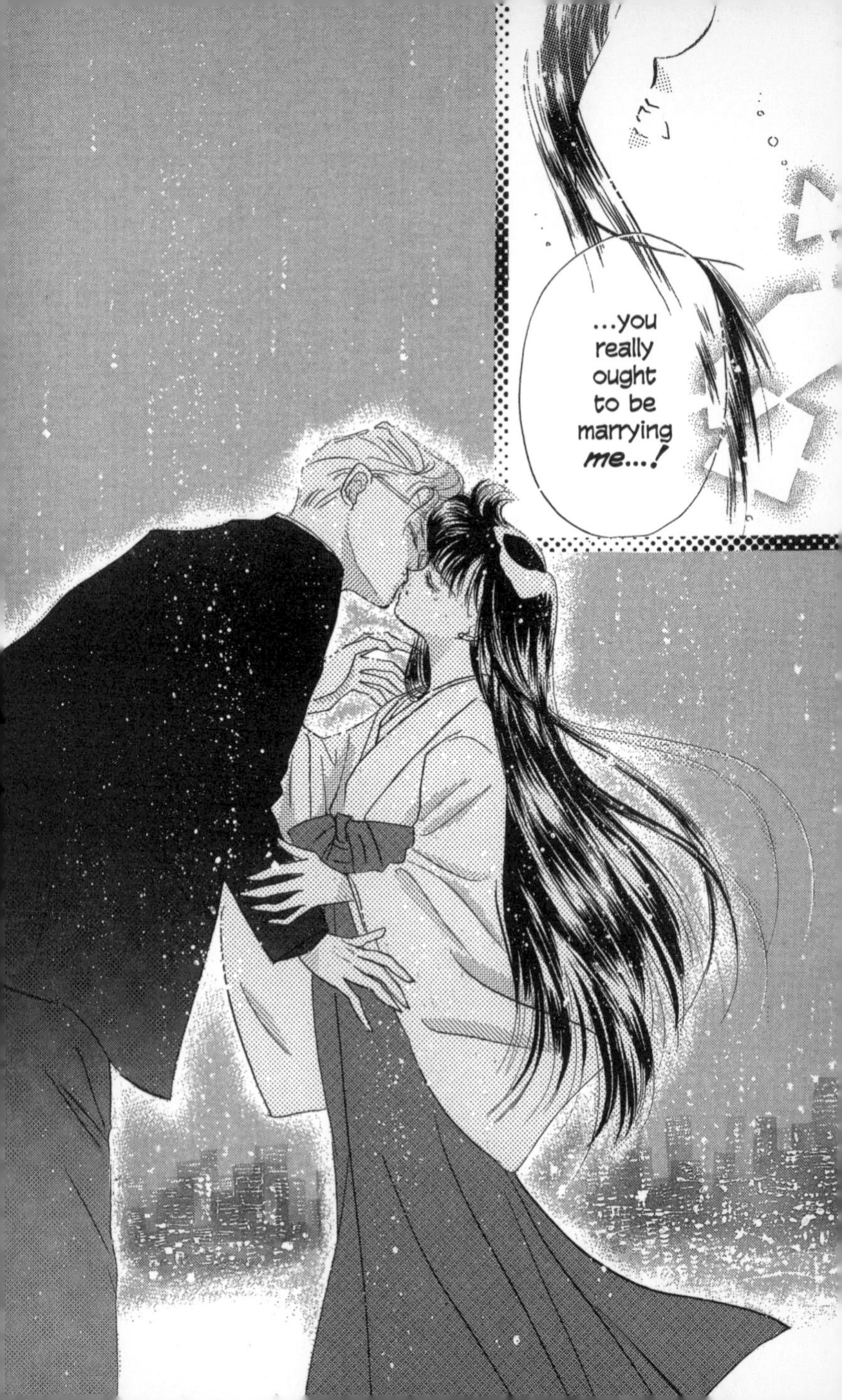
...you really ought to be marrying *me*...!

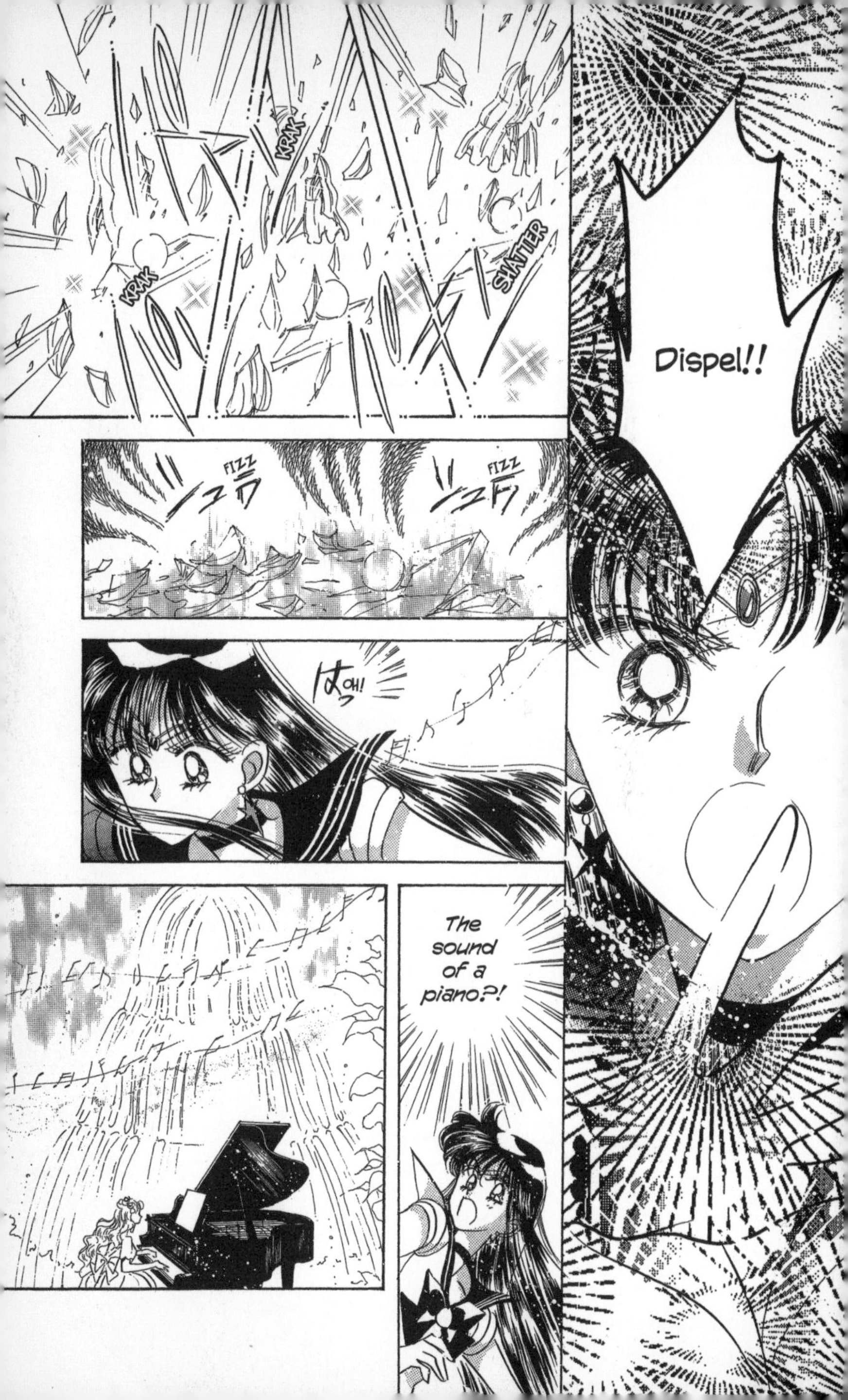
Dispel!!
SHATTER
KRAK
KRAK
FIZZ
FIZZ
はっ GAH!
The sound of a piano?!

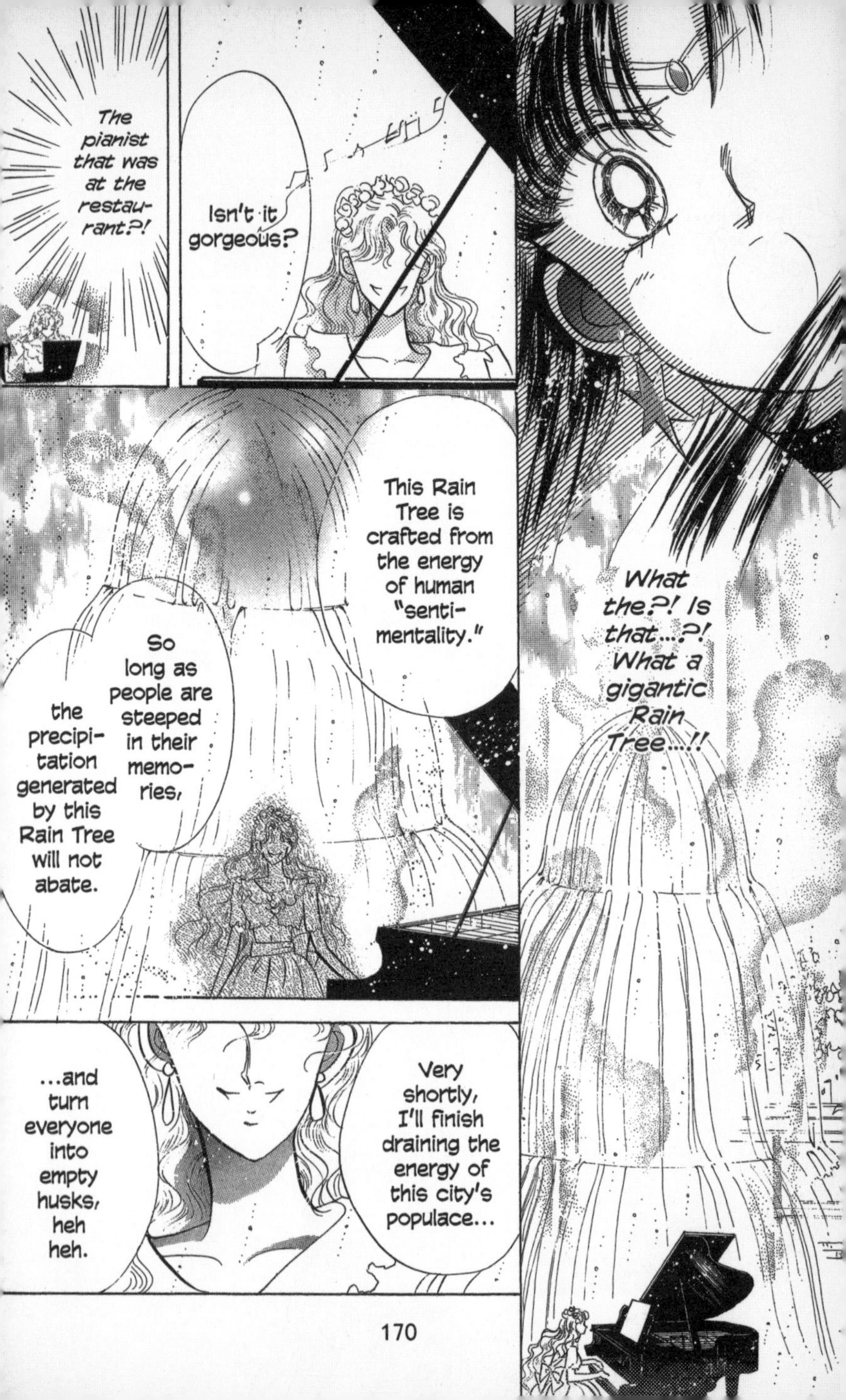
What the?! Is that...?! What a gigantic Rain Tree...!!
Isn't it gorgeous?
The pianist that was at the restaurant?!
This Rain Tree is crafted from the energy of human "sentimentality."
So long as people are steeped in their memories,
the precipitation generated by this Rain Tree will not abate.
Very shortly, I'll finish draining the energy of this city's populace...
...and turn everyone into empty husks, heh heh.

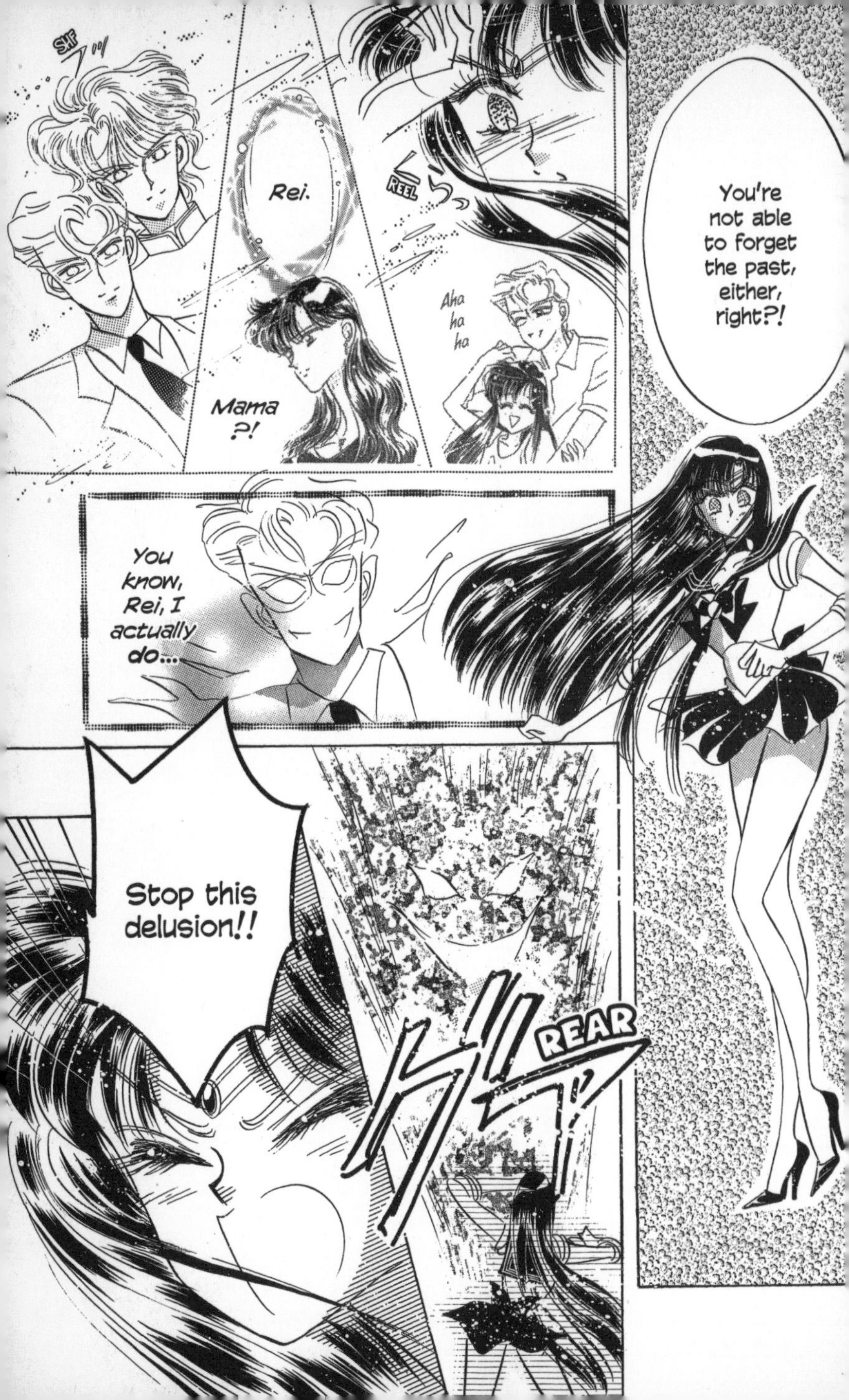
You're not able to forget the past, either, right?!
REEL
Aha ha ha
Rei.
Mama?!
SHF
You know, Rei, I actually do...
Stop this delusion!!
REAR

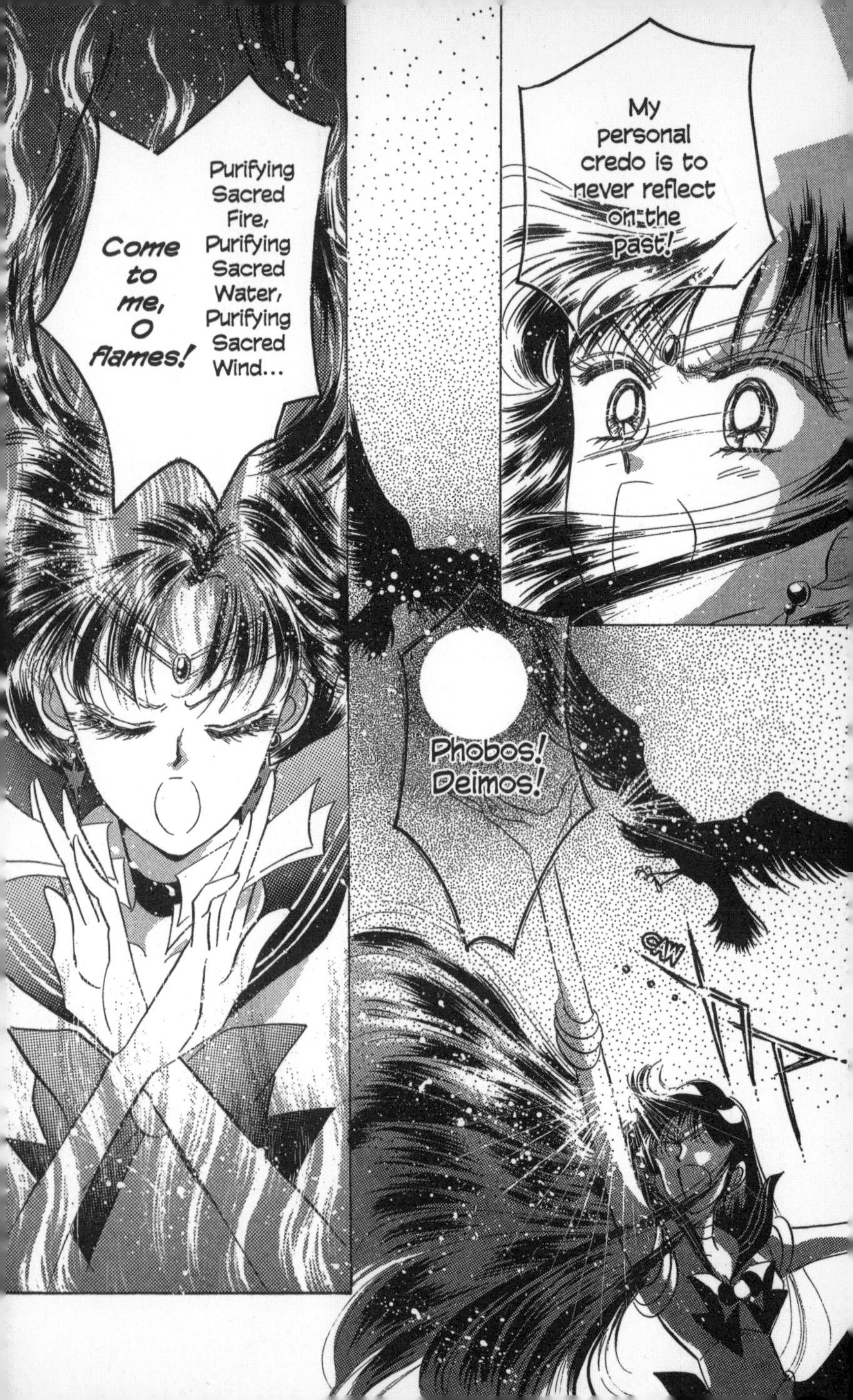
My personal credo is to never reflect on the past!
Phobos! Deimos!
CAW
Purifying Sacred Fire, Purifying Sacred Water, Purifying Sacred Wind...
Come to me, O flames!

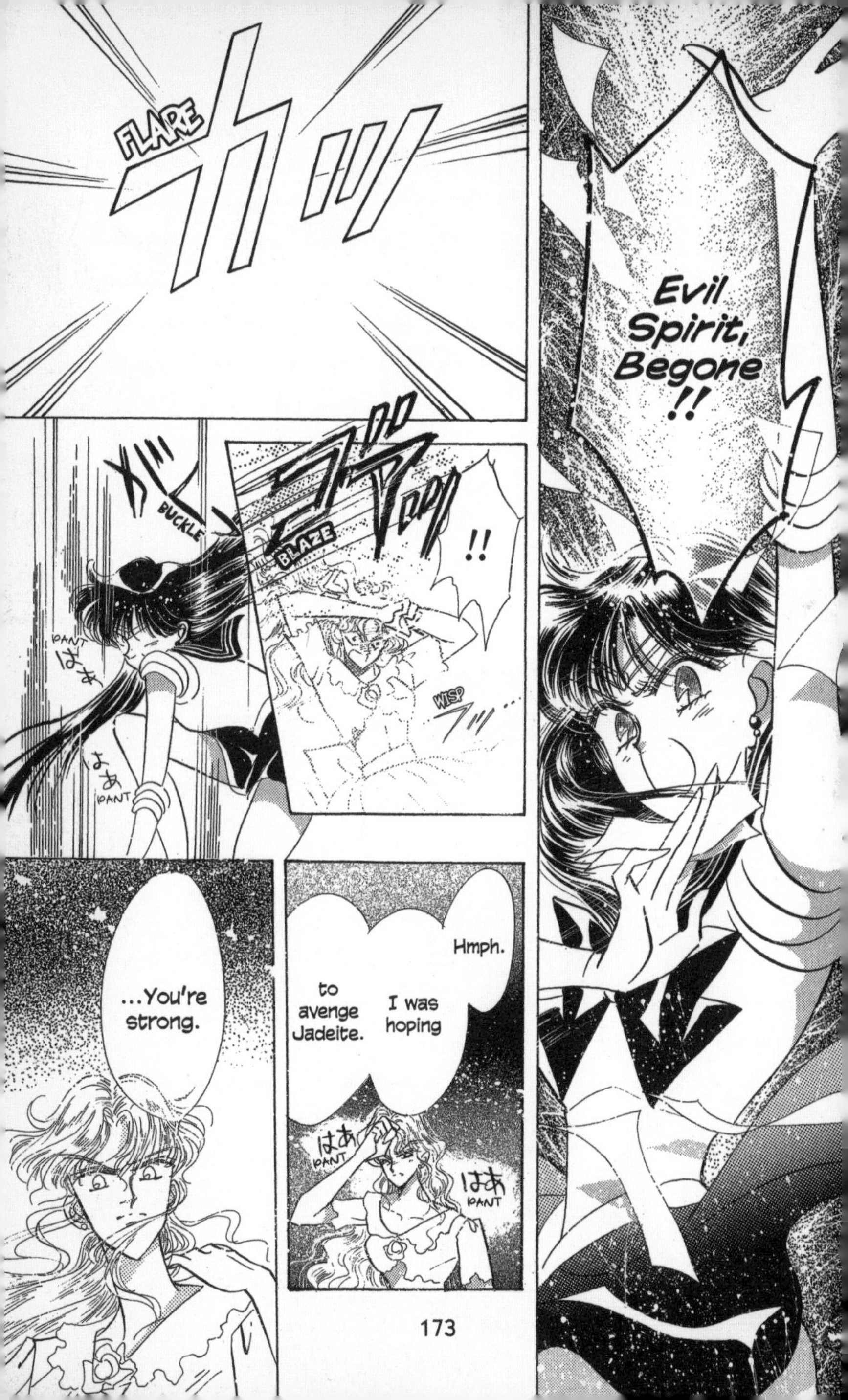
Evil Spirit, Begone!!
FLARE
BLAZE
!!
WISP
BUCKLE
はあ PANT
はあ PANT
Hmph.
I was hoping to avenge Jadeite.
はあ PANT
はあ PANT
...You're strong.

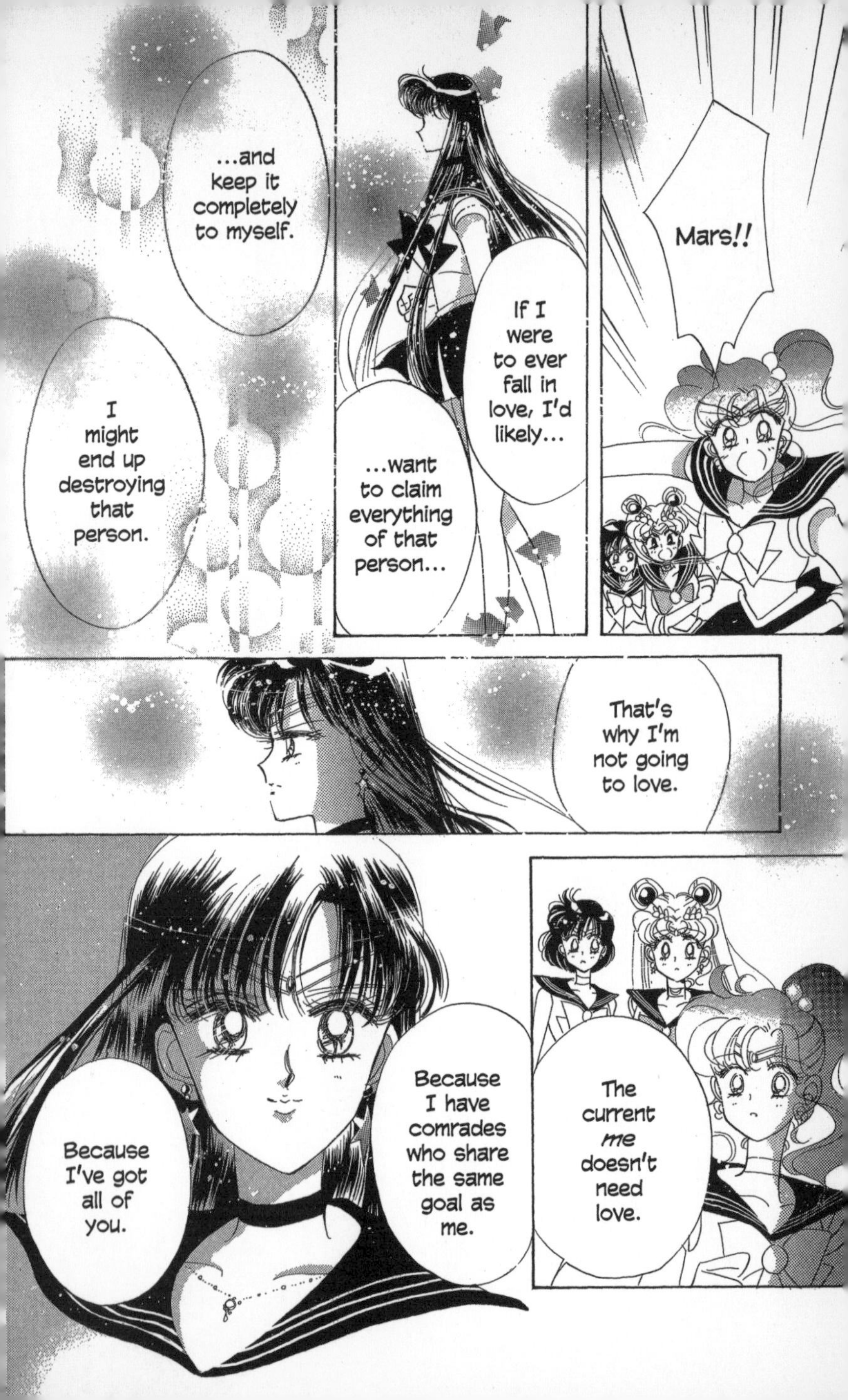
Mars!!
If I were to ever fall in love, I'd likely...
...want to claim everything of that person...
...and keep it completely to myself.
I might end up destroying that person.
That's why I'm not going to love.
The current *me* doesn't need love.
Because I have comrades who share the same goal as me.
Because I've got all of you.

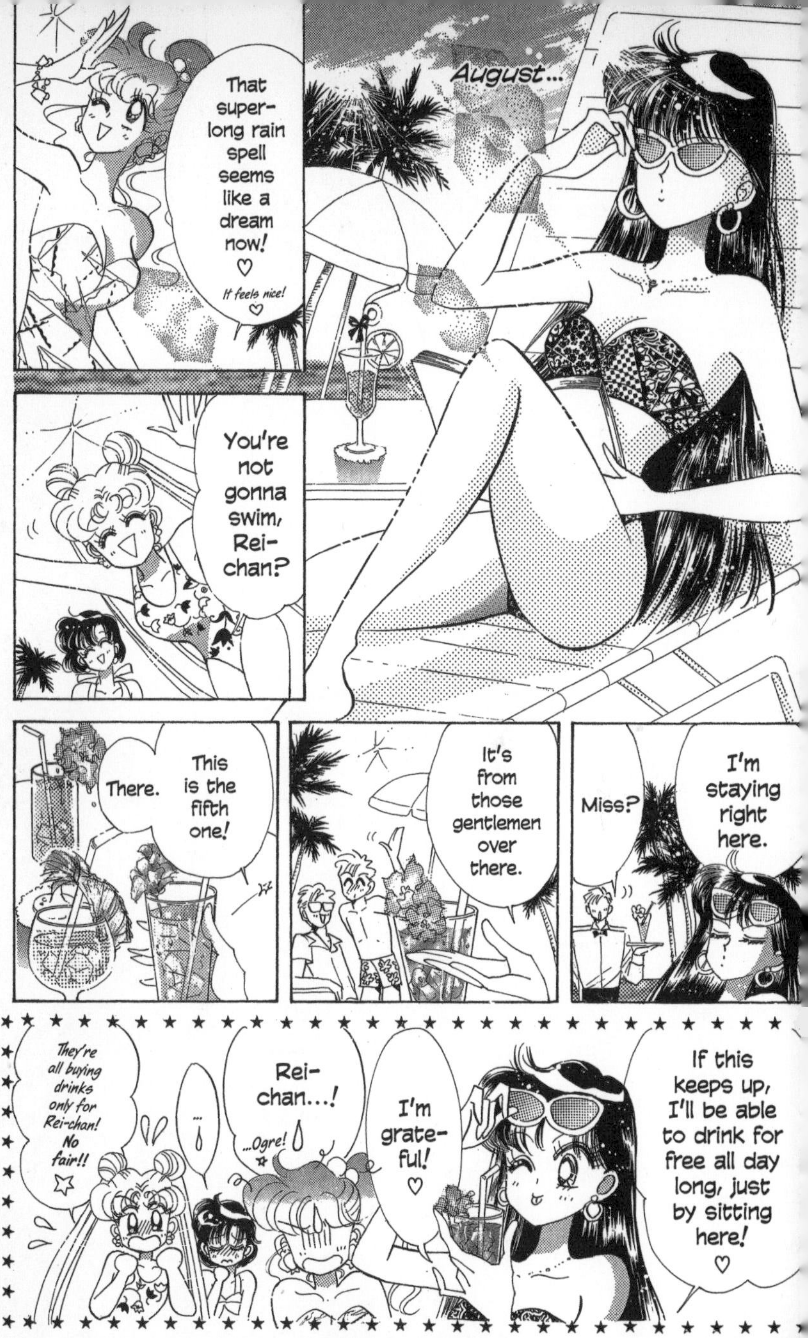
August...
That super-long rain spell seems like a dream now! ♡
It feels nice! ♡
You're not gonna swim, Rei-chan?
I'm staying right here.
Miss?
It's from those gentlemen over there.
This is the fifth one!
There.
If this keeps up, I'll be able to drink for free all day long, just by sitting here! ♡
I'm grateful! ♡
Rei-chan...!
...Ogre!
...
They're all buying drinks only for Rei-chan! No fair!!

• The End •

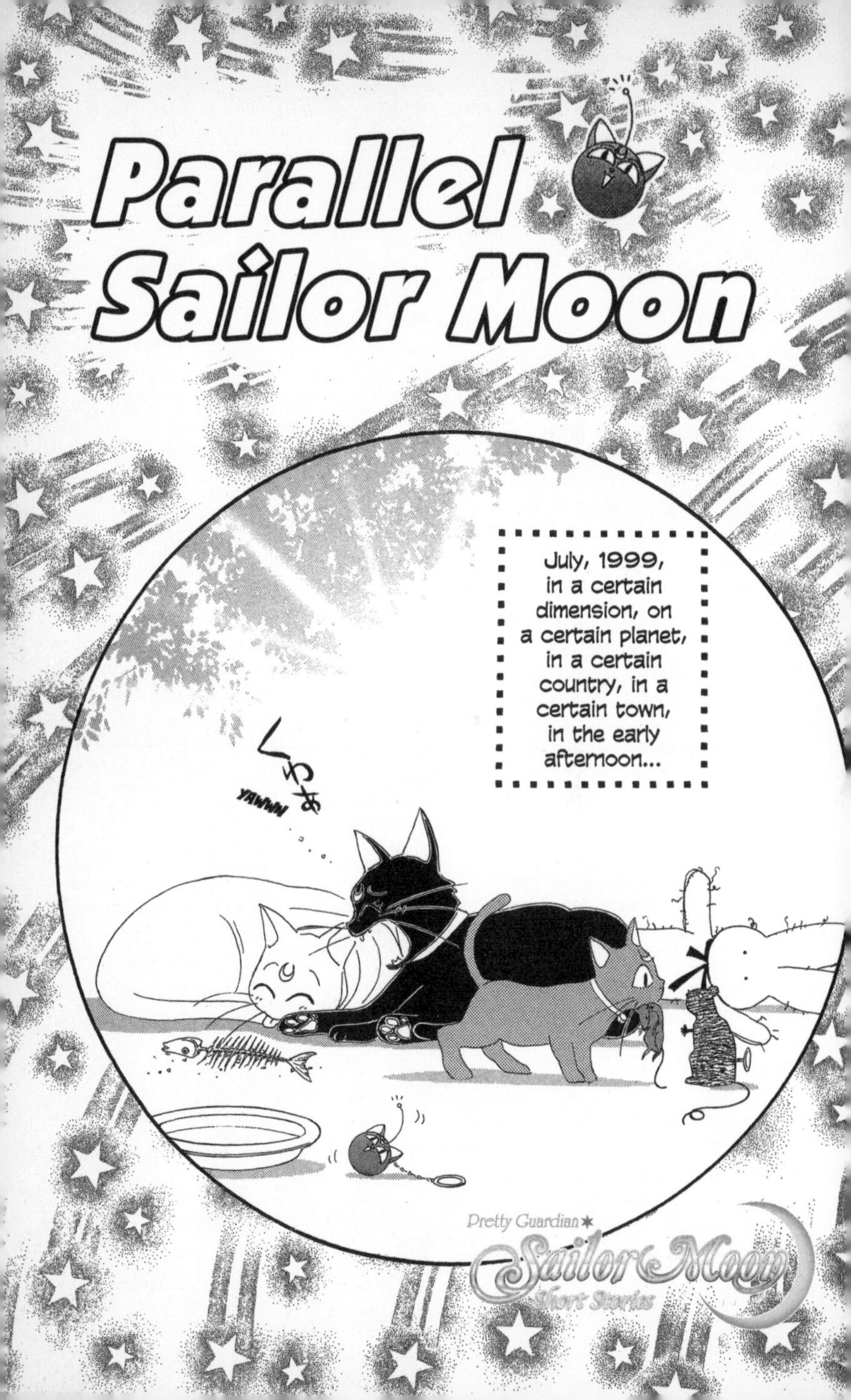
Parallel Sailor Moon
July, 1999, in a certain dimension, on a certain planet, in a certain country, in a certain town, in the early afternoon...
YAWWN
Pretty Guardian Sailor Moon Short Stories

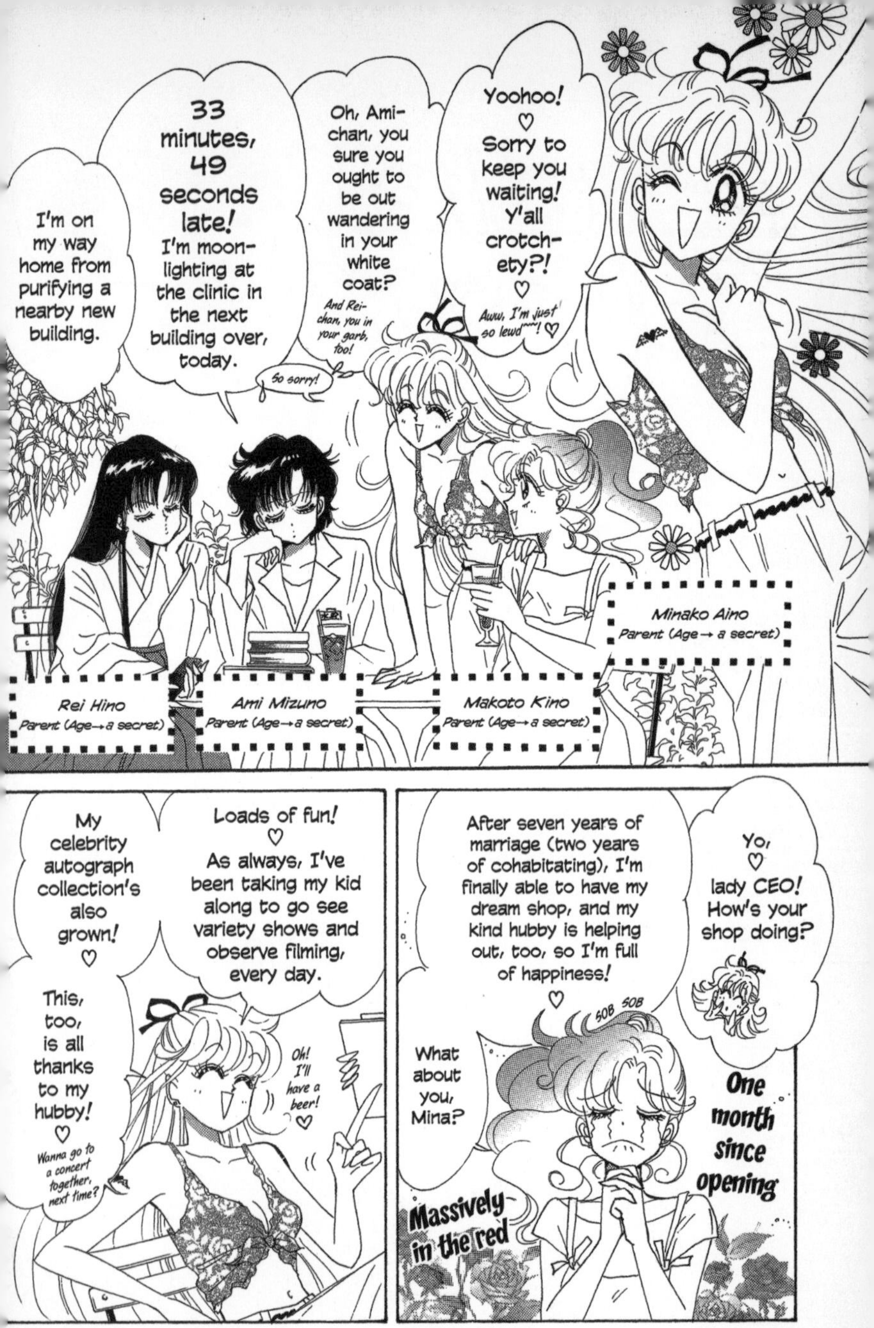
Yoohoo! ♡ Sorry to keep you waiting! Y'all crotchety?! ♡
Aww, I'm just so lewd~~! ♡
Oh, Ami-chan, you sure you ought to be out wandering in your white coat?
And Rei-chan, you in your garb, too!
33 minutes, 49 seconds late! I'm moonlighting at the clinic in the next building over, today.
So sorry!
I'm on my way home from purifying a nearby new building.
Minako Aino
Parent (Age → a secret)
Makoto Kino
Parent (Age → a secret)
Ami Mizuno
Parent (Age → a secret)
Rei Hino
Parent (Age → a secret)
Yo, ♡ lady CEO! How's your shop doing?
After seven years of marriage (two years of cohabitating), I'm finally able to have my dream shop, and my kind hubby is helping out, too, so I'm full of happiness! ♡
SOB SOB
What about you, Mina?
One month since opening
Massively in the red
Loads of fun! ♡ As always, I've been taking my kid along to go see variety shows and observe filming, every day.
My celebrity autograph collection's also grown! ♡
Oh! I'll have a beer! ♡
This, too, is all thanks to my hubby! ♡
Wanna go to a concert together, next time?

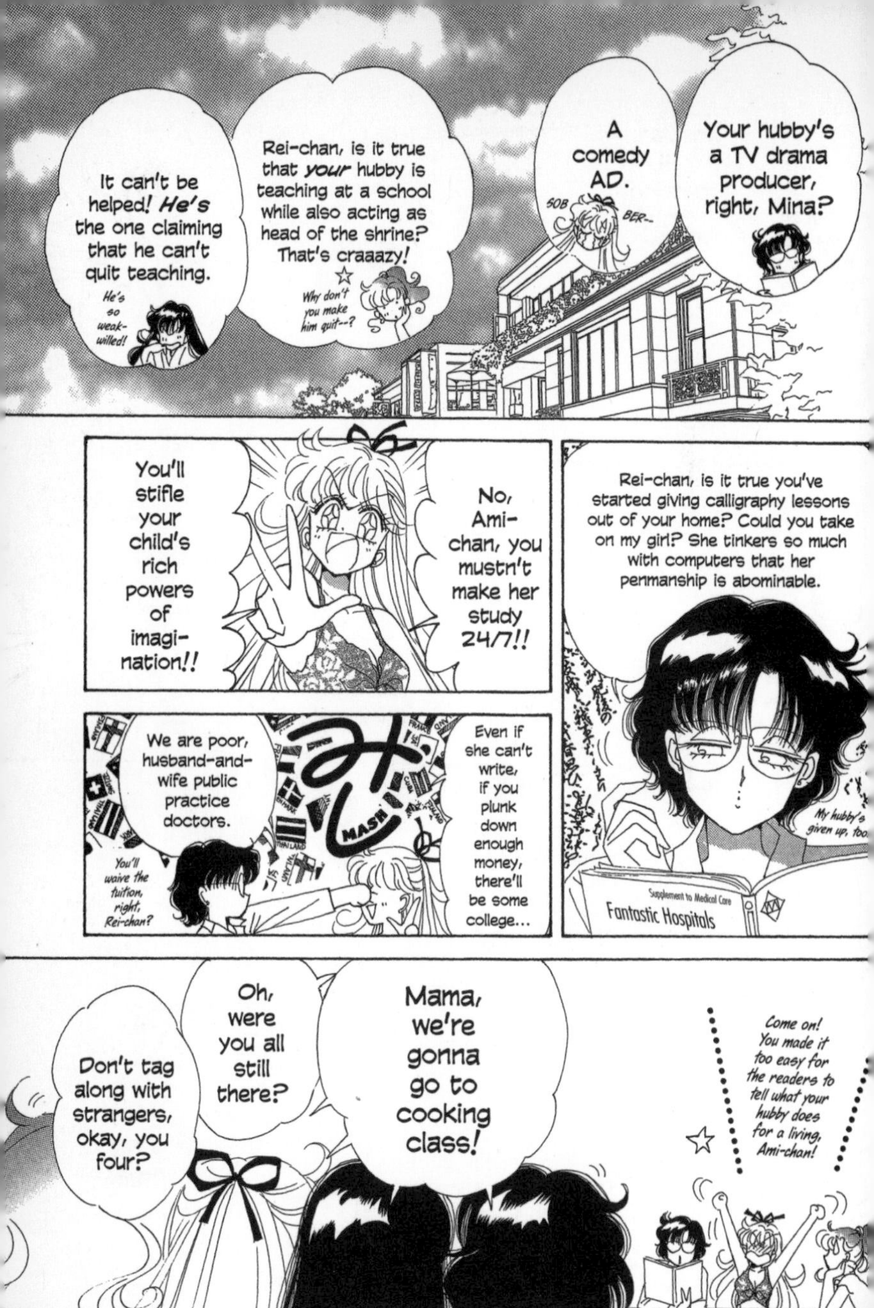
Your hubby's a TV drama producer, right, Mina?
A comedy AD.
SOB
BER--
Rei-chan, is it true that *your* hubby is teaching at a school while also acting as head of the shrine? That's craaazy!
Why don't you make him quit--?
It can't be helped! *He's* the one claiming that he can't quit teaching.
He's so weak-willed!
Rei-chan, is it true you've started giving calligraphy lessons out of your home? Could you take on my girl? She tinkers so much with computers that her penmanship is abominable.
My hubby's given up, too.
Supplement to Medical Care
Fantastic Hospitals
No, Ami-chan, you mustn't make her study 24/7!!
You'll stifle your child's rich powers of imagination!!
Even if she can't write, if you plunk down enough money, there'll be some college...
MASH
We are poor, husband-and-wife public practice doctors.
You'll waive the tuition, right, Rei-chan?
Come on! You made it too easy for the readers to tell what your hubby does for a living, Ami-chan!
Mama, we're gonna go to cooking class!
Oh, were you all still there?
Don't tag along with strangers, okay, you four?

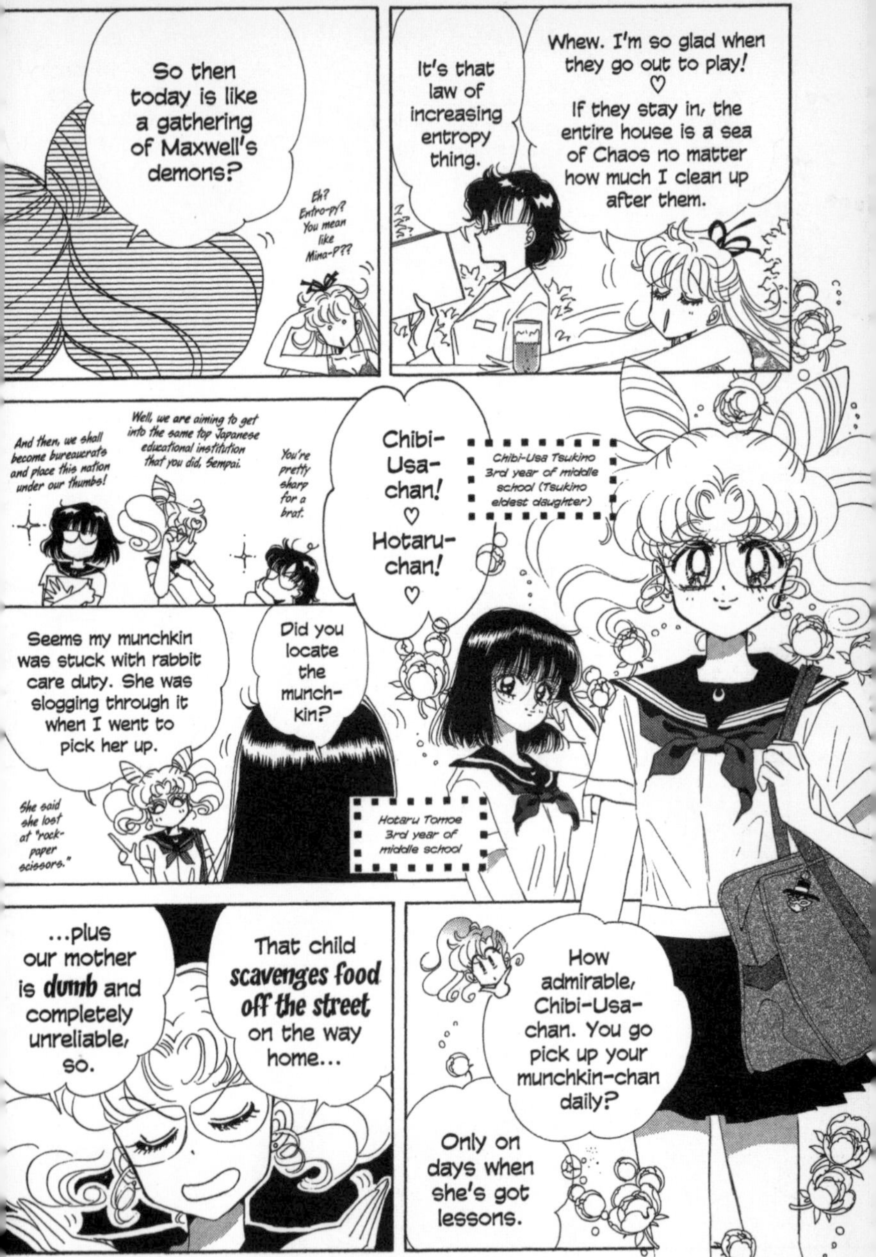
Whew. I'm so glad when they go out to play! ♡ If they stay in, the entire house is a sea of Chaos no matter how much I clean up after them.
It's that law of increasing entropy thing.
So then today is like a gathering of Maxwell's demons?
Eh? Entro-py? You mean like Mina-P??
Chibi-Usa-chan! ♡ Hotaru-chan! ♡
Chibi-Usa Tsukino 3rd year of middle school (Tsukino eldest daughter)
You're pretty sharp for a brat.
Well, we are aiming to get into the same top Japanese educational institution that you did, Sempai.
And then, we shall become bureaucrats and place this nation under our thumbs!
Hotaru Tomoe 3rd year of middle school
Did you locate the munchkin?
Seems my munchkin was stuck with rabbit care duty. She was slogging through it when I went to pick her up.
She said she lost at "rock-paper scissors."
How admirable, Chibi-Usa-chan. You go pick up your munchkin-chan daily?
Only on days when she's got lessons.
That child scavenges food off the street on the way home...
...plus our mother is dumb and completely unreliable, so.

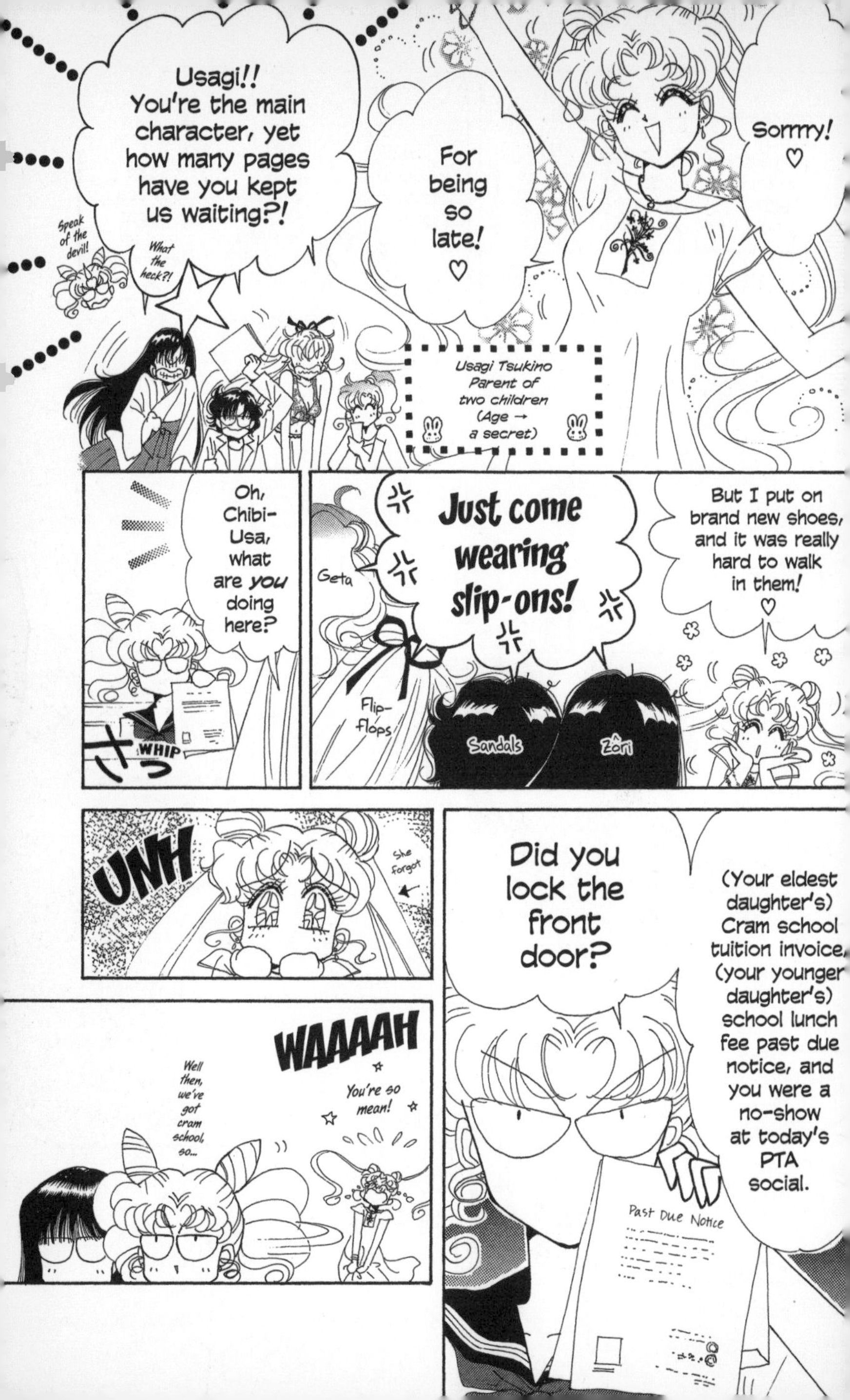
Sorrry! ♡
For being so late! ♡
Usagi!! You're the main character, yet how many pages have you kept us waiting?!
What the heck?!
Speak of the devil!
Usagi Tsukino Parent of two children (Age → a secret)
But I put on brand new shoes, and it was really hard to walk in them! ♡
Just come wearing slip-ons!
Geta
Flip-flops
Sandals
Zôri
Oh, Chibi-Usa, what are *you* doing here?
WHIP
Did you lock the front door?
(Your eldest daughter's) Cram school tuition invoice, (your younger daughter's) school lunch fee past due notice, and you were a no-show at today's PTA social.
Past Due Notice
UNH
She forgot
WAAAAH
You're so mean!
Well then, we've got cram school, so...

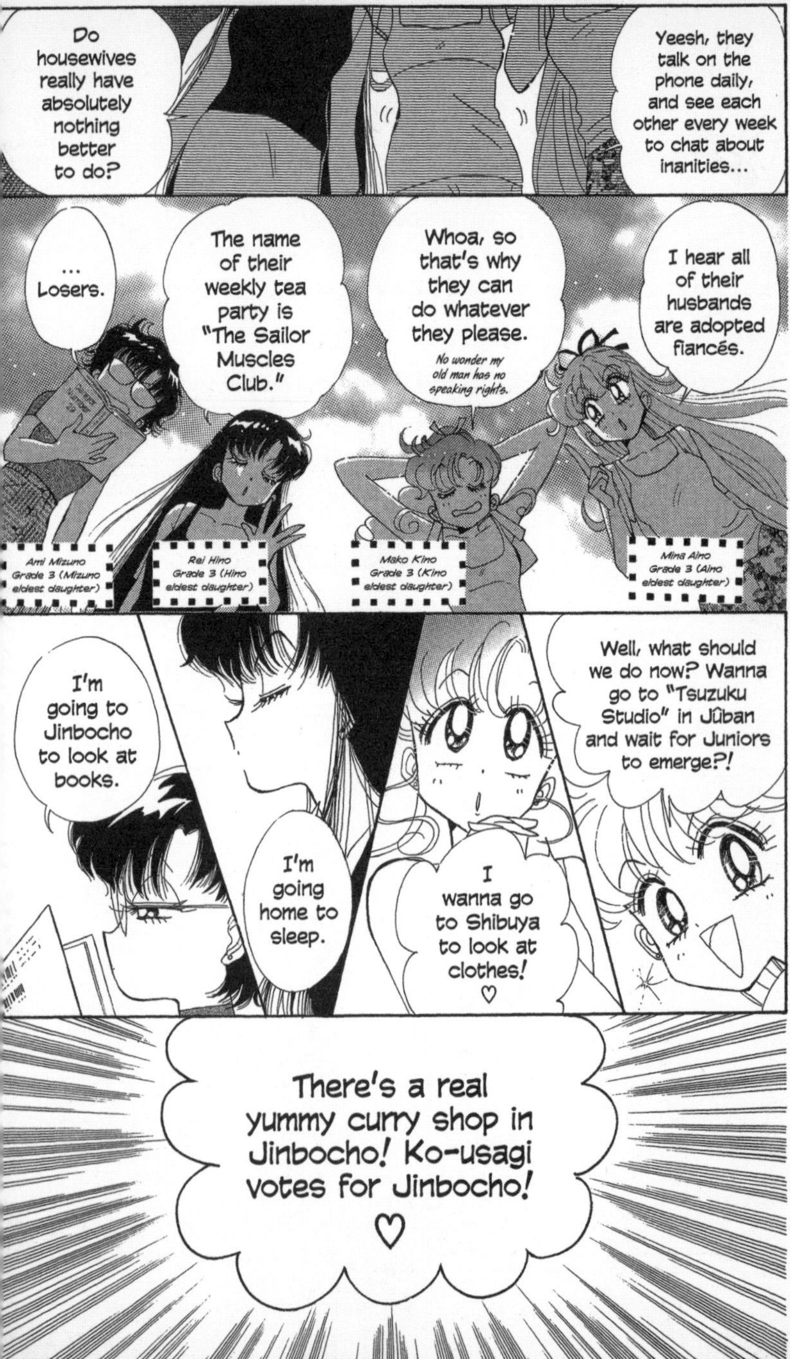

Yeesh, they talk on the phone daily, and see each other every week to chat about inanities...
Do housewives really have absolutely nothing better to do?
I hear all of their husbands are adopted fiancés.
Mina Aino Grade 3 (Aino eldest daughter)
Whoa, so that's why they can do whatever they please.
No wonder my old man has no speaking rights.
Mako Kino Grade 3 (Kino eldest daughter)
The name of their weekly tea party is "The Sailor Muscles Club."
Rei Hino Grade 3 (Hino eldest daughter)
... Losers.
Ami Mizuno Grade 3 (Mizuno eldest daughter)
Well, what should we do now? Wanna go to "Tsuzuku Studio" in Jûban and wait for Juniors to emerge?!
I wanna go to Shibuya to look at clothes! ♡
I'm going home to sleep.
I'm going to Jinbocho to look at books.
There's a real yummy curry shop in Jinbocho! Ko-usagi votes for Jinbocho! ♡

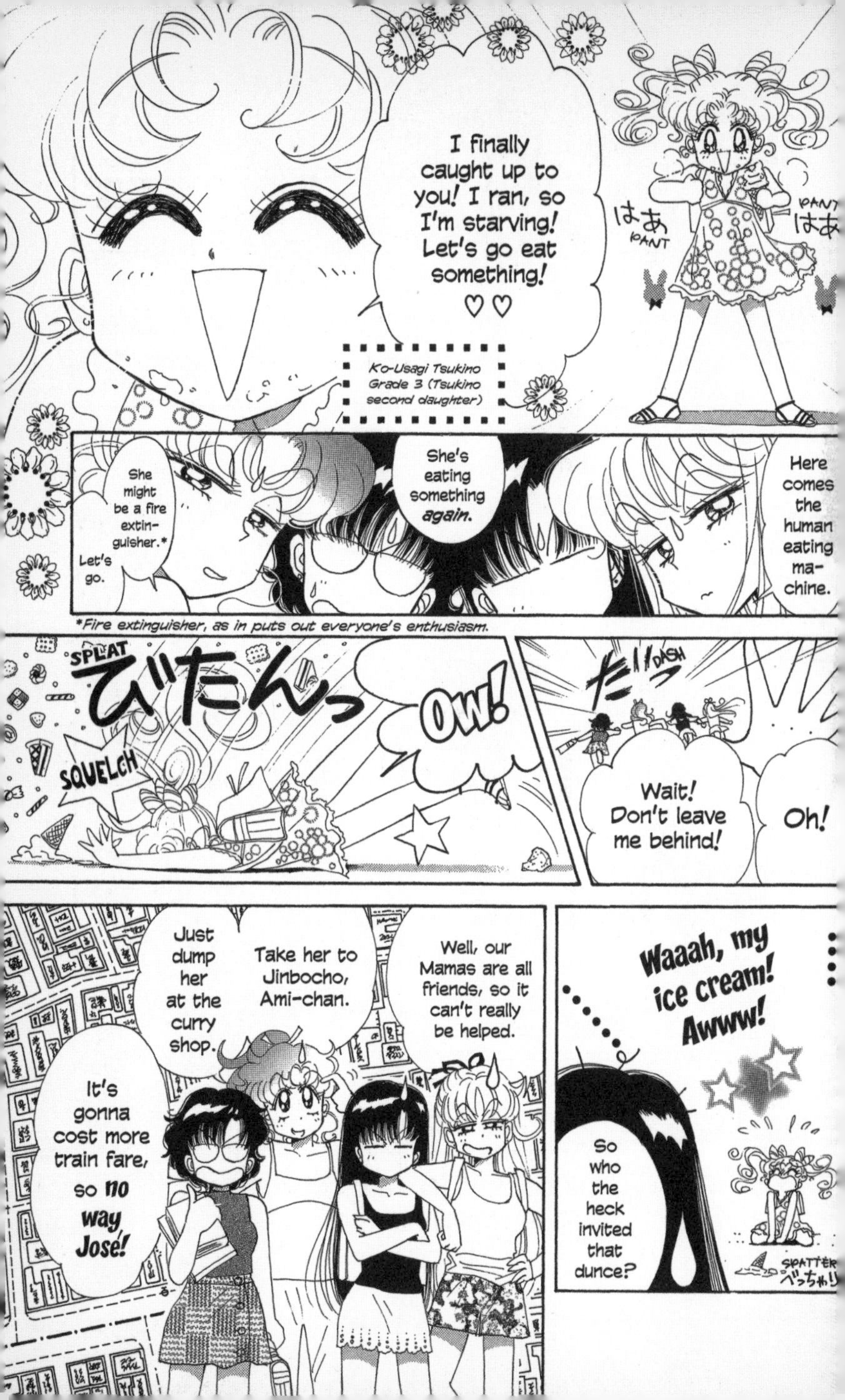
はあ PANT
はあ PANT
I finally caught up to you! I ran, so I'm starving! Let's go eat something! ♡♡
Ko-Usagi Tsukino Grade 3 (Tsukino second daughter)
Here comes the human eating machine.
She's eating something again.
She might be a fire extinguisher.*
Let's go.
たっ DASH
Oh!
Wait! Don't leave me behind!
OW!
びたんっ SPLAT
SQUELCH
Waaah, my ice cream! Awww!
......
So who the heck invited that dunce?
べっちゃ SPLATTER
Well, our Mamas are all friends, so it can't really be helped.
Take her to Jinbocho, Ami-chan.
Just dump her at the curry shop.
It's gonna cost more train fare, so no way José!

*Fire extinguisher, as in puts out everyone's enthusiasm.

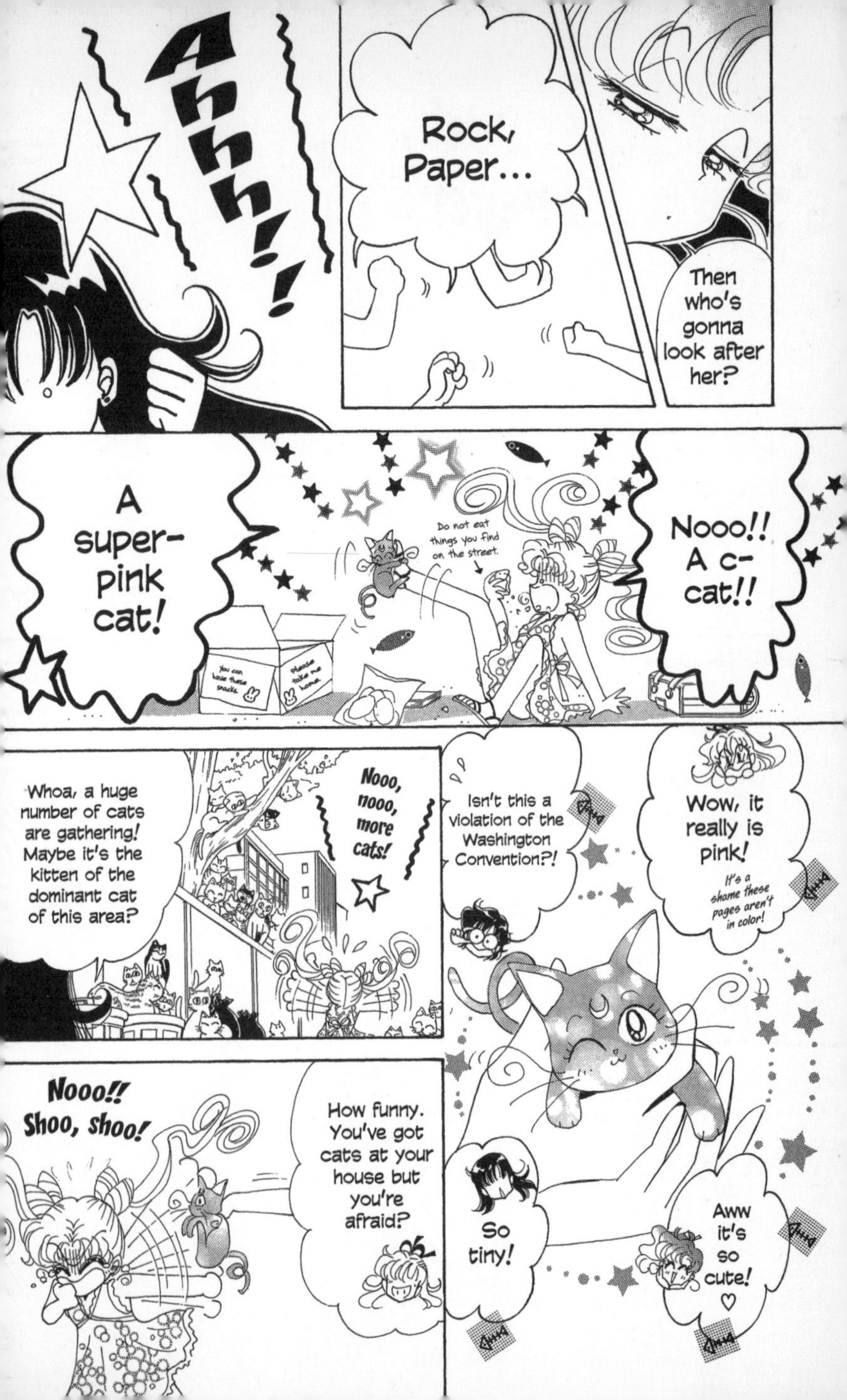

Then who's gonna look after her?
Rock, Paper...
Ahhh!!!
Nooo!! A c-cat!!
A super-pink cat!
Do not eat things you find on the street.
please take me home.
You can have these snacks.
Wow, it really is pink!
It's a shame these pages aren't in color!
Isn't this a violation of the Washington Convention?!
Aww it's so cute! ♡
So tiny!
Nooo, nooo, more cats!
Whoa, a huge number of cats are gathering! Maybe it's the kitten of the dominant cat of this area?
How funny. You've got cats at your house but you're afraid?
Nooo!! Shoo, shoo!

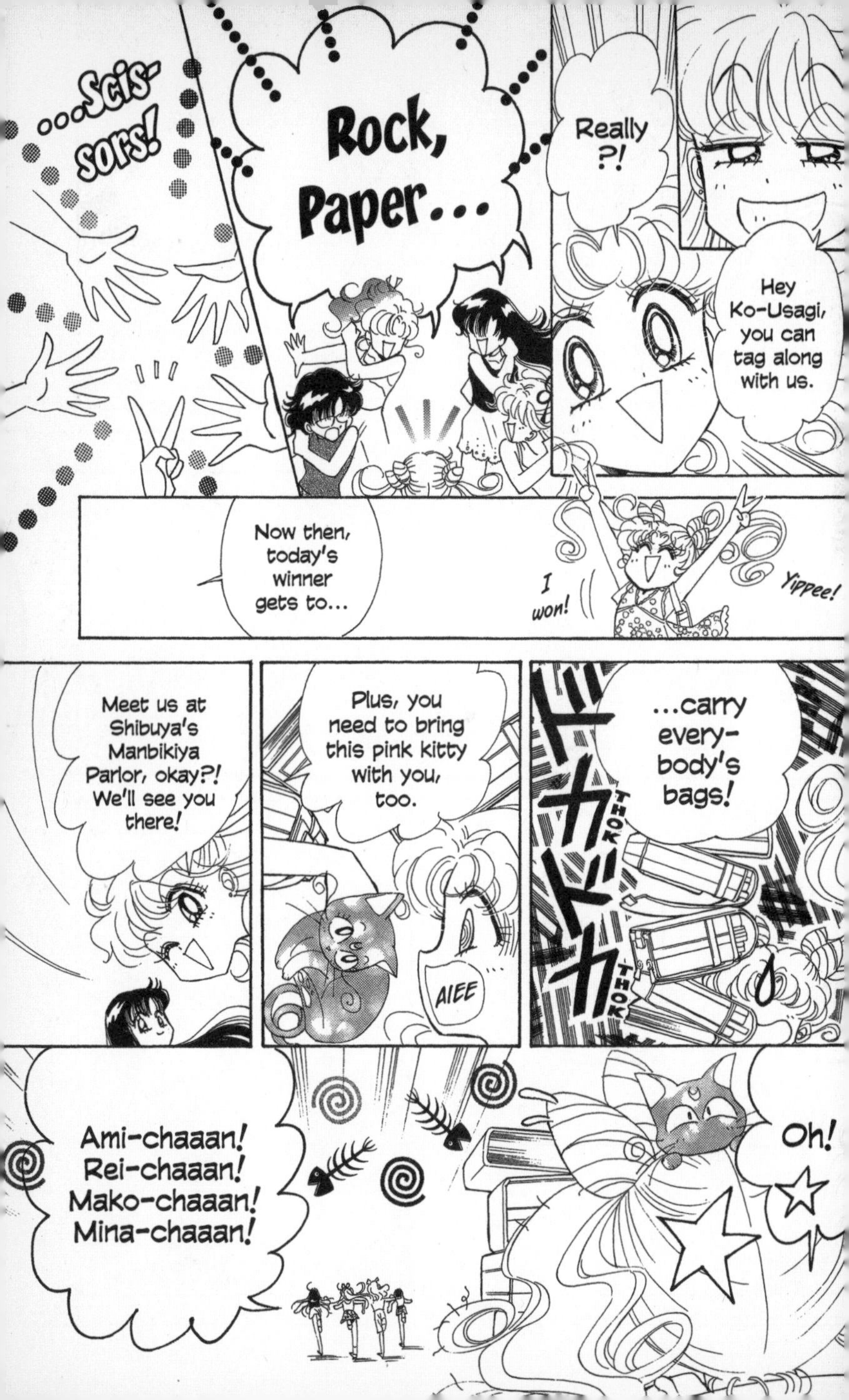
Hey Ko-Usagi, you can tag along with us.
Really ?!
Rock, Paper...
...Scis-sors!
Yippee!
I won!
Now then, today's winner gets to...
...carry every-body's bags!
THOK
THOK
Plus, you need to bring this pink kitty with you, too.
AIEE...
Meet us at Shibuya's Manbikiya Parlor, okay?! We'll see you there!
Oh!
Ami-chaaan! Rei-chaaan! Mako-chaaan! Mina-chaaan!

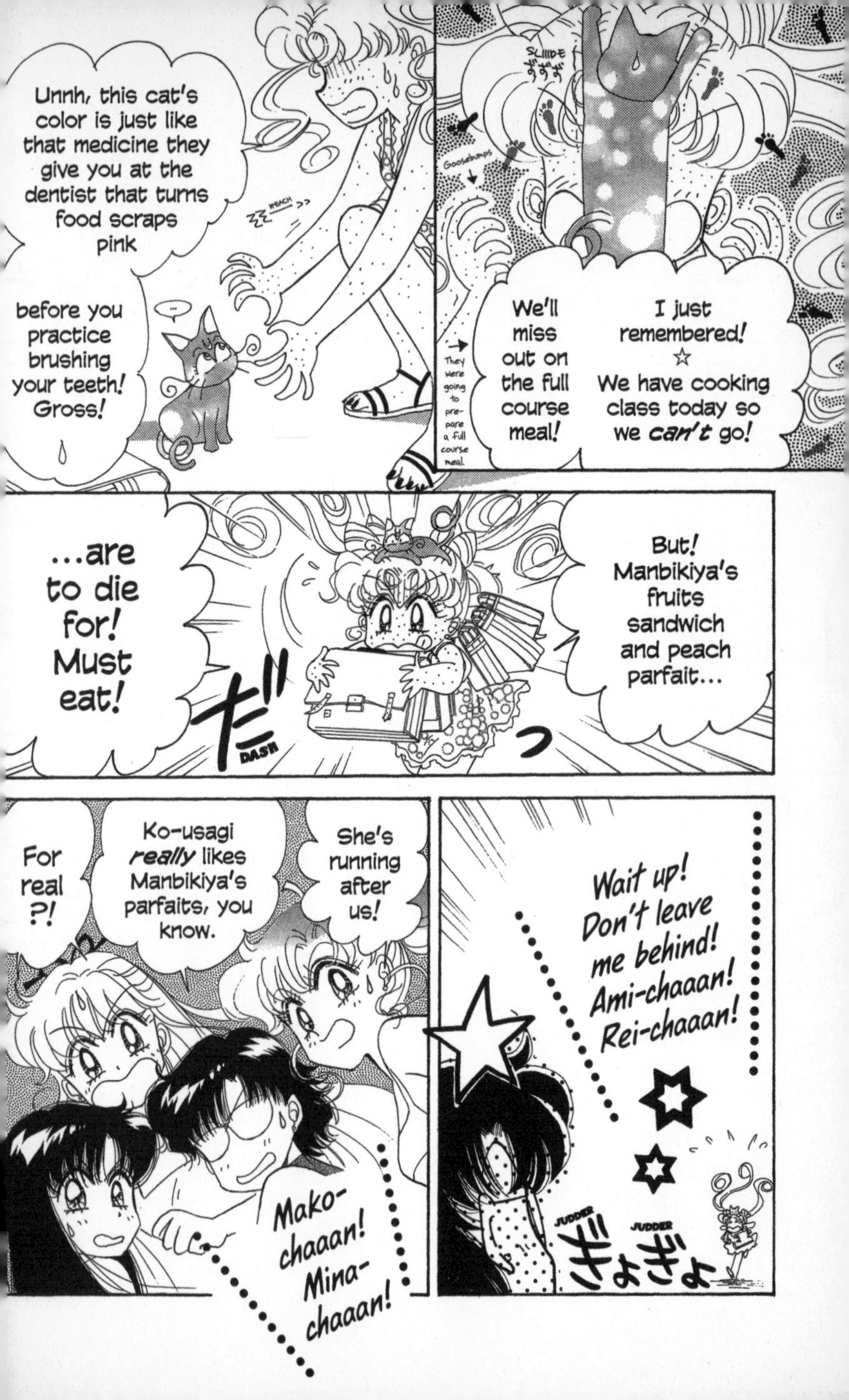
SLIIIDE
Goosebumps
I just remembered! ☆ We have cooking class today so we *can't* go!
We'll miss out on the full course meal!
They were going to prepare a full course meal.
Unnh, this cat's color is just like that medicine they give you at the dentist that turns food scraps pink
REACH
...
before you practice brushing your teeth! Gross!
But! Manbikiya's fruits sandwich and peach parfait...
DASH
...are to die for! Must eat!
Wait up! Don't leave me behind! Ami-chaaan! Rei-chaaan!
JUDDER
JUDDER
She's running after us!
Ko-usagi *really* likes Manbikiya's parfaits, you know.
For real?!
Mako-chaaan! Mina-chaaan!

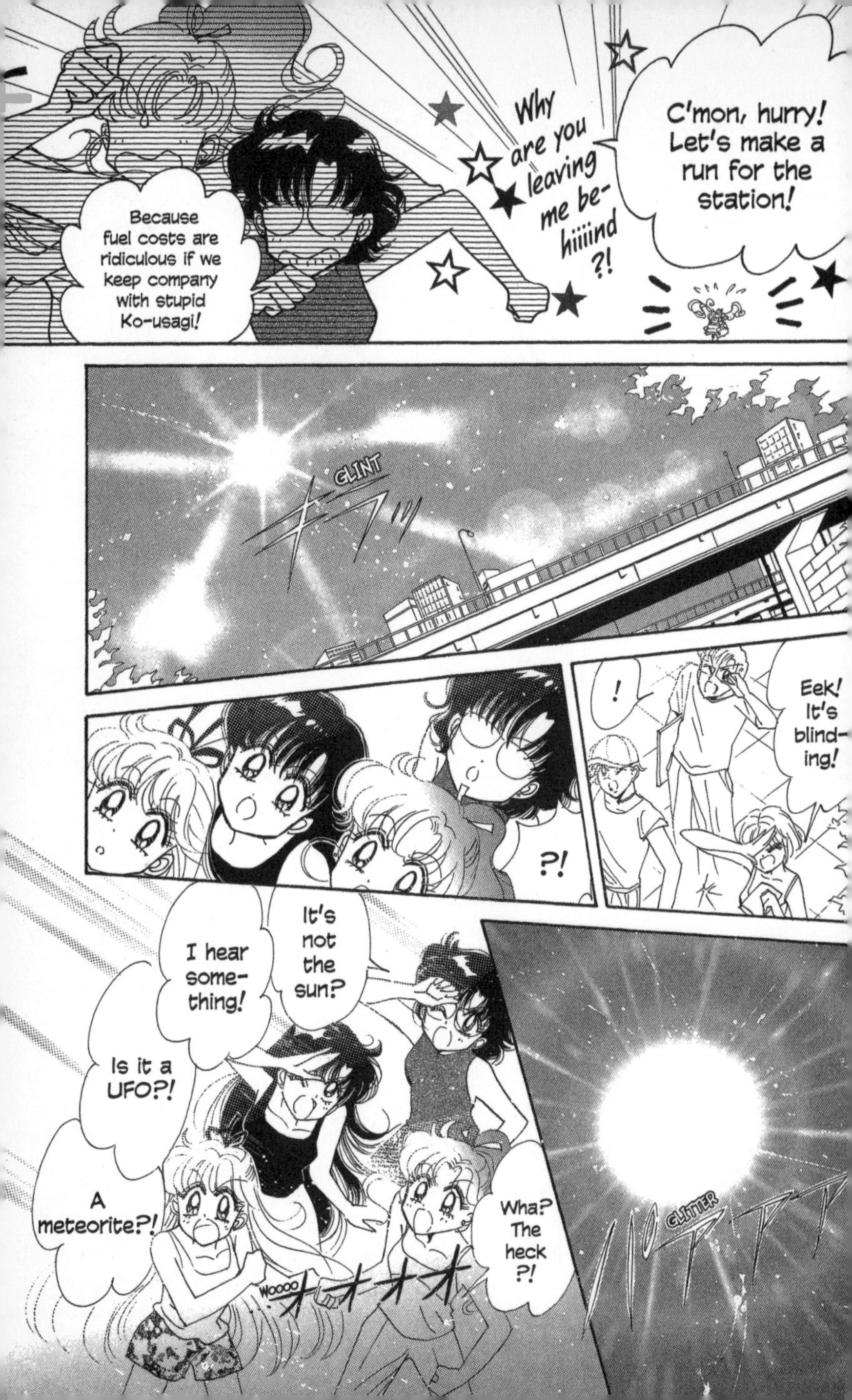
C'mon, hurry! Let's make a run for the station!
Why are you leaving me be-hiiiind?!
Because fuel costs are ridiculous if we keep company with stupid Ko-usagi!
GLINT
Eek! It's blind-ing!
!
?!
GLITTER
Wha? The heck?!
WOOOO
It's not the sun?
I hear some-thing!
Is it a UFO?!
A meteorite?!

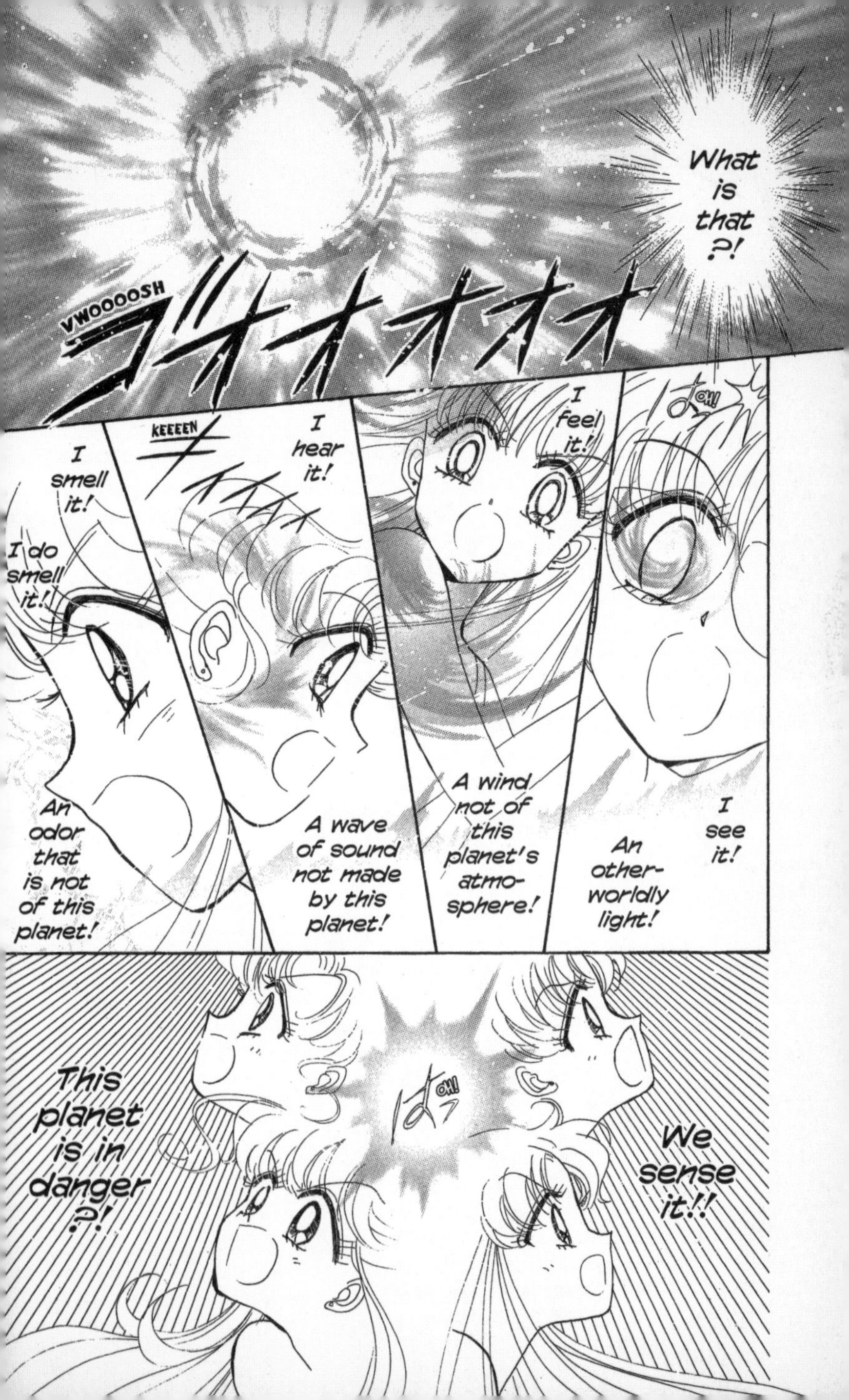
What is that?!
VWOOOOSH
OH!
I see it!
An other-worldly light!
I feel it!
A wind not of this planet's atmosphere!
I hear it!
KEEEEN
A wave of sound not made by this planet!
I smell it!
I do smell it!
An odor that is not of this planet!
We sense it!!
OH!
This planet is in danger?!

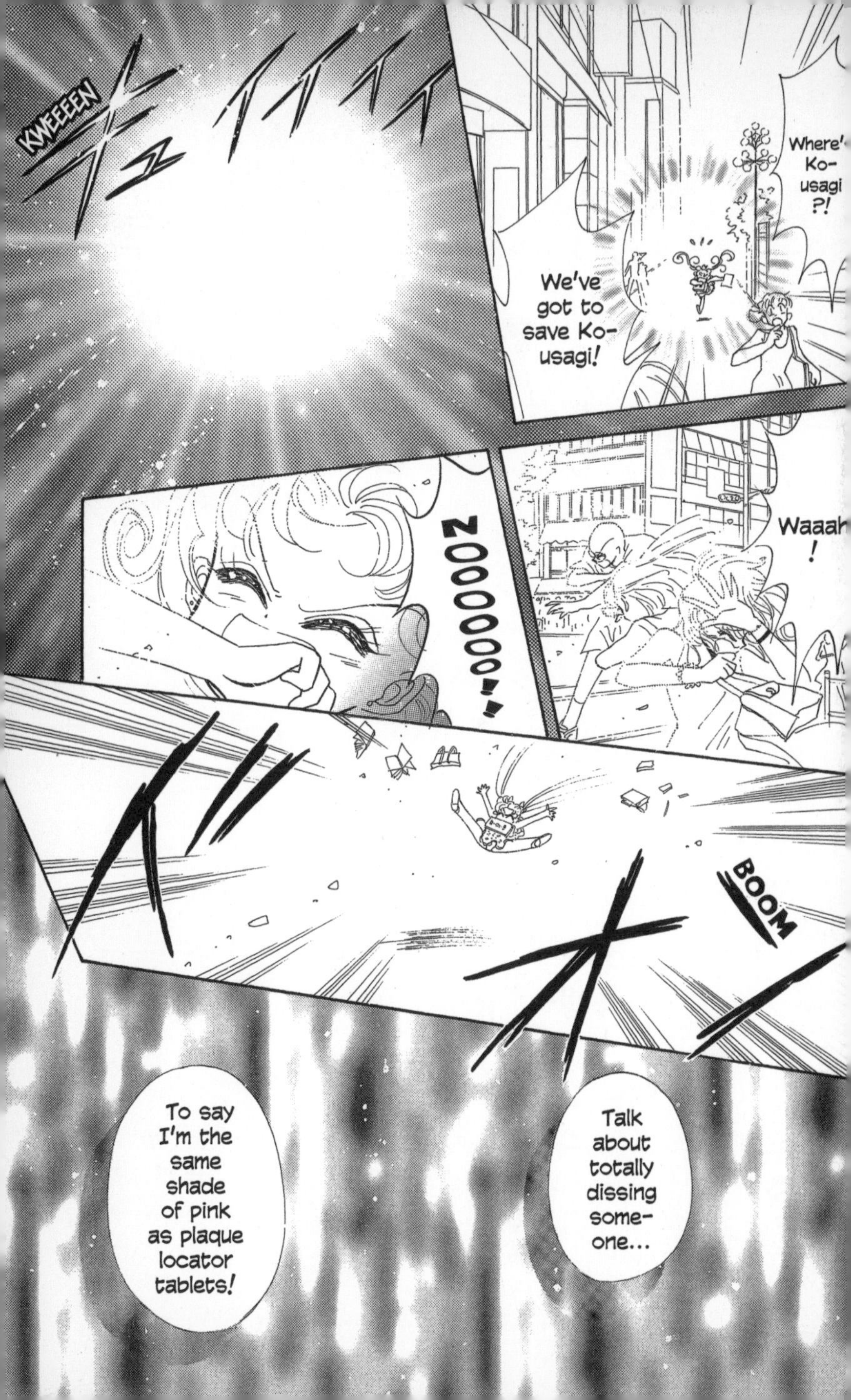

Where' Ko-usagi ?!
We've got to save Ko-usagi!
KWEEEEN
Waaah!
NOOOOOOO!!
BOOM
Talk about totally dissing some-one...
To say I'm the same shade of pink as plaque locator tablets!

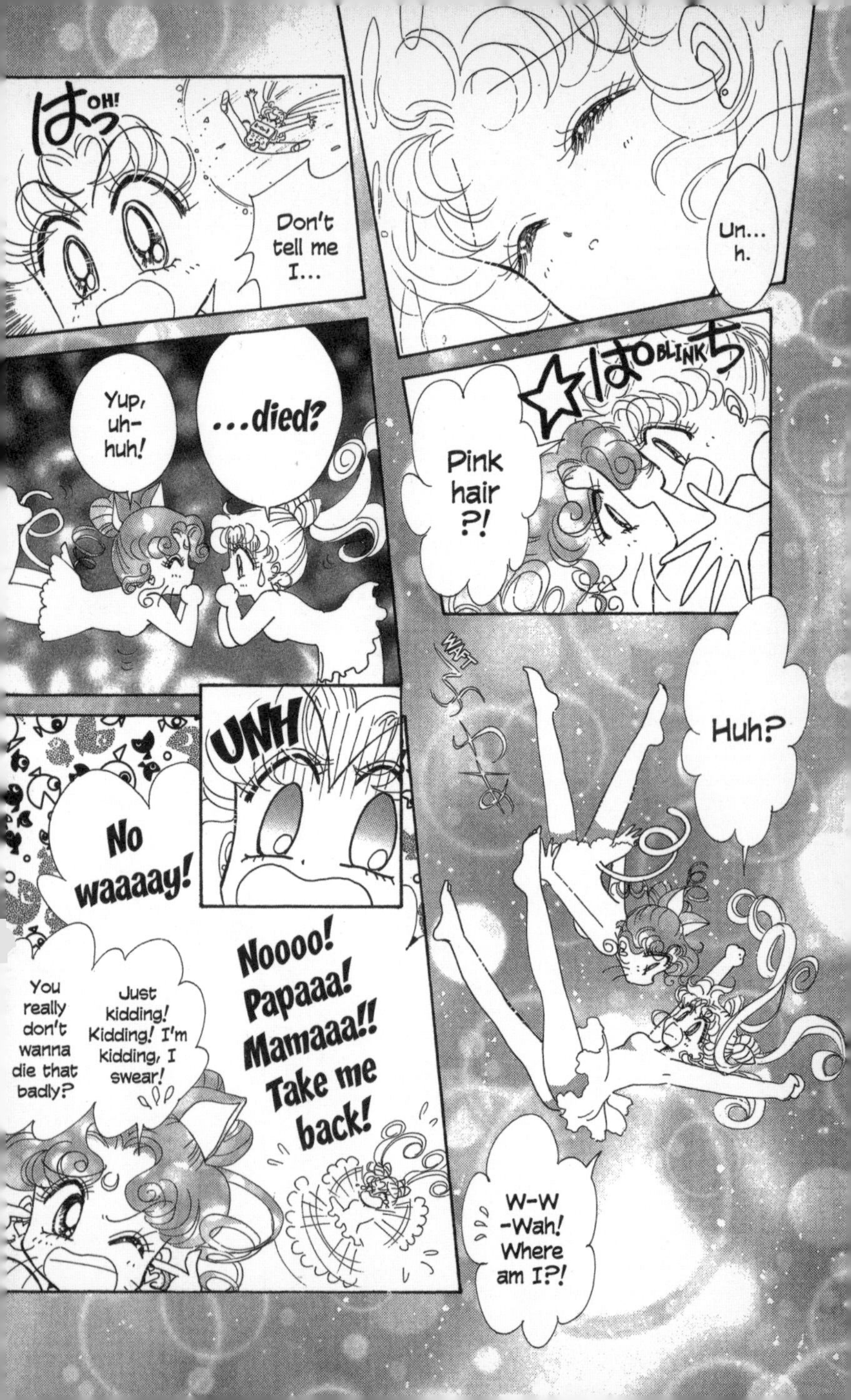
Un... h.
はっ BLINK ち
Pink hair ?!
WAFT ふわ
Huh?
W-W -Wah! Where am I?!
はっ OH!
Don't tell me I...
...died?
Yup, uh-huh!
UNH
No waaaay!
Noooo! Papaaa! Mamaaa!! Take me back!
Just kidding! Kidding! I'm kidding, I swear!
You really don't wanna die that badly?

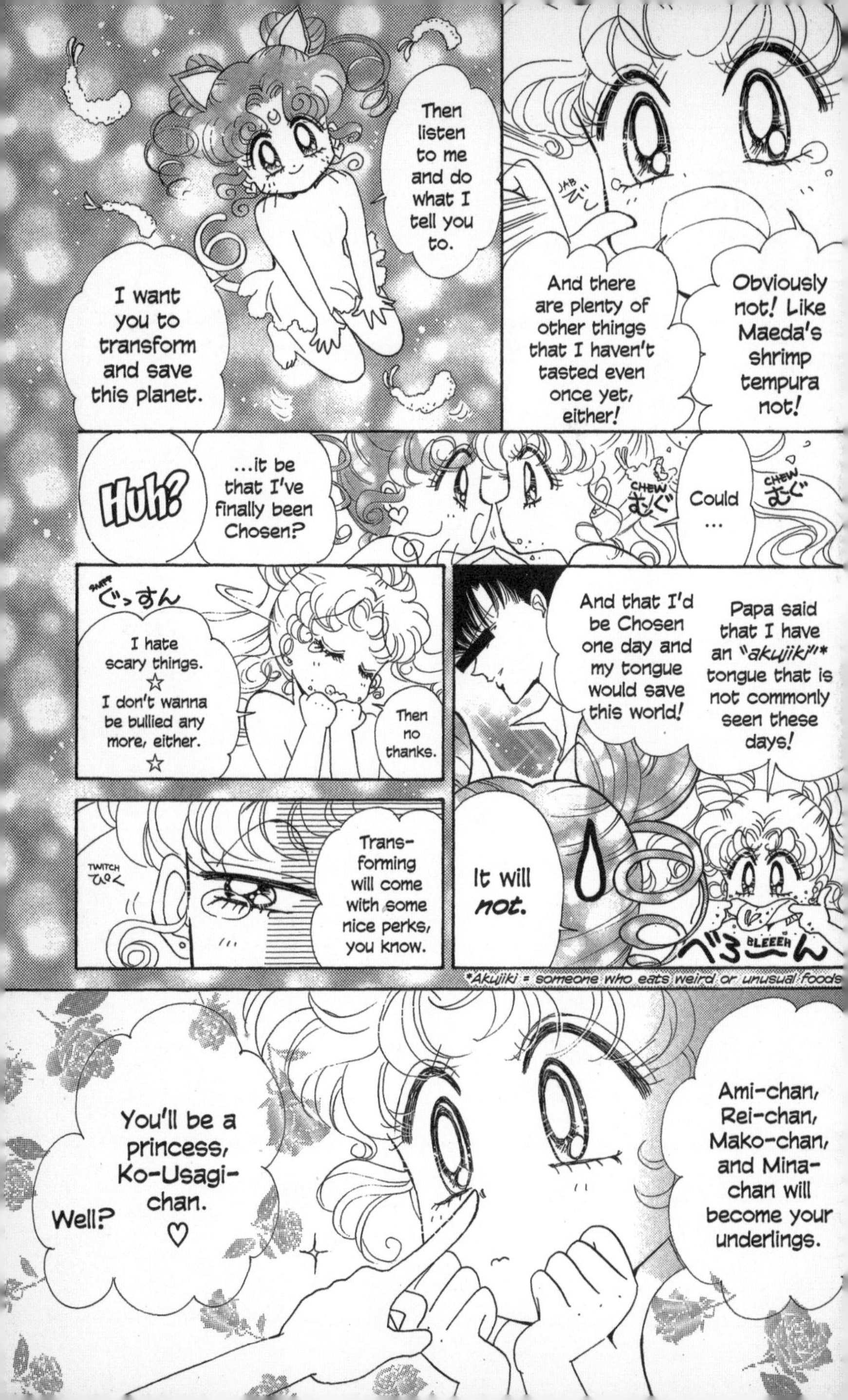
JAB びく
Obviously not! Like Maeda's shrimp tempura not!
And there are plenty of other things that I haven't tasted even once yet, either!
Then listen to me and do what I tell you to.
I want you to transform and save this planet.
CHEW むぐ
Could ...
CHEW むぐ
...it be that I've finally been Chosen?
Huh?
Papa said that I have an "akujiki"* tongue that is not commonly seen these days!
And that I'd be Chosen one day and my tongue would save this world!
SNIFF ぐっすん
I hate scary things. ☆ I don't wanna be bullied any more, either. ☆
Then no thanks.
It will not.
べろ〜ん BLEEEH
Trans-forming will come with some nice perks, you know.
TWITCH ぴくっ
Ami-chan, Rei-chan, Mako-chan, and Mina-chan will become your underlings.
You'll be a princess, Ko-Usagi-chan. ♡
Well?
*Akujiki = someone who eats weird or unusual foods

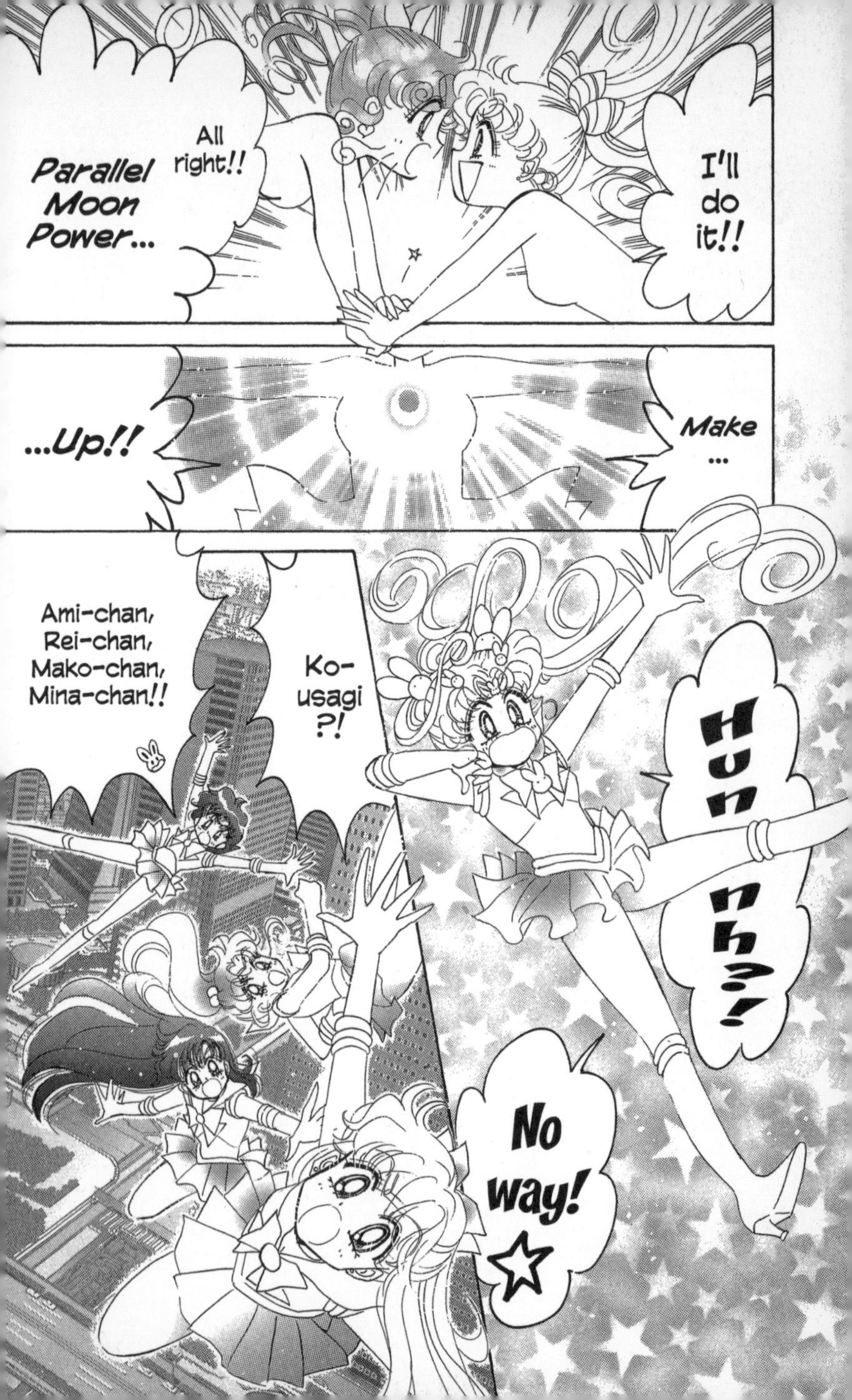

I'll do it!!
All right!!
Parallel Moon Power...
Make...
...Up!!
HUNNH?!
Ko-usagi?!
Ami-chan, Rei-chan, Mako-chan, Mina-chan!!
No way! ☆

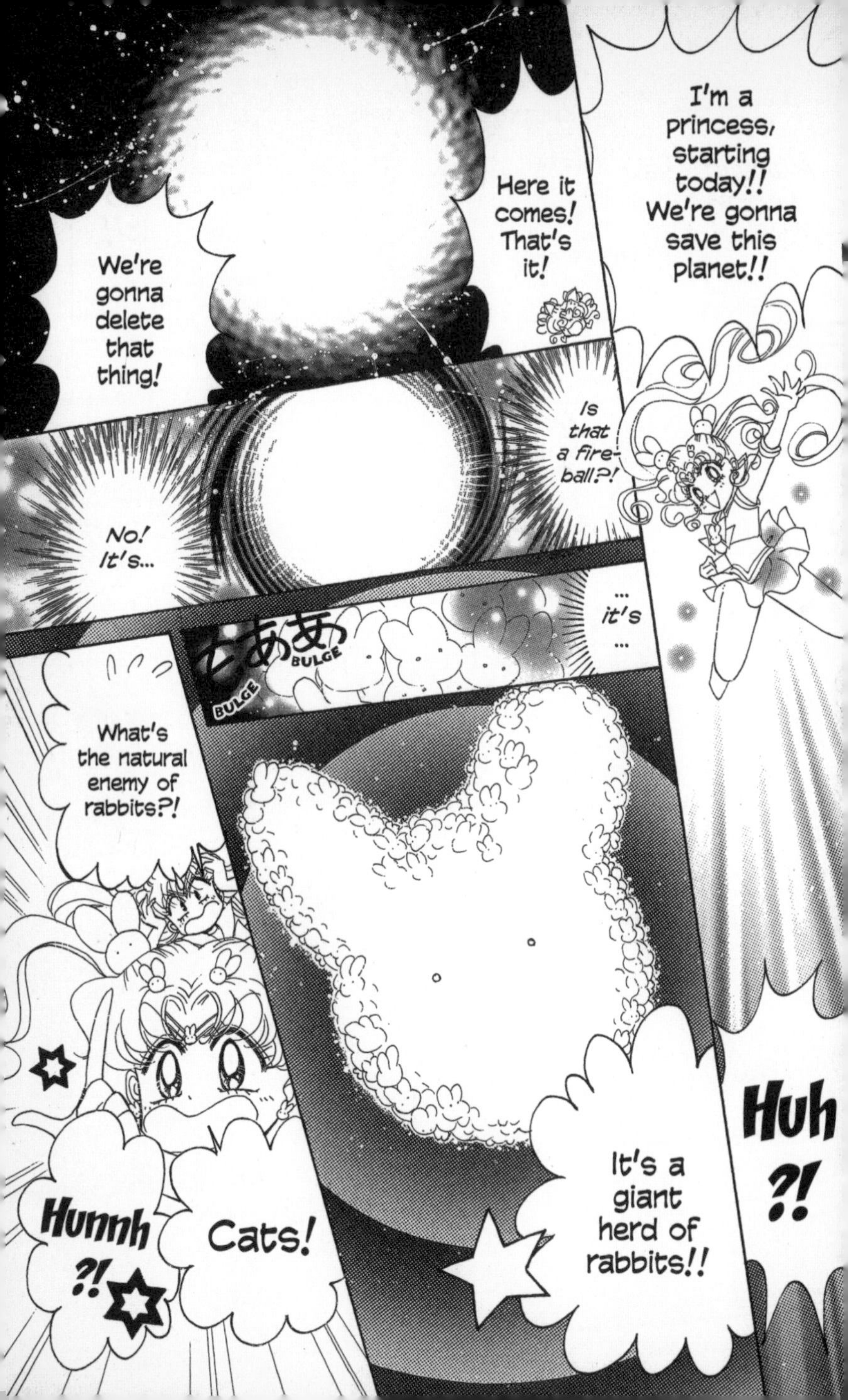
I'm a princess, starting today!! We're gonna save this planet!!
Huh ?!
Here it comes! That's it!
We're gonna delete that thing!
Is that a fire-ball?!
No! It's...
... it's ...
BULGE
BULGE
It's a giant herd of rabbits!!
What's the natural enemy of rabbits?!
Cats!
Hunnh ?!

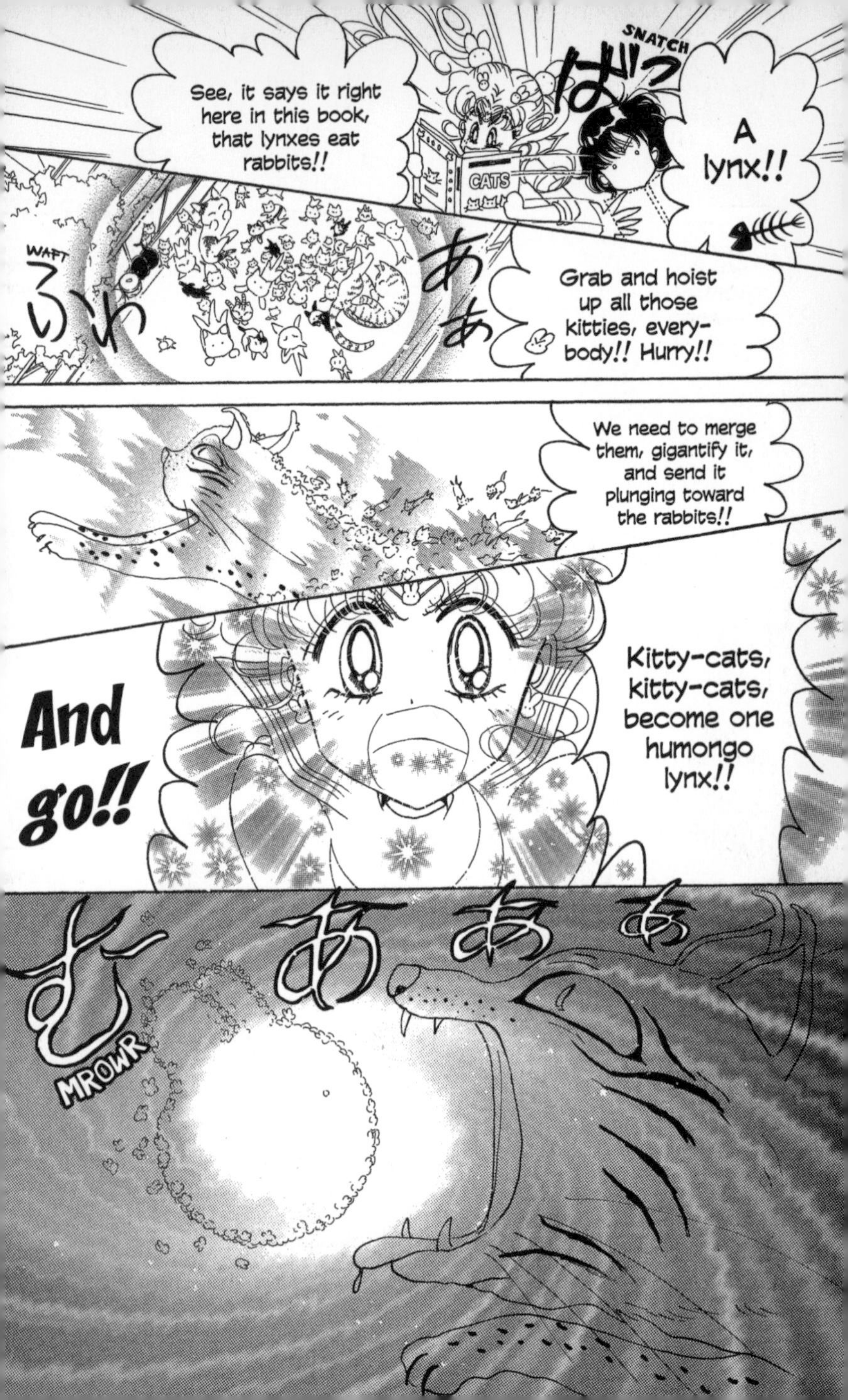
ぱっ
SNATCH
A lynx!!
See, it says it right here in this book, that lynxes eat rabbits!!
CATS
Grab and hoist up all those kitties, every-body!! Hurry!!
ああ
ふわ
WAFT
We need to merge them, gigantify it, and send it plunging toward the rabbits!!
Kitty-cats, kitty-cats, become one humongo lynx!!
And go!!
むあああ
MROWR

All these tales are works of fiction. Any resemblance to actual persons, organizations, and/or events are purely coincidental.

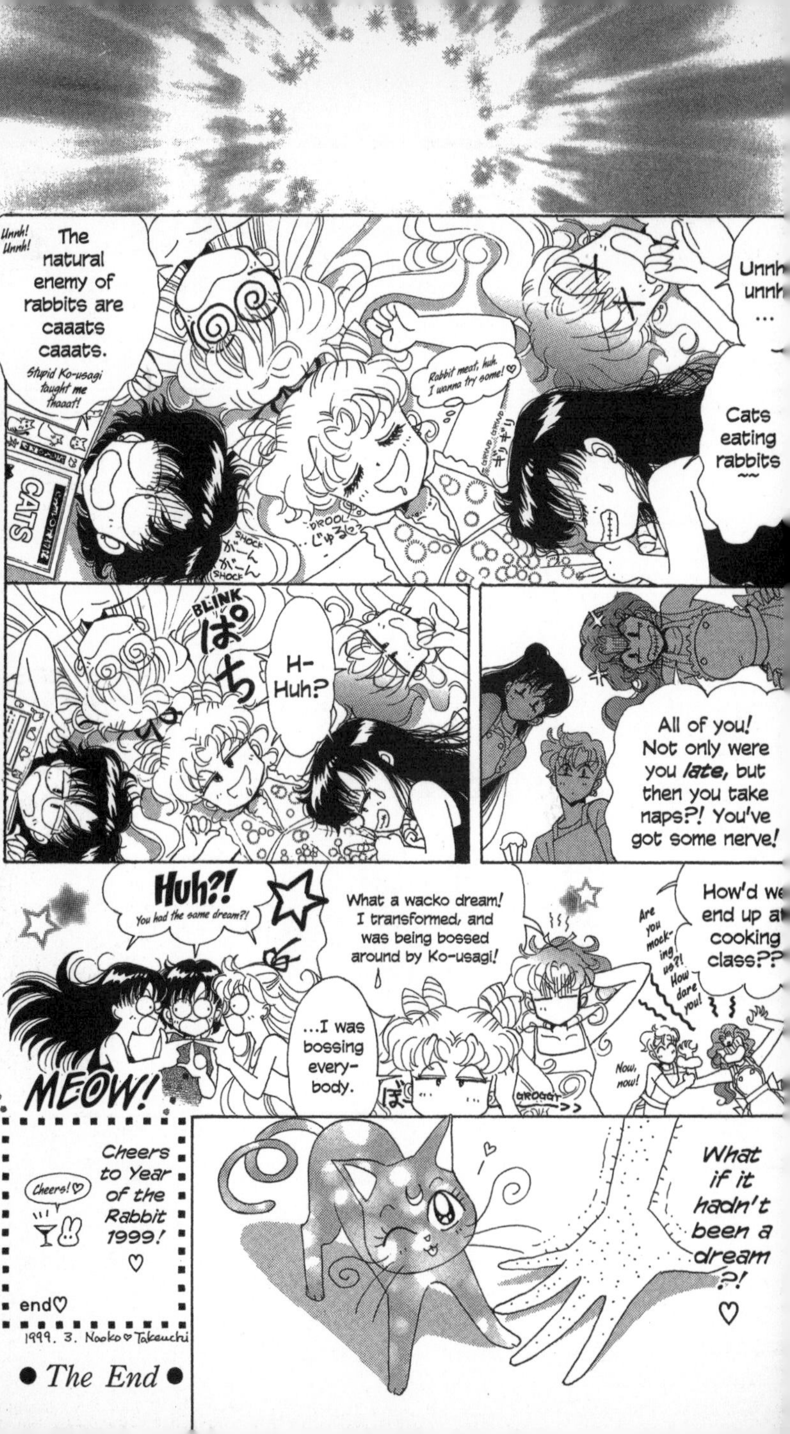

Unnh unnh ...
Cats eating rabbits ~~
GRIND GRIND キリキリ
Rabbit meat, huh. I wanna try some!
DROOL じゅるる
Unnh! Unnh!
The natural enemy of rabbits are caaats caaats.
Stupid Ko-usagi taught me thaaat!
SHOCK がーん SHOCK
All of you! Not only were you *late*, but then you take naps?! You've got some nerve!
H- Huh?
BLINK ぱち
How'd we end up at cooking class??
Are you mock-ing us?! How dare you!
Now, now!
What a wacko dream! I transformed, and was being bossed around by Ko-usagi!
...I was bossing every-body.
Huh?!
You had the same dream?!
MEOW!
What if it hadn't been a dream?!
Cheers to Year of the Rabbit 1999!
Cheers!
end
1999. 3. Naoko Takeuchi
• The End •

etty Guardian ★ Sailor Moon Short Stories

~ 10 years of love and miracles ~

Phase One Series

The Birth of Pretty Guardians of Love and Justice in Sailor Suits!

Appeared in *Nakayoshi* February 1992 ~ March 1993 issues / Revised Edition KC DX volumes 1 ~ 3

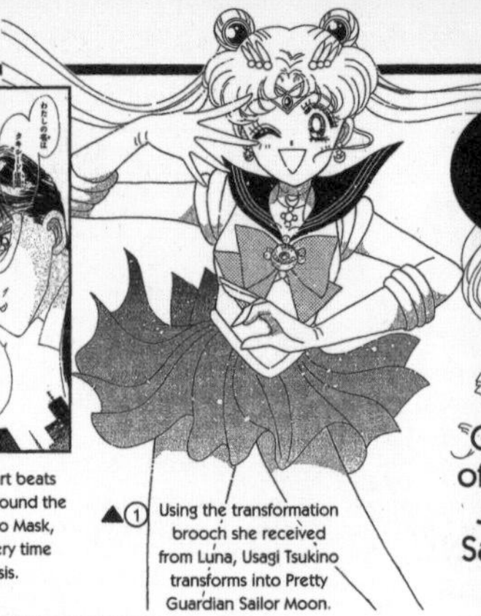

▲① Using the transformation brooch she received from Luna, Usagi Tsukino transforms into Pretty Guardian Sailor Moon.

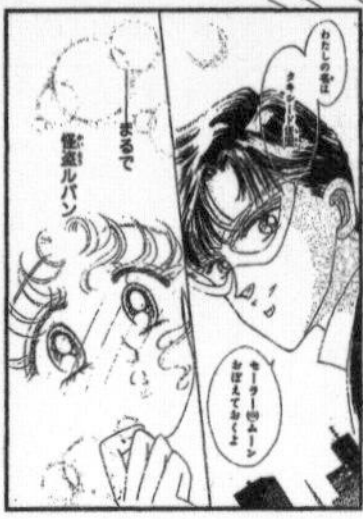

わたしの名は
まるで
怪盗ルパン

▲② Sailor Moon's heart beats just a little faster around the mysterious Tuxedo Mask, who appears every time there is a crisis.

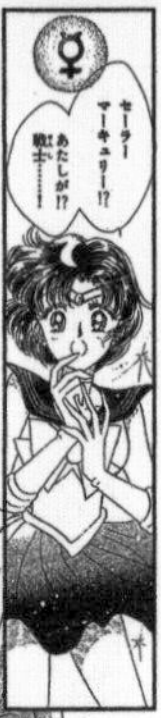

セーラーマーキュリー!? あたしが!? 戦士……!

Starting with Sailor Mercury, ▶③ other companion Sailor Guardians start appearing one after another.

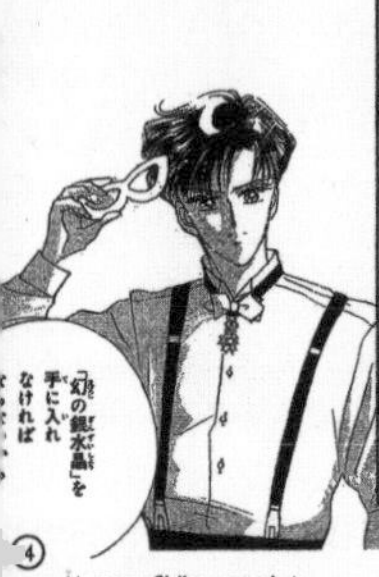

「幻の銀水晶」を 手に入れ なければ

④ Mamoru Chiba reveals to Usagi Tsukino that he is the true identity of Tuxedo Mask.

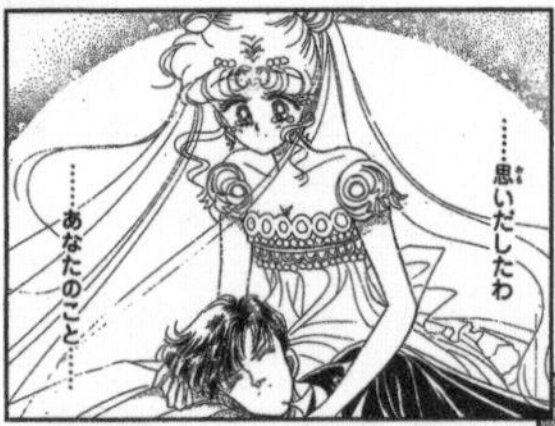

……思いだしたわ
あなたのこと……

◀⑤ The Moon Princess, Princess Serenity, who they have been looking for, turns out to be Usagi Tsukino herself.

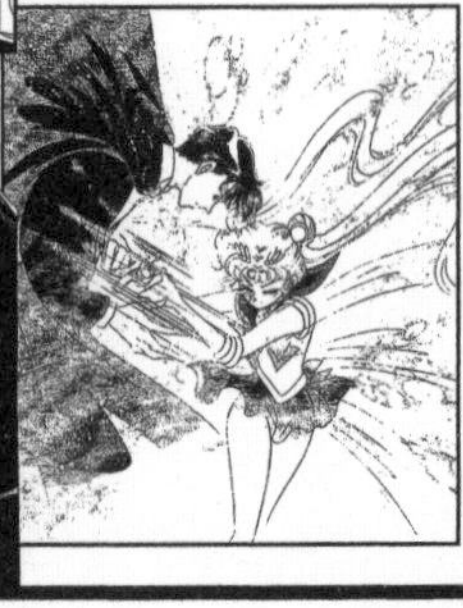

▼⑥ In order to free Endymion, whose heart has been tainted by evil, Sailor Moon arrives at a bitter decision!

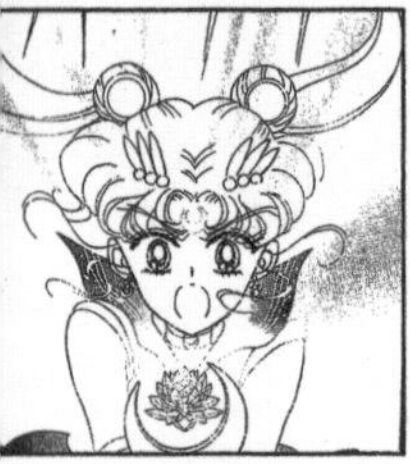

◀⑦ Sailor Moon invokes the power of the "Legendary Silver Crystal" and destroys Queen Metalia.

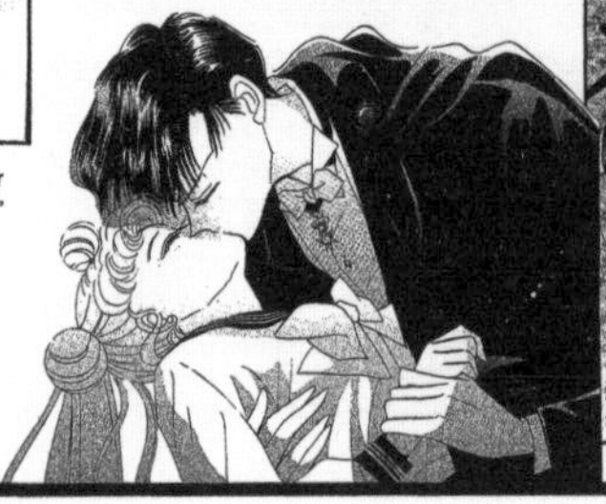

⑧ What revives Sailor Moon, who had used up all her strength, is a kiss of love.

Pretty Guardian Sailor Moon Eternal History

• August 1991 / "Codename: Sailor V" debuts!!

Naoko Takeuchi-sensei's one-shot short story, "Code-name: Sailor V," which becomes the basis for "Sailor Moon," appears in *RunRun's* Summer Break issue.

• December 1991 / "Pretty Guardian Sailor Moon" series launches!!

The long-awaited manga serialization finally begins, in *Nakayoshi's* February issue.

• March 1992 / "Pretty Guardian Sailor Moon" animated television series begins airing!

Broadcast of the Toei Animation-produced animated television series begins on TV Asahi. New episodes air every Saturday, closely following the original work.

• March 1992 / "Moonlight Densetsu" main theme song CD released

Becomes an explosive hit for an anime CD single, and even spreads to karaoke rooms in a flash.

• March 1992 / "Codename: Sailor V" appears again in *RunRun's* Spring Break issue!!

"Sailor V" also becomes serialized, and appears concurrently with *Nakayoshi's* "Sailor Moon." The following April, *RunRun* gets re-launched as an every-other-month magazine.

• July 1992 / KC Nakayoshi 'retty Guardian Sailor Moon" graphic novel volume one released!!

The ommemoration-worthy first collection of stories into graphic novel form. The first dition sells out in the blink of an eye.

The Chibi Guardian That Arrives From the Future!!

Phase Two Series

■ Appeared in *Nakayoshi* March 1993 ~ March 1994 issues / Revised Edition KC DX volumes 3 ~ 5

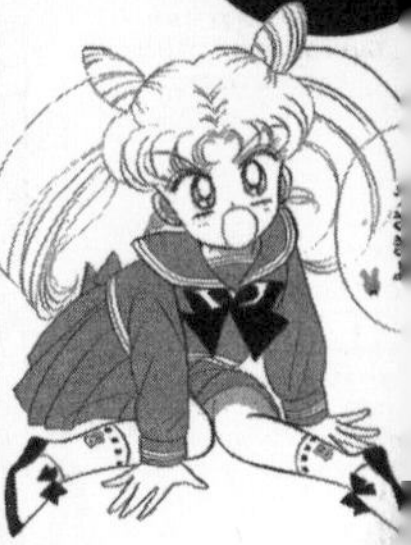

▲① The mysterious little girl "Chibi-Usa," who suddenly falls from the sky one day. What is her true identity?

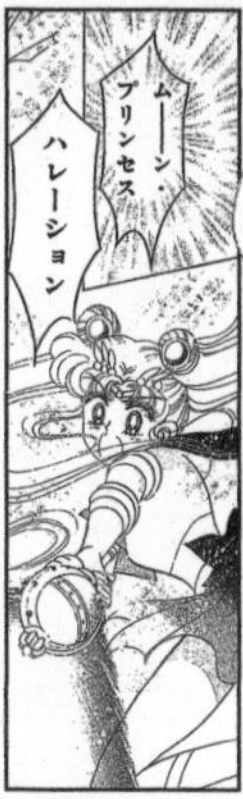
ムーン・プリンセス
ハレーション

▶② Sailor Moon, who undergoes a power-up in response to the new enemy, Black Moon, fights them with a new special move.

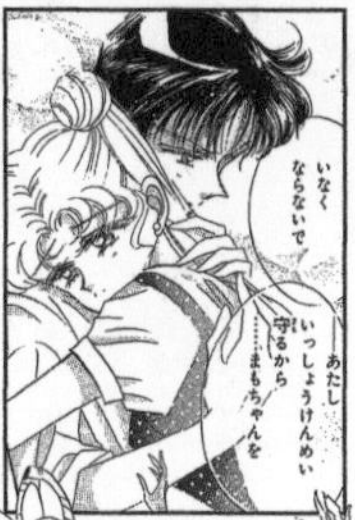
いなくならないで
あたし いっしょうけんめい 守るから ……まもちゃんを

▶③ Anomalies occur in the future world of the 30th century...?! An indescribable uneasiness descends upon Usagi and Mamoru's hearts.

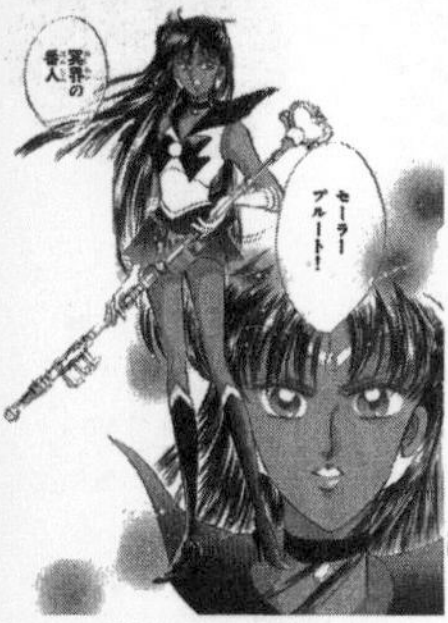
冥界の番人
セーラー プルート！

▲④ The Guardian of Time, Sailor Pluto, appears before the time-traveling Sailor Moon and company.

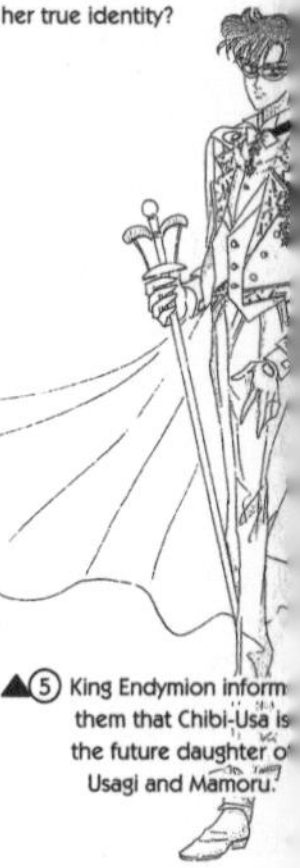

▲⑤ King Endymion informs them that Chibi-Usa is the future daughter of Usagi and Mamoru.

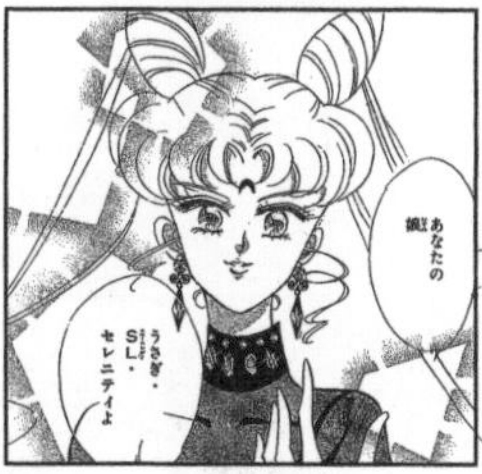
あなたの娘よ
うさぎ・SL・セレニティよ

▲⑥ The evil will of Wiseman transforms Chibi-Usa into the Queen of Darkness, Black Lady.

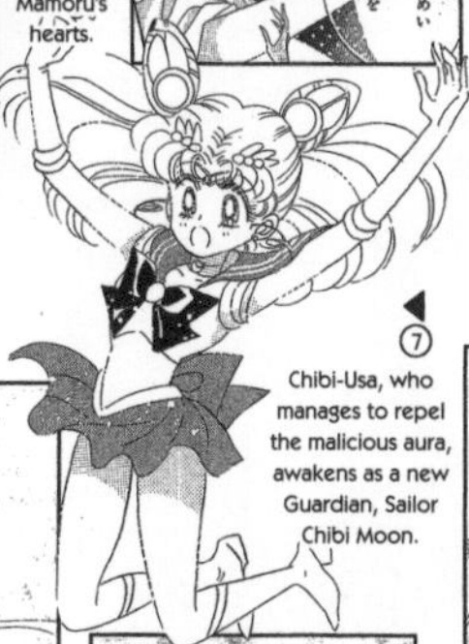

◀⑦ Chibi-Usa, who manages to repel the malicious aura, awakens as a new Guardian, Sailor Chibi Moon.

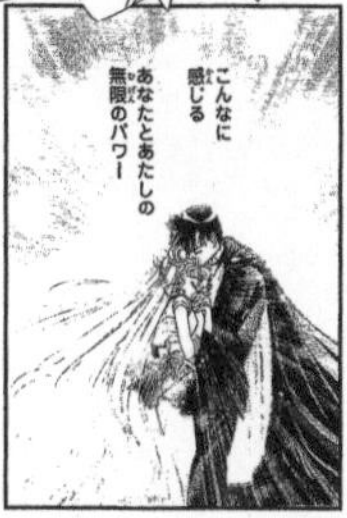
こんなに 感じる
あなたとあたしの 無限のパワー

◀⑧ The moment their two hearts become one, the "Legendary Silver Crystal" brings about another sacred miracle.

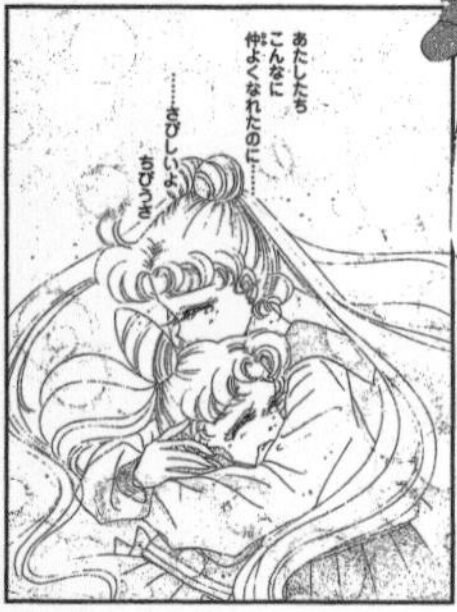
あたしたち こんなに 仲よくなれたのに……
さびしいよ ちびうさ

▲⑨ The actions of the Double Moon restore peace to the future. And leads to a sad parting with Chibi-Usa...

• August 199[2] / "Pretty Guardi[an] Sailor Moon" anime book series publication begins!

Volume one o[f] the film comic utilizing scene clips from the anime, is released. Late[r] books based o[n] the theatrica[l] films are also produced.

• August 1992 / "*Nakayoshi* Festival" is a roaring success!

A "thank you" festival for faithful *Nakayoshi* readers is held at PAO in Shibuya. Because tickets were not absolutely necessary, 4500 fans line up, almost all the way to Shibuya Station, on Takeuchi-sensei's day.

• December 1992 / The "First Sailor Moon (Character) Popularity Poll" is carried out in *Nakayoshi's* January issue!

Total entry count reaches 150 thousand, with Sailor Moon shining grandly in first place.

• March 1993 / "Pretty Guardian Sailor Moon R," season two of the animated television series, begins airing.

• March 1993 / LD's and videos of the television series start being released!

Laser discs and videotapes of the television series are released on a simultaneous schedule from Toei Video.

• June 1993 / Naoko Takeuchi-sensei wins the "17th Kodansha Manga Award"!!

Due to the high acclaim of its subject and popularity, Takeuchi-sensei's "Pretty Guardian Sailor Moon" takes the "17th Kodansha Manga Award."

• December 1993 / "Pretty Guardian Sailor Moon R" movie premieres!

"Pretty Guardian Sailor Moon R," a new work created just for theatrical release, premieres simultaneously nationwide. Its co-feature is a short called "Make Up! Sailor Guardians."

riends or Foes? Mysterious Sailor Guardians Appear!

Phase Three Series

Appeared in *Nakayoshi* March 1994 ~ March 1995 issues / Revised Edition KC DX volumes 6 ~ 8

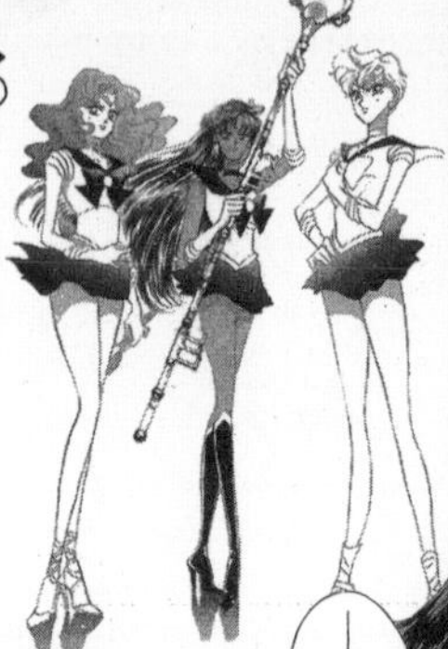

Pluto, ranus, and ptune, the three Outer Solar ystem ardians, onfront Usagi and mpany over otaru. ▶⑤

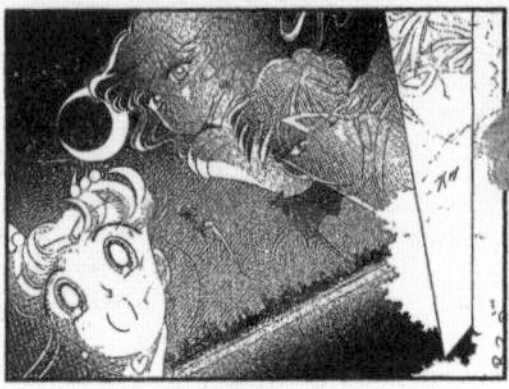

▲③ Mysterious shadows that leave the scene where a monster appeared. Could this be the arrival of new Sailor Guardians?!

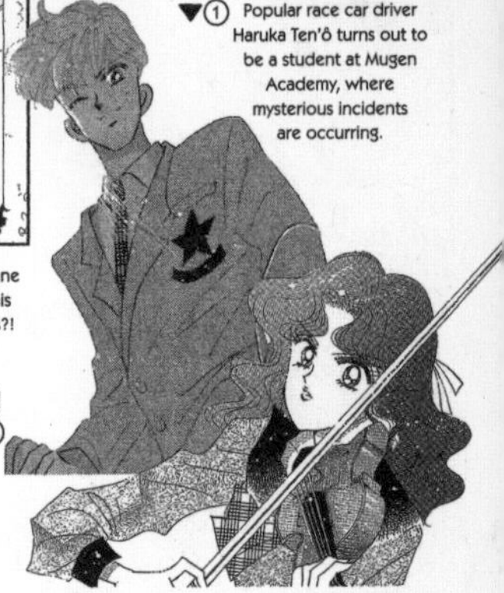

▼① Popular race car driver Haruka Ten'ô turns out to be a student at Mugen Academy, where mysterious incidents are occurring.

▲② Along with Haruka, violin virtuoso Michiru Kaiô also lurks around these incidents.

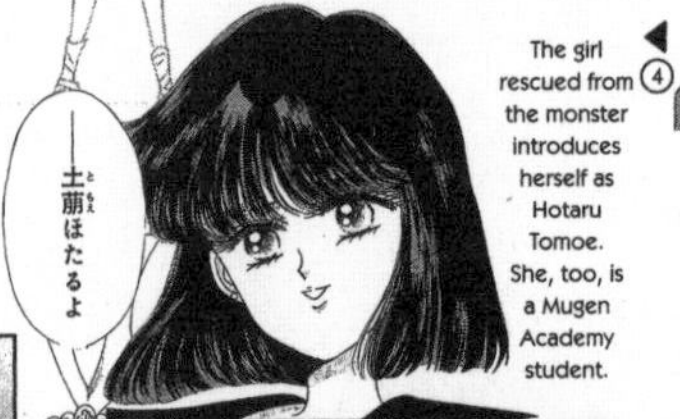
——土萠ほたるよ

◀④ The girl rescued from the monster introduces herself as Hotaru Tomoe. She, too, is a Mugen Academy student.

▼⑨ Usagi awakens as the "messiah" and revives Hotaru's life and body with her miraculous powers.

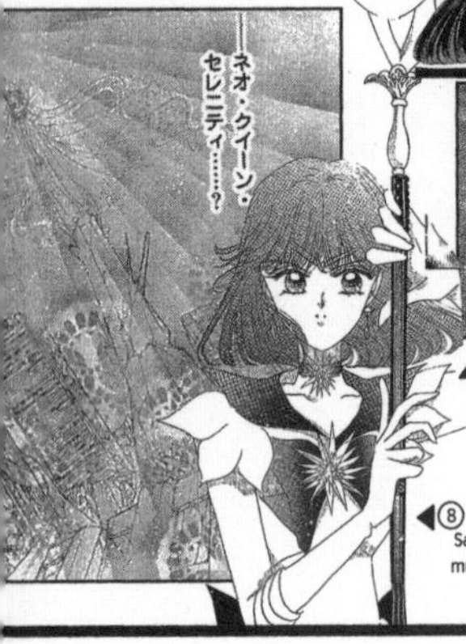
——ネオ・クイーン・セレニティ……?

◀⑧ Hotaru turns out to be Sailor Saturn, the Guardian of Ruin, who must never be allowed to awaken.

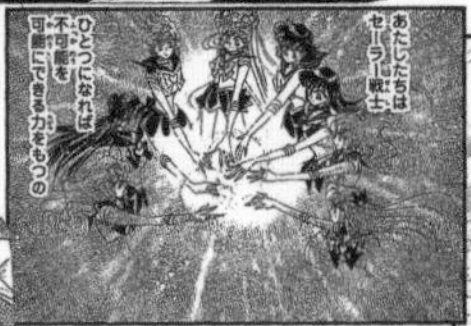
あたしたちはセーラー戦士
ひとつになれば不可能を可能にできる力をもつの

◀⑦ The antagonistic Uranus and company end up joining forces and fighting together as fellow Sailor Guardians.

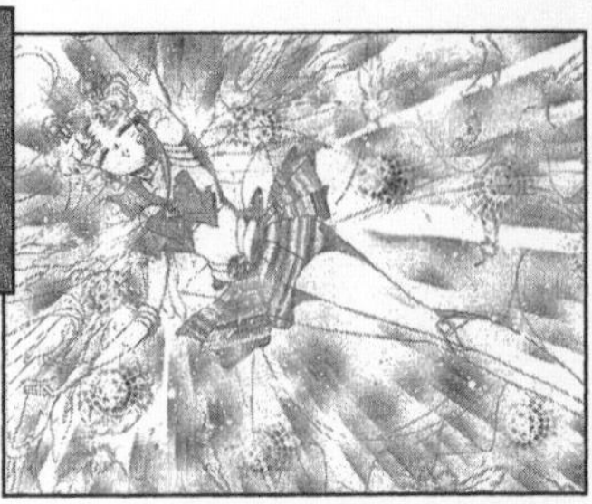

▲⑥ The three talismans assemble, and the Legendary Holy Grail appears. Super Sailor Moon is born!

• March 1994 / "Pretty Guardian Sailor Moon S" season three of the animated television series, begins airing.

• August 1994 / An art exhibition is held to commemorate the release of art books volumes one and two!

• August 1992 / "Pretty Guardian Sailor Moon" anime book series publication begins!

Volume one of the film comics, utilizing scene clips from the anime, is released. Later, books based on the theatrical films are also produced.

• December 1994 / "Sailor Moon S" movie premieres

A film adaptation of Takeuchi-sensei's (extant) work finally hits theaters. It is replete with noteworthy highlights, such as Chibi Moon's first Make Up and Luna's fantastical transformation scene.

• December 1994 / Greatest ever Christmas event is held!

A large-scale event entitled "Sailor Guardians Greatest Ever Christmas Party" is held at Tokyo Bay NK Hall.

• March 1995 / "Pretty Guardian Sailor Moon SuperS" begins airing.

• April 1995 / Elaborate triple-feature television special airs!

Starting off with an adaptation of the first "Chibi-Usa's Picture Diary" tale, the one-hour triple-feature "SuperS Special" airs.

June 1995 / rsts through miraculous er-milestone for KC Nakayoshi!

With the release of volume 10, e aggregate rint volume of "Pretty Guardian ailor Moon" mics exceeds a landmark 10 million.

A White Steed Prince? A Tale of Tiny Love.

Phase Four Series

■ Appeared in *Nakayoshi* April 1995 ~ March 1996 issues / Revised Edition KC DX volumes 8 ~ 10

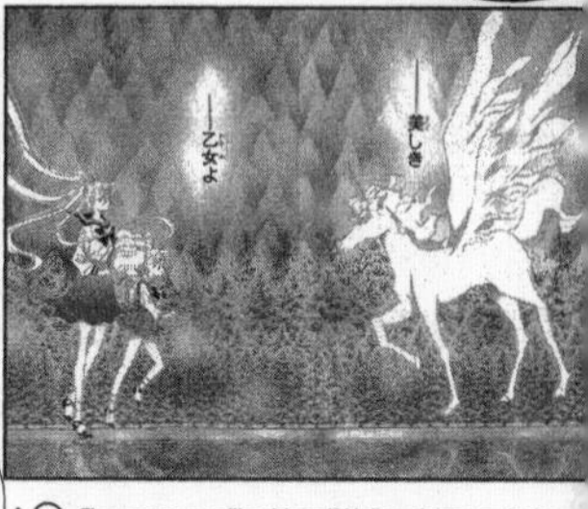
——乙女よ
美しき

▲① The pegasus calling himself Helios claims to desire the aid of a young maiden in order to save Elysion.

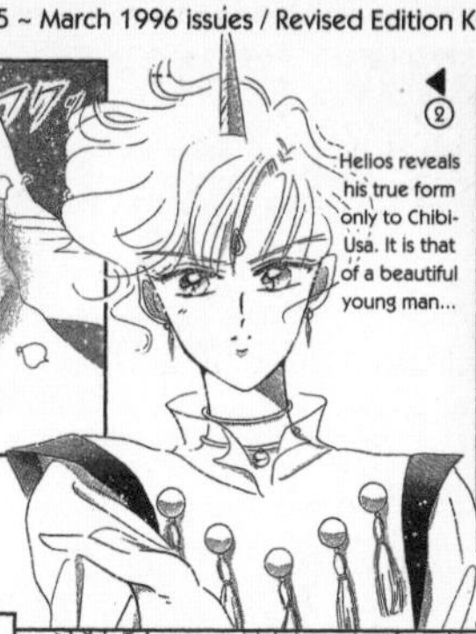

◀② Helios reveals his true form only to Chibi-Usa. It is that of a beautiful young man...

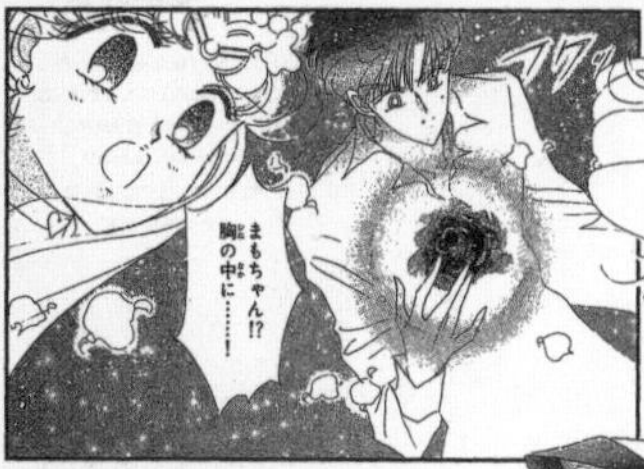
まもちゃん!? 胸の中に……!

▲③ The crisis befalling Elysion, the sacred land of Earth, is also eating away at Prince of Earth Mamoru's flesh.

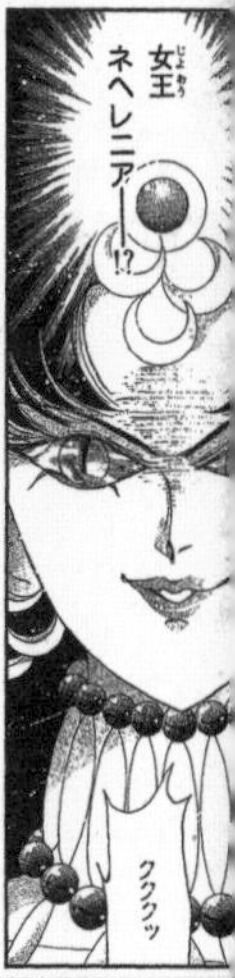
女王ネヘレニア——!?
ククッ

▶④ Nehelenia, queen of the new moon's darkness, has revived. Inside her burns fierce flames of vengeance towards those of the White Moon Kingdom: Usagi and company.

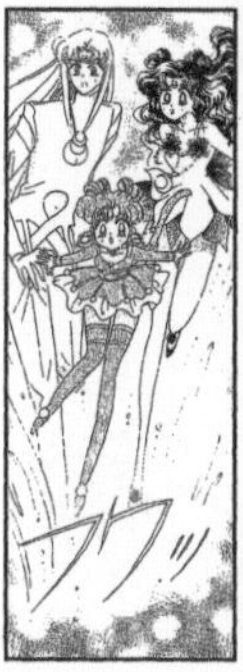

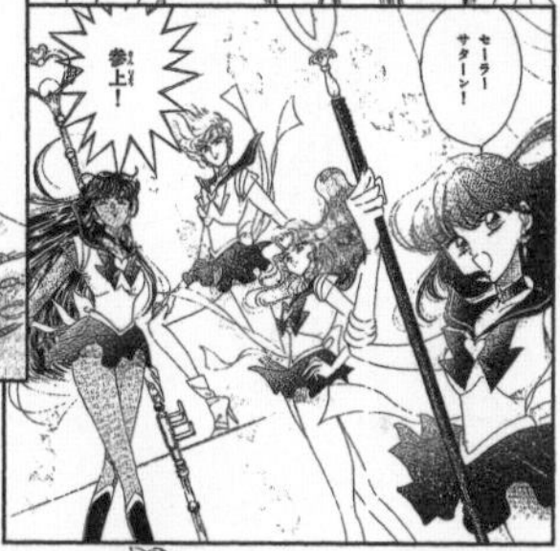
セーラーサターン!
参上!

▲⑤ The newly impending crisis causes infant Hotaru to undergo accelerated development. The four Outer Solar System Guardians assemble once more!

▶⑥ Luna, Artemis, and Diana are also restored to human form, and aid and fight alongside the Sailor Guardians.

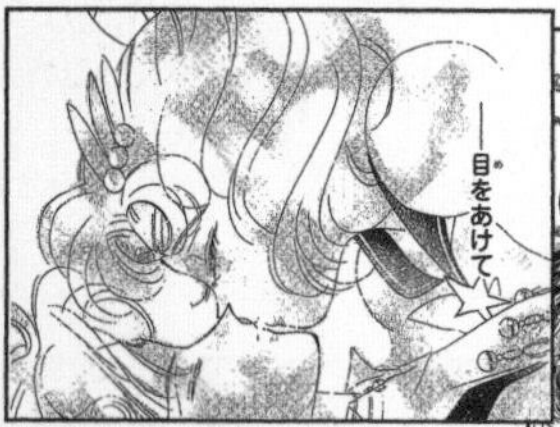
——目をあけて

▲⑦ Helios is reawakened by the kiss of the true "young maiden" that he had never stopped seeking.

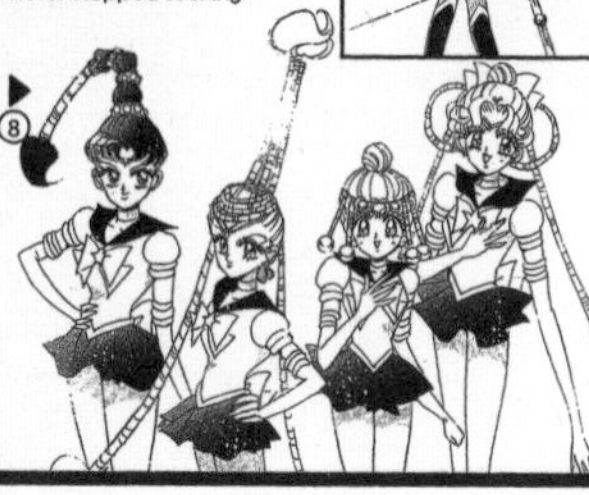

The enemy Amazoness Quartet actually turn out to be Sailor Guardians that are supposed to protect Chibi Moon. ▶⑧

• August 199 Performance of the "Prett Guardian Sail Moon SuperS musical begir

• August 1995 / "Sailor Moon" appears on an auction program!

A cameo opportunity in Takeuchi-sensei's original manga work goes for a winning bid of two million yen in Fuji TV's popular variety show "Hammer Price."

• September 1995 / "Sailor Moon" finally arrives in America!

Starting with Spain and France in December 1993, the anime airs worldwide and becomes hugely popular internationally, as well.

• December 1995 / "Sailor Moon Express No. 2" appears

In commemoration of the theatrical release, the "Sailor Moon Express No. 2" runs to Seibuen Amusement Park, just like back in 1994. Other events such as "lookalike contests" are also held that day.

• December 1995 / The long-awaited double-feature new films finally premiere!

The "Pretty Guardian Sailor Moon SuperS" and "Ami-chan's First Love" films hit theaters. The day before, a commemorative event assembling the five (main) voice actresses is also held at the Shinjuku Toei (Hall).

• February 1996 / "Sailor Moon" anime begins airing in Australia and New Zealand

• March 1996 / "Pretty Guardian Sailor Moon Sailor Stars" (animated) television series begins airing.

• July 1996 / Special "Hammer Price" manga (story) appears!

In *Nakayoshi's* August issue, "Chubster Mask," modeled after the aforementioned "Hammer Price" auction winner, appears in "Chibi-Usa's Picture Diary."

ierce Clash?! Sailor Guardians VS. Sailor Guardians!!

Phase Five Series

Appeared in *Nakayoshi* April 1996 ~ March 1997 issues / Revised Edition KC DX volumes 11 ~ 12

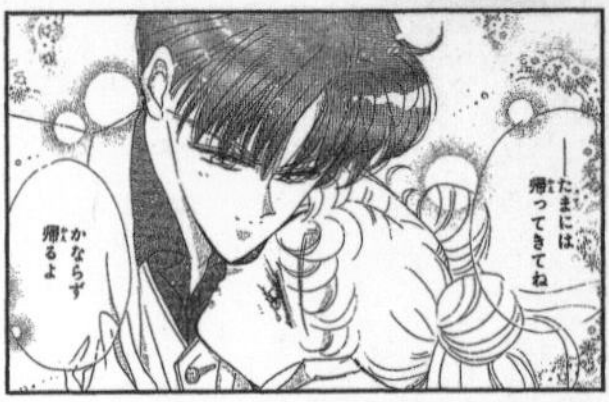
——たまには帰ってきてね
かならず帰るよ

① Mamoru leaves to study abroad in America. The shock of the incident that occurs in that moment is so great that it induces amnesia in Usagi.

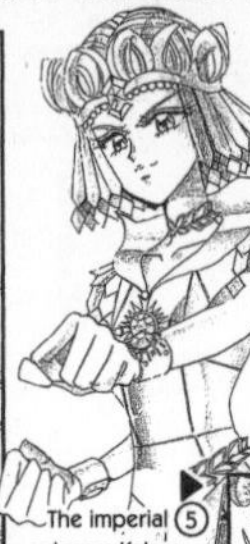

② Galaxia, who burns with the ambition to rule the entire universe, steals Sailor Crystals from Guardians' bodies one after another.

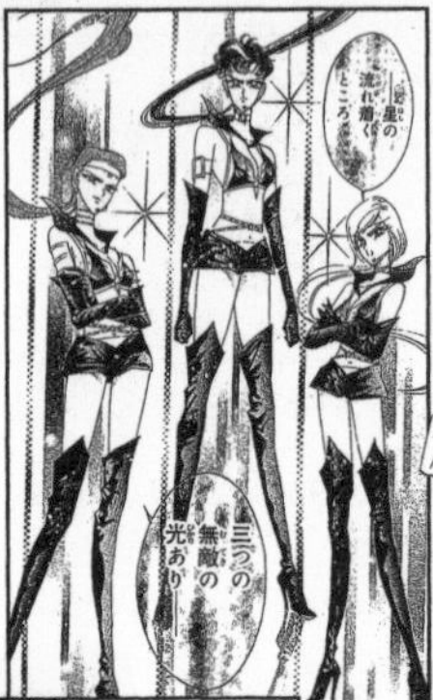
——星の流れ着くところ
三つの無敵の光あり——

③ mbers f the ·pular dol ·oup nree ghts are tually e Star ghts, ailor ardians f an lien anet.

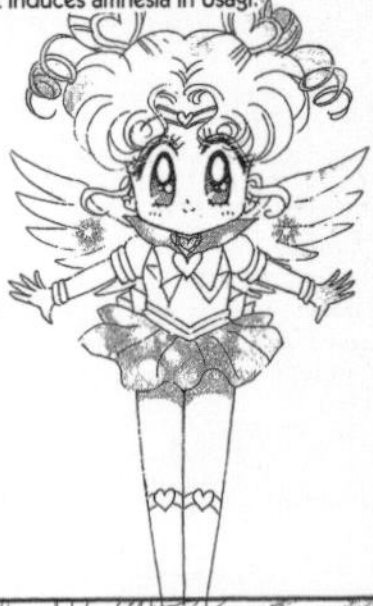

④ The mysterious little girl Chibi-Chibi also transforms into a Sailor Guardian. What is her true identity...?

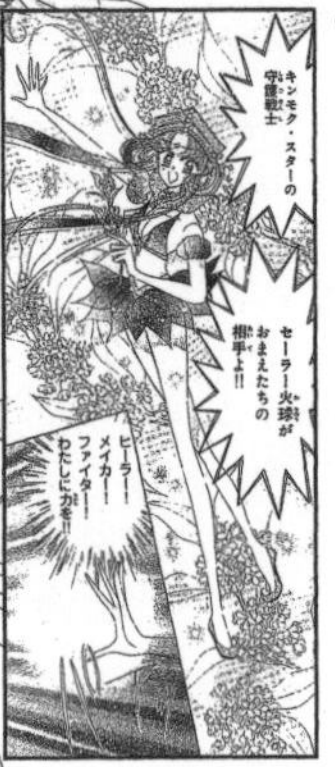
キンモク・スターの守護戦士
セーラー火球がおまえたちの相手よ!!
ヒーラー! メイカー! ファイター! わたしに力を!!

⑤ The imperial princess Kakyu, whom the Star Lights have been searching for, undergoes Make Up! She fights alongside Sailor Moon.

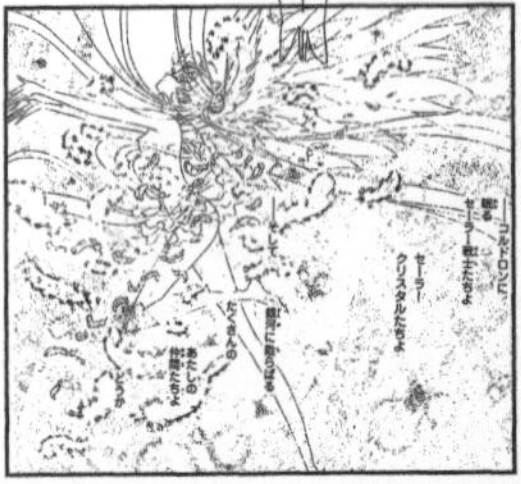

⑥ Sailor Moon risks everything and challenges Chaos, who has merged with the Cauldron.

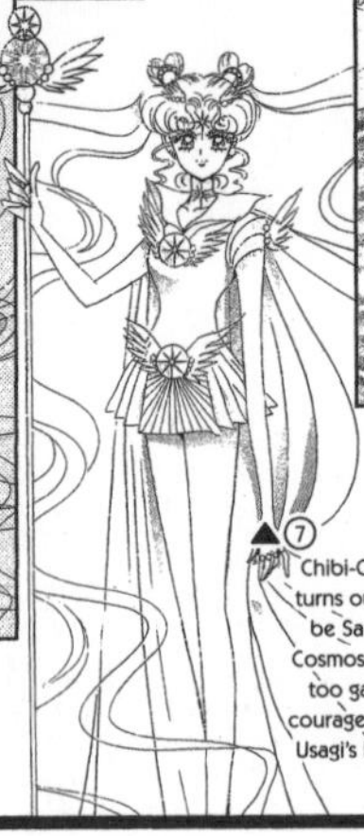

⑦ Chibi-Chibi turns out to be Sailor Cosmos. She too gains courage from Usagi's love.

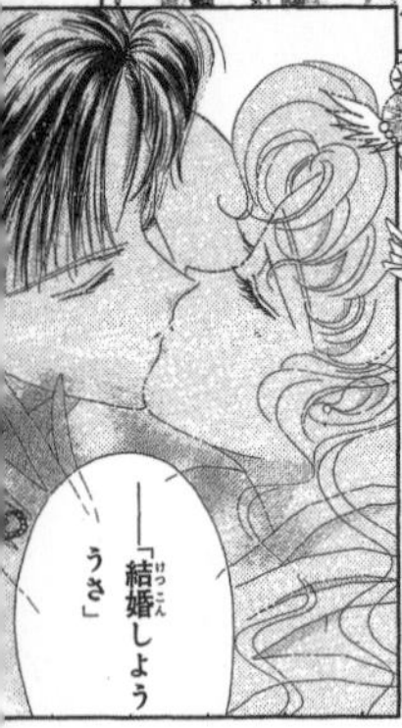
——「結婚しよう うさ」

⑧ Sailor Moon's actions bring true peace to the universe. Usagi returns to her beloved Mamoru's side...

• August 1996 / Performances of the "Pretty Guardian Sailor Moon Sailor Stars" musical begin

• August 1996 / The widely popular Naoko Takeuchi Art Books appear yet once more!

Naoko Takeuchi-sensei's "Pretty Guardian Sailor Moon Art Book" volumes three and four are released.

• February 1997 / "Sailor Moon"'s emotional finale!

The manga series that has spanned five years' time comes to a happy end in *Nakayoshi's* March issue.

• February 1997 / The entire staff holds a toast at the End-Commemorating Party!

In celebration of the conclusion of both the manga and animated television series, an End-Commemorating Party is held at the Prince Hotel Takanawa. On that day, Takeuchi-sensei and all the other staff view the emotion-filled final (anime) episode on a television set specially installed in the venue.

• April 1997 / The emotional final volume of the comic book series is released!

• August 1997 / The final performance of the "Pretty Guardian Sailor Moon Sailor Stars" musical is held.

• September 1997 / "Pretty Guardian Sailor Moon Art Book" volume five is released!

Naoko Takeuchi-sensei's widely popular art book series also finally comes to an end with this fifth volume!

• November 1997 / "Codename: Sailor V" reaches a climax!

The finale of the Sailor Guardian series originator, "Sailor V," appears in *RunRun's* November issue.

Side Stories & Additiona Tales

The Infinitely Expanding Sailor Moon World!

■ Appeared in *RunRun* July 1993 issue, etc. / Revised KC DX Short Stories volumes [1] & [2]

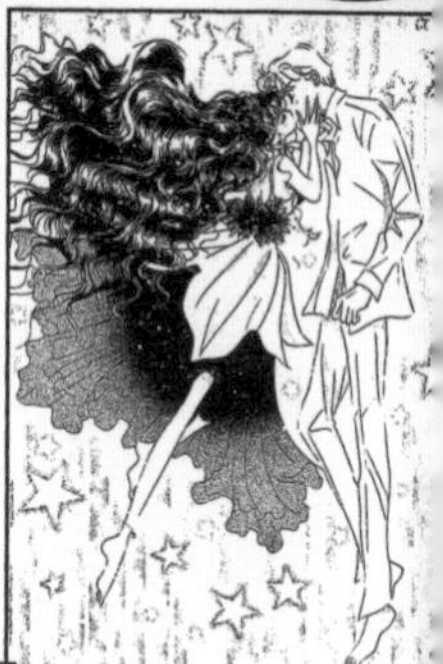

▶① Naoko Takeuchi-sensei's extended original story "Princess Kaguya's Lover," into which she pours her heart and soul. It is a fantastical love story involving Luna, which becomes the basis for the "S" movie.

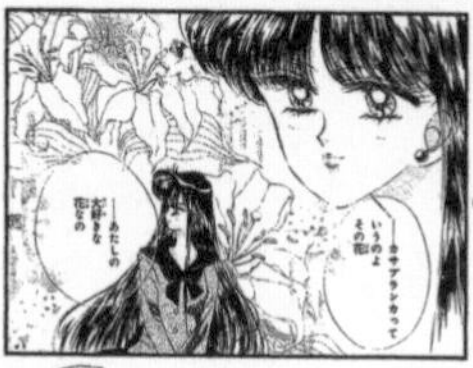

—カサブランカって いうのよ その花
—あたしの 大好きな 花なの

"Casablanca Memory," where Rei-chan is center stage. A work with voice actress Michie Tomizawa-san's favorite flower as its motif. ▶③

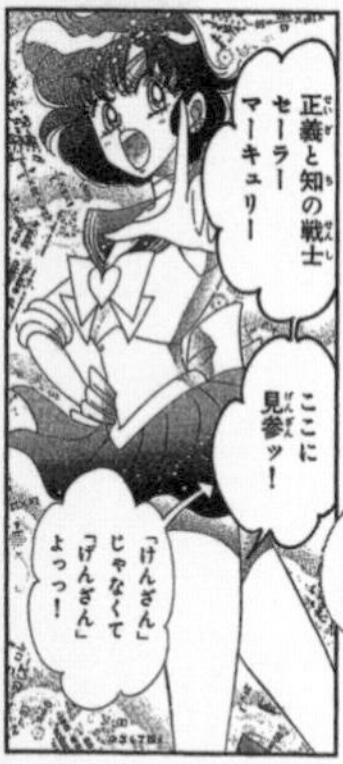

正義と知の戦士 セーラーマーキュリー
ここに 見参ッ！
「けんざん」 じゃなくて 「げんざん」 よっっ！

▲⑦ "Ami-chan's First Love," whose title is identical to its corresponding movie (short). It depicts Ami's epic battle against her archenemy (?) Mercurius.

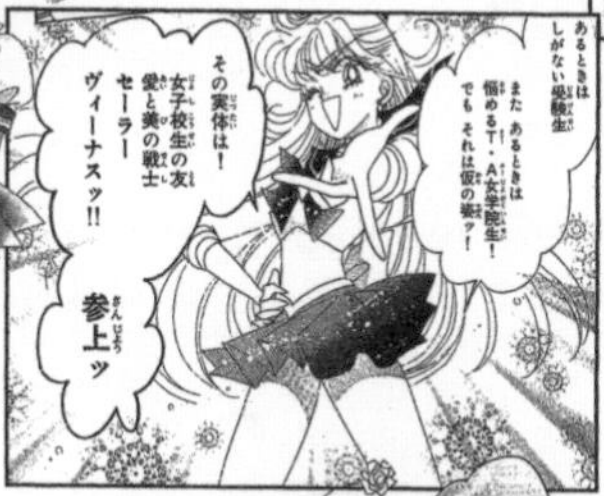

あるときは しがない受験生
また あるときは 悩めるT・A女学院生！ でも それは仮の姿ッ！
その実体は！ 女子校生の友 愛と美の戦士 セーラー ヴィーナスッ!!
参上ッ

◀④ "Rei & Minako's Girls' School Battle," which is also the final tale in the Entrance Exam Wars arc. Powerful Minako runs amok at T•A Academy for Girls?!

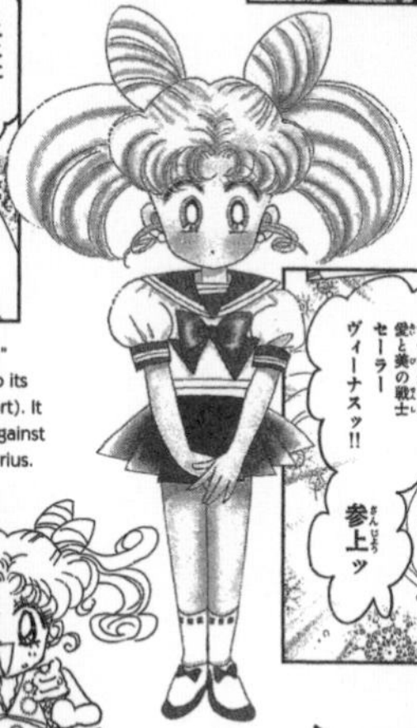

◀② The first "side story," tale one of "Chibi-Usa's Picture Diary." It was even animated into a TV special.

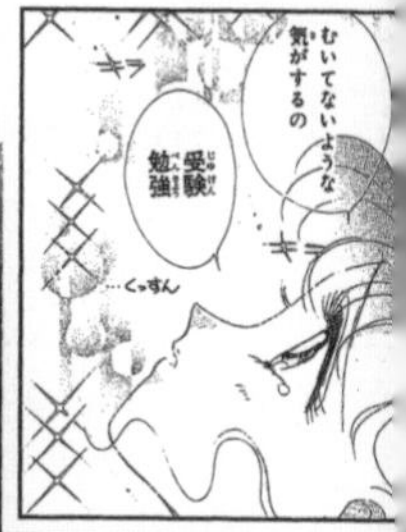

むいてないような 気がするの
受験 勉強
…くすん

▼⑤ "Mako-chan's Melancholy," a short story depicting the much-troubled Makoto's slapstick entrance exam war.

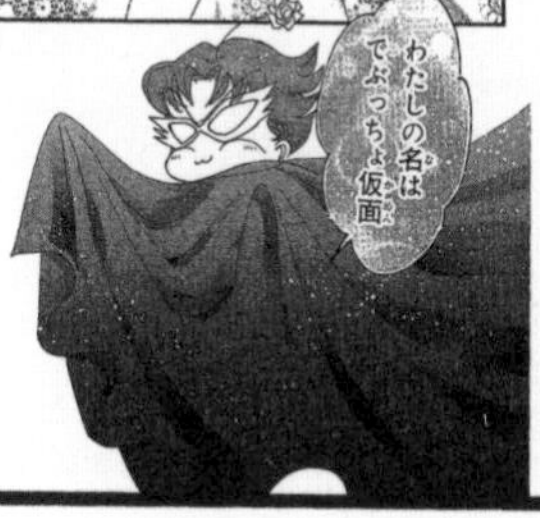

わたしの名は でぶっちょ仮面

"Chibi-Usa's Picture Diary," an original story which was specially written for a charity auction program. ▶⑥

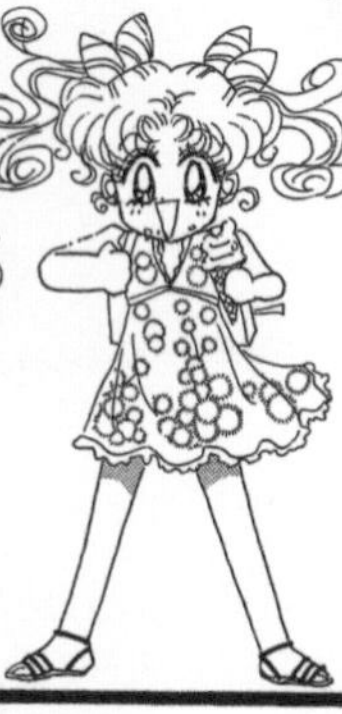

Usagi's second child Ko-usagi appears!! A special piece written just for the reference data book. ▶⑧

• Feb 199 Perf man of t "Pre Guar Sai Mo ~Ete Lege rem mus ar hel

• July 1998 / Performances of the "Pretty Guardian Sailor Moon, Beginning of the New Legend" musical are held.

• January 1999 / Naoko Takeuchi-sensei weds (fellow) manga artist Yoshihiro Togashi-shi!

• March 1999 / Performances of the "Pretty Guardian Sailor Moon, Legend of Kaguya Island" musical are held.

• September 1999 / Naoko Takeuchi-sensei's "Pretty Guardian Sailor Moon" reference data book is released.

• January 2000 / Performances of the "Pretty Guardian Sailor Moon, Overture of LAST-DRACUL" musical are held (Exceeds 500 performances!).

• April 2000 / "Pretty Guardian Sailor Moon" anime begins rebroadcast!!

• November 2001 / "Pretty Guardian Sailor Moon" 10th Anniversary commemoration event is held.

• December 2001 / "Pretty Guardian Sailor Moon" official website launches!!

• March 2002 / "Pretty Guardian Sailor Moon" 10th Anniversary commemoration festival is held.

• September 2003 / "Pretty Guardian Sailor Moon Revised Edition" (12 volumes en toto, plus 2 additional volumes) begins publication!!

• October 2003 / "Pretty Guardian Sailor Moon" live action (television) series begin airing nationwide on CBC/TBS!!

• October 2004 / "Codename: Sailor V Revised Edition" (two volumes in total) begins publication!!

Translation Notes

Japanese is a tricky language for most Westerners, and translation is often more art than science. For your edification and reading pleasure, here are notes on some of the places where we could have gone in a different direction with our translation of the work, or where a Japanese cultural reference is used.

Princess Kaguya (page 5)
Princess Kaguya is the main character in the "Tale of the Bamboo Cutter," which, dating back to the 10th century, is considered the oldest known Japanese folktale. As this space is woefully insufficient to do justice to the story, the translator urges readers to check it out for themselves. However, the salient points are that Princess Kaguya is a princess of the Moon who was sent as a baby to Earth, but eventually returns to the moon despite offers of marriage from various princes and even the Emperor of Japan. Thus, it is not only this short story, but the entire *Sailor Moon* storyline that has elements taken from the Princess Kaguya folktale, in particular the pairing of Moon Kingdom Princess Serenity with Earth Prince Endymion.

Spousal quarrels are raw giraffe meat (page 10)
As is typical, Minako misquotes an existing idiom, of which the literal translation is "even dogs don't pay attention to spousal quarrels," and it means, "one should not interfere in lover's quarrels."

***Nakayoshi* (page 14)**
The Kodansha monthly shojo manga magazine in which *Sailor Moon* was originally serialized.

***Konpeitô* (page 16)**
Small and colorful star-shaped sugar candy somewhat similar in concept to rock candy. Their cute appearance and sweetness make them a popular gift item.

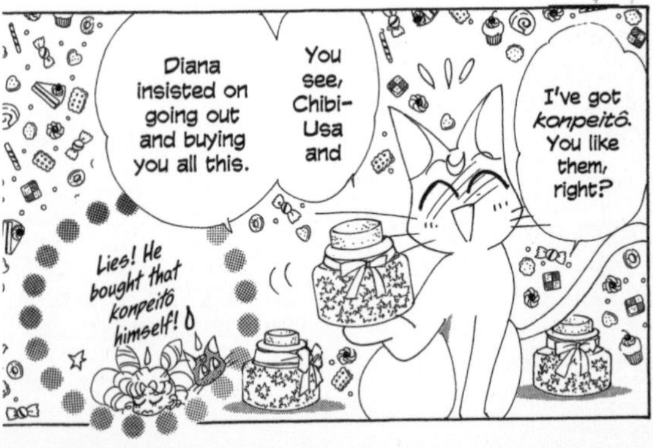
I've got *konpeitô*. You like them, right?
You see, Chibi-Usa and
Diana insisted on going out and buying you all this.
Lies! He bought that konpeitô himself!

Kakeru Ohzora (page 17, 18)

Our good Samaritan astronomy professor character's name means "Shard Cosmos" ("Cosmos Shard" in the original Japanese name sequencing), an apropos name considering the plot of the story.

Himeko Nayotake (page 19)

Our female astronaut character's name means "Princess-child Bamboo" ("Bamboo Princess-child" in the original Japanese name sequencing), another apropos name.

NSDA (page 22)

The National Space Development Agency was the Japanese national space agency from its establishment in 1969 until October of 2003, when it was merged with ISAS (Institute of Space and Aeronautical Sciences) and NAL (National Aerospace Laboratory) into a new entity, JAXA (Japan Aerospace Exploration Agency), which still exists today.

Comet demises (page 25)

According to various sources, comets, especially those of this size (10-kilometer diameter), do not just "vanish," "fade out," or get annihilated without leaving some visible evidence of said destruction...

Kuro, Miké, Tama (page 29)

All popular Japanese cat names, these three are also coat color or pattern descriptives. "Kuro" means "black," i.e. "Blackie," "miké" means "tri-colored" or "calico," and "tama" can mean "spotted" or "splotched," i.e. "Spot."

***Sempai* (page 62)**
Sempai is a Japanese word that refers to someone senior to oneself in the context of academic year or office hierarchy, with some inference of a mentor-mentee relationship. It is the opposite or counter term to *kôhai* (the junior/younger mentee).

The undone ribbon bow (page 108)
It is said to be an ill omen if an object breaks or comes undone out of the blue or without obvious provocation, such as an untouched plate or cup falling off a shelf and breaking, or as in this case, the ribbon bow that Kakeru had tied around Luna's neck coming undone and falling off.

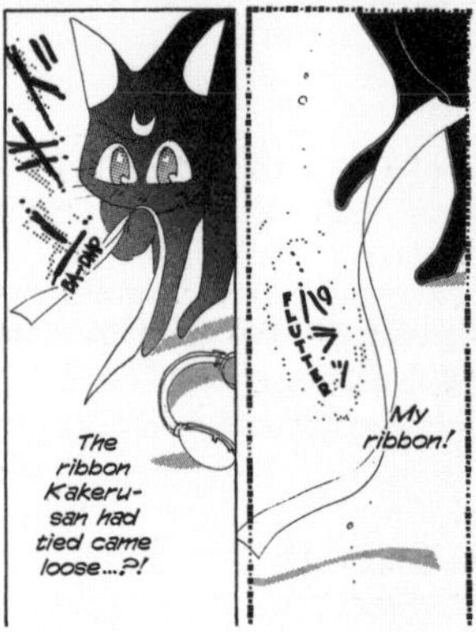
FLUTTER
My ribbon!
BA-DMP
The ribbon Kakeru-san had tied came loose...?!

Nagata-chô (page 160)
Located within the Chiyoda Ward of Tokyo, Nagata-chô, Nagatachô, or Nagatacho is Japan's political center, with both the Diet (Parliament) and Prime Minister's residence found here. In this sense, it is the Japanese analog to Downing Street, and many often just say "Nagata-chô" to refer to the national government.

Democratic Liberal Party (page 161)
Historically, the Democratic Liberal Party was a right-wing political group that existed briefly from 1948 until 1950. It came about from the merging of the Japan Liberal Party with the Democratic Club in 1948, and then in 1950, when a faction of the Democratic Party joined it, it was renamed the (Yoshida) Liberal Party. Incidentally, the merger of the Liberal Party with the Japan Democratic Party in 1955 is what led to the birth of the current powerhouse Liberal Democratic Party. However, it is hard to say if Takeuchi-sensei was truly referencing Japanese political history or was simply doing a word switcheroo (Liberal Democratic <-> Democratic Liberal).

***Katsu!* (page 169)**
"Katsu" (dispel) is a word shouted out in Zen and some other sects of Buddhism, as well as some East Asian martial arts schools. While it literally means "to yell" in Chinese, it is uttered to help focus one's energy and thus induce an enlightened state in oneself or another. Because of this, however, it is also often inferred to be verbal punishment.

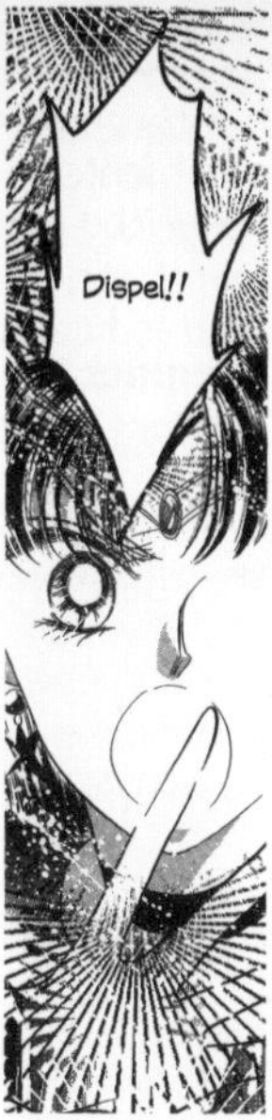
Dispel!!

***Geta* and *zôri* (page 181)**
Geta and *zôri* are two types of traditional Japanese footwear. *Geta* are made of (often unfinished) wood, with a thonged rectangular base elevated by two parallel "teeth" that are fixed perpendicular to the long side of the base, and are most similar to clogs. *Zôri* are also thonged, but flat, and can be made of rice straw, lacquered wood, rubber, or recently even plastic. *Zôri* are most similar to flip-flops, although interestingly, it is said that modern-day rubber flip-flops were actually inspired by *zôri* that servicemen observed during World War II.

Adopted fiancés (page 182)
There is a centuries-old tradition in Japan of well-to-do families with no or only female children to adopt a male adult to carry on the family name and business. When there are no heirs at all (or no capable male heirs), the individual may be a younger male blood relative such as a nephew or second cousin, who then weds outside his adopted family. In cases (such as the Sailor Guardians) where there are only daughters, the man is usually a non-relative who takes the adopting family's surname and marries the (oldest) daughter.

Jinbocho (page 182)
Also located within the Chiyoda Ward of Tokyo, Jinbocho or Jimbocho is the center of Tokyo's used-book stores, as well as antique shops.

Tsuzuku Studio, Juniors (page 182)
An homage to Tsuzuki Studio, a rehearsal and recording studio for the Johnny & Associates, Inc., talent agency that grooms and promotes male idol groups and solo artists. Semantically, "tsuzuku" is the present-tense verb form of "tsuzuki." Its trainees, artists that have yet to debut, are known as Johnny's Jr., which is likely the source of the "Juniors" mentioned by Minako. The actual studio *is* located in Azabu Jûban.

"Eating machine" versus "fire extinguisher" (page 183)
The words "fire extinguisher" and "digestive organ" are pronounced the same (shôkaki) in Japanese and are written almost identically, kanji-wise, as well. "Fire extinguisher" is written "erase-fire-instrument," and "digestive organ" is written "erase-chemically-vessel," where "instrument" and "vessel" are the same kanji. Here, the girls are using both to refer to Ko-usagi, so the translator elected to use "eating machine" as opposed to "human digestive organ." "Fire extinguisher" refers to how Ko-usagi douses the enthusiasm of everyone around her.

Washington Convention (page 184)
The Washington Convention, aka CITES (Convention on International Trade in Endangered Species of Wild Fauna and Flora), is a multilateral treaty meant to protect threatened and endangered species of plants and animals within the context of international trade.

Manbikiya Parlor (page 185)
An homage to Senbikiya Fruits Parlor. Fruit parlors are Japanese eating establishments based on the concept of ice cream parlors, except that dishes feature fruit (in various forms) as the main ingredient. The "sen" in Senbikiya is written using the kanji for "1000," and one way of writing "man" would be "10,000." However, in this case, the actual kanji used means "stuffing-filled bun."

Obviously not! Like Maeda's shrimp tempura not!
And there are plenty of other things that I haven't tasted even once yet, either!

Maeda's shrimp tempura not! (page 193)
This is a play on words that doesn't really have an equivalent in English. The literal translation is "atarimaeda" as in "of course not" but mashed up with the name of a restaurant "Maeda."

Idol (page 200)
Usually refers to young female or male media personalities, such as J-pop artists, actors, and models (but occasionally also foreigners). However, this Japanese phenomenon can also extend to civilians, i.e. the prettiest student or company employee.

Pretty Guardian Sailor Moon Short Stories volume 2 is a work of fiction. Names, characters, places, and incidents are the products of the author's imagination or are used fictitiously. Any resemblance to actual events, locales, or persons, living or dead, is entirely coincidental.

A Kodansha Trade Paperback Original.

Published in the United States by Kodansha Comics, an imprint of Kodansha USA Publishing, LLC, New York.

Publication rights for this English edition arranged through Kodansha Ltd., Tokyo.

First published in Japan in 2004 by Kodansha Ltd., Tokyo, as *Bishoujosenshi Sailor Moon Shinsoban Short Stories*, volume 2.

ISBN 978-1-61262-010-7

Printed in Canada

www.kodanshacomics.com

9 8 7 6 5 4 3 2 1

Translator/Adapter: Mari Morimoto
Lettering: Jennifer Skarupa

TOMARE! DISCARD
STOP

You're going the wrong way!

Manga is a completely different type of reading experience.

To start at the beginning, Go to the end!

That's right! Authentic manga is read the traditional Japanese way—from right to left, exactly the opposite of how American books are read. It's easy to follow: Just go to the other end of the book and read each page—and each panel—from right side to left side, starting at the top right. Now you're experiencing manga as it was meant to be!